SO THAT'S A WRAP

50 Years of Fun and Adventure
Making Documentary Films

David Kennard

FEATURING

Carl Sagan, Joseph Campbell, Jane Goodall, Leonardo DiCaprio, Arthur C. Clarke, John Cleese, Richard Nixon, Edward Heath, Ronald Reagan, Peter Jennings, David Attenborough, James Burke, Richard Gere, Michael Bentine, Jacob Bronowski, Michael Tilson Thomas, J.K. Galbraith, Brian Swimme, The Duke of Edinburgh, George H.W. Bush and many more...

InCA
PRODUCTIONS

First published worldwide in 2020 by InCA Productions, Mill Valley, CA, USA
Distributed by Kindle Direct Publishing

ISBN: 9798686299498
A catalogue record for this book will be available from the Library of Congress

This book is a work of non-fiction based on the life, experiences and recollections of the author. To the best of his knowledge and memory, it is a true record.

For Lizzie, with so much love

and for Amanda, Juliet, James and Pippa

with thanks for all the joy you have given me
and for all the fun and adventures we have had

CONTENTS

PART ONE: MY FIRST LIFE

INTRODUCTION

BACKSTORY

THE TRAVELER'S JINX

1. Radio Days

2. From Hitler to Quiz Games

3. The Ascent of Man

4. From Science to Religion

5. The Great Galbraith Fiasco

6. James Burke's Connections

7. Carl Sagan's Cosmos

8. From Walter Cronkite to Joseph Campbell

9. The Heart of the Dragon

10. The West of the Imagination

11. Founding InCA and Finding Lizzie

PART TWO: MY SECOND LIFE

INTRODUCTION

12. We the People, with Peter Jennings

13. Frequent Flier: Tahiti to Maida Vale

14. Dangerous Years: From Nixon to Bush

15. Nanotechnology and Things to Come

16. The Heart of Healing: Around the World in 80 Weeks

17. Pulling Out All the Stops: from Pipe Organs to Levi's

18. Arthur C. Clarke: Master of the Imagination

19. Amelia Earhart: Recreating Her Final Flight

20. Play, Fun and Creativity: Jane Goodall and Company

21. Churchill's Granddaughter and the New York Scene

22. Keeping Score with Michael Tilson Thomas

23. Journey of the Universe: The History of Everything

24. The World of Wine: From John Cleese to Gevrey Chambertin

25. The Ones That Got Away

EPILOGUE: The Book Makers

Acknowledgements

David Kennard: Principal Credits as Director and/or Producer

INTRODUCTION TO PART ONE

Even to contemplate writing a memoir is an act of hubris, I admit. It raises many questions. What is so special about *my* life, that you should bother to read about it? What have I learned? What are my failings? Is this simply the reflections of a hardened narcissist? What was it like, working on film and video with famous and famously clever people for 50 years? Have I thereby discovered any tiny part of the meaning of life? All these questions buzz round in my head, as I sit at my keyboard.

Writing this introduction in the autumn of 2020, there's one thing I do know. I'm finally hanging up my stopwatch and clapperboard. I'm bowing out from making non-fiction television programs and films – over 150 of them, it turns out, including multiple episodes of several long series. As I've said so many times at the end of a shoot, "So, that's a wrap."

I have proudly passed the torch to my son James, whose excellent film *The Book Makers* premiered at film festivals in the autumn of 2020 and then ran on national public television in the US, followed by international distribution. I've worked with him on three documentary features over the past few years and may have passed on a few techniques I have learned. But James is far more skilled than I am. Not only can he produce, direct and write, he is a talented artist who can also operate a complex camera and edit a film digitally to the highest broadcast and movie standards – things I have never learned how to do. I played a modest role in finding the money for *The Book Makers* and have hovered in the background as "Senior Producer," offering suggestions and trying not to get in the way. But the film is entirely his, creatively.

The book you are reading was completed during the onslaught of the worldwide Coronavirus pandemic of 2020. This ongoing nightmare scenario causes me to reflect on two things: what a lucky break I had, trying to forge a career in film in the window between 1970 and 2020, and what a fortunate and richly rewarding personal life I have been able to lead since 1945.

On the professional front, I joined the BBC as a trainee at a moment when British television was flowering into one of its most creative periods. Most shows were in color by then – still a novelty, for many people in the UK. The audiences were becoming more open-minded: think of the impact of the Beatles, mini-skirts and sexual freedom in Britain, and civil rights and the Vietnam war protests in the US. British TV budgets were becoming more generous, and the management at the BBC bolder and more imaginative. At the same time, the Boeing 747, introduced in 1970, transformed international travel: it cut the cost of flying by half, making it possible to create all-encompassing globe-trotting series like *The Ascent of Man* – my first big break in television.

In 2020, of course, the shutters came down on that kind of life: all Hollywood and much TV documentary production, let alone fancy-free international travel, came to a screeching halt. How James will manage to make a living in film from here on is a deeply troubling question.

On the personal front, I had the luck to be born in September 1945, just after the horrors of World War Two, which had drastically impacted my parents' generation. Though the first few years of my life were spent in modest circumstances, while Britain recuperated from the war, I was too young to understand the meaning of austerity. By the time I entered my teens, I could spread my wings. I had the chance to learn languages and spend time living with families in both France and Germany while at High School. I had caught the travel bug.

Now in my mid-70's, I have a loving, supportive wife and family, including four children and (so far) five grandchildren. That's the good news. The bad news is that, since I now live in the United States, the Coronavirus has cut me off from my British daughters Amanda and Juliet, and their children. At the same time, I have had to face up to the fact that I am living with cancer, and that I might never be able to see them face to face again. Only time will tell. But even if I died tomorrow, I am profoundly grateful for all the opportunities and all the fun I've had.

In fact, I feel that I have had two lives for the price of one. The first was based largely in London and spanned the years 1945 to 1986: it features in Part One of this book. Everything changed when I married my second wife, Lizzie (also English by birth, like me), and we made the decision to start a new life in California. That is where I raised my second family – Pippa and James. That is where I started to create and produce my own films and series, through an independent company that I co-founded, rather than working as a writer, producer and director on other people's projects. In a sense, that is when I finally grew up – yes, aged over forty. I also developed a vision of what else I wanted to achieve in life – if my luck held. That is all to be found in Part Two.

∎∎

So… that's a wrap. What the heck have I been doing for the last 75 years?

In my professional life – and indeed, when I'm off-duty too – I have always tried to tell stories that make people smile (or even laugh), give them hope and joy, and to stimulate their own creativity. Not for me the "piss and moan" school of non-fiction, which concentrates on the bad news that surrounds us. I admire people who dedicate their lives to promoting social justice in their films, and revealing all sorts of wicked and criminal behavior, but I just cannot do it. I have never been a journalist. I am an optimist. I want to spread the good news, to help people say "Aha!" and experience revelation, as they discover some of the extraordinary people and ideas that surround them on this pale blue planet.

But, to create anything, I have always needed to be part of a team, however small. Not for me the life of the lone auteur, the maverick filmmaker surviving in poverty, scraping together a subsistence living, to finish a film that has taken a decade to create. I love to work with other people: to share jokes and adventures, along with the insights and ideas that make a good film. I also love to work as efficiently and swiftly as possible:

filmmaking like this becomes a high-speed thrill ride and keeps my adrenaline pumping. What could be more fun?

To make this happen at any level, I realized early on that, if I could, I needed to find people with a similar attitude to life – top-flight producers, directors and writers who were not cynical and world-weary – people I could learn from, if they'd let me. I was lucky to have such brilliant mentors as Alasdair Clayre, Peter Dunkley, Lawrence Gordon-Clarke, Adrian Malone and Dick Gilling, early in my career. I also understood that I could never master the range of subjects that I so longed to explore and explain. If possible, I had to work as an apprentice with world-class experts, if I wanted to help create resonant films.

That has meant working with Big Names, some of whom, of course, have egos as large as their CVs. The only way to survive in a world of super-stars and wizards is to know that they need respect – indeed, many of them crave it, and cannot live without it. So, whenever writing with them, or directing them, or editing and producing what they have said and trying to craft it into a decent film, I have had to remember to stay behind the scenes. I am not the expert, they are – at least in principle. There have been a few projects where the 'expertise' of the experts has turned out to be laughable, as I will recount. But, once we had started a project, I had to feel we were all in it together.

Of course, being the man behind the curtain is much the safest place to be. If the film turns out to be a turkey, it will be the on-screen star who takes much of the blame, or at least the hurtful criticism. Those who did not like *Cosmos* tended to blame Carl Sagan, rather than the producers and directors who did so much to create it. The price of lurking in the shadows, of course, is that everyone has heard of Carl Sagan, and nobody has heard of David Kennard. And Dr. Sagan made a ton of money, and Mr. Kennard did not. But that is fine by me. I am happy to be unknown, in the wider scheme of things. (No, honestly!)

I am still proud of many of the shows I have helped to create. Which ones have stood the test of time? Is Bronowski as relevant now as he was forty-five years ago? Was Carl Sagan more of a showman than a scientist? Is Jane Goodall right to judge human relationships on the basis of the habits of chimpanzees? Is Michael Tilson Thomas stuck for ever in a Mahler-Ives-Copland-Bernstein hall of mirrors? How weird is John Cleese? Well, you will be the judge.

I have learned one cardinal lesson. What a good documentary consists of is never 'reality.' Reality is what a CCTV security camera captures. A 'non-fiction' film offers a highly nuanced form of what takes place. Every time that filmmakers set to work, they create something original: certain scraps of remarkable behavior, unusually interesting people and special events are carefully selected, filmed, edited and re-edited into a unique story, with a beginning, a middle and an end. When you settle down to watch a 'documentary,' you are stepping into a world created by the producer, the director, the camera operator, the editor and the writer. You are actually stepping into a quasi-fiction, lightly sprinkled with a topping of facts.

But I am getting ahead of myself. Time for some background briefing, and if you really don't care about what I did before I started to make radio and television documentaries, then please skip ahead to Chapter 1.

So, how did it all start? I was never specially gifted or artistic, as a child – or later, if it comes to that. I studied Modern Languages at Oxford, because I found it fun to speak another language: it was a form of play-acting. It also meant that I would have a passport to travel. When I was a teenager, my parents told their friends that I might become an interpreter at the United Nations, because that sounded important and purposeful, but I knew that, for me, languages had to be one skill among many, not the final goal.

I never formally studied "The Yartz," as the Australian humorist Barry Humphries calls them, in his persona of Sir Les Patterson, the drunken Australian Cultural Attaché. My degrees are not in film, television or – horror of horrors – media studies. I did once spend a hair-raising month on a BBC Production Training course (along with the famously self-regarding BBC Arts panjandrum Alan Yentob, of all people), but this training happened long *after* I had already produced and directed both radio and TV shows at the Corporation. Of course it did. Dear old "Auntie" BBC.

Instead, my graduate study was in Business Administration, at Indiana University ("IU") in the deepest Midwest of America, and I did that purely and simply because they offered me a scholarship on a plate. I could not resist the opportunity to try something different, to see a new continent and relish some new experiences.

I certainly never wanted to be a businessman. I was not a natural entrepreneur: too timid, perhaps, or too prone to imagining the disastrous consequences of poor decisions. For some reason, I never really wanted to make money either – at least, not serious money. I am sure that my parents shaped my attitude to wealth. They taught me that enough was all you should ask for. This made me the odd man out in the Business School.

At the end of my time at IU, I told the Dean of Business Studies that I was turning down a job offer in Chicago that would pay me $20,000 a year – a great starting salary, fifty years ago. Instead, I had decided to join the BBC. They would pay me the princely equivalent of $2,000 a year – one tenth of the Chicago offer. The Dean laughed out loud.

"Good Lord," he said, "Have we taught you *nothing* here?"

Why the BBC? Because it was, and I believe still is, the best public service broadcasting organization in the world. I wanted to be part of it. One thing after another seemed to propel me towards thoughtful, non-profit documentary making, initially in radio, then in TV: sheer curiosity, the need to ask questions and get answers, the lure of travel to faraway places, a fascination with maps and foreign cultures (shared with my father) and with visual creativity (shaped by my mother). It was all that, plus a deep desire not to spend my entire life sitting on my rear end in an office.

I also realized that I wanted to be a teacher – to communicate ideas. I knew I would not have the patience to teach a small roomful of spotty, resentful children. I wanted to teach anybody and everybody who would listen. I finally realized I wanted at best to teach the world – no small ambition. Documentary film making seemed to offer that opportunity.

Of course, other alternatives for a job, if not a career, had presented themselves. From time to time, I was tempted by the world of comedy. I had sometimes been seen as the class clown, as a child. As recounted later, I was expelled from my English private high school for writing and performing in a satirical show. Happily, I never thought of trying to make a living that way. Just as well, because I was never much good at it, unless I was throwing a joke into the conversation – creating an impromptu piece of 'improv' theatre. Conversation came easily to me: I have always talked too much. I was known as Polly Parrot at my pre-school in London, and nothing has changed. Ask Lizzie, my wife.

If I have to follow a comic script, even one I've written myself, my onstage performance is often dire. At Oxford, it often reminded my friends of Leslie Crowther, a famously unfunny British TV host, who was prominent in the 1960's and 70's. He had a penchant for cozy woolen pullovers and a creepy avuncular chuckle: a bit like Mr. Rogers, except that he was talking in similar vein to adults.

I am slightly better as a writer of comedy sketches than as a performer, but most of my early skits used to be pale copies of other people's material. Only later, in semi-retirement, have I been happily turning out comic one-hour versions of Alice in Wonderland, Aladdin, Cinderella and other old British pantomime chestnuts, for the delectation of a San Francisco men's club that appreciates highbrow smut. Americans find my humor "very British," which is not entirely a compliment, but means I can get away with risqué material that would not easily pass muster in polite company in the US.

So, for about fifty years, my professional life has centered on making non-fiction films and TV shows. In this memoir, I have tried to capture what was unique, interesting or special about these projects. But I have also tried to remember some of the funnier and more curious as well as the most remarkable or significant episodes. I have tried to avoid cheap jokes and slander, where possible, but this stuff would be unreadable if I kept a straight face all the time. There is still a facetious eleven-year-old trying to get out somewhere.

More importantly, there is one thing, which has brought me untold happiness, and made it possible for me to stay fairly sane and optimistic in the high-stress world of film and television. By great good fortune, as I suggested before, I have been able to marry twice and help raise two families, one in England and one in California, without going bankrupt or resorting to crime.

"Family life" can often turn out to be a byword for stress, complexity and conflicting emotions, but as I have got older, and particularly under the influence of Lizzie, I have found that it can also mean peace, love, trust, hope and simplicity. Whatever thrills I have had while making the radio, television and movie shows, in working with famous people or in traveling round the globe to the most exotic locales, nothing can compare with the joy and peace of mind created by returning to a simple, loving life at home.

So I have dedicated this book to Lizzie and to my four children: Amanda, Juliet, James and Pippa. May they get as much happiness out of life as I have, and may they give as much as they get.

••

BACKSTORY

Please indulge me, while I sketch in what Hollywood calls the 'backstory' and describe some scenes from my first twenty years. What follows may shine a light on who I am, why I made the choices I did, and what became of me.

In classic Hollywood style, cue a harp arpeggio and a ripple dissolve to a scene seventy-five years ago in grimy north London, immediately after World War II...

∎∎

I was born at home, in a small flat in London's inner-city Chalk Farm district, in September 1945. Today, it is a hip enough neighborhood, just up the road from the market stalls of Camden Lock, but back then, it was known for its immense, dark engine shed – or Roundhouse, as it came to be called in the 1970's, when it was converted into a theatre. Great snorting steam locomotives were coaled and fired there, prior to taking express trains to the North. My earliest aural memories are not of my mother's voice, or baby rattles or mechanical toys, but of steam whistles and puffing, clanking trains of every size. No wonder I still love railways.

And my earliest visual memory? I was three years old. I have a vivid picture of being wheeled in a pram or buggy through a park, past giant gaping holes in the ground and devastated streetlamps standing at crazy angles. Apparently, I asked my nanny why the lamps were all falling over, and, according to family legend, she said it was because they had not eaten up their spinach. In fact, I later learned, these were the sad remnants of the war. Primrose Hill, as the park is quaintly named, was at the bottom of the list of places to be refurbished, after the Nazi bombing of London was finally over.

My mother had very advanced ideas about the benefits of natural birth, with only a midwife in attendance. Luckily, all went well, but I think it was typical of my mother to make that decision. Though her father (a surgeon at Guy's Hospital) thought she was crazy, she insisted on having her only child at home. Though cloaked with elegance, and possessed of a kindness beyond measure, she had an iron will.

To the very last, Irene Dorothy Kennard (née Relph, known to her grandchildren as "Beanie") was a wonderful mother and an extraordinary mixture. She was painfully shy as a girl, I learned, but was determined to overcome her shyness by becoming an actress. This did not find favor with her parents. With their soundly middle-class professional values, they considered actresses to be little better than high-class tarts. But Irene Dorothy did a deal with her parents: if she agreed to go to a fancy Swiss finishing school, and learn what young ladies needed, so as to snare a suitable husband (elocution, deportment, cooking, sewing, French), would she then be allowed to go to a reputable acting school? The deal was done. She spent a docile year in Switzerland becoming a nice young lady, and then entered LAMDA (the London Academy of Music and Dramatic Art) in 1930, aged nineteen.

After a spell in touring companies and repertory theatre in the provinces, she got her first acting job in London's West End. A good friend, Patricia Hastings, pulled some strings, and she was hired by the prestigious H. M. Tennent management company to do walk-on parts and minor roles in their many theatres. Slowly, she rose to "having her name in small lights", as she put it. Here, in 1937, she met her first husband, my biological father, Frank Arden.

He was what was then known as a "Stage-door Johnnie." These were obsessive theatre-lovers who visited many shows and would hang around after the show to get some autographs or, perhaps, to ask the less famous actresses out to dinner. Astonishingly, one of his group turned out to be my future mother-in-law, Betty Ross (née Davis): see later for tantalizing details.

It was already clear from Hitler's actions in Europe that war might be on the horizon. Fearful of what that might mean, like many couples at the time, Irene and Frank married in late 1937: marriage seemed like a safety net. So far, so good. Eventually, war was declared in 1939.

It is pretty clear what Frank did. He looked for a nice easy billet. He was enlisted as a Second Lieutenant in the Royal Naval Reserve and spent most of his war in a bleak posting in Suffolk, on England's east coast, as far away from danger as possible. One way and the other, Irene and Frank saw very little of each other during the war.

But what of my mother? To her dying day, she maintained that, soon after war started, she enlisted, and took up a clerical job at the Navy HQ. She would tell comical stories of senior officers doing ridiculous things like drying out their damp cotton handkerchiefs, encrusted with snot, on the hot radiators of the classical Admiralty building. But my mother never typed very well, so she cannot have been a secretary. And I could not see her spending the war as a filing clerk.

So, what else was she doing? Much later, when she retired, she decided to move with her second husband to Winslow, a small town 50 miles to the North-West of London. She explained that her old friend, the actress Patricia Hastings, also lived near there. But still, she had many friends elsewhere in the country, so why Winslow? She seemed to have had no roots out there. To me, this was a mystery.

For sixty years, it made no sense. It was only after her death that Patricia Hastings revealed the truth: my mother had been involved with top-secret activities at the now-famous Bletchley Park, just a few miles east of Winslow. She was a "runner", taking decrypted messages from Bletchley's Nazi Enigma machines to the Admiralty HQ in London. She went to her grave without ever telling me about this – even though the world had learned about Alan Turing and his de-coding work at Bletchley Park by the 1970's. But my mother was sworn to secrecy, so she never even hinted at what she'd been doing, except to her closest friend, Pat Hastings. Their training as actors stood them in good stead. No-one else ever knew – with one exception: her future husband.

While at the Admiralty, Irene met someone else, who was also involved in secret business: Vernon Esmond Kennard. He so hated his Edwardian Christian names that he preferred to be called Mick, and that is how my mother knew him. Mick had been a senior officer in the merchant marine almost all his working life. When war was declared, he promptly joined the Royal Naval Volunteer Reserve. Within months, he was a skipper on cruisers, accompanying the vital convoys across the Atlantic, carrying food and weapons from America to Britain. Twice, the ship he was commanding was torpedoed, and he found himself in the freezing North Atlantic with his crew. Twice he was rescued. Third time unlucky, he must have felt, but happily the Navy had other plans for him.

He was seconded to the Admiralty, to engage in a highly secret venture connected to the planned invasion of France on D-Day. There, he met my mother. At this stage, I am fairly sure that they were just good friends. In any case, Mick was often away, developing and practicing a covert project called PLUTO – Pipe-Lines Under The Ocean. This turned out to be one of the more bizarre and remarkable technological feats of WWII. It required ice-cold nerves.

While working as a First Officer for the British India Line before the war, Mick had gained experience of laying oil-carrying pipelines from Bandar Abbas (in present-day Iran) down the Persian Gulf to terminals in British-held territory. Now, he was asked to do the same thing, to deliver diesel oil to the beaches of Normandy, in preparation for the D-Day invasion. The catch was that he and his crew had to lay the pipelines in broad daylight from a small boat, disguised as a fishing trawler.

They adapted real trawlers, to be able to roll out fishing nets on the surface, at the same time as they rolled out flexible oil piping below the waves. From the air, German spotter planes would assume that they were fishing boats and ignore them. Or so they hoped. Near the British coast, they flew the British Union Jack. Near the French coast, at night, they painted a new name on the boat and flew the Tricoleur flag of France. Had they been discovered, not only would it have been clear to the Germans where the invasion was going to take place, but they would all have been shot as spies.

Long story short, it all worked. Mick Kennard was not shot. Irene Arden was not discovered with Top Secrets on her person. And the war eventually ended.

By December 1944, it was fairly clear that the Allies were going to win. But just what the post-war world would look like – with London half-destroyed from bombing and with shortages of food and fuel – was not clear at all. Frank, my mother's husband, came home for Christmas, and in a final burst of passion and optimism, he and Irene got together and created me. I suspect that there was not much love between them any more, and I also suspect that my mother carefully calculated her dates, to ensure she got pregnant. Again, the consummate actress.

By 1947, the marriage was definitely over. Frank left a home where I suspect he never really felt that he had belonged. The last time he saw me, I believe, I was eighteen months old. He never contacted me or my mother again. When I was about to turn twenty-one, in my last year at Oxford University, my godfather asked me whether I'd like to meet my "real" father, because he was still occasionally in touch with him. I said yes, why not? But Frank refused to see me. He could not face the idea, apparently. So I never met him.

The rest of the story I learned from Betty Ross, my future mother-in-law, in the 1980's. She was fascinated by the way my father had been "allowed" (as she put it) to disappear. Long before Google or the Internet were available, this required real work. She was partially disabled and therefore could not act like a traditional gumshoe, pounding the pavement to discover the facts. She went to work like a super-sleuth, however, phoning local government offices around South London, writing letters, getting copies of the marriage, birth and death certificates of everyone named Arden, who might be roughly the right age.

"People do not tend to move far from their roots," she said. "Unless they emigrate."

She had had great success tracking down members of her own family, back to the eighteenth century. She had unearthed some of them as far afield as New Zealand, so finding traces of my father somewhere in south-east England was a piece of cake.

One day in the late 1980's I was briefly over in England, working on a film. I visited Betty with my daughters Amanda and Juliet, and she revealed what she had discovered: Frank had gone on to marry another woman, also called Irene, in 1953, and had fathered another son. She told me that I had a half-brother, called Andrew, whom I had never met and never even knew about. She smiled, and pointed to a pile of telephone directories, covering all of south London.

"Your father died many years ago," she said, "But you'll find Andrew in there…"

Amanda, Juliet and I divided the pile of phone books into three, and thumbed through them, fascinated. There were no Andrew Ardens, until Amanda came to the very last directory, covering a south-east London suburb called Dartford. There he was: listed at Darenth Park Crescent. I looked up at my mother-in-law.

"Dartford's only half an hour's drive from here," she said, mischievously.

"Oh Dad, come on!" chorused Juliet and Amanda. "Let's get in the car and go! We can pretend to be doing a survey for our schoolwork, and knock on his door, and see if he looks like a nice guy! He'll probably be getting home from work any time now."

It took me all of five seconds to decide: let sleeping dogs lie. I was not going to be driving to Dartford to knock on a door, meet a perfect stranger and say "Hello, Brother Andrew."

Did I fear being rejected for the second time – first by my father, then by his other son? Did I really need another close relative, who might want to bring his family to California, to come and visit? Or did I want to maintain the strangely special status of an only child, in my own mind at least? I am sure that psychologists (my wife included) will have much fun with all this, but, as luck would have it, I had acquired a new father when I was five years old – one who could not be bettered – and I did not want to conjure up the ghost of the old one, when I was in my late 30's.

∙∙∙

Back in 1949, aged four, I was taken to Chalk Farm tube station by my nanny for a trip to London's West End. I had a succession of nannies, not because we were rich, but because my mother had to work as an actress, to keep bread on the table. One of them, who did not last very long, rejoiced in the name of Miss Harness, but my favorite was a smiling

Irish woman called McNamara – "Miss Mac" to me. I kept in touch with her till her death in the 1970's.

Occasionally, I would be allowed to take the tube with Miss Mac to Shaftesbury Avenue – London's theatreland –. for a matinée. I became a Stage-door Johnnie myself. Very rarely I would be allowed to stand in the wings, awestruck by the glamor, watching my mother pretending to be someone else on stage, and usually making people laugh. Her greatest hit was in a comedy about a boarding school called *The Happiest Days*, where she played a character part opposite Patricia Hastings, the star. The play ran for eighteen months – a long time for a show to run, back in the 1940's. I was very proud of her, once I was old enough to understand what Shaftesbury Avenue meant.

Not surprisingly, I suppose, Mick Kennard and Irene Arden had started seeing each other soon after Frank had done a bunk. I was soon introduced to "Uncle Mick." They would take me on long and exciting tube train journeys out to the edge of London, where the trains emerged from their mole-like burrows and scuttled along in the sunshine: nobody owned a car if they were not stinking rich, back in the late 1940's. We would have picnics in verdant semi-suburban nooks like Mill Hill – my first memory of the countryside.

Much later, my future mother-in-law, Betty Ross, had her own view on all this. She loved a mystery, and always enjoyed stirring things up.

"Oh, I bet your mother and Mick were close, much earlier on," she said, eyes glinting over a cup of tea. "It was the war! All sorts of things went on in the war."

She even hinted that I might be Mick's child, not Frank's. But there I drew the line: I am sure that my mother was a faithful wife, right to the bitter end. She was that kind of person. And anyway, looking today at the two photos of Frank that my mother kept, I look just like him.

In 1950, my life took a sharp turn. For a start, we moved from cozy, grimy inner London – Chalk Farm, with its warm tube station, just 15 minutes from the glamor of theatreland – to the bleak southern suburb of Croydon. We moved from a modern, 1930's centrally-heated three-room flat into a cold, ugly Victorian 'maisonette' – the upper half of a big house, which was the most that Mick could afford to buy. But it was near a nice big park, with swings and slides, and quite close to a busy railway line. What more could a five-year-old want?

My mother was stoical about the whole thing, because she loved Mick very much, but secretly I am sure she was appalled. Croydon was *ten miles* from the center of London – why, it was not even on the tube. How could she go on acting. when she would have to run to Victoria Station to catch the last train home after the show?

She coped with her exile to the suburbs for a few years by acting on television (in some of the very first TV drama productions in England), but we didn't get a television till 1956, so I never saw them. She did some radio, too: I remember sitting on my grandfather's lap, hearing her playing some stodgy part in a serious radio play. But she soon lost interest and decided to start a high-class lingerie and couture business with her actress friend Patricia Hastings. What is more, they decided they would run the business from our home. "Outworkers" would come in to do the machining, and my father would do the accounts.

So here I was, suddenly surrounded at home by women making frou-frou nighties for posh London stores like Harrods and Fortnum & Mason. All that, and the acting background as well? It's a miracle I'm straight. As an only child, I retreated to my large (and cold!) attic bedroom and lost myself in model trains and fantasy worlds. I really was quite lonely, much of the time. Until, that is, it was time for school.

Every weekday, in winter, my father would bring hot, strong tea up to my bedroom at 6.30 a.m. Many mornings, there would be frost inside the windows, making silver fern-like patterns on the glass. I would get up in this freezing un-centrally heated house, gulp down some porridge (oatmeal) and then walk the mile and a half to school, alone, from the age of five to nine.

In the early 1950's, London was still heated by coal, and still suffered from its famous 'pea-souper' fogs, where you literally could not see more than a few feet in front of you. I knew every sidewalk and turning by feel. Near our house, I would cross the railway lines on a high footbridge. If it was foggy, I would be stunned and frightened by the sharp bang of the military detonators automatically placed on the tracks to warn the drivers to stop, if they could not see the signals.

Down at the High Street, traffic crawled through the pea-souper at walking pace, following the tram tracks: it was the only way the drivers could figure out where the road was. Leading the string of trucks and cars through the fog were fantastical, red, lumbering double-deck trams (US: read trolleys or streetcars) that groaned and whined and clanked their way along, brightly illuminated like fairground attractions. I could ride them for part of the way to school, at the princely fare of one penny for a child's ticket: salmon-colored, neatly printed with the name of every stop, and canceled by the conductor punching a hole opposite your destination. That's one *old* pre-decimal penny: value today less than $0.01.

When the weather was good, however, I walked and saved the pennies, to buy tooth-rotting old-fashioned candy at the kiosk in the park, on the way home: black licorice sticks, bags of sherbet that fizzed in your mouth and barley sugar (hard candy). No wonder English dentistry has a bad reputation in the US: it has had a lot to cope with.

The principal challenge, going to and from school on sunnier days, was to avoid the heaps of horse manure in the roads. When we first moved to Croydon, our household had five separate deliveries by horse-drawn conveyances. Yes, this was 1950, not 1850.

Milkmen delivered daily, before dawn: traditionally, they woke you up with a cheery whistle and the clink of glass milk-bottles. In our street, there was lots of clink but not much cheery whistle. The horse-drawn drays were on their way out, slowly replaced by electric vans, but our milkman liked his horses, and was one of the last to use them, apparently.

It needs to be said that English milk is treated and pasteurized in a different way from the milk in America. Traditional English milk is engineered to spoil within a day or two, even in a fridge. This hugely benefits the milk industry, because it ensures that everyone needs a daily delivery – particularly if you do not have a fridge, which we did not get until 1955 – one year before the TV.

Later in the day, the baker would arrive, in another, much taller horse-drawn wagon – almost a Conestoga. The horses would wait patiently in the road, wearing their blinkers (to prevent them seeing anything to one side, which might frighten them), and chewing the oats in their permanently attached nosebags. The baker came to the side door with a large basket, urgently trying to persuade his customers to buy a little more than their regular daily loaf. And would you believe, the bread, like the milk, was also engineered to go stale within a day or two, to ensure that frequent delivery was maintained. When sliced and wrapped white bread was introduced, it was snootily dismissed by the middle classes as "American," fit only for the working class, who apparently preferred it.

Once or twice weekly, the laundryman called, with an altogether flashier horse-drawn vehicle, to pick up and drop off a package of freshly washed and ironed white towels and sheets. No-one in our road had a washing machine, back then. To wash such things at home, which we occasionally needed to do, required boiling the laundry in a giant galvanized iron tub, which took up all four gas hobs on the top of our cooker. Our cleaner, Mrs. Hall, supervised this operation, with many a muttered curse under her breath. Her performance increased my vocabulary from an early age.

Once a month, the coal men would arrive and cheerfully tip sack-loads of coal through a special manhole into our cellar. Their horses were always jet black: whether from breeding or simply from the coal dust, I could never figure out. Our cellar was a large, damp, ill-lit nest of rooms, and I loved being down there when the coal came in: it roared like an earthquake, and the dust seemed to hang in the air for hours.

Our final horse-drawn visitor was the most unpredictable, the most Dickensian, and the longest lasting: the rag and bone man. Why were they looking to buy (not sell) rags and bones? Because until recently, the paper industry urgently needed linen rags to make good non-wood-pulp paper, and the bones went to make glue. The men uttered an inarticulate street-cry, every ten seconds, as their horses ambled along, pulling a cartload of junk. The cry was meant to sound like "rags and bones," but suggested instead that the man was being forcefully strangled. You could still see them around London into the 1970's. The BBC had a smash hit TV comedy series, *Steptoe and Son*, featuring a particularly smelly and bad-tempered one. They picked up all manner of stuff, at no charge. If the junk contained substantial metal – an old stove, perhaps – you could try and get "half a crown" from them: two shillings and sixpence in the old pre-decimal money.

"They're OK," my father said reassuringly. "Better than the gypsies, anyway." He was always trying to get my mother to turn things out. "I've lived in a ship's cabin for too much of my life," he said. "I've no room for junk." How he would have hated the basement of our house today, and my Museum of Bad Taste, featuring questionable objects collected from film trips all over the world.

Whenever my grandmother was babysitting me and saw one of the many horse-drawn carts arriving, she would say:

"Get your bucket, David! Remember the roses."

It was commonly agreed that horse manure was excellent for promoting the growth of rose trees – second only to animal blood, they claimed – and we had plenty of roses in our front garden. So out I would go to the street, deeply embarrassed, and wait for one of the horses to relieve itself. I never had to wait for long. Once they had moved on, I scraped the steaming pile into my gaily painted metal beach bucket with a small shovel and spread it around the flowerbeds. For this, my grandpa would give me a large sticky lollipop (read: popsicle) and sometimes, if the haul was extravagantly prolific, an eight-sided three-penny coin as well. They were exciting times, indeed.

■■

My first school was a modestly priced private institution, called Coombe Hill House. My parents could barely afford it, I am sure, but my grandparents may have helped with the fees. They were very clear that no grandchild of theirs was going to mingle with *hoi polloi* at the nearest state school, so off I went.

The headmaster was a bald and grumpy disciplinarian, whose name was Dr. Uphill. Mick, or Dad as I was learning to call him, delighted in calling my education "the Uphill struggle."

The staff were all elderly and included various dog-eared individuals like Major Pannett, who had been invalided out of the war with shell-shock and could not control a cage of white mice, let alone a bunch of rambunctious kids The most impressive teacher was Miss Prest, the size of whose bosom was a wonder, even to boys as young as we were. To be "Prest to her Bosom" was a super joke for seven-year-olds and incurred a severe rapping on the knuckles with a twelve-inch ruler, if overheard. Learning was ninety percent by rote. Miss Prest would find the longest and most complex words she could and have us memorize and repeat them ad nauseam.

"Aurora Borealis" she would say. "Aurora Borealis" we chanted in return. But quite what these Northern Lights in the sky were, she never could quite explain.

When I first went to the school, I was still called David John Douglas Arden, just as I had been christened by my mother and father. Frank was a Catholic, and therefore so was I. The "Douglas" was a family name in the Arden family. In my first term at school, I was teased endlessly because of my family name.

"I beg your pardon, Mrs. Arden, for doing poo-poos in your garden" was a time-honored English playground rhyme that was incessantly repeated, and it sometimes reduced me to tears. Children are so kind.

So, in November 1950, Mick and Irene made an important decision. They would marry and Mick would adopt me as his son. They would drop the Douglas, and I would become David John Kennard. And what is more, I would now be officially a member of the Church of England – none of this papist nonsense, much to the relief of my grandparents. The name change was a small thing, but it meant a lot to me.

At school, none of the boys could believe you could change your name as easily as that. Before Christmas, I was Arden; after Christmas, I was Kennard. First names were never used, at an English private school, of course. It was felt that this might lead to an unwholesome intimacy. It was some years before I realized that the name Kennard has its pitfalls too: once we started learning French, the name sounded awfully like Canard, a duck. There was much quacking in the schoolyard. You cannot win. Thirty years later, in Los Angeles, I was still being teasingly called "Hollywood Dave the Duck," by my good friend, the cameraman H.J. Brown.

But more importantly, together with my new father, I also acquired an elder step-brother (Peter) and step-sister (Pamela), the product of Mick's failed first marriage. They were much older than me, and had already left home, but to this day they treat me like a blood brother. To me, Mick became a real caring father and role model – in many ways, the greatest father I could have wished for. I slowly realized that he deeply loved my mother: as a couple, they were inseparable for almost 40 years. It is hard to overestimate what a strong foundation this gave to my life.

In 1953, Queen Elizabeth II was crowned, on a typically rainy day in London. My father's side of the family gathered in the house of his sister Hilda Mary and my Uncle Victor. It was a posh house, half a mile from our more modest quarters. It had a gravel driveway, a billiard room and that most exciting invention, a black and white television set – the first I had ever seen. The screen was about nine inches wide and six inches tall. There was a magnifying device in front of it, which made the picture slightly more visible, but distorted human faces at the edge of the screen, like a funfair mirror. The entire machine was housed in a substantial wooden cabinet, with a large loudspeaker built in.

Uncle Victor herded the family into the Morning Room, as he called it. I had to sit cross-legged in the front row, with cousins I had never met before. Granny and Grandpa Kennard had traveled up from their home in the sedate seaside resort of Folkestone, for the event. Granny was hard of hearing, so the volume was set to maximum. For the kids in the front row, it was like being shouted at by pompous adults, for three solid hours.

I remember being told to stop wriggling, stop whispering, stop giggling and finally to leave the room for five minutes until I was sorry. I recall the voice of the chief narrator, Richard Dimbleby, who solemnly explained every last boring detail of the coronation procedure. I remember one image: Queen Salote of Tonga, riding to Westminster Abbey in an open horse-drawn carriage, defiantly smiling and waving in the pouring rain. I kept wondering when the horses would poo, and someone would rush out with a bucket. But most of all, I remember the TV set itself: the idea that these were actual real live pictures, coming from somewhere else, fired up my imagination more than any of the children's movies and newsreels I had seen in cinemas.

That was the biggest excitement of my life until 1954, when I came down with scarlet fever. At that time, antibiotics had barely arrived in Britain, and scarlet fever was a potentially fatal disease. Most kids caught the less dangerous form, called scarlatina, but "you couldn't be sure which one it was," said my mother.

I had red rashes and felt poorly and very sorry for myself, so I was quarantined in my bedroom, and damp sheets were hung at the bedroom door, apparently to prevent the disease from spreading. My mother wore a mask as she came and went, with comforting drinks and soft foods. Our family doctor, a whiskery old fellow named Bentley, looked increasingly worried, and then announced that I should be taken off to hospital. My parents were aghast. I, of course, thought it all sounded very exciting.

Even at eight years old, I felt a bit of a fraud: I had a nasty rash or two, but I did not feel very ill. So why the drama? I still remember lying in the ambulance en route to the Waddon Isolation Hospital. At that time in England, ambulances did not have sirens. They had a little bell, which went ting-a-ling in a polite but vaguely urgent manner. Anything more would have been considered vulgar and was quite unnecessary in an era when most people traveled by tram, bus or bicycle and the streets were relatively empty.

When we arrived at Waddon, I was told that I had to make a choice as to which soft toys I took in with me. Any teddy which was admitted to the isolation hospital with me would have to be left behind and burned when I came out. The choice was stark: be accompanied by my favorite friends (Bonzo and Quacker) into this fearsome place – and then have them cremated in a month's time? Or take the second-best toys (Bambi and Little Duck and a nameless cat with sharp edges) and pretend that they would see me through OK? I chose the latter, waved my parents goodbye – a kiss or hug would have been infectious – and disappeared into the belly of the beast.

Waddon had been a Dickensian workhouse in the nineteenth century, and not much had changed. Being male and over the age of seven, I was assigned to the Men's Medical ward: thirty or forty beds in long rows, and everyone considerably older than me. I was ignored entirely until the first night. After 'lights out', a small gang of urchins arrived, to break all my pencils, tear up my books and drawing paper, disembowel my soft toys and show me who ran the place.

For two days, I was distraught. I realized that I was not going to be allowed to go home, or even to talk to my parents, for a long time. When they came to see me, they had to wave at me through a thick double-paned observation window. I could not even hear what they said. "Isolation" was the word for it, indeed. Later, I wondered quite how that worked. I am sure most of the other inhabitants were not there because of scarlet fever. They must have had any one of a number of other highly infectious diseases. I think the hospital chucked us all in the same pit, and it was sink or swim. The logic must have been: if you had one disease, you probably would not catch anyone else's. Strange medical habits of the past... but at least the general public was safe from us poor sick brutes.

Then, after a few days, a miracle occurred. I started to really enjoy myself. In part, this was because I really was not very sick. In part – my savior strategy throughout life – I discovered how to make at least some of the other inmates laugh. We developed rude names for all the hard-pressed hospital staff. When they came to polish the linoleum floors with giant industrial scrubbers, we would 'help' by pushing the beds, on their squeaking wheels, to the other end of the vast dormitory, making long trains which crashed into the wall, to the consternation of the staff, who were always on the lookout for the ringleaders of such anarchy. And how could the ringleader be eight years old?

I made two or three good friends, about the same age as me. As soon as I started to feel better, we would sneak out into the wild gardens and climb the apple trees and try to smoke clandestine cigarettes. They made me cough and gag, but I wanted to look like a man, so I persevered, and threw them away when no-one was looking. One time, we managed to get up onto the hospital roof. We could not be sent home, because we were all still infectious, so there were very few ways to punish us. It was springtime, the weather was good, and it suddenly all seemed like a glorious holiday, without parental or any other form of supervision.

When I finally came home after six weeks, I was a changed person. I had twice as much self-confidence. I knew a string of undesirable youths with bad habits. I had acquired a strong quasi-Cockney "Sarf London" accent, and I had learned to swear like a sailor. I had also been reading tattered books from the hospital children's library, which told far-fetched tales about the adventures of boarding school life: *Tom Brown's Schooldays, Jennings and Darbyshire* and the like.

"I want to go to boarding school!" was my cry. Life as an only child with Mummy and Daddy and Granny and Grandpa now seemed distinctly tame.

My grandparents in particular were appalled at my transformation. What could be done to make me into a nice little middle-class boy again? Reluctantly, they agreed that a sharp dose of boarding school was probably the only remedy. The trouble was that Mick and Irene were not earning enough to pay for it. Coombe Hill House cost £68 per term, ('inc. Lunch & Extras') but even a modest boarding establishment cost at least three times that much. My kindly grandfather stepped forward once again. He had a little reserve in his retirement pot and would pay the difference for the next three or four years.

So we set out to find a boarding school that was both affordable and respectable – always the delicate balance that faces the British middle classes. In Mick's 1939 sit-up-and-beg black Vauxhall 12, we drove sedately round the counties of Surrey, Sussex, and Kent, visiting one school after another, out in the countryside. The school had to be far enough from home that I could not easily come home for weekends – strictly disallowed, back then – but near enough that my parents did not bankrupt themselves, when driving down to see me on occasional weekend 'Exeats.' That is Latin and translates as time off for good behavior – maximum eight hours: a day out.

We visited many a pleasant school – ivy-clad mansions and quaint, castellated compounds, with smiling teachers who were more than happy to show us round. But none of them appealed to me. Then, one afternoon, when my parents were starting to lose patience with this treasure-hunt, we arrived, in the pouring rain, at St. John's College, Hurstpierpoint.

Gaunt and forbidding at the best of times, clad in grey Sussex flint, its chapel tower rearing up like a gothic fantasy, Hurstpierpoint in the rain looked like a set design for the Rocky Horror Show. But I was instantly captivated. This is what I had imagined a boarding school ought to look like, from all those grim, manly novels about school life that I had read in Waddon Hospital. And of course, back in the day, like Coombe Hill House, it was a school for boys only. That was clearly what God intended, in the 1950's.

We were welcomed, if that is the right word, by Mr. Kenneth Mason, MA (Oxon), the Deputy Headmaster (read: Assistant Principal). His dour face suggested that he would have liked to be paid extra for the inconvenience of seeing us. He led us round an empty school: it was the spring vacation. He showed us echoing cloisters and the massive chapel. Anglican services were held every day, *de rigueur*, he explained.

We poked our noses into fusty Victorian day rooms, where every boy had a wooden stall called a horsebox, in which he kept his books, pens and a very small number of personal items, which had to be listed and approved. We saw the gaunt, echoing Tuckbox Room, where every boy was allowed to sequester a few treats and candies in a padlocked wooden box, to supplement the meager school fare. I still have that tuckbox in our basement, and my school trunk and suitcase too, all with my initials painted on. Opening them still makes me shiver.

Through the lead-paned windows of the main school, Mr. Mason pointed out the classrooms – still a row of wartime wooden huts in a field. It was not thought necessary to show us the inside of these drab classrooms, for reasons that became obvious later: they were a disgrace. Much more important was to point to the soggy playing fields and the quaintly gabled cricket pavilion.

"*Mens Sana in Corpore Sano* is our guiding principle," said Mr. Mason, drily. "A healthy mind in a healthy body!" If only the staff had known what the pupils got up to with their bodies, they might have chosen a more appropriate motto.

Finally, as the grand climax to the tour, Mason decided to show us the central school lavatories, known for some reason as The Courts: long rows of old-fashioned pull-chain toilets with half-doors, so that school prefects could look underneath, to ensure there was only one boy in each cubicle. They were set in an outdoor courtyard, with the rain pouring down.

"Every boy is expected to move his bowels after breakfast, during the homework hour between 7.45 and 8.45 a.m.," explained Mr. Mason proudly. "A prefect keeps a register in the dayroom, and the boys report to him, upon successful conclusion of their business."

I saw my parents exchange a glance – half horror, half humor. My mother preserved a perfect rictus of approval, however, as she shook Mr. Mason's hand and bade him goodbye. More great acting.

Of course, Mason had said virtually nothing about the academic prowess of the school. He explained that Hurstpierpoint aimed to turn out "a fully rounded boy", who could turn his hand to a little of everything, who had good manners and of course "the right attitude." Most of the boys, he said, went into the church, the military, or the City (read: business): the suggestion was that the school – and God – preferred to think of those careers in that order.

As we drove away, my father let out a great lung-full of air and reached for a cigarette.

"I thought I had a rough tour of duty in the Navy," he said, "But *that* place – my God!" My mother could not stop laughing.

In the back of the Vauxhall, however, I was appalled. "I thought that place was *great*," I said. "I want to go there! Pleeeeease!"

There was a long silence, and then my Dad said, "Well, it's your funeral." That was a favorite expression of his. "I thought that place was a real bugger's muddle." That was another.

"Vernon!" said my mother, disapprovingly. She always called him Vernon rather than Mick, when she disapproved. "Language!"

"Well it was," said my father. "Wasn't it?" There was silence for some time in the car.

In fact, "Hurst", as we were invited to call it, reminded me vividly of the Waddon Isolation Hospital. It had been built around the same time in the 1830's, when England was a no-nonsense place with a burgeoning empire, and needed lots of churchmen, military officers and businessmen to make that empire reputable, functional and profitable. To me, it was the embodiment of a challenge: surely, once inside, I would have as much fun as I had had at Waddon?

Well, no surprise, I did not. In the first three years at the Junior House (also known as the Prep School), things were tolerable. I was quite good at soccer – a saving grace at such an institution. I did well in class too, being quite a smug little "swot," as boys said back then. I could also make the whole dormitory laugh after "Lights Out" with smutty jokes and improvised one-liners. For this, I was beaten on half a dozen occasions. (See the start of Chapter 20).

At the age of thirteen, all the boys sat an important examination called Common Entrance – they do like jazzy names in England. If successful, you were transferred to the Senior School, as is customary in the British private school system. Luckily, at this stage, I won a small scholarship on academic merit, which meant that my parents could afford to keep me at Hurst, without my grandfather's help. Later, I wondered whether this was good fortune or not.

On the one hand, there was good news: corporal punishment had recently been discontinued in the Senior School, because, I later learned, the authorities worried that it might be over-exciting the boys – let alone the staff –rather than disciplining them. I have to say, however, that the Senior School was so tightly regulated and disciplined that there was little opportunity for the "sin that knows no name," as the Headmaster put it. We all masturbated furiously, but for the most part kept ourselves to ourselves. We were too frightened to do otherwise.

The Headmaster never ceased to warn us about vice. Headmaster Howard was officially a Canon of Chichester Cathedral as well as School Principal, and wore his black, clerical garb, together with his academic robes, twenty-four hours a day, as far as we could see. The idea of him in pajamas with a nightcap was too weird to contemplate. He had been at the school since 1937, and already seemed a relic from the Dickensian past. Known as "Chops" from the sinister jowls that adorned his face, he would sweep along the cloisters that served as corridors in the main building. Woe betide the boy who did not step to one side to let him pass. He preached long, fire and brimstone sermons at the Sunday chapel services. He was genuinely scary.

The bad news about getting to the Senior School for me was everything else that came with puberty. My body went haywire. I grew about four inches; my face erupted in acne spots; my eyesight collapsed, requiring National Health spectacles of the sort that Harry Potter wears; and, finally I lost almost all hand-eye and other physical co-ordination. This meant that I was suddenly useless at all sports. And that meant that I joined the ten per cent of lowest-caste boys at the school. To be bad at sports – and what was worse, to be cynical and satirical about school life in general – was the cardinal sin at Hurst. It probably cast you into a deeper circle of Dante's hell than even blasphemy or sodomy.

That, I think, is why I started to get interested, deep down, in the media. Initially, curiously enough, it was a way of avoiding public attention. With two equally unsporty friends, I started the Printing Society. In a bitterly cold flint-covered outhouse, we struggled with a small Adana printing press that the school had been given, and produced business cards, invitations and cricket "Fixture Lists" of matches against similar schools. Unofficially, we also produced an irregular one-page news sheet, with school scandal of every sort: the Samizdat of Hurstpierpoint College. Incredibly, these rags were never discovered, or traced back to the Printing Society. Probably the school authorities would never have imagined we had the patience or the skill to sit in the freezing cold, using tweezers to pick out enough 10-point Times Roman type to fill a page or two.

In my final year, entirely due to the encouragement of my French teacher, "Johnny" Sturrock, I sat the entrance examinations for a group of Oxford colleges. Sturrock was a legend: he wore cool clothes – for 1962 – including shockingly narrow trouser legs and suede Hush Puppies. He drove an open-top Sunbeam Alpine, which was considered very racy. He had worked as a copywriter in advertising. Indeed, he had been one of the team which invented a famous advertising campaign for Smarties (British M&Ms): "Wotalotigot" was the slogan, endlessly repeated on the single British commercial TV channel. Whenever Johnny Sturrock gave us good marks on a French test, we'd say "Wow, sir! What A Lot I Got," and he took it with good humor.

The school had not put up a boy for Oxford for several years and was somewhat baffled by how it all worked. Luckily, Sturrock had been a student there, and had thoroughly enjoyed his time at a small, ancient institution within the University: Lincoln College.

"Apply to Lincoln," he told me, "You'll love it. It's friendly, and it's right in the center of the city. John Wesley studied there, and he founded Methodism, so do watch out for the God Squad. But the cellar bar's five hundred years old, and the faculty is good." It was valuable advice, coming from someone with Sturrock's experience. He left Hurst a couple of years later and went on to a distinguished career at the Times Literary Supplement and the London Review of Books. I was lucky to have had such a sophisticated mentor.

But wait… Oxford? Nobody from my family had ever been to university before. And if I was accepted, I would matriculate (i.e. enroll at the University) only one month after my 18th birthday. Help! I had always been considered "young for my age." And I came from dreary Croydon and Dickensian Hurstpierpoint, so how would I survive in this bastion of privilege?

I took a train up to snowy Oxford in February 1963. Knees knocking and teeth chattering – partly from the fright, partly from the extreme cold of that winter – I sat the examination papers in a gaunt, empty hall. It seemed even grimmer than the cloisters at Hurstpierpoint. But, incredibly, I passed the exams and was accepted by Lincoln College, to start in October. Forty-five years later, our son James was to follow in my footsteps, though I don't think he enjoyed the Lincoln experience quite as much as I did. He hadn't had five years of training behind the gaunt flint-stone walls of Hurstpierpoint College.

To celebrate receiving my "Get Out of Jail Free" card, and to enjoy the rest of the school term, I joined a couple of friends – The Gang of Three, we portentously called ourselves later, echoing Chairman Mao's language – and sketched out an idea for an end-of-term entertainment.

Britain had been stunned, the previous autumn, by a new, topical Saturday TV show called *That Was The Week That Was*. Hosted by David Frost, with a cast of comedians and singers, it was in some ways the precursor to the American *Laugh-In,* with Rowan and Martin. But TW3, as it was known, was far more bitingly satirical and up-to-the-minute. It was so 'live' that scripts for the finale were apparently updated while the show was on the air. It was allowed to run on, from a start time at 10 p.m., for as long as the producers decided – sometimes for a couple of hours – past midnight, even! Unheard of, on British TV in 1962. When I asked to see the show at home, my parents went to bed, saying it was probably not to their taste. How right they were...

The Gang of Three suggested to the school authorities that they would like to write and perform a topical news show for three performances in the school theatre, shortly before the Easter vacation began. Tongue in cheek, we suggested that it would be good for the students to keep up with current affairs, that there would be scenes depicting interesting school events during the past three months, and that there would be musical interludes too. It sounded, on the face of it, like a mild Victorian concert party, and no mention was made of TW3.

Robert Bury, the master in charge of the theatre, only rarely allowed the boys to perform anything but Shakespeare, poetry readings and Christmas concerts: they were all thoroughly safe. But he thought our current affairs plan sounded like a wholesome enterprise and gave us the green light. What he had neglected to consider was that there would be no script, which could be vetted and pre-censored: it was, we insisted, a news show, a *topical* show – a live show...

In retrospect, our material was pretty tame. There was a theme song, predictably *That Was The Term, That Was,* which referred scathingly to highlights of the school's activities. There were a couple of genuinely funny sketches, including an attempted piano recital by a music scholar, who had to keep stopping to remove bizarre items from his concert grand: a cabbage, a motor horn, a dead rat. There was a sports report, in which we excitedly recited details of the only games the school had *lost*, in hockey, rugby, etc. There was a small band, which was intentionally terrible. There were many parodies of teachers in the school, mocking their mannerisms and foibles. Plus, of course, we had to include a few double entendres of a schoolboy sort. But as the comedian Ronnie Barker once pointed out:

"The best thing about double entendres is that they can only mean one thing."

The curtain went up on the first performance of *That Was The Term, That Was* at 7.00 p.m. on the final Wednesday of March, 1963. The theatre was packed. Word had obviously got out that the audience was in for something unusual. Most of the seats were filled by pupils – as the school still called them – but there was a fair share of teachers and their wives and families, school staff and other local well-wishers. Remember, there was no official script. It was all improvised, though the performers had scraps of paper in their pockets to remind them of key jokes and punch lines.

I still have a reel-to-reel tape of the show. It was, frankly, terrible: very amateur indeed. No pacing, long pauses, laugh-lines trodden on by other over-eager actors. But there were undoubted highlights, and it provoked a lot of laughter. One of the boys – "no names, no pack drill," as my father would have said – did an uncanny imitation of the Headmaster. Plagiarizing Alan Bennett in the great satirical London stage show of the era, *Beyond the Fringe*, he imitated Canon Howard giving one of his fire and brimstone sermons, and this brought the house down.

The following day, we were preparing for the second performance, when the Headmaster himself entered the auditorium, black robes swirling around him, and took up a seat in the center of the front row, flanked by two of the teachers, who were known to be strict disciplinarians. They folded their arms, looked like thunder, and sat facing straight forward. The theatre filled up, seven o'clock came round, and up went the curtain.

About fifteen minutes into the show, the Headmaster stood up and bellowed: "STOP! Stop this disgraceful nonsense immediately!"

You could have heard a pin drop. Howard looked like the angel of death, as he turned to the audience.

"I beg your pardon for this farrago of filth, ladies and gentlemen. It will cease immediately. Boys, you will go back to your dormitories in single file and complete silence. There, you will await further instructions."

He then turned to the stage: "As for everyone involved in this so-called entertainment, you should be ashamed of yourselves. I will see all those who are responsible for it in my study at 9 o'clock tomorrow morning."

He swept out of the theatre like a battleship at full steam.

"All those responsible" had to be really just us, the Gang of Three. Although the entire cast and stage crew turned up at the Headmaster's office at 9am, to offer moral support, most of them were sent away with only a firm ticking-off. Then the Headmaster turned to us three.

"How DARE you?" he said, seeming almost lost for words – an unusual occurrence for him. "HOW DARE YOU? Bringing the name of the School into disrepute! Do you realize how many of the school staff were present in the theatre, let alone the masters and their families? News of this disgraceful show will be all over the village by now. We'll be fortunate if we do not get into the local newspapers. Do you realize what you've done to me? You've undone the work of a lifetime. HOW DARE YOU?"

We were all quite scared by now. We had never seen Canon Howard quite as angry as this. Would it mean reinstatement of corporal punishment? Three days in the coal cellar with only bread and water? But worse was to come.

"You are all hereby expelled from the school. I shall be telephoning your parents this morning, to instruct them to come immediately and remove you from the premises. Go to your dormitories and pack your clothes."

So I left Hurst under a cloud. Luckily, all three of us ringleaders had already gained university places, and the School could not take those away from us. We did not need to stay on for the summer term at all. Things started to look a little brighter.

My father arrived in the family Ford, and picked up me, my trunk and my tuckbox. I felt the eyes of the school upon me, peeping from behind the lead-paned windows in the old flint buildings, as the pariah was removed from the premises. Goodbye, Hurstpierpoint.

But the clouds soon parted. My father, once we had passed the school gates, asked me tentatively why exactly I had been expelled. When I told him, he heaved a sigh of relief, and laughed.

"Oh, thank God for that," he said. "Your mother and I were afraid you'd been found in bed with the Captain of Cricket." He laughed, and added: "Every cloud has a silver lining, you know. I won't have to pay the fees for the summer term."

In fact, he went one better than that: he put the money that he and my mother had set aside for the fees into a savings account for me, to enable me to travel abroad during my Oxford days. I am sure I learned more from those travels than I ever would have done in that final summer term at Hurstpierpoint College. Thank you, Dad, for this and for so much more – including my sense of humor.

There is a small postscript to this story. My father had insisted that I spend the summer "in the real world." He had arranged for me to be taken on as a lowly intern at Fuller, Wise and Fisher, a City of London firm of accountants, to see what actual work felt like. Needless to say, it was not my choice of career, but it had its amusing side: some of the other young people who worked there were also pranksters. It helped them to relieve the tedium of auditing company accounts.

When they heard how I had been expelled, one of them suggested the perfect way of getting my own back on the school. They helped me print a series of black and white postcards, ostensibly from a pornographic film company in London's Soho district: the Spanky Panty Film Club. We typed brief messages on several of these cards, ostensibly asking the head of the school's Film Society to return copies of blue films that, of course, had never existed or been sent to the school.

I knew that the school mail was routinely inspected by the School Porter before distribution. He was a little weasel, a tattle-tail who was roundly hated by all the pupils. We could imagine his glee at reading a postcard, addressed to the Film Club, saying "Regret that we cannot supply a copy of *Nudes in the Snow* for your meeting on the fifteenth of next month. Can we replace it with *Nuns on the Go* or *Who's A Big Boy Now?*" The news would get to Canon Howard within minutes.

The prank succeeded beyond my wildest expectations. I was told that the Headmaster preached a sermon on smut, filth and the moral dereliction of the school. The president of the Film Society, a friend of mine, was in turn called to the Headmaster's office for some unspeakable punishment. But he had rightly guessed that I might be behind this business. He asked for permission to phone me, to find out if it was so. Using the single publicly available telephone from an English boarding school in 1963 was an enormous privilege, usually confined to emergency situations. This was certainly an emergency – for him at least. He pleaded with me, to confess to the prank and save his bacon: he still did not have a university place or a job lined up.

So I penned a neat, sober-sided, hand-written letter to the Headmaster, admitting everything, assuming all blame, and requesting that my friend should not be hung, drawn or quartered. In return, two weeks later, I received an anonymous letter from the school, without even the Head's signature, informing me that, as a result of my gross misdemeanors, I would be barred from the School premises for life. But my friend was spared any punishment.

Today, Hurstpierpoint College is utterly transformed. Canon Howard offered his resignation to the School Governors in the summer of 1962 and was replaced by a modernizing headmaster called Griffiths. They have admitted girls as well as boys for more than quarter of a century now. Imagine that! They have invested in fine new buildings; their exam results are impressive; the atmosphere is completely different.

I couldn't resist going back to Hurst one last time ten years later, with my own young son and daughter, James and Pippa. We casually strolled across the campus to the school's Bury Theatre, named after my old Housemaster. It was empty and nothing seemed to have changed. I walked across the stage with my children, memories flooding back. I told them that this was where their Daddy had produced and directed a very naughty show, thirty-five years before, and had been severely punished. Now it was their turn to laugh: they didn't seem to think that their father had changed that much.

· ·

THE TRAVELER'S JINX

Before I plunge into tales of radio, TV and film production, and the quirks and egos of those who work there, there is one more ingredient to add to the recipe that has made me what I am, for better or worse: a deep desire to travel – to be somewhere else, to enquire into other people's lives – even to try and live other people's lives. But my early attempts to do so were accompanied, earlier in my life, by one near disaster after another.

Right from the start, I was cursed with the curiosity that killed the cat. It damn nearly killed me too on a few occasions. I am sure that the urge to look round the next corner, or the next country, is one of the driving forces that lead people to become journalists or documentary filmmakers. People like me are just too nosey. We are the kids who persist in asking "why?" long after our parents and teachers have lost patience with us.

From the age of eight, I roamed around London on the tubes and buses by myself. Astonishingly, my parents were happy to let me do this. For sure, the mid-1950's were a safer age in many respects: most people in England "knew their place," I suppose. But I had no idea when and if I was journeying into dangerous areas of the big city. In retrospect, I was like Christopher Robin, wandering naively through the Hundred Acre Wood. On school vacation weekdays, as an only child with nothing else to do, I bought a cheap Red Rover day ticket, which allowed travel everywhere in London on the red buses and tubes. I would set off after breakfast for who knows where: 750 square miles to investigate and discover.

Armed only with a large London Transport foldable paper map, I left our house in Croydon, to poke around the furthest reaches of the metropolis. I made it out to the far north east, to sunny Ongar, an Essex village way out in the countryside,
at that time still served by a limb of the tube's Central Line. I followed in the footsteps of Dickens and Sherlock Holmes, into the bowels of Whitechapel and Wapping, when these areas were still ancient, decrepit and dangerous. No-one told me about the Kray brothers and their infamous East End gang. No-one told me about the terrible murders that had recently happened at 10, Rillington Place in Notting Hill, long before that area became fashionable and expensive.

But never once was I accosted, molested or even lost in London. I would arrive home at dusk, and tell long stories about how I'd been to Highgate Cemetery and seen Karl Marx's grave, whoever he was, or down "the drain", the bizarre one-stop shuttle line that connected Waterloo mainline station with the Bank of England, or run down the deepest spiral staircase on the tube (at Hampstead).

"That's nice, dear," said my mother. "Supper's nearly ready."

But my good fortune in traveling was to change, the moment I went abroad by myself. From then on, almost every trip seemed to invite disaster, for the next ten years. Was I jinxed, as my parents came to believe?

My first trip outside England was a family camping vacation to France in July 1957, when I was nearly twelve. My parents had recently bought their very first new car, a pale gray Ford Consul, which my father christened Lady Jane, in honor of the historical character, Lady Jane Grey. Like many men, when car-ownership was still a novelty, he thought it was fitting to name cars, the way that ships were always named. Custom dictated that the names had to be female. The old 1939 Vauxhall 12, registration FLW 365, had been called Flo (short for Florence, apparently), and had recently been put out to pasture.

The British government, being in a parlous economic state ever since World War II, only allowed each family to take a tiny quantity of cash abroad, and credit cards weren't introduced in the UK till 1966. Before we left home, my mother crammed every nook and cranny of the new Ford with frugal rations. Most of it was canned English food: Spam, Luncheon Meat, Salad Cream, Baked Beans, Condensed Milk, Tapioca Pudding, Vegetable Salad, Peach Slices in Syrup – a veritable orgy of the bland comestibles of the 50's, packed full of artificial preservatives, colorings and flavorings. And we were going to France, the legendary home of fine food! Along with two tents and a couple of naval kitbags, there was also just room for a "Camping Gaz," (a two-burner device for making tea and warming up the tinned food), and an old-fashioned cooler that looked like a giant Thermos vacuum flask.

For two weeks, we struggled through France, pitching our tents in fair weather or foul, and preparing our modest English banquets every evening, under the incredulous gaze of German and Dutch campers, who tended to drive into the nearest town for dinner. But nothing very dangerous happened, apart from the constant hair-raising experience of overtaking large trucks on those picturesque two-lane French highways, which plunge southwards through avenues of plane trees.

In England, of course, we drive on the left. In Europe they drive on the right. Our holiday driver was always my father. He had to operate with the steering wheel 'on the wrong side.' I sat next to him, as chief map-reader and port-side look-out.

"Do be careful, Mick," my mother would say, somewhat unnecessarily, and then shut her eyes. She had never learned to drive, and always chose to sit in the back and have one of her migraines, so as not to witness our constant dicing with death.

My father used to put the nose of the car out very gently, so that the front-seat passenger (me) could see if it was safe to try and overtake.

"NO!" I would usually shout. Or, more often, "NOOOO!"

But occasionally I'd say "Well, maybe," in which case my father would pull out and estimate if Lady Jane had enough oomph under her bonnet (read: hood) to make it past the truck in front, before the oncoming bus hit us. No holiday journey on the French Routes Nationales was ever boring.

But the sense of danger increased, when I made my first foreign trip alone.

My cousin Helen had spent a very enjoyable six weeks with a French family in the city of Lyon, during the summer of 1960. The Bechetoile family had a flat in the city – the father was a banker – and a ramshackle chateau some fifty miles south, near Annonay, on the banks of the River Rhone. The following spring, Helen was eager to return. I was soon to find out why. She begged my mother (her aunt) to give this plan the green light and explained that there would be plenty of room for both of us in the Bechetoile's homes.

This seemed the perfect opportunity to pick up some conversational French, so my parents were pleased to accept. At some stage in the future, we would need to have the young son to stay with us in London, to reciprocate the hospitality, but that seemed very possible.

"What a good plan," my mother said, tying a metaphorical blue ribbon round the arrangements, as she often liked to do.

Cousin Helen communicated with me at my boarding school by writing letters. I should prepare myself, she said, by learning bridge: all the French teenagers played bridge to while away the hot afternoons and long evenings at the chateau.

"You don't need to be good at it, but at least you need to join in," she explained.

Then there was the question of alcohol: from the age of eight, Helen told me, the children drank red wine, watered down, with the cheerful permission of their parents. Indeed, outside the evening meal, the kids seemed to subsist on nothing but bread (the crispy, French baguettes), dark chocolate and red wine. Best not to tell my parents about that, we agreed.

Most of the kids smoked, too, so Helen told me I had better get used to that before leaving for France. I sneaked a couple of mild Abdullah filter cigarettes from my father, when he was not looking, and duly coughed and spluttered and threw up a couple of times, as I went through the training. Little did I know that, in France, I would be expected to smoke unfiltered Gauloises Caporals – about as strong as tobacco gets before it explodes.

So off I went, in the month-long Easter vacation of 1961, to experience the most exciting weeks of my life so far. The family was large, the number of young people down in Annonay – where we spent most of the time – was huge, and there was virtually no parental supervision whatsoever.

On a Friday morning, we would all pack into the three rows of a Peugeot "shooting brake", as they called it – or estate car, or station wagon, or whatever name you give these extended cars – and drive south for two hours. All our luggage was roped to the top of the car. Everyone would talk at once, with Madame usually at the wheel. She had a way of gesticulating vigorously as she talked and smoked, and things did not change when she was driving. She would often use both hands to emphasize a point, leaving nothing but pressure from her ample thighs to keep the steering wheel from spinning wildly. Bechetoile car journeys were like a claustrophobic fairground ride, with thrills aplenty.

I was always in the back of the three rows, along with at least two other people, one of whom was Madeleine, the maid. Madeleine was a sad-faced woman who cooked and cleaned and never seemed to get any time off. No wonder her expression was one of gloomy resignation. She was treated like a dog, frankly, and lived in a tiny room no bigger than a walk-in closet. She was kind enough to me, in her taciturn fashion, but she had one big drawback: she stank.

It is easy today to forget that the French had a Europe-wide reputation for being unhygienic until well into the second half of the twentieth century. "It's why they invented the perfume industry," adults would tell me in England. The water was "non-potable" in many of the taps: enamel signs warned you against drinking from them. Many of the older generation of French men and women seemed to feel that washing frequently was an unnecessary luxury. Indeed, the smell of the Paris Metro, until quite recently, was a potent mixture of sweat, garlic, cheap perfume and cigarette smoke. Thank goodness, the date they finally banned smoking on the trains coincided more or less with general French acceptance of modern plumbing, sanitation and effective soap.

Anyway, in the back row of the Peugeot, there were no windows that opened, and there certainly was no air-conditioning. So the temperature rose to well into the thirties, centigrade – somewhere near blood temperature – and Madeleine's aroma dominated the car. I later learned that the other kids used to pick straws to determine who else shared the back seat with Madeleine, but it was always me who got placed right next to her.

That spring was in many ways idyllic, however. Down in Annonay, I learned to ride a motorbike on one of the insanely dangerous French VeloSolexes. They were like oversized bicycles, with a small motor balanced on top of the front wheel, powering the wheel by friction. All the weight was up front, so, if you hit a pothole, too bad: over the handlebars you went, and onto the road, whereupon the VeloSolex would then probably run over you. Helmets were unheard of. I came off two or three times and was lucky to escape serious injury. On one occasion, I was somewhat stunned. I was carried indoors to a dark room, Madeleine sponged my wounds, and I was given a stiff brandy. That was French First Aid. But it worked.

I also got to kiss and canoodle with one or two of the family's many cousins and friends. After about 10 p.m., after some wine and a few hands of bridge, every evening seemed to conclude this way. A sweet girl called Geneviève must have taken pity on this gauche English boy with spectacles and acne, and taught him how to kiss and cuddle. It did not go much further than that – this was 1960, after all, and I was not yet sixteen – but it did wonders for my morale. Smoking, drinking, playing cards, riding motorbikes and now – sex! No wonder I decided to go on and study French at Oxford.

So, why does this happy story figure in the *Traveler's Jinx* chapter? For one good reason. As my vacation drew to a close in mid-April, we drove back to Lyon, so that I could prepare to return to England. I had tickets from Lyon to Paris, Paris to Calais, Calais to Dover (by ferry), and Dover to London.

For once, Monsieur Bechetoile was listening to the car radio throughout the journey: "*C'est grave, la situation,*" he told us all.

I noticed that there were long military convoys on the highway, and the main road was blocked in two places, requiring long deviations. The atmosphere was tense, but I could not fathom what was going on.

The following morning in the Lyon flat, we were woken at 6am by the sound of rumbling and clanking. Looking out of the windows up on the third floor, we saw tanks rolling past on the streets: it looked like a cinema newsreel. There were no cars or buses. There were plenty of police and soldiers. France had woken up to find that the country was on the brink of civil war.

The radio news was running just one story: rebel generals in the French colony of Algeria were trying to launch a right-wing coup. They had joined the Nationalist political parties and refused to countenance France giving up its colony. Several bombs had exploded in various parts of the country, one at the Gare de Lyon station in Paris, which had been closed. The airports had all been shut, the ports were blocked, and the country was in a state of lockdown. General de Gaulle, the French President, was calling for calm, but it seemed that half the French military were preparing to fight him.

Around lunchtime, my father managed to get a phone call from London through to the Bechetoile's flat. It had taken him all morning. This was back in the day when every international call had to be pre-booked through the operator and cost a fortune. That morning – no surprise – all lines to France were particularly busy.

How could the Bechetoiles get me out of France? No-one knew if the situation would deteriorate, and a real civil war would spread.

"Do whatever you need to," my father said to Monsieur B. "Whatever it costs."

There was a council of war immediately after the call. The family proposed that the only way out would be via Switzerland: this border might not be as heavily guarded as the maritime ports. This plan would require a train to Geneva and a flight from Geneva to London's Heathrow airport – provided that the trains were still running between Lyon and Geneva.

I stepped out into the street with Madame Bechetoile, past the military trucks and tanks, which had closed down the main streets. We took back alleys to a travel agent.

There, we learned that a few express trains were getting out to Switzerland, though none were being allowed back for the time being. Madame B booked a ticket. When the travel agent tried to find a seat on a plane to London from Geneva, she discovered that only First Class was available.

"Book it!" said Madame B. To me, she said, "We will send the bill to your father."

So, the following morning, my journey began at Lyon's Perrache station, just around the corner from the flat. I felt like a secret agent, slipping across the border into Switzerland. In Geneva, I had no Swiss francs to pay for the bus to the airport, and no-one wanted French francs, with the country poised on the brink of civil war. Luckily, I had a few British pound notes, and they were accepted. By the skin of my teeth, I reached the airport in time. All was chaos: many other people had had the same idea – to get out of France as soon as possible.

Just an hour later, I was sitting in a British European Airways turboprop plane, luxuriating in First Class. I was given a pre-flight glass of champagne by the stewardess, who seemed quite unconcerned that I was only fourteen years old. This was the first time I had ever been in an "aeroplane", as the English still called them back then. It remains the only time I have ever flown First Class. It was a great introduction to air travel. The anxieties of the previous 36 hours vanished in a moment.

●●

My parents were relieved to have me back in one piece, and I duly embroidered the story for telling to my friends at school. Tanks in the street sounded just like a war movie, though I had not heard a single shot fired. But all the adults told me this was just a one-off. France had not eventually collapsed into civil war, and I was safe and sound, so what was the big deal?

My next travel adventure came less than a year later. I had started learning German at school as well as French, and it was considered necessary to have total immersion in the language, since I had started to learn it fairly late, by European standards. So the school arranged that I should spend two months in Hamburg at a Grammar School, or Gymnasium, as the Germans call it, rather confusingly. I would swap places with an unfortunate German boy, who would be sent to Hurstpierpoint College at exactly the same time. I would stay in a nice warm modern flat with his family, and he would stay in a large unheated dormitory, in the bleak embrace of Hurst. I thought I had the best of the deal.

My mother duly packed a bag, with some warm clothes and my school raincoat, and came to London's Liverpool Street Station, to see me off, at 8pm on 16 February, 1962. The weather was foul: rain and low scudding clouds. The Harwich-Hook of Holland Boat Train was still pulled by a steam locomotive at that time, and the goodbye scene felt like a sequence from a World War II movie. Little did I know, as the train pulled out into the darkness, how close I was going to come to a WWII experience.

The first hint that all was not well came during the voyage of the good ship Duke of York. There had been some suggestion that the ferry might not even sail, because of the extreme winds and bad weather. But the skipper apparently had seen worse, and nothing was going to stop him. We were told to batten down the hatches, stay below, and on no account go for a stroll on deck. We left the dismal east coast port of Harwich shortly before midnight, and immediately hit rough seas.

The first problem was that no-one was allowed out on deck, though more than half the passengers were soon violently seasick. The "heads" (as sailormen like to call the bathrooms) were running in vomit, as were the bars and lounges. I had a berth in a two-bed cabin, and my roommate was a great deal sicker than I was. The entire ship stank, as it bobbed around like a cork in the teeth of the gale.

We arrived at first light and limped into the port of Hoek van Holland. The wind had died down, but it was still raining. Drenched to the skin, I had my passport stamped and found the Hamburg train. In fact, the train went on to Warsaw in Poland, but I had a reserved seat in a carriage with an enamel plate on the door, saying Hamburg Hauptbahnhof

(Central Station), so all I had to do was get in and stay warm until we got there, right? Wrong.

The train was late leaving, and then seemed to stop for longer than usual in the principal stations en route: Rotterdam, Utrecht, and on into Germany. I had reset my watch to European time, an hour ahead, and could see that there was no way we were going to make Hamburg on schedule. Slowly, I realized that something was wrong. People in the compartment were chattering anxiously, in Dutch or German, but I could not understand a word of what they were saying. Then the ticket-controller arrived and made a short official announcement in German. I tried to understand and was helped by a friendly woman sitting next to me.

"Big flood," she said. "Hamburg *zerstoert* – destroyed, you say? No bridges remain. No station. A big tragedy."

I was shocked. This was getting more and more like the World War II stories my parents had told me. What should I do? I was due to be met at Hamburg Central Station by the family who had invited me. But the apocalypse had apparently got there first.

The train trundled on, very slowly now, and we could all see that the fields surrounding the track were inundated. We came to an unscheduled halt at a wayside station: Buxtehude. A station announcement (in German) was being made: it seemed to be a list of some kind. Suddenly, in the midst of incomprehensible words, I thought I heard my name. I asked the woman next to me. She said the list was being repeated. I listened.

Yes, "*David Kennard... Aussteigen, bitte.*" Get off the train! If I had not done so, I would have been carried on to East Germany and Poland.

There on the platform at Buxtehude, I found the Hansel family, holding up a very wet piece of cardboard with my name on. They looked a great deal more worried than I felt, but I did not yet know the extent of the damage: freak high tides, the Elbe river had burst its banks, more than three hundred were dead, twenty-five thousand homes destroyed, winds of one hundred and thirty miles per hour, sixty dykes collapsed, bridges washed away, rail operations suspended. My two- month stay in Germany was not going the way I had expected.

The suburb of Harburg, where the Hansels lived and the children went to school, was on higher ground, and had not been badly damaged. But between them and Hamburg was the low-lying suburb of Wilhelmsburg, which was devastated. It took two weeks to reinstate the tram service, and for some time thereafter, the tram offered the only way to get into Hamburg itself. Perched on temporary wooden trestles, it trundled and clanked along at fifteen miles per hour. Looking down at the surrounding lake of water, stretching as far as the eye could see, was a sobering sight. The center of the city was covered in mud and looked like a war scene once again, less than seventeen years after the conclusion of hostilities.

"*Ach, du lieber Gott!*" (Dear God!) said Mrs. Hansel.

Once again, my parents tried desperately to make an international phone call, to see how I was, or indeed where I was. The Hansels tried to call London, too, but the wreckage was so extensive that it took two days before international phone calls were possible. Two days of white-knuckle worry for my parents. Finally we got through.

"You're jinxed," my father said. "Every time you go abroad by yourself, something dreadful happens. The country falls apart. We should send you to Russia for a holiday – that'd put a spoke in their wheels." My mother was less inclined to make a joke of it all.

Much to my relief, the Hansels were the complete opposite of the humorless German stereotype. They enjoyed jokes, even if the jokes were peculiarly Germanic.

"We are the Hansels of Hamburg, the H Family," Papa told me. "I am Heinrich Hansel, and my wife is Heidi Hansel. Our son, who is visiting your school, is called Hans. So he is Hans Hansel of Hamburg. This is his younger brother Heiko. All the H's. Ha Ha Ha. So you never forget us, huh?"

Every night, we would sit and watch the evening news on television and see the slow progress of repairs to the city. We would eat black bread and more varieties of dried sausage, steamed sausage and fried sausage than I knew existed. Sauerkraut was the vegetable, with some spicy pickles on the side. Tea, with lemon and no milk, was the beverage. I came to love this diet, and still do. I had no nostalgia whatsoever for British cooking, and particularly Hurstpierpoint school cooking. Poor Hans Hansel was stranded at my school, faced with boiled gray meat and gravy, with suet pudding to follow: what would he make of England?

On Saturday nights, Heinrich Hansel liked to invite a few friends round, open some beers and play some ribald games. Young Heiko, being only 10, was sent to bed before these parties, but I was encouraged to stay up and join in the fun.

Heinrich did a disturbingly accurate impression of Adolf Hitler, with a black comb under his nose, representing the moustache. He would march round the apartment, his voice rising as he warmed to the task of reproducing a Hitler speech. His friends all had their party tricks too: one played Goebbels, one played Himmler, one played Goering. They would work themselves up into a fine lather, laughing and shouting and marching around as if practicing for a rally.

"Sieg Heil!" they would shout, shooting their arms out. Were they serious, or was it all a parody? They would collapse into fits of giggles.

"Those people were all clowns!" said Heinrich, wiping the tears from his eyes and cracking another beer. "David, why don't you play Winston Churchill, eh?"

I found this embarrassing and pretended I did not know how to imitate Churchill's accent. I need not have worried. Heinrich could impersonate Winston as accurately as he did Hitler. He found a cigar.

"Never," he said ponderously, "In the field of human conflict", (pause) "has so much", (longer pause) "been owed… by so many… to so few… and so often!"

There was more hearty laughter from all concerned, except from Heidi, his wife. She gave me a pale smile and left the room. Later, the men, fortified with beer, often had a belching and farting contest, trying to imitate the sounds which might be made by a nun, say, or Chancellor Adenauer, or singer Charles Aznavour, as they attempted to break wind politely. At that stage I would make my excuses, as they say, and go to bed.

How could I know that, a few years later, in my first year at the BBC, I would meet and direct television interviews with two *genuine* senior Nazis? That experience, however surreal, was no laughing matter. (See Chapter 2)

••

There was one final journey, before I finished my studies, that really did go wrong. I had thought my travel jinx had been broken, after several successful vacation trips with school and university friends to European destinations. But then the opportunity arose to join a very special expedition – overland to India.

I heard about COMEX in 1965, while singing in a musical comedy, at the end of my second year at Oxford. The show was set in the 1920's and called *You Can't Do Much Without A Screwdriver*. It was very silly but quite tuneful, and featured almost every notable performer at the University, plus a lot who were not, like me. I was just one of a chorus of twenty, somewhere in the back row probably, because I cannot sing any better than I can act.

We were touring the show to the Arts Theatre in Cambridge, when one of the other chorus members asked me if I wanted to join a Commonwealth Expedition: COMEX. Apparently, five buses representing five universities would be leaving London in July, to travel by road to India. Each busload would put on plays and comedy sketches, as we drove through Europe and into Asia, in the interest of international understanding. The grand climax would be a reception by Mrs Indira Gandhi, the Indian Transport Minister, in New Delhi. It sounded like a daft idea, but really intriguing. And thanks to philanthropic support and commercial sponsors, it would cost me precisely nothing.

If I had stopped to think about what we were attempting to do, I might never have left the shores of Britain. The journey was going to be longer than 8000 road miles We would be driving very ordinary old-fashioned English tour buses, with heavy-duty springs and tires and extra fuel tanks, but no air-conditioning or on-board bathroom. The drivers were all students, none older than twenty-three: they were given no more than a week's training on how to drive a bus at the British Army's Catterick Camp. My Oxford friend Jeremy Gibson was one of them.

"My God," he said when he got back from Catterick. "The buses are really heavy. There's no power steering, and most of the roads between here and Delhi are unpaved. Oh yes, and of course we'll be driving on the wrong side of the road from Belgium to Pakistan. But the steering wheels will be on the right, because they're British buses."

The navigators were all students too. I was one of them. We were given a one-day briefing by the expedition leader, Colonel Gregory, whom we came to know as Greg. He was a tireless leader, who made light of every problem and had single-handedly put this whole undertaking together. He had even secured the patronage of His Royal Highness the Duke of Edinburgh.

"You navigators have two jobs," Greg told us. "To make sure you don't get lost, of course, and to make sure you don't get everybody killed. You'll act as deputy drivers. Overtaking is a bit tricky, with the steering wheel on the wrong side, so you navigators have got to act as the drivers' eyes. He'll pull out a bit if he wants to overtake, and then you've got to shout NO if there's something coming, or NOW if there is not. Don't get those two mixed up, or there'll be tears.

"Once you get beyond Turkey", he said, "The roads are mostly unmarked, unpaved and rather narrow. They're quite dangerous really, because long-distance trucks travel at high speed in the center of the carriageway, so watch out for them. They kick up a hell of a lot of dust.

"By the way, there are very few road signs anywhere from Syria onwards, and if they do exist, they're all in funny script – Arabic or Farsi or whatever – so they'll be no use to you. The maps are not very reliable either, and in some areas the authorities refuse to publish maps for security reasons, so you'll have to rely on the sun and your common sense. You'll all be given a compass, too. We've got five buses, so obviously we can't all stick together the whole time. I'll be going ahead in the Land Rover, to scout the trail, and I'll come back to warn you, if there's trouble ahead."

He then handed out a small pile of assorted paper maps, covering various stretches of our proposed route. Many were in the local language and not much help. Today, in the era of GPS and the iPhone, it is almost impossible to understand what travel was like just fifty years ago. You never really knew where you were, and you could not contact anyone, if you got lost. The local people were unlikely to speak any European language, at least until you reached Pakistan and India. The nearest British consulate or embassy could be up to a thousand miles away.

We departed Britain with only the vaguest idea of what lay ahead. My parents were very supportive, but I knew they were anxious. If I was still cursed by the family travel jinx, anything could happen, and undertaking a trip like this was like putting my head in the lion's mouth.

Just for a minute, consider our itinerary: London – Dover – Ostend – Frankfurt – Vienna. Then behind the Iron Curtain into Communist Hungary and Yugoslavia. Back to the "free world" with the Greeks, then across the border to their traditional enemies, the Turks. From Istanbul we took a ferry across the Bosphorus – there was no bridge back then in 1965 – to Eastern Turkey and Asia Minor.

Unusually, there was no war going on in the Middle East that year. It was possible to drive through Syria – Damascus, Homs, Hama, Aleppo – and Jordan to the magical Old Town sector of Jerusalem. This was still a divided city, with the East administered by Jordan. Two years later, in the Six Day War, Israel overran and occupied the entire area. But in 1965, we could stroll through the Garden of Gethsemane, ascend the Calvary hill where Christ was crucified, stop off at Bethlehem to visit the Church of the Nativity and float in the briny waters of the Dead Sea, six hundred feet below sea level.

From here it was out across the Great Salt Desert, seven hundred and seventy miles of bleak emptiness, with only the barest traces of a road. We were making for Baghdad.

Remember, it was the end of July, the hottest month of the year. Why on earth had Colonel Gregory planned this trip for the height of summer?

We did the desert runs at night, struggling to stay awake. Wherever possible, we followed in the wake of the local trucks, whose drivers knew the roads, but our staid British tour buses could not keep up with them, and they would disappear into the darkness ahead of us.

Somewhere in the loneliness in the Great Salt Desert, we stopped for a pee-break – girls to the left of the coach, boys to the right, a custom we had agreed on since the second day of the trip. A giant moon was rising over the hills to the east. We gulped down water from the locally made clay pots we all carried in the bus, and someone suggested that we should dance. There was a battery-operated record player in our bus, which we used as part of our skits and entertainments, so we hauled it out and played Beatles songs, dancing barefoot in the warm sand.

When I went to put on my shoes, after the dancing had finished, I absent-mindedly tapped them on the side of the bus, as we had been taught to do. A giant scorpion fell out of my right shoe, raised its tail and made a lunge at my right foot. I leaped backwards.

"Missed," I think I said. There was laughter from everyone around me, and then a shocked silence. I shivered. Was the travel jinx stalking me?

A large, colorful book of photos was produced a couple of years ago, to celebrate the fiftieth anniversary of that epic trip. There are photos of Jeremy Gibson, Richard Holloway, Robin Denselow (later a much-admired music critic for *The Guardian*) and all the others I knew on the Oxford bus. Alas, there were no photos taken at night: we only had simple cameras, taking precious celluloid film shots with weak flash units. There were also very few photos of our theatrical performances, for which, perhaps, we should be glad.

Along our route, the idea was that we accepted accommodation in student hostels wherever possible, in return for entertaining our hosts with whatever amusements we had concocted. In the Oxford bus, our main attraction was a production of *The Importance of Being Earnest*, by Oscar Wilde. We put on our first performance of this classic comedy at the British Embassy in Vienna: it was a disaster. Only the Ambassador and about twenty per cent of the audience apparently spoke English. Laughs were few and far between, and the audience was half the size after the interval.

"Sorry about that," said the Ambassador afterwards. "Austrians don't always go in for comedy of course. Bit like the Germans, eh? And dear old Oscar Wilde is subtle stuff, for a beginner."

We made a mental note to stick to our less-verbal cabaret acts, until we got to the next English-speaking country – Pakistan. Cabaret was the name we had given to a series of sight gags, age-old comedy routines and sing-along songs that we had cobbled together, to entertain the natives east of Turkey. We had various silly props like rubber chickens and chamber pots, plus a few traditional British costume bits and pieces – a constable's helmet, army officer's hat, Queen Victoria's crown, silly wigs – and whatever else we could find in the local bazaar on arrival at each of our overnight stops. Luckily, we also had the guitar and singing talents of Richard Holloway.

From Damascus to Amman, from Baghdad to Tehran, and on through the wastelands of Baluchistan into Quetta and Lahore, we mugged and gurned and practiced the occasional pratfall for a series of bemused audiences. Most of them spoke not a word of English but were unfailingly kind. Indeed, they were often so astonished to see this group of thirty-five white – or, rather, scarlet/pink – boys and girls fooling around like idiots, that they could not stop laughing, even when we were not trying to be funny.

What is remarkable about the expedition, from the perspective of 2020, is that it was possible at all. Fifty years ago, there was no immigrant crisis between Turkey and Greece, no war between Turkey and the Kurds, and no battle for control of Syria. Jerusalem was still accessible from the Arab side. Iraq and Iran were not daggers drawn, between Sunnis and Shia Muslims. There was no tribal unrest or Al Qaeda presence in Baluchistan. Driving all the way from London proved to be perfectly possible, however dangerous the hurtling trucks, lack of signposts, wandering cattle and unmade roads. For sure, it was exhausting and hellishly hot, but the scorpion had not got me, so where was the jinx?

In Pakistan, we first heard the bad news. We were told that the border ahead had been closed: tensions had risen, saber rattling was the order of the day, and the country was on the brink of invading its neighbor, India. The British Ambassador in Rawalpindi explained regretfully that our Commonwealth Expedition was unlikely to reach its final goal, New Delhi, because two Commonwealth countries were preparing to go to war with each other. How ironic was that?

The indomitable Colonel Gregory was having none of it. He insisted on meeting some top brass in the Pakistani Army. We simply had to be allowed to cross into India, he told them. The Duke of Edinburgh was our patron. The British Raj would not be stopped. After much debate and a two-day delay, we were given a special permit.

"But it's at your own risk," a senior Pakistani official told us. "We can't give you an army escort, because that might precipitate a war."

So, feeling somewhat apprehensive, we approached the Indian border in our convoy of five buses, led by Colonel Gregory's Land Rover. A red and white pole stood lowered, blocking the road. It had started to rain. The monsoon season was upon us.

"Good morning," said Gregory to the Border Guards, handing over nearly 200 passports and some other official papers for rubber-stamping. "We're the Commonwealth Expedition, and we have all the permits to proceed."

There was some hectic phoning, and much talking in a language other than English. Then the chief border agent stepped out of his hut.

"I cannot stop you," he said. "Please proceed. But be very careful."

Our convoy crept forward through the rain, across the one-mile no-man's-land between the two countries. I was navigating. Jeremy Gibson was driving.

"What happens if they don't let us in?" Jeremy asked me. "We're stuck here in the middle, if the war starts. Stuck in the mud. Like World War I."

By the time we reached the Indian border, the rain was torrential. Indian army tanks blocked the road, and we were being observed by senior officers with binoculars. What they made of this surreal sight – a convoy of English tour buses led by a crazy colonel in a Land Rover, sporting a Union Jack – is hard to imagine. But once again, Colonel Gregory bluffed and blustered his way through.

"We have an appointment in Delhi with Mrs. Indira Gandhi, your Transport Minister," he said, as if this explained everything.

Faced with Greg's implacable will, and not sure what else to do with us, the army let us enter India, but not before they had ransacked every single bus. Perhaps they imagined we were concealing a division of Pakistani troops. All they found were rubber chickens, theatrical costumes and back-packs full of unwashed clothes.

"Keep your headlights off," said an Indian Army officer, as we left the border post. "There'll be a blackout tonight, in case the enemy is planning air raids."

By the time we reached Delhi, it was completely dark. Such few streetlights as might have been available had been turned off. Traffic was moving at walking pace, with occasional sidelights on. The monsoon rain was like a waterfall. The road was a foot deep in water. Ahead, there was a mass of bicycles, rickshaws, tuk-tuks, sacred cows and peasants carrying impossible loads on their back. Jeremy Gibson asked for two volunteers to walk in front of the bus, to test how deep the water was and to prevent us running over unseen children and animals.

On my lap, I had an old street map of New Delhi, and a flashlight. I could not make head or tail of where we were, because it was too dark to read any street signs. I am sure we went round in pointless circles at least a couple of times, and then we emerged into Connaught Circle, the official center of town.

Here it was possible to orient ourselves, and we made for the University campus and the hostel where we would be staying for several nights. One by one, as the night wore on, the five buses arrived. The last to come was the Welsh bus, shepherded in by the indomitable Colonel Gregory. They had been halfway to Agra before he found them and turned them round.

"Well done, chaps," he said, to boys and girls alike. "All present and correct? Jolly good show. We'll sort out a plan of action when we've had some sleep."

There was not much chance of sleep: thunder and lightning had developed around the monsoon rain, and the sultry heat demanded that all available windows in the dormitories were left open. Everyone was swapping tales of what had happened in the previous twenty-four hours. Our Indian hosts, the students at the University, were impatient to hear of our adventures.

"You mean you drove right through Pakistan?" they asked, agog. "Did you see many soldiers? They say they are going to invade, or at least bomb our cities." It was not easy to sleep under these conditions.

Daylight brought no news. Greg was away, meeting with John Freeman, the British High Commissioner, and Mrs. Gandhi, the Transport Minister, to discuss what was still possible under the circumstances. The rain was continuous. We all felt suddenly deflated. Thirty-three days on the road, eight thousand miles of driving, all for this?

The plan had been for the five buses to split up at Delhi, and for each to go to a different city – Lucknow, Calcutta, Bombay, Madras, Jaipur. But unnecessary travel in wartime was frowned on, and diesel had been rationed. We heard that the first artillery fire had been heard at the border we had recently crossed. The war had started. If we had tried to cross into India even a day later, we would have been out of luck. But now what?

As you might expect, my dear parents were once again beside themselves with worry, back in London. The BBC and the British newspapers were dominated by urgent bulletins and scary headlines. My traveler's jinx had been bad enough before, but a full-scale war? This was too much.

They tried to call the Indian High Commission in London, but they were not answering the phone. It proved impossible to phone India from the UK. Never easy at the best of times, wartime regulations had shut down all the lines. The British Foreign and Commonwealth Office made bland announcements that, to the best of their knowledge, fighting had so far been sporadic, and no UK nationals were known to be in danger. So far.

Colonel Gregory returned to our dormitories in Delhi, to announce that our trips to the five Indian cities would go ahead as planned. It was considered safer to have us out of Delhi, which would be a prime target for Pakistani bombers, if the border incident escalated. So we packed up our meager belongings and, in the words of Willie Nelson, we were on the road again.

India, like Marmite (the British savory spread) is something you tend to either love or hate. So many people, such poverty, such cruelty to children and animals, such squalor: it can all be too much. But at the same time, there is such natural beauty, such kindness, so many architectural and cultural wonders to behold. We visited the Taj Mahal on a cloudy day, under a light rain: it gleamed like a giant white dream-palace in a fairy-tale, and the feel of its cool, damp marble terraces under our bare feet was unforgettable. We visited Varanasi, one of the holiest cities in India. At dawn, in the ghats on the shore of the wide River Ganges, we watched as dead bodies were wrapped in cloth and slid into the water, and a widow was burned on a giant bonfire, in the terrible ritual act of suttee.

Nothing was too much trouble for our Indian hosts. We met hundreds of students and professors at the universities, which hosted us. In Lucknow, we put on the first full-scale production of our showpiece, Oscar Wilde's *The Importance of Being Earnest*. We were so excited by the response of the huge, enthusiastic audience that one of the Oxford actors, Richard Samuel, skipped about a dozen pages of script and plunged straight into Act II, not long after the curtain had gone up. Unfazed, we plowed on. I was playing a small comedy character part, Canon Chasuble, and found that one of my two scenes had been lost entirely. I was also the director of the play – and was in somewhat of a panic.

To our surprise, at the end of the performance, there was thunderous applause. As we collapsed in our dressing rooms, thankful to have made it through to the end of the play, a visitor was announced. The University's Senior Professor of English had come round to the stage door and wished to see us.

"Oh God," said Richard Samuel. "What are we going to tell him?"

The Professor entered the room, beaming.

"I thought it was marvelous!" he exclaimed. "I was following the performance line by line in the original text."

He shook me vigorously by the hand.

"Are you the director? I thought it was very clever to make that big cut in Act One. The play is too long anyway. Reducing it to two acts makes the whole thing go down like a spoonful of honey."

The performance which really sticks in my mind, however, was up in the breezy hill town of Simla, to the north of Delhi. This was where the British Raj retired in the hot summer months, back in the day when India was part of the Empire, and the town had not changed much since 1900.

We were astonished to be accommodated in the old Vice-Regal Lodge, and even more astonished when we saw the Gaiety Theatre. It was a perfect bijou English music hall, complete with red plush and all the original first-generation electric lighting. We had twenty-four hours to rehearse and get programs printed. Two hours before Curtain Up, there was a line a hundred yards long outside the theatre: word had spread that the Raj were back, and performing a play from the 1890's, just as if nothing had happened in the intervening seventy years.

Reality hit us when we were halfway through Act One – at more or less the same place in the script where we had gone off the rails in Lucknow. All the lights went out, and we heard the wail of air-raid sirens. It was twenty years since World War II, but we all knew what air-raid sirens sounded like. The Pakistani Air Force had apparently decided to bomb Simla, which was uncomfortably near the border. We heard a couple of muffled booms: anti-aircraft fire. There was consternation and near panic in the darkness of the over-full auditorium.

"Do something!" said the stage manager. Colonel Gregory took the initiative, and strode onto the stage, with a flashlight in his hand.

"Ladies and Gentlemen," he bellowed, in his best authoritative voice. "Please stay in your seats. While we are waiting for the lights to come back on, our students will entertain you with songs and cabaret. Quiet, please!"

The audience rapidly stopped talking, astonished to hear the voice of British authority, eighteen years after independence. Then they broke into sustained applause. At this moment, two eager air-raid wardens rushed into the theatre. One of them had a bullhorn.

"Be silent!" he shouted at the audience, in both English and Hindi. "What use is a blackout if the enemy planes can hear your clapping? Do you want the bombs to drop on your own head?"

Meanwhile, backstage in the dark, we were rushing around, trying to find guitars, side-drums and appropriate props and costumes. The local theatre manager found some candles. He appeared completely unfazed by the situation.

"Oh, we're always having power cuts up here in Simla," he said pleasantly. "People are used to them. Don't worry."

I remember grinning nervously, as the boom of distant anti-aircraft fire continued.

"OK, ready?" I asked the cast. "Let's start with *No Business Like Show Business.*"

This was a cod version of the song, with new lyrics, full of double entendres, which happily went over the heads of most of the audience. For almost half an hour, we improvised some sort of ramshackle entertainment. At the end of each number, skit or mime everyone generously laughed or clapped, ignoring the air-raid wardens entirely. When we were finally scraping the barrel and launching into Kumbaya a second time, the lights came back on and the All Clear siren sounded. The audience went wild, cheering and stomping.

"Continue the Earnest play!" they shouted. "More! More Earnest!"

So, after a few minutes to restore our Wildean personae, we dived back into *The Importance of Being Earnest.* We were the toast of the town and did not get out of the theatre till after midnight. It turned out that the Pakistani plane had been a lone intruder, scouting the territory, and no bombs had been dropped. So all was well that ended well.

There was one further unexpected punch line to the COMEX story. We were told we would be unable to drive back to London, as originally planned, because the frontier was still an impassible war zone.

Mrs. Indira Gandhi, as Transport Minister, came to see us in our hostel, accompanied by the British Ambassador, John Freeman, and a smiling Colonel Gregory, who had fixed up a deal. Mrs. Gandhi told us that her government was going to buy our buses and swap them for one-way air-tickets to London on Air India – via Moscow. Cheap buses for India, and salvation for us! That sounded fair enough.

I cannot say that I was unhappy to forego that 8000-mile drive back. In future years, the COMEX expedition was repeated once or twice, but the round trip was grueling for the students involved. Subsequent wars, local insurrections, misunderstandings and one bad accident made the journey more dangerous and less fun. We had been very lucky.

The cherry on the COMEX cake for me was the five hours we spent at Moscow's Sheremetyevo airport, waiting for the London connection. To add to the souvenirs and gifts we had bought in India, we loaded up on vodka, super-cheap caviar and communist propaganda posters. It was a surreal finale to a fantastic summer.

And the travel jinx was finally dead and gone, it seemed. Well, apart from the time we were all arrested by Russians in the Afghan desert... But that story will have to wait for Chapter 3.

■■■

1.   RADIO DAYS

Strangely enough, I think I can thank the Thornton Heath Tape Recording Club (THTRC) for the start of my professional career in radio, if not TV and film. Thornton Heath is a suburb of a suburb, two or three miles north of Croydon and south of London. It boasts rows of identical late Victorian and semi-detached houses of the sort that encircle London in their millions. It's lower-middle-class "Sarf London" personified, and the memory of it makes me deeply grateful that I now live in Northern California.

I had a cousin, Clive, my Aunt Hilda Mary's son, who lived just half a mile from us, in the house where I had watched the Coronation on TV in 1952. He was much older than me and had been born blind. Every day, in an act of routine bravery, he made his way on a commuter train to the City of London, to work for the General Electric Company as a stenographer, tapping his way through the rush-hour crowds with his white stick.

His pleasure was to listen to the then-new 33 rpm vinyl discs of classical music, on a simply stupendous sound system, with loudspeakers that would rattle your teeth and dislodge the foundations of the house. This is where I first heard good music that was perfectly reproduced and indistinguishable from the live event. Clive also possessed a professional-quality reel-to-reel tape recorder, quite a novelty for the 1950's, with which he used to record his mother (a concert pianist) and any local musical luminaries who visited their house.

I lusted after that tape-recorder. My family could not afford any such wondrous, professional device, but I wanted *something* that would record sound, and on my sixteenth birthday, my parents gave me a portable plastic Philips recorder, which boasted tiny reel to reel tapes, that turned at the modest speed of one-and-seven-eighths revolutions per second. Not broadcast quality, then.

But I could record birds and – of course – steam trains, and… oh yes, people! I still have all the tapes. I recorded the memories of my grandmother in her ninetieth year. I recorded conversations between my parents that I was not supposed to hear, and best of all, ownership of the device entitled me to membership of the THTRC.

One of the activities of the club was to record local concerts, with permission, which were re-broadcast on the free hospital radio networks of various medical facilities in the Croydon and Thornton Heath areas. Back in the day, when the BBC only offered three radio channels, and commercial radio was not permitted in the UK, bedridden patients enjoyed hearing special "radio" shows through headphones on the hospital audio network, with requests for the latest pop songs and goodwill messages from friends and relatives.

So, one day, I found myself inside Croydon's newly constructed Fairfield Halls, a local concert facility billed as 'rivaling London's Festival Hall.' With a team of THTRC stalwarts, I was preparing to rig up our microphones, to record a concert by a new pop group called

The Beatles. Their first big single, called *She Loves You, (Yeah Yeah Yeah)*, had just been issued.

Frankly, I had never heard of the Beatles at that stage, and nor had most other people in 1963, let alone the members of the THTRC. But the functionaries at the Fairfield Halls had been forewarned about what had happened at other venues. A uniformed official explained:

"The place will be full of young girls, under sixteen years old many of them, and they'll all be screaming, and half of them will wet themselves and we'll have to change the seat covers. And watch they don't nick your gear, too."

It all seemed most unlikely, as we set up our microphones and recorders, but it turned out to be all that and more. The needles on our audiometers peaked in the red zone, time after time. We could barely hear the music for the sound of ecstatic, shrieking sixteen-year-old girls.

"Where were they," I asked myself "when I was trying to get dates at the Croydon Young Conservative Club?" It sounded like something between an orgy and a revolution.

When the show was officially over, we packed up our gear, shaking our heads at these wild shenanigans, and went outside to load up our van. We found ourselves trapped between the stage door (where the Beatles were about to emerge) and a horde of several hundred teenage girls, in the last stages of screaming joy. When the doors opened and John, Paul, George and Ringo appeared, the girls surged forward and trapped us poor sound guys right in the middle. The electric smell of female sweat and lust was unforgettable.

We survived, and I hope the ensuing hospital radio show brought a smile to some of the listeners. Quite possibly, it hastened the end of life for some of them, because it was nothing if not scary to most people over the age of thirty. No, make that twenty. Whatever had happened to the polite enthusiasm that had greeted Frank Sinatra or Doris Day? Not even Elvis Presley had managed to shake the foundations of Britain in quite this way.

It all made a great impression on me. It demonstrated that I could be a peripheral part of showbiz without becoming an actor. I promptly started saving for a professional tape recorder of my own: one that would spin round at the dizzying speed of fifteen inches per second and record broadcast-quality sound.

• •

And now, we must fast-forward the tape a few months, to the start of my second term at Oxford, where I was studying French and German Literature – not always a bundle of fun. I decided, as a break from Descartes and Goethe, to join the University Broadcasting Society (OUBS). It had just been founded by a budding student actor, Nigel Rees, who went on to become a successful writer and broadcaster. He has remained a lifelong friend.

OUBS was in many ways an excuse to invite eminent stars and alumni from the world of TV and radio, to make their way from London to Oxford, to be wined and dined. Once relaxed, they would face the prospect of speaking to a small and somewhat nerdish group of enthusiasts and describe what they had achieved in the big wide world. Incredibly, many of them were really quite famous. They included Sir Hugh Carleton Greene, the longtime Director General of the BBC, brother of the novelist Graham Greene, and John Tydeman, Head of BBC Radio Drama, who judged an early tape-recorded comedy competition (which I had entered, with a dire montage borrowing much from the Goon Show). They all agreed to come with minimal payment, drawn to the dreaming spires of Oxford, no doubt, by the sheer nostalgia of their own time there as an undergraduate. And, of course, by the free wine and dinner. This was England, after all.

In November 1964, a young and brilliant Prize Fellow from All Souls College approached the Society and asked whether any of its members had experience with recording location sound on a tape recorder. He had secured funds from the BBC to create a radio documentary about night-work at the Cowley motor works, on the outskirts of Oxford. Back then, the factory produced famously unreliable Morris cars, though in recent years, it has been rescued and taken over by BMW to produce the new Mini range for international consumption. I drive one: they're great.

Happily, I was the most appropriate candidate for the post of recording assistant, because I knew how to use my own professional-level tape-recorder. So I met with this academic researcher and we immediately hit it off. His name was Alasdair Clayre, and I became firm friends with him, right up to his tragic early death in 1984.

Twice a week, we would leave the center of Oxford on Alasdair's Vespa two-wheeler, sometime after eight o'clock in the evening, and roar and putter our way out to Cowley. I had to ride pillion, without a crash helmet. Who wore crash helmets, back then? I would have to carry what the BBC called a "portable" tape-recorder: a dark-green fifteen-pound monster with a brace of extra heavy batteries and a bag of microphones. In rain, sleet and snow we would venture out into the darkness, with me sitting behind on the bike, holding onto Alasdair for dear life. There was nothing else to hold onto. Though religion was not my strong suit, I prayed that God would look after us and we would not meet an Oxford Corporation double-decker bus coming the other way.

We would then spend hours talking to workers during their breaks, and recording their deepest thoughts, their hopes and anxieties, amid the mind-numbing crash, rumble and roar of an old-fashioned car factory.

One night, arriving back at Lincoln College in the rain, and making my way back to my room shortly before midnight, I bumped into three imposing figures walking through the Chapel Quadrangle. I recognized the Rector of the college, Professor Walter Oakeshott, and was startled to see that one of the others was the Duke of Edinburgh, the Queen's husband. A single security man was holding an umbrella over his head.

"Ah," said the Duke, stopping to mingle briefly with *hoi polloi,* "You must be an undergraduate."

"Yes, sir," I said, water pouring off both me and my bags of equipment.

"And what have you been up to?" said the Duke affably. He had evidently thoroughly enjoyed his dinner and port with the Rector, who was also Vice-Chancellor of the University.

The Rector gave me a very stern glance, as if willing me to say something sensible, and hoping that I had not been drinking too.

"I've been recording the night shift up at the Cowley Motor Works," I said. "They hate night work, but the Union makes sure they're paid well for it."

"Ah, yes. Good," said the Duke, momentarily nonplussed. "Very interesting. Part of your studies, is it?"

"It's for the BBC," I explained.

"Oh, right you are. Well, er, carry on the good work," said the Duke, and off they went, with the Rector giving me another of his grim glances. Was I some sort of journalist in training, or even a communist sympathizer? A "red under the bed," as they used to be called?

The resulting tapes were transcribed by a patient secretary, to whom Alasdair had access because he was, after all, in a most prestigious academic position. Then we would mark up the best parts of the interviews, cut them out of the transcripts, and Sellotape them (US: read "Scotch Tape them") to all four walls of his college rooms in All Souls.

To this day, I have never encountered a better way of structuring a documentary, in sound or film. You can literally visualize the whole thing: step back from it all, move the bits of paper around on the wall, step back again and consider the rhythm and pace and structure of the end product. Alasdair persuaded his Scout, the elderly man who cleaned his room, that these bits of paper must never be touched or moved – for weeks, that is, till the show was ready to be edited on tape. That final process and the sound mix had to be done at the BBC Regional HQ in Birmingham.

Alasdair's program was destined to be part of a series called *Landmarks*, produced and eventually broadcast on the BBC's main current affairs channel (the "Home Service", later Radio 4). Each documentary depicted the realities of working life for men and women in factories, coalmines, fishing boats and so on. There was no narrator, giving a God's eye view. The audience just heard the voices of the workers, interspersed occasionally with authentic location sound effects and excerpts from traditional work songs, often more than a hundred years old, which celebrated and mourned the toughness of hard physical work. The songs were sung by the well-known folk-singers Peggy Seeger and Ewan McColl, and occasionally by Alasdair, an impressive composer and singer in his own right. The project was produced by the legendary Charles Parker.

In my spare time, while studying at Oxford and during the vacations, I went on to do two more radio documentaries with Alasdair Clayre. He generously gave me credit as assistant producer and eventually co-writer, besides being the sound recordist. One of the shows featured the barges and small freight boats of the River Thames, whose skippers participated in a competition for the Doggett's Coat and Badge – a trophy awarded since the time of Queen Elizabeth I. By 1965, this was already a fast-disappearing way of life. We called the one-hour program *A Gentle Easy-flowing River* – a title taken from one of our interviews and made into a beautiful new song by Alasdair.

The final radio documentary we made together was a series of very moving interviews with survivors from the Auschwitz concentration camp. Here, there were no sound effects and no music: just the haunting words of those who testified to the horror. Eventually, all three of the radio documentaries we made were preserved in the BBC Archives, and two of them won prizes. We were both very proud of that.

∎∎∎

One of the incidental pleasures of working on these shows was receiving letters from the BBC in my mailbox (or "pigeonhole") at Lincoln College. Some were large brown envelopes with big blue BBC labels on them, containing transcripts of our taping: very good for elevating one's status among other undergraduates and the college porters, who inspected and sorted the mail. There were echoes of my time at Hurstpierpoint College, when the school porter had stumbled upon my postcards from the Spanky Panty Film Club. This time, however, the college porters were impressed by the envelopes I was receiving.

In time, other envelopes arrived, containing BBC checks – payment for my labors with Alasdair Clayre. They would often be for three guineas, sometimes for as much as ten guineas – a princely sum, when that would buy almost a hundred pints of beer in a pub. I should explain that, in those pre-decimal times, a guinea was one pound and one shilling (£1.05 in today's money). It was considered a classy way to pay people. Eminent lawyers and doctors would present their bills in guineas, rather than pounds: it made their pecuniary demands seem so much more elegant.

But it was an envelope of a very different nature that was to switch my life in a completely new direction.

Come my final year at Oxford, I had to try and decide on what I would do, when I was ejected into the real world. As I was studying French and German, I had been allowed a year away from Oxford in Paris, to study at the Sorbonne and try to improve my French. To cover my costs, I had been given a part-time job, sharing conversational English with young, cynical teacher trainees, who only wanted to hear about the Beatles and Rolling Stones. It was an experience that decided me against teaching for a living, though I have come to realize that making documentaries is a bit like teaching hundreds of thousands – even millions – of people, all over the world.

But if I did not want to teach, what *did* I want to do? I made an agreement with Peter Cole, a friend at Lincoln College, and we decided we would apply for literally dozens of jobs in business, as a way of taking our minds off the fearsome "Finals", the two weeks of examinations that faced us at the end of our university life. The UK Atomic Energy Authority, London Transport, the BBC, British Airways, Imperial Chemical Industries, The Sunday Times, J. Walter Thompson (a big advertising agency) – we divided them into two piles: Peter would apply to one batch, I would apply to the other. Only in very special cases, where we both craved the job, would we both apply. We got quite good at it, and were, between us, offered nearly a dozen jobs, but none of the initial offers appealed to me much.

One morning in spring, Ian Small, a graduate student who had that prized possession, a *car* (forbidden to undergraduates), asked me if I'd like to go to London with him for the day, to take my mind off the upcoming examinations. He told me he was visiting something quaint called the ESU – the English- Speaking Union – an Anglo-American friendship organization that dated from World War II. They handled applications for graduate study at dozens of American universities. Why not try my luck? What was there to lose? We leaped into his Morris Minor and chugged off to London.

At the ESU in Mayfair, we were met by a couple of elderly ladies, who told me that the deadlines for application had almost passed. Ian had already applied, but I would have to fill in application forms there and then, on the spot, for the last few remaining opportunities. My mind went blank. What should I study? It would be pointless to go three thousand miles or more to the USA, and then continue with French or German. I did not have the pre-requisites, the talent or the inclination to study atomic physics or medicine.

"How about Business Studies?" one of the welcoming ladies asked. "We still have a few places left for that."

Not, she explained, at Harvard or Columbia, but there were a few state universities of good repute, whose deadline was still a week or two away. I frantically filled out some paperwork, handed it over to my kindly advisors, and left to have a pint of beer with Ian in a nearby pub.

I completely forgot about my job applications, as I immersed myself in the final three months of hectic "cramming" for the upcoming exams. But within a few weeks, the BBC sent me a letter, asking me to go to London for an interview. This was stunning: I had been short-listed, at least, for the BBC! The interview, conducted by three sober middle-aged white men in suits, chaired by a dull civil servant aptly named Mullins, was even more daunting than the interview to get into Oxford. I was convinced that I had done very badly.

Three weeks later, another BBC letter arrived. They were offering me a position as a General Trainee! Incredibly, my friend Peter Cole was also offered the same job. We had secured two of the ten similar positions offered annually to graduating students by the BBC. We must have become quite good at writing job applications, or in pulling the wool over people's eyes.

"General Trainee" sounds pretty dull. But it was in fact the most coveted way to enter the Corporation: a guarantee of two years' training and practical production work in radio and TV, with the chance of applying for a full-time job during the second year. As I learned later, it was also a fast track towards a life of senior management in the bureaucracy of the BBC. If I had known that, I might never have applied, but happily I just saw it as a golden key to creative production for the first few years, which indeed it turned out to be.

But I had other things on my mind at the time. All too soon, we had the Oxford finals to sit, in the forbidding University Examination Halls. This is a grim endurance test: more than a week of three-hour sessions, both morning and afternoon on several of the days, with three papers or essays to write in each session. At Oxford, the University only test you twice, if you are taking an arts degree: once, a few months after you arrive – and if you fail that test, you are sent down from the University immediately, with no chance of retaking the examination. The second occasion is at the end of your three or four years.

Finals present a grueling, thoroughly medieval experience. You have to memorize everything you have learned in the previous years, and be prepared to select a few topics from a very short list of alternatives, presented to you on a single sheet of printed paper on the stroke of 9 a.m. and 2 p.m. You can take no notes into the hall. You write in longhand. You sweat for three hours – up to a hundred of you, in this vast, forbidding room. All you can hear is the ticking of a large clock and the sound of a hundred pens scratching, with the occasional nervous cough to relieve the tension.

Exactly at the end of the three hours, the invigilators announce "Pens down," and the papers are collected. There are seven or eight such sessions, covering the various topics you have chosen to study. For linguists, there is the added torture of a "Viva" in each language you are studying: a panel of three distinguished academics cross-question you, in my case in both French and German, and you have to defend and explain what you have written – speaking entirely in the relevant foreign language.

I still don't know how I got through it. Some people go temporarily crazy before, during or after this prolonged torture. The local Warneford Hospital is the psychiatric institution, which looms large in the mind of all students in their last term at Oxford. With luck, most people manage to avoid being sent there – and so did I, more by luck than judgement, I think.

With the exams finally over, I enjoyed my last days at Oxford: dallying with ladies in punts on the River Cherwell, enjoying the goodbye parties with college friends, and trying to forget the looming world of real work and responsibility, even if it *was* with the BBC.

"Time to grow up", I thought, but put such depressing thoughts out of my mind. At twenty-one, it is easy to convince yourself you will be Peter Pan forever. Heck, at forty-one, it's still possible, if you're as immature as I am. Even *sixty*-one.

On one of my last few days at Lincoln College, I had a big surprise. I found an unexpected airmail envelope in my pigeonhole. It was from the University of Indiana. Thanks to my efforts at the English-Speaking Union, I had been offered a Ford Foundation grant to study for a Master's Degree in Business Administration, plus a Fulbright travel grant, and a stipend for living expenses. Would I like to accept the offer?

"If so, kindly write back by 30 June, and be prepared to present yourself at the Business School on the Bloomington campus at 11 a.m. on 31 August."

I could not believe my eyes. I had to dig out an atlas from the college library to find where Indiana was. I had never been to the USA. And what about the BBC job? Was I going to leave them in the lurch, and deny myself the fun of working in TV? I convened a group of friends in Deep Hall, the college's 500-year-old bar, below the medieval dining hall.

Over pints of warm beer, we discussed the conundrum. Nick Young, a professional theatre director in the making, and still a good friend, came up with a blindingly simple solution. Why not phone the BBC and ask them if they could postpone my job for a year?

So I did, and, miraculously, Mr. Mullins, Chair of the Board that had interviewed me, said that the BBC would hold my job open for one calendar year, so that I could get this extra experience.

"Mind you," he said, with an eye on the BBC's pocketbook, "We won't be able to offer you any more money, just because you'll have the extra experience. The salary will still be £1,072 per annum."

That was only $2,500 *per year* at the then-current exchange rate: a pittance, even by UK standards, even in 1967. But it simply did not matter to me, as I put the phone down: I was going to America *and* I could join the BBC.

∙∙

The journey itself was the start of the adventure. It was still possible to travel to the US by regularly scheduled ship, and the Fulbright Foundation would cover the cost of a single bunk somewhere beneath the waterline of the stately Queen Elizabeth I. So I found myself at Southampton Docks in mid-July 1967, with my parents, my very dear girlfriend Hazel Carroll and my Oxford traveling companion George Taylor, who had landed a scholarship to Cornell University. Tearful goodbyes, ships' hooters, baggage swung aboard in nets by giant cranes (each big bag labeled 'Not Wanted On Voyage'), a last-minute dash up the gangplank: it all seemed like a scene from an MGM musical.

Then we were off, into the grey waters of the North Atlantic. Five days was the scheduled crossing time: five days of rough seas, for the most part. George and I played squash before breakfast every day, in the bowels of the giant ship. We giggled like fools as the ship rolled and plunged, and we kept running to hit the ball and instead hit the walls of the squash court. We followed each game with a massive English Breakfast, while most of the passengers were outside, losing theirs over the ship's railing as the waves rolled by.

One glorious evening, a steward took pity on us poor waifs in steerage class, lent us tuxedos and white shirts, and spirited us into the First-Class-Only Captain's Ball: a full orchestra, a hundred elegant participants, and us. It only occurred to me later that the ratio of women to men at the event was about three to one, and an extra couple of eager young lads with British accents was probably very welcome – particularly since our presence reduced the average age of the dancers to somewhere nearer seventy.

Just after dawn on the final day of the voyage, an announcement came over the loudspeaker system: we should prepare for disembarkation. The City of New York was on the horizon. I will never forget the next half-hour. We passed under the newly constructed Verrazano Narrows Bridge, high above us, saw the Statue of Liberty off to the port side, and there, dead in front of us, was Manhattan, glittering in the early morning sun. It was, once again, like a scene from a movie.

Tugs were roped to the enormous ship, and nudged it into the 57th Street pier, on New York's West Side. Dockers and stevedores were running everywhere. The gangplanks were rolled up to the ship, giant cranes swung nets full of baggage onto the docks. You had to find your bag under the first letter of your last name – an easy job if your name began with X,Y,Z or even K, because your pile of bags would be modest, but a nightmare if you were called Smith or Brown.

The English-Speaking Union had fixed up small windowless rooms for George Taylor and myself on the lower ground floor of the renowned Biltmore Hotel – all part of the Fulbright Travel Grant. I almost expected F. Scott Fitzgerald to be standing at the bar. We had two glorious days in New York, getting invited to a skyscraper rooftop party at a *Mad Men*-era advertising agency, getting drunk in Greenwich Village, and then, our ways parted. George went off to Cornell, and I set off for Indiana University (IU), far to the west.

In the Fall of 1967, the grand American railroads were on their last legs. The nationally subsidized Amtrak organization was not invented for another few years. So my train, the Pennsylvania Railroad's famous *Spirit of St Louis*, consisted of just one locomotive, one 'day car', one parlor/bar car, one dining/kitchen car, one sleeping car, one baggage car, and that was it. I could not believe my luck: I had a berth in the sleeping car. A black conductor from central casting smilingly explained how to tuck away the seat and magically pull down a narrow bed from the wall. He took one look at my shabby student shoes and valiantly offered to polish them. I was so embarrassed that I left him an enormous tip the next morning – probably larger than the value of the shoes.

I went to the bar car, ordered myself a drink and fell into conversation with a traveling salesman, who was going to Pittsburgh. It felt like the start of a joke or an Arthur Miller play. I took some paper and envelopes, embossed with 'En Route: Pennsylvania Railroad,' and wrote letters to my parents, to my girlfriend Hazel,and to everyone else I could think of. I was really here, and it was all just like the movies. I kept humming "I want to be in America" from West Side Story. I had fallen in love with the US of A in the first few days of being there, and this initial sense of excitement was going to shape my whole life to come.

The magic sparkle disappeared with a bang at Indianapolis, when I left the train. Union Station was dark and damp and almost empty. The Greyhound bus to Bloomington (site of the IU campus) left from a terminal half a mile away, in about three hours' time. The dereliction of downtown was equaled by the desperation of the derelicts, chugging Night Train liquor from brown bags on the sidewalk. Welcome to real life, David.

• •

And so began a wonderful year, studying business and acclimatizing myself to this whole new culture. Instead of the tightly walled quadrangles and dreaming spires of ancient Oxford, there was a vast campus, housing more than 30,000 students in myriad faculties, from dentistry to business and music. In these three spheres, I was told, IU excelled. For the rest, it was generally considered "a good school." As a bonus, that year, for the first time in living memory, IU also got to the finals of the Big Ten, whatever that was. (American college football, I later discovered, was one of the principal secular religions of the country).

I soon realized, after starting classes at IU, that the Ford Foundation fellowship, generous though it was, covered the costs of basic food and tuition, and nothing else. No pocket money: no money for beer, or movies, or taking girls out to Dairy Queen for a hot fudge sundae. Everyone told me I should get a job in radio. With my English accent and my BBC experience, they suggested it would be easy.

This was a revelation. In England at the time (1967) there were four national BBC radio channels and nothing else: no local radio, no legal commercial channels. The idea that a modest burg like Bloomington would have a radio station – no, *three* radio stations – was incredible. So I took myself along to the one that sounded most promising: the classical music station on campus, WFIU.

Here, I was subjected to a studio test by the kindly head of the station, who was also a professor of the Radio & TV department. That was incredible too: no university in the UK had such a department at that time. They were all far too academic. I had to do a speech test, and also demonstrate that I could place the needle onto a 33 rpm vinyl record in the right place at the right time, without scratching the hell out of it.

"Read this," said the professor, and gave me a long list of tough-to-pronounce composers and works which an announcer might have to contend with. He then went and sat in the control booth with the engineer, and both listened to me intently, through headphones, and watched me through the double-paned window. I cleared my throat nervously. Luckily, having studied French and German at Oxford, the list was not too daunting.

"L'Après-Midi d'une Faune, by Claude Debussy," I intoned. "Aran Khachaturian's Violin Concerto in D Minor, dedicated to the violinist David Oistrakh… Ludwig van Beethoven's Third Symphony, known as the Eroica."

The one blooper I made was to pronounce the American conductor André Previn's name as if he were French. The squawk-box from the control booth instantly buzzed.

"No, David, that's PREVINN. Like a car *revvin'* up. Not PRAYVUNG please."

I passed the test, however. They had a job opening, three nights a week, from ten p.m. to midnight, when the station closed down. It was called the "graveyard shift." They would pay me $2.75 an hour: a fortune, it seemed to me at the time.

It was a perfect job. I followed the list of records they had prescribed, and just before 11 p.m. I had to go the newsroom and rip off the latest news bulletin, which had come through on the chattering teletype machines from the offices of the Associated Press. Night owls in Bloomington heard my dulcet English tones describe the latest horrors from the Vietnam War and the price of Live Fat Hogs at auction. Meanwhile, during those great long symphonies that I played – thank you, Gustav Mahler: some of yours are over an hour long – I sat and wrote my papers for the Business School: "Econometrics: an Introduction to the Field" and other riveting stuff.

My compadre was called Jack Tracy. He was the engineer. Since I was not an American national, the station had to have someone in attendance in the technical booth, in case, presumably, I started uttering treasonous or foreign thoughts. We amused each other by swapping off-color jokes over the intercom. We wrapped up the station's output at midnight, by playing the State of Indiana's official anthem - a stark contrast to the elegance of the music that had preceded it. Then we took off and went down to Bloomington's only all-night eatery.

Here, Jack and I treated each other to piles of muffins, lashings of bacon and egg, and wallowed in a huge early morning breakfast. Round us sat jovial, overweight cops, tucking into similar spreads: there was not too much crime in Bloomington in 1967. Random other night birds filled the remaining tables, and the waitresses were always cheerful. I felt I was starting to experience the real America.

Sometimes, I would fill in for other announcers on weekend afternoons. On one occasion, Jack Tracy squawked me from the engineer's cabin.

"Come in here. Look at the weather. Holy Mother of God!"

He showed me that the temperature had plunged from sixty-five degrees Fahrenheit to forty-two degrees in the space of a minute, and the barometer was going crazy.

"It must be a twister!" he said.

We left Mahler playing on the turntable and went outside to look. Sure enough, we saw the ominous black spout of a tornado about three miles away, and apparently bearing down on us. There was a distant roar, but immediately around us, everything was deathly still.

We dashed back into the building, and I interrupted the music to announce the imminent arrival of the twister. I read from a pre-written State warning.

"Remain in place. Seek shelter in a basement if possible…"

Luckily, it passed the campus by about a mile, though part of the town was hit. I was still quaking in my boots some hours later. We do not have tornados in England.

Then, there was the afternoon when IU were playing their deadly rivals, Purdue University, in the semi-finals of the Big Ten football contest. So important was this game that it was being relayed live from the IU Stadium, through the relay station at WFIU, and across the world to American forces in Vietnam, Frankfurt, Guam - everywhere. I had to be in attendance, in case something went wrong, but I was lost in the magical world of a paper for Accounting 501. Suddenly Jack broke into my reveries.

"We've lost the line from the stadium," he shouted. "We can't have dead air. Say something! Do something! Play something!"

I panicked. Without even clearing my throat, I opened the mike and said something along the lines of:

"Um, well, sorry about that, ladies and gentlemen, we appear to have some sort of technical problem."

Remember, hundreds of thousands of red-blooded American football fans – troops on front-line operations in Vietnam, among others – were listening to this weedy British voice, bumbling an apology. What had happened? A British take-over? Remembering a BBC standard apology, I stammered:

"Normal service will be resumed as soon as possible. Meanwhile, here is a little light music."

I put the needle down on a very fairy-like guitar sarabande by some Spanish composer, which I happened to have cued up. The phone lines at the station all lit up at once. The General Manger came into the booth and shouted at me.

"For God's sake, put on a marching band, can't you? And explain what the hell's going on!"

I never lived that episode down. It was my very own *Good Morning Vietnam* moment. Other employees at the station, when they passed me in the corridor, would affect an exaggerated English accent and say, in a nervous voice:

"We appear to have some sort of technical problem."

Luckily, there were two other radio stations in town. $2.75 an hour was good money from WFIU, but I did not get offered many hours. Sure, a weekly income of about $20 was pretty good for a student fifty-plus years ago – it bought a lot of beer, pizza and cinema tickets. But, to travel, I would need a lot more. So, taking a deep breath, I went to visit WTTS, the local commercial radio station that was Midwestern through and through.

WTTS was in the rough, tough industrial area of town. It was owned by the Sarkes Tarzian company, which manufactured FM radios and even color TVs right there in little old Bloomington. It is incredible to think, today, that TVs and radios were still being hand-built in Southern Indiana, rather than Shenzhen, Shanghai or Bangladesh. Happily for me, Sarkes Tarzian also owned several radio and TV stations.

"You'll have to see the General Manager," said the receptionist when I arrived. "He's the one who hires and fires round here."

Within minutes, a big man with a florid face and forearms the size of hams strode out into the reception area.

"You lookin' for voice jobs?" he asked. "Got any experience?"

I told him that I had, but did not mention WFIU: in Sarkes Tarzian land, classical music stations, I am sure, were a joke. He gave me a sheaf of papers, each with big type, so it could be read by the hard of thinking in the dim studio lighting. All of them were thirty or sixty-second commercials for local companies.

"You're a Brit," he said, "Try the ones for Redwood and Ross."

R&R was a Mid-Western chain of preppy men's outfitters, which specialized in button-down shirts, 'Oxfords' and brogues. He went into the control room.

"Do the top two."

I cleared my throat and went at it, trying to sound mid-Atlantic rather than Oxford English.

"Redwood and Ross, for the smarter man. Dress suits, casual wear, everything you need. This week, three shirts for the price of two…"

He interrupted me on the squawk-box.

"Jeez, you don't sound British at all. Amp it up, will you? Close your eyes and think of England, isn't that what you guys say?"

I took another run at the advertising copy, giving him the full English rendition, with hints of upper-class toff thrown in. Redwood and Ross was a classy store, obviously. He came into the studio and looked at me as if I was a moron.

"Talk REAL BRITISH," he said. "Put some hot stones in your mouth or something. Talk real classy, like – well, like the Queen or –," he struggled to remember the name of a British actor. "or David Niven. You gotta be the snootiest guy we've ever heard."

I considered this for a moment, put my nose in the air, and read the copy like a strangulated butler in a comedy sketch.

"Hey, that's more like it!" he said. "Read a couple more, and then we'll tape some."

So I did, praying that none of my English family or friends would ever get to hear this linguistic sacrilege. At the end of the session, the manager came back in and pulled a fat roll of twenty-dollar bills out of his pants pocket. He peeled one off and thrust it in my hands.

"You did good, kid," he said, "Come down here every week. Wednesday's best. Those Redwood and Ross guys always need new ads: the promotion of the week, starting Fridays. Heck, they might even give you free shirts."

So, suddenly, I was in the money. Twenty dollars in cash for an hour's work, *every week?* Plus my WFIU income…? In 1967, a gallon of gas cost twenty-seven cents. A dozen eggs cost thirty cents. I was rich.

The final radio bastion to attack was, funnily enough, the hardest to get into: WIUS (today, WIUX), the student station. All the ambitious undergraduates majoring in Radio & Television had shows on the station, which at that time was run from a modest house a few blocks from the campus. There were no commercials and the content was supervised at arm's length by an academic committee. It was mostly rock music, with inane chatter and – very daring for its time – phone-ins from listeners. These were tape-delayed, in an attempt to prevent bad language and un-American thoughts being expressed. Controversial conversations – about the Vietnam War for example – were not encouraged by the university.

I spoke several times to an informal group of station DJ's and a couple of graduate students who seemed to have some vague management role. Eventually one said:

"OK. If you can come up with a good idea for Sunday afternoons – some talk, some music, something British maybe – we'll give it a try."

Nobody told me that Sunday afternoons are considered virtually dead time on American radio. Students, particularly, are out at some ball game, or having fun in general. But the airspace had to be filled.

Peter Morrell, another British business student with a puckish sense of humor, agreed to join me as co-host in the studio. We agreed we would ad lib the script entirely, except for the obligatory station identification breaks. We would play exclusively British music – not just the Stones and the Beatles, but Herman's Hermits and all the other feel-good stuff that was washing across the Atlantic in the late sixties. Plus, we would add short clips of comedy from British radio shows – lifted, without permission, from a number of LP records I had brought over with me from the UK. We might even interview any interesting Brits who were passing through and seemed like they could raise a laugh. We decided to call the show *The Illustrated London News*.

In its own way, it became quite a success. We started writing three-minute comedy sketches, which ran during the program. We called these *The Edwin Pode Show*, as if some strange character had insisted on doing his own thing, in spite of us. Some really good student announcers and comedians like Mike Ballard and Jan Bina joined us to help write, perform and record these.

To my amazement, the station kept the tapes of the Edwin Pode shows, and continued to use them as short interstitials (between other programs) for many of the last fifty years. At a fifty-year re-union, I was told that they had digitized them in their archive, and still occasionally ran one, for nostalgia's sake. There was even a compilation hour-long Pode show called *Radio is Alive and Well.* Jan Bina went on to join Second City, the renowned improvisation theatre group in Chicago, and Mike Ballard became a professional radio host, so they can't have been that bad.

But time was ticking on. I stayed for the summer semester to get the final credits I needed towards my MBA. Then I took a month traveling by car with George Taylor, Brendan O'Regan and a French friend, to the West Coast: I saw San Francisco, one year after the Summer of Love, and Manhattan Beach in LA, where I would live for a time, fifteen years later. I was intoxicated by it all.

Regretfully I returned to Bloomington to wrap up my affairs in July 1968. I had to be back in London by mid-August, to present myself to the BBC and start work. My year's sabbatical was over.

∙∙

There, on the docks at Southampton, as I arrived back in England, stood my parents and my much-loved English girlfriend, Hazel Carroll. Hazel and I had kept in touch the whole time I was away, and even met for a romantic tryst in Iceland halfway through the year, because it was symbolically halfway between London and Indiana.

It felt so good to see them and hug them once again. I felt I was home, after a roller-coaster ride through a giant Disneyland of a country – my first realization that I had been through the looking glass into a strange mirror-world. Already, in my mind, I saw the US as the best of all possible worlds and at the same time – for its grimmer aspect of poverty and inequality – the worst. England seemed small, quaint and fairly safe by comparison. But it still seemed like home.

I duly reported for duty at Broadcasting House, the BBC's imposing HQ in central London. I was given an identity card and a staff number: 131706L – it is ingrained forever in my memory. I was then given a stern lecture by a Health and Safety Officer, who handed me a large book called Standards and Practices of the BBC. It was like indenture into a branch of the armed forces, the civil service or the Jesuits. I was informed that my first posting would be two miles away, in another impressive and storied building – Bush House, home of the BBC World Service.

It was a jump from the ridiculous to the sublime: from facetious skits on WIUS to the world's most influential radio broadcaster – transmitting twenty-four hours a day in more than fifty languages. The Bush House cafeteria looked like the United Nations: broadcasters and staff from every corner of the globe, hundreds of them. Perhaps even thousands. The BBC employed more than 22,000 people at the time.

"Pleased to meet you, old man," said my new Head of Department, Brian Sharpe. He called everyone "old man", even a nervous twenty-three-year-old recruit. It was a strange piece of archaic banter, even then.

"Now, I see from your file that you've had some radio experience. Good show."

He mentioned the Birmingham-based documentaries I had done with Alasdair Clayre, which were all listed in my file. I told him some of the things I had been doing with a microphone in the United States. He seemed to doubt that I was telling the truth. In the UK, there was only one broadcaster – the giant BBC. How could a one-horse town like Bloomington have three radio stations?

"Well, anyway..." he said ruminatively, looking at a giant hand-written chart on the wall. "I've put you into the schedule for *The World Today*. It goes out four times daily, in English of course, and its audience is pretty much global. It's mostly live, as you probably know. Pretty simple stuff really. The news, then an in-depth interview or two. fifteen minutes total. I thought you might shadow one of the producers for a few days, and then take it on by yourself. How does that sound, old man?"

It sounded terrifying. At least the consolation was that I would be scheduled to look after the 3 a.m. transmission, and who would be awake to hear that? What I had not considered was that much of the BBC's vast worldwide audience would be very much awake at 3 a.m., Greenwich Mean Time, to hear whatever went out.

The first week was fun, shadowing an experienced producer, who knew all the short cuts and tricks of the trade. I got a crash course in current-affairs production in five days.

"We get most of our interviewees from the LSE – that's the London School of Economics," he said. "It's just across the road, and those people will get out of bed any time to run across here and earn their five guineas for an interview. Anyway, most of the stuff on the 3 a.m. broadcast is pre-taped at nine o'clock the night before. You can re-use that most of the time, unless some big news breaks."

I started on Monday night, 19 August 1968. All went well for my first edition: it was the summer vacation period. Not much news around in the Northern Hemisphere. 20 August was my mother's birthday, and Hazel and I went to have tea and cake with her and my father, out in leafy Winslow, Buckinghamshire.

Late that night, my second night alone at the wheel, so to speak, the Russians invaded Czechoslovakia. A rumor flashed round the building. People were running along corridors. Tanks were moving towards Prague, and alarm bells were ringing in Bush House, as *The World Today* was about to go on the air. Many of the staff were still in bed, catching a nap in the informal dormitory made available for people working the night shift. The newsreader arrived in the studio, ashen faced in his pajamas, with copy ripped from the wire services only minutes before.

"Holy Mary," he said, or some such godly phrase. "This could be the start of World War III." Turning to me, he said, "Find someone for me to interview."

The studio manager, a veteran I am glad to say, was already on the phone to Prague, and had dug up a correspondent who would talk live to us in London. My only thought was to dash to the cafeteria, which was always open. I stood at the door, and shouted:

"Is anyone here from the Czech service, or Central Europe?" There was no time to get anyone over from the LSE.

Happily, there were two volunteers. We ran back to the studio, just as the live link from Prague was coming to an end. I handed the newsreader a piece of paper, with the name of the Czech volunteers scribbled on it. The names had too few vowels for an English newsreader to pronounce at first sight. But, luckily, he was a professional. As the Czechs sat down, he announced that he had two expert current affairs analysts at his side and invited them to introduce themselves.

"What do you think this will mean for East-West relations?" asked the newsreader. The two Czechs improvised desperately, suggesting that this was a very serious development, and that everything would depend on the NATO military reaction. Only time would tell.

The studio manager gave us the "one minute to wrap up" sign, the newsreader wrapped things up, the theme music played and we were off the air. I nearly passed out with relief. It had been a baptism of fire. But flying by the seat of your pants is what real radio is about, I had learned.

Alas, the excitement of my training attachment to the BBC World Service came to an end just before Christmas, but ahead loomed the exciting heights of television.

2. FROM HITLER TO QUIZ GAMES

The next two years were some of the happiest of my life. My old Oxford friend Jeremy Gibson, who had traveled with me to India on the COMEX expedition, kindly found a room for me in an enormous, ramshackle flat he shared with four other former students. It was right in the middle of Queensway, just a few hundred yards from London's Kensington Gardens. The street was pulsing with activity from dawn to midnight: completely multi-cultural, with Arabic clothing stores, Italian restaurants, Cypriot betting-shops, a tired old department store (Whiteley's), and small garages, where repairs were constantly being made to my first car, an old Triumph Herald.

The flat was the fulcrum of a wonderful communal life. We shared two kitchens, two bathrooms, five bedrooms, a living room, three internal staircases and a large entrance-hall, which sported an old upright pub piano, ideal for fun and general creativity. My Oxford friend and comedy co-writer Nick Young joined us: he was a dab hand at improvising on a pub piano, and every night seemed to include some sort of singalong.

During the next few years, we held Christmas extravaganzas, birthday parties with costumes and themes, and 'Summer Village Fetes', offering skittle games, three-legged races – down the long corridor – food and drink stalls, raffles and bingo, and musical and magic performances. From a rather dodgy second-hand shop in Clapham, I acquired a fully working, all-American pinball machine.

Every party was an excuse for everyone to dress up, and we kept a closet full of hats and dresses and props, for those who arrived without them. My girlfriend Hazel moved in with us, followed shortly after by her sister Mary. While Nick Young gave us saucy vaudeville songs, Hazel played Chopin.

Happily, Queensway also boasted two tube stations. With no trouble at all, I could take the Central Line out to my next BBC assignment: in Villiers House, Ealing, which liked to brand itself "The Queen of the Suburbs." This was the headquarters of BBC Further Education (FE) TV, and here I was due to be posted for up to six months, starting January 3, 1969, to learn the mysteries of television, as part of my training.

As luck would have it, I was attached to a major series that was already under way. Bismarck had unified Germany into one country about a hundred years before, and the BBC were preparing a series, imaginatively titled *Germany 1870-1970*. This ten-part historical overview was an ambitious gambit for FE. They had modest budgets, and still produced all their shows in black and white. In the UK, color TV had only been launched in 1964, and then only on one channel. It took the BBC seven years to switch over entirely.

The small team creating the Germany series was led by Peter Dunkley. He concealed his anxiety with a steady stream of jokes and impressions of Kaiser Wilhelm, Hitler, Goebbels, Konrad Adenauer and other notables of the Reich and the Bundesrat. His deputy was a German expert, John Eidinow: he was the principal location director and had an impressive academic background. Being Jewish, he rolled his eyes when Peter Dunkley put a black comb under his nose, and goose-stepped down the corridor to the toilet, ranting at length from one of Hitler's speeches at the Nuremburg rallies, just as Herr Hansel had done in Hamburg. Political correctness was not high on the agenda in 1969.

Rounding out the main team was the researcher, a very jolly woman called Joy Curtis. Her principal job was to find historians and Germans to interview, and to wade through dozens of cans of historical archive film, and mountains of stock photos of events and Nazi artwork. I remember her laughing heartily as she held up a poster, featuring statues of two naked Wagnerian soldiers facing each other with swords, somewhere in the Nazi Valhalla.

"They are so manly," she said. "But it must be awfully cold, fighting without any clothes on, in the Northlands. And look at their willies: nasty long carroty things. I suppose they had to be sculpted like that, to prove they weren't circumcised."

I was given a small desk and a genuine welcome. They were so short-staffed that any new pair of hands, even if they belonged to the village idiot, would have been welcome. When they learned that I could also read and speak German, they were in ecstasy.

"That's splendid!" said Peter Dunkley, looking at me owlishly through his big round glasses. "What are you doing at the end of the month?"

I told him I had no special plans.

"Well, John Eidinow is going to film in Germany on the twenty-fifth, and the main fixer and translator we use over there has just told us he's unavailable. Can you go? We'll book you a ticket immediately. Pack your bags!"

So, three weeks after starting at FE(TV), I was sitting with John Eidinow and a BBC camera crew on a British European Airways Vickers Viscount turboprop, rumbling slowly towards Berlin. I had only the dimmest idea of what was planned for this two-week trip, but I knew that funds were short, and we had to shoot the maximum footage possible: mostly interviews, but also establishing shots of the cities we visited. I was present as the general dogsbody, to help lift gear for the crew, to argue in German with traffic policemen, to get lunch and so on. I was called "Man Friday" – or actually, "Freitagsmann" – by John. It was not entirely a compliment.

Berlin was a shock. It was divided into four zones of occupation: the British, the French, the American, and the Russian. Slicing through the middle was the infamous Berlin Wall, closing off the Russian zone from the rest. There were still signs of wartime devastation everywhere: gaunt, bombed-out buildings, vast holes where bombs had dropped, roads and tram-tracks that led nowhere and stopped at the Wall.

We were hosted (and protected) by officers of the British Command, who had decided to let us film the remains of some of the wartime Nazi HQ buildings, which lay undisturbed in no-man's land, near the Wall. A very casual army Major accompanied us, driving a jeep, with another jeep following, carrying the cameraman, the film gear, and a further soldier with a serious-looking light machine gun.

"Keep your heads down," said the Major affably, as we got out of the jeep. "This is right on the border of our territory and theirs, and the Russkies can get a bit trigger-happy if they're bored. Of course, they pretend they're all East Germans, but that's bollocks."

He trained his binoculars on a nearby watch tower.

"Russkies, for sure. So, don't make any sudden moves. They're watching us. Just make your way slowly into the building and take the shots you can. Be careful though: the whole place is falling apart, and it's meant to be off limits."

Inside, the building looked like a film-set for an Armageddon movie. It had been bombed and set on fire, the windows and bits of wall were all blown out, but so strong was the concrete construction that staircases, bits of Nazi insignia, even the odd desk and chair, were still in place. Doors could be gently pushed open and creaked ominously on their hinges. It had been abandoned twenty-four years before, and (being right on the line between two military zones) had never been touched again. It was truly spooky, and, when edited, made a strange, sad, evocative sequence about Germany's last war.

Within days, after interviews with Willy Brandt and others, we were on our way by train to Southern Germany. We filmed the Eagle's Nest, Hitler's eerie mountain-top redoubt, and Neuschwanstein, the fantasy castle built by mad King Ludwig II of Bavaria between 1869 and 1883. There could hardly have been a starker contrast between the era of comical Germanic principalities, and the era of the Third Reich, just fifty years later.

If you are ever in Bavaria, do not miss Neuschwanstein, by the way. This huge, kitsch, multi-turreted edifice was built by the king in homage to his favorite composer, Richard Wagner. Alas, Wagner was not moved to set foot in the building, and died in 1883, shortly before it was complete. Ludwig was distraught, and only ever spent a total of 170 days in the palace. The whole edifice is such a Looney Tunes piece of architecture that Walt Disney took it as the basis for his own much smaller castle, the one that graces all the Disney theme parks. It is part of the Disney empire's logo to this day.

Our final few shooting days in Germany were to be interviews in and around Munich. But, with just three days to go, the Director John Eidinow received the news that his father was gravely ill and that he would have to return immediately to London.

"I'm sorry", he told us all, "But we'll have to wrap up the trip early."

"Wait a minute", said the cameraman, a veteran called Henry Farrar. "It's only the interviews that need to be done, isn't it? It seems a shame to go home without those in the can, and then have to slog back here and do them some other time. Why doesn't David Kennard direct them? He speaks German, and I can do all the lighting and the set-up. We'll do fine."

John surveyed me bleakly. "Well, if I could write out the questions we need to ask," he said, "I suppose... Well, I'd better phone Peter Dunkley at home and get the OK." He called London and was given the green light.

I, of course, was very excited – until John explained what the work would entail. I would have to interview two of the last remaining senior Nazis of the Third Reich: the head of the Hitler Youth, Baron Baldur von Schirach, and the head of Hitler's Foreign Press Office until 1937, "Putzi" Hanfstaengl. Both of them had escaped execution at the Nuremburg trials of 1948, and von Schirach had only recently been released from his 20-year sentence in prison.

I was only twenty-three, and it felt like a daunting task. They would eat me for breakfast, wouldn't they? But at least I had the crew with me, and they were seasoned professionals.

The next morning, John left for London. The rest of us, following the schedule, drove south to the Bavarian mountain town of Trossingen. Lightly covered in snow, the roads grew darker and darker amidst the pine trees as night fell. We finally pulled into the town square, shut off the engine, and heard... virtually nothing. There was nobody out walking, no cars moving, no snow falling. Just the façade of our hotel, which looked like a stone-clad military ski lodge, built to withstand the next couple of wars as well. But, on listening more closely, we detected a continuous whining, mewling, occasionally moaning sound in the background. What could that be?

At the hotel reception desk, all was made clear.

"Ah yes," said the male clerk in perfect English, "This is why Trossingen is famous. What you hear is the headquarters of the Hohner Music Company, ja? They make the world's best harmonicas and accordions, and this is where they tune them: from seven o'clock in the morning, till seven o'clock at night. I expect this is why you are here, ja? To film the mouth organs, no?"

Henry Farrar insisted that the crew needed rooms as far from the Hohner Works as possible, plus a pair of earplugs each, if it was not too much trouble. He explained politely that the sound man had delicate ears, which could not possibly be endangered by the music of a dozen accordions on test. Meanwhile, I explained what we were really there to do: could the receptionist give me the directions to the Schloss Von Schirach, please? We were here to do an interview in the castle. There was a definite pause in the conversation.

"Ah yes," the desk clerk said, coolly. "The Baron has only recently returned. He was incarcerated for twenty years in Berlin's Spandau Jail, as you may know." He paused, for effect. "By the British."

I felt as if he was holding me personally responsible for this unforgiveable breach of etiquette.

"Er, yes, so I believe," I muttered. "But, um, would you be so kind as to give me the directions?"

The next morning, we were served our breakfast in complete silence. The otherwise empty dining room had barely a couple of lights switched on. The waitress refused to look at us in the eye and took our orders wordlessly.

"Gruss Gott!" I said heartily to the Receptionist, as we left. There was no answering welcome to the new day. The only sound was the continuous moaning of accordions being tuned, somewhere in the background.

It is hard not to exaggerate the impact of the next few hours. Driving up to the imposing gates of the von Schirach family castle in the snow, I felt we had arrived in Transylvania. I looked for a brass-plate inscribed with the name Dracula or Frankenstein. I pulled a large metal bell-pull at the gate and heard nothing. I waited, muffled up in a weather-proof coat that looked like the lagging for a domestic boiler. I pulled the bell-pull again, and then saw an elderly retainer struggling out through the snow towards the gate. I cleared my throat and tried to sound twice my age and look twice my height.

"Wir kommen vom BBC," I ventured.

I think I must have sounded like Minnie Mouse, with a high-pitched voice and big, oh-so-big and frightened eyes. But the manservant opened the gate and we drove up to the house. House? What am I saying? It was a proper German Schloss - a large castle that must have been in the von Schirach family for hundreds of years. I was shown in at the front door, and the crew was taken round to the servant's entrance, which they did not appreciate. But, apparently, technical equipment and technicians had to enter via the back door: the customs of four hundred years were not going to be altered for a British film crew.

A majordomo of some sort took us to an imposing library, and, in German, explained where we should set up. The room was not warm. Henry Farrar came in, blowing on his fingers.

"God," he said, "I don't want to operate with my gloves on."

He started setting some lights. A modestly sized log-fire was flickering in the enormous fireplace and having very little impact on the temperature. The Baron's chair was situated so that the wide shot of him would show the fireplace on one side of his chair, and part of the four-story rows of books on the other side. Two large deer heads, resplendent with antlers, adorned the wood-paneled walls. The set-up was pre-ordained and gave the impression of restrained wealth, good taste and worldly wisdom.

Suddenly, there he was: Baron Baldur von Schirach, scion of a noble family and former head of the Hitler Youth, standing in the doorway.

"Good Morning, gentlemen," he said, in perfect English.

His voice was perfectly modulated, suave and elegant. It reminded me of Shere Khan, the tiger in the Disney version of The Jungle Book. I was surprised that he had not said, "Good Morning, Man Cub."

He was still a handsome figure. Someone had obviously been helping him with some subtle make-up. As he sat in the high, wing-back chair, it was not difficult to imagine him inspiring tens of thousands of the 'Hitlerjugend.' He surveyed me with an ironic smile. No doubt I looked a lot younger than my twenty-three years.

"How crafty of these British," he must have been thinking, "To send me the youngest of their producers. Why, this stripling could have been one of my junior lieutenants, back in the good old days."

He was completely unrepentant, in the interview. Most of the senior Nazis had been condemned to death at Nuremburg, but he had been given just twenty years in prison. His military defense lawyers had claimed that he had in no way been responsible for the deaths of anyone. Of course, he had poisoned the minds of an entire generation, he had drilled boys and girls from eight to eighteen in their fanatical shouting of "Sieg Heil!" He had urged them to prepare for their coming of age, when they would join their older brothers in the German army or the Luftwaffe. He had urged them to spy on their parents, to check that there was no anti-Nazi sentiment or trace of Judaism in the family. And in the last few months of the war, many of the older Hitler Youth *did* pick up arms against the invading allies.

But Baron Baldur von Schirach had had a good defense lawyer, who had managed to persuade the court that this elegant man, part of the German aristocracy no less, had not stooped as low as the vile creatures of the central Nazi leadership. Together with Albert Speer, Hitler's architect, he had escaped the noose or the firing squad. And now, here he was, sitting by the fire, telling me and the camera how misunderstood he had been.

"You see," he said, "Our Hitler Youth was modeled on your Boy Scouts and Girl Guides. You remember Mr. Baden-Powell, who founded the Scouts? He believed in the open air – clean-minded, clean-limbed activities, like hiking and making campfires. Well, so did I. You have no idea the moral morass that Germany was in under the Weimar Republic, before the Third Reich was established: drugs, alcohol, sexual misconduct of every sort, undesirable literature, communism – all this was poisoning the minds of our young people. Something had to be done."

When pressed to explain how much he knew about Hitler's excesses in the real world of Blitzkrieg and Auschwitz, he brushed aside my questions.

"War is war," he said, as if Hitler had not started it. "Dreadful things happen. We tried our best to shield the flower of Germany – her young people – from the grimmest realities. We gave them holidays up here in the mountains of Bavaria, taught them how to help old people, and rebuild the homes which you British had bombed. We were building a new, fresh, pure Aryan civilization, and I make no apology for that."

He invited us to stay for lunch, and, after some hesitation and discussion with the crew, we did, since there was nowhere else to eat. In the dining hall, ancient flags with German heraldic symbols hung from the high rafters. An elegant table had been set, with places for us all. It looked like a film set for a Wagnerian opera. Indeed, von Schirach's entire life had been lived, in his own mind, as a Wagnerian opera. There had been that little misunderstanding which landed him in jail after Nuremberg, but now, life was back to normal, for him.

A butler served us a fresh Moselle wine. Four courses of haute cuisine were brought out: no simple German sausage or sauerkraut here. I remember some excellent veal cutlets, and finally the traditional Black Forest Cake, a delicious and highly fattening chocolate extravaganza.

I am not sure whether von Schirach actually said "It was all most unfortunate," about the war, as if it had been a trivial misadventure, or even "I have been gravely misunderstood." But, as we took our leave of him, he was talking about the many cultural links between Germany and England.

"After all," he said, "Even your Royal Family is German, you remember. They are from the family of Saxe-Coburg-Gotha. It was just local politics that made them change their name to Windsor, I've always felt."

• •

As we drove away from the castle at Trossingen, it was hard to believe we had spent four hours with such a prominent villain. Henry Farrar, the cameraman, had very obviously not participated much in the conversation at lunch, though it had all been in English. The entire crew had swallowed their meals in virtual silence, while I prattled on, sometimes showing off my German. Later I reflected: what had I been doing? Trying to impress this monster?

"That bugger's a real smooth operator," said Farrar in the car. "I wouldn't have trusted him for five minutes with one of my children." I suggested that the children had had no choice, back in the 1930's.

"They didn't all join the Hitler Youth," said Henry. "Their parents had to be real fervent Nazis." We drove on for a few more minutes before Henry spoke again. "I'd have strung him up at Nuremburg, quick as a flash."

Our next and final appointment could not have been more different. We were due to meet Ernst 'Putzi' Hanfstaengl in his modest flat in the center of Munich. He had been one of Hitler's oldest friends, from back in the Munich Bierkeller days, when Adolf had tried and failed to launch a putsch to overthrow the government in 1923. Putzi, like von Schirach, had impeccable, colloquial English, and had eventually risen to become Hitler's Foreign Press Chief.

It was, frankly, hard not to like him. His flat was overflowing with books, papers and old furniture. He welcomed us with a pot of strong English tea, together with milk, sugar and biscuits. At eighty-two, he was no youngster, but his big, beaming face, his generous, booming laugh and his great interest in everything we were doing for our TV series made him seem no more than sixty.

There is no room here to go into Putzi's amazing life-story in much detail. His father was German, and his godfather was one of that Saxe-Coburg-Gotha royal family much respected by von Schirach. But his mother was American, and he spent many years in the US, initially as a student. He composed songs for Harvard's football team in 1909 and joined the New York office of his father's business soon after. Eventually, he seemed to have known everyone from William Randolph Hearst to Charlie Chaplin. He returned to Germany in 1922, where he found the country in political chaos. There, in his native Munich, he met Hitler. He admitted that he had been immediately dazzled.

"What Hitler was able to do to a crowd in two and a half hours will never be repeated in 10,000 years," Hanfstaengl said. "Because of his miraculous throat construction, he was able to create a rhapsody of hysteria."

"You see," he told us on camera, "I don't think I was ever considered to be one of the really wicked Nazis. It's true that I hung around with Hitler in the early days. I was one of his confidants: he had a magnetic personality. I was probably one of the first people to read *Mein Kampf*, though I didn't believe most of it. I suppose you could call us friends: Hitler was godfather to my son Egon. But the most important thing for Hitler was that I was part of high society in Munich, and he really needed those connections, before he could take power."

Hanfstaengl seemed curiously modest about his achievements, and sprinkled jokes throughout his interview. Once again, I felt, an old Nazi was pulling the wool over my eyes: his charm was different from Schirach's, but just as effective. During the interview, Henry Farrar rolled his eyes at me, and crossed his fingers. He obviously did not believe a word of it.

"I spoke four or five languages," Putzi continued, "so Hitler put me in charge of the Foreign Press Bureau. I had a wonderful time, because there was so much good news at the start: he got everyone back to work, building freeways and Volkswagens, and lifting people out of the depression they felt. It all really seemed like a huge success until…" His voice drifted away.

By 1937, Putzi was having severe doubts about the direction in which Germany was being driven by Hitler. At the same time, Joseph Goebbels was having severe doubts about Hanfstaengl: he seemed to have too little enthusiasm for the emerging vision of the Third Reich. Putzi got on with the English-speaking press a little too well. He was becoming, Goebbels apparently suggested to Hitler, a liability.

An elaborate hoax was hatched by the German government: Putzi was put on a plane, and told he was going to Spain on a secret mission, to report back on how the Civil War was going. Soon after takeoff, however, the pilot took pity on him and revealed that Putzi was intended to be pushed out of the plane without a parachute. The pilot landed at Leipzig airport, claiming an engine malfunction, and Hanfstaengl escaped. He made for the Swiss border as fast as he could, and arranged for his only son, Egon, to be smuggled out of Germany and meet him in Zurich.

The rest of Putzi's life story is equally astonishing: he was imprisoned as an enemy alien in Britain, and then in Canada. Finally, he ended up working for the OSS (forerunner of the CIA) in Washington, spilling the beans about the Nazis' plans, and describing the innermost workings of Hitler's mind. He even became good friends with President Roosevelt: they were both old Harvard men.

But the big surprise for us was when Egon Hanfstaengl, Putzi's son, walked into the room during our interview. A handsome man in his early fifties, with impeccable English, he too had special memories of Hitler, as he told the camera.

"Around 1928 or 1929, 'Uncle Adolf' would often come to supper here in this flat. If my father knew he was coming, we would have to re-arrange the sofas and all the furniture in the living room, to make a giant maze that you could crawl through. I was about ten years old, so this was a great adventure."

"But why?" I asked, nonplused. "What was the point of that?"

Egon grinned. "Hitler loved to play First World War with me. He'd cover his eyes and tell me to go and hide somewhere in the maze. Then he'd get on all fours, as if he was crawling along a trench on the battlefield, and start looking for me. He was really quiet, and it was quite scary as I waited, trying not to breathe, trying not to be found. But he always found me."

"And then?" I asked.

"Then he would put a pretend machine-gun up to his face and started firing it at me. 'Ack-ack-ack-ack-ack-ack-ack. Got you!' he said. 'You're dead! I win!'"

∙∙

Back in London, editing was starting, and we had to shoot the video links, to tie the films together. Our presenter John Tidmarsh would be in studio, in front of a giant map of Germany, and would interview a couple of historians too. By chance, I had worked with John at the World Service on the daily *Outlook* magazine show. It was reassuring to see a familiar face.

Peter Dunkley had been so pleased with the Von Schirach and Hanfstaengl interviews that he let me direct some of the final studio sequences and put together two of the complete shows.

"This is splendid," he effused, in typical Dunkley mode. "You know Mr. Tidmarsh already? What a small world the BBC is. First rehearsal is on Monday, at Riverside."

I could not believe my luck: hands-on television directing experience, within a few months? At Riverside Studios, near London's Hammersmith Bridge, we were one of the last productions to use the old, heavy black-and-white cameras. We had to cue the edited film-clips to run at exactly the right moment in the show, and we had to roll credits and wrap the shows exactly on time: 27 minutes and 30 seconds per episode. We were not allowed to edit the videotapes, because back then, that would have meant physically cutting them with a razor blade, and thereby preventing the two-inch tape from ever being used again. And who could afford that kind of luxury in Further Education (TV)?

After six months with FE, I was officially credited on four programs as a Director and even (on two) as a Producer as well. For sure, Further Education shows were generally transmitted at 11 a.m. (for schools) or 11 p.m. (for insomniacs), but a credit was a credit. I couldn't believe it. My family and friends couldn't believe it. I still looked about sixteen years old, but at least I had contact lenses now, and had shed the Harry Potter glasses.

As the last part of my two-year internship, I was given an attachment to General Features (TV), an all-purpose department, which made high profile programs for primetime consumption. This was a big step up the totem pole and parachuted me into Kensington

House, a notorious den of creativity in London's Shepherds Bush district, a mile south of the iconic Television Centre.

Except for News and Current Affairs, almost all other BBC-TV documentaries were produced here: sport, science, the arts, religion, tales of adventure, quiz shows – you name it. Producers and directors were always arriving back from some improbable location shoot in Tooting or Timbuktu and telling tall stories of their adventures in the BBC Club bar. Yes, all BBC buildings had a bar: it had been official policy since the 1920's. Lord Reith, the BBC's first Director General, had decided that it was better for the BBC's image if staff got drunk inside the building rather than at a pub round the corner.

To my surprise, I was initially attached to a splendid, unflappable producer called Patricia Owtram. She was queen of the studio programs for General Features. She started me out on a series of fifteen-minute shows called *The Sky at Night*, which featured a much-loved and ageless amateur astronomer called Patrick Moore. This, to me and many other younger viewers, was the dullest quarter hour on television. Moore would usually sit in a high-backed chair next to a brass telescope and enthuse about some planetary body at great length, while waving his arms about a lot.

The single episode I helmed featured Phobos and Deimos, the two moons of Mars, which had recently been discovered. We had three smudgy black and white photos of them, and they looked like giant misshapen potatoes. Those were the only visuals we had, except for a card on a stand with a graphic, showing their orbit. Cut from Patrick to the potatoes; cut back to Patrick; cut to the orbits; cut back to a close-up of Patrick; cut to a different view of the potatoes.... You get the picture. Actually, there was barely any point in having a picture: it was fifteen minutes of perfect radio.

After that exciting ride, I was thrown in at the deep end: I would be directing two sixty-minute quiz shows in an occasional series called *So You Think...* Mine were: *So You Think You're a Good Husband* and *So You Think You're a Good Wife.* I was just twenty-four, so this was a subject about which I knew not one solitary fact.

Happily, the object of the shows was to entertain rather than instruct, so I set to work with Pat Owtram, writing scripts and coming up with silly ideas. I was allowed to hire some of my ex-Oxford friends to write and perform humorous skits for inclusion in the shows. We held a complete fake marriage in a church, with a dozen actors and extras. My mother's friend Patricia Hastings, a famous actress in her day, agreed to play roles as a door-to-door opinion-poll canvasser, a department-store saleswoman, and a local politician.

Questions in the quiz would be based on the scenes: we would freeze frame, pose the multiple-choice questions, and the audience at home would try to answer them, filling in blank spaces in that week's edition of the Radio Times, the BBC's weekly flagship program guide:

"Who has a legal right to come into your home?"
"Can you return an item you've bought more than 30 days afterwards?"
"At what point in the wedding proceedings are you actually married?"
"Which has more calories, a glass of wine or a half pint of beer?" – that sort of thing. A ton of fun for all the family, back in those simpler days.

The shows were taped in a large studio, with a fairly large audience, an avuncular host called Cliff Michelmore, and a panel of 'stars' who also tried to answer the questions. A famous comedy actor, Brian Rix, was the biggest star we landed for these two shows: he was famous for acting in slapstick farces, in which, one way and another, his trousers always came down, as he rushed from his hiding place in one closet to his hiding place in another. His wife, Elspeth Gray, also agreed to participate. At least she was not trying to be funny all the time, since Rix's antics and one-liners on our show became somewhat tiring.

We filled the rest of the studio with friends, family – my parents included – and coachloads of "the general public." We cued the band, and away we went. The programs made the front cover of the Radio Times on two successive weeks, and both scored a huge audience. I had seriously started to cut my teeth in television. But did I really want to get known as a director of quiz shows?

∎∎

My final production as a General Trainee was called *Seven Seconds to Run*, and could hardly have been more different from *So You Think…* It was a half-hour docudrama on film, shot on location, as one of a six-part series called *He Who Dares*. You will note the 1970 gender bias in the title…

The Executive Producer and Senior Director of the series was Lawrence Gordon-Clarke, a brilliant filmmaker on his own account, and a charming man. It was the height of generosity for him to offer me (a trainee with barely a year of television experience under my belt) the chance to create a half-hour film of my own. He gave me gentle, witty guidance and many a helpful hint, but always made it clear that this would be *my* film, sink or swim.

The idea was to re-create some feat of heroism and survival in microscopic detail, using the people who had been involved in the escapade, and running extensive interviews with them over the location filming. The whole thing would combine the experience of undergoing extreme stress with psychological insight into what the participants actually thought, minute by minute, during their ordeal.

We had episodes in the Australian desert (where a family's car broke down, leaving them stranded for weeks), and of course one in the obligatory icy crevasse (where the climber reconstructed the hell he'd gone through to get out), and several others. The short straw I picked was to recreate the heroic defusing of a giant World War II bomb in the center of London.

Major George Fletcher and Sergeant Major Stephen Hambrook had achieved this scary feat together, just a few months before we filmed. They were both professionals, from the UXB (Unexploded Bomb) Unit of the Royal Engineers (RE), and they had done this type of work many times before on old bombs that were slowly disintegrating. But this bomb was much bigger than anything they had tackled before.

I went down to the RE headquarters outside London and interviewed them both. Sergeant Major Hambrook had obviously been the hero of the day, and I am pleased to say he became quite a good friend: we held the premiere of the completed film at a grand party thrown specially for the event, and anyone who knows the British Army know that the Sergeants' Mess throws the best parties of all. My head was still spinning thirty-six hours after it had finished. Luckily, an Army staff car was on hand to take me and my girlfriend Hazel home.

In October 1969, Fletcher and Hambrook had led a UXB team to a building site just north of Camden Town, in London, near the flat where I had been born. Workmen had discovered the tip of a complex Type C German parachute mine. Nine feet long and packed with more than 1,500lb of explosives, it was capable of devastating entire streets in the area. The Northern tube line passed thirty yards away and terraced houses and tall blocks of flats were all within the quarter-mile danger zone. We went to see the site, and a stunning realization hit me: if this bomb had gone off during the war, when it had been dropped, it could easily have killed my mother. Her flat was in one of those blocks... In which case, I would not be here to write this book. The story became suddenly very personal.

What had happened in 1969 (and what we had to recreate a year later) was that the entire area – hundreds, if not thousands of people – had been evacuated. Very, very carefully, the UXB team exposed the mine, which was found to be equipped with six different fuses and a triggering device set for seventeen seconds. Ten seconds were left to run because it had jammed after seven seconds. If the clock restarted, they would have three seconds to try to "choke off" the fuse and seven seconds to get clear. Hence the title of the film: *Seven Seconds to Run.*

At four o'clock in the afternoon, Hambrook and Fletcher had gingerly started work, removing the filling plate and setting about the desperately dangerous task of steaming out the explosive. They both knew that the rise in temperature caused by the steam could restart the clock at any moment. The steaming process lasted the whole night and into the morning: this was the nail-biting heart of the scene we had to recreate.

Major Fletcher had been in charge, but it was clear right from the start who had been closest to the danger, with his hands actually inside the bomb. Stephen Hambrook gave us a wonderful interview. He was only thirty-six, but his craggy face suggested how many tight spots he had been in, before this one.

"I remember looking down into this deep trench and thinking 'This could be my grave'", he said. "With the big arc lights we had, glimmering through the swirling steam, it looked like the entrance to hell."

The mine was declared safe at seven o'clock the following morning. In the film, we cut back to local news footage, as the population returned to their homes in relief. In fact, the close-ups for the film - the trench itself, and the bomb (using the original casing and clock, but happily minus the explosive) - were filmed at a similar building site in Rochester, Kent, because the inhabitants of Camden did not want to go through the whole nightmare again, just for a film. I think we all understood their feelings.

In recognition of Stephen Hambrook's bravery, he was awarded a George Medal for this exploit. In all, he dealt with two hundred unexploded missiles and ten bombs in his distinguished career, receiving many further decorations. He died on February 6, 2015. I have never met a more modest or a braver man in my life.

In some ways, Hambrook reminded me of my father, Mick. Both were quiet men, never willing to talk about their bravery, and generous to a fault. Our film, though it was atmospheric and well received, gave only the most sketchy idea of what Stephen Hambrook had really gone through. I learned later that a block of flats had been built on the bombsite and named after him. When I went back once or twice, out of pure nostalgia, to see the flat where I was born in Chalk Farm, I always made a detour to the block that was named after Hambrook.

3.   THE ASCENT OF MAN

If I had applied for the production job on *The Ascent of Man* just six months earlier, I would never have been offered it. I would have been labeled as a studio quiz-show director, who mucked around with farceurs and music-hall comedians, creating popular fun for the less intellectual end of the market – or else as a director of *The Sky at Night*, the dullest show on television. But *Seven Seconds to Run* had been quite a sensation in its own small way. This was thanks largely to advice given to me by the Series Producer, Lawrence Gordon Clark, by a great cameraman, Henry Farrar once again, and by a great editor – Paul Carter. I had a big credit on the end of it, and, most importantly, it was shot on 16-millimetre color film, and entirely on location. These were subtle indicators, inside the BBC, that this was a real "film", not just a "program," and that made me a proper *filmmaker.* I had won my spurs.

Not that I believed I had a snowball's chance in hell of getting the job on *The Ascent of Man.* It was labeled Production Assistant at the lowly grade of MP2, but it would represent the end of my trainee internship phase, and the start of a real staff job. If I got it, I would be starting to climb the BBC production ladder, even if I was only clambering onto the bottom rung.

The interview was hair-raising. Facing me was the Head of Science and Features TV, Robert Reid. I had never done any science beyond the age of fifteen at school. There was also a VIP from the BBC's personnel department, whose name and face escape me, plus the Series Producer Adrian Malone, and last but not at all least a large roly-poly man called Aubrey Singer. Singer was a legend: you either loved him or hated him, I had heard it said. As head of the entire Documentary Features Group, he was a man with a mighty sword. He had personally gone to bat for big documentary series, signing very expensive international contracts to co-produce what he liked to call "world-beating television."

"I have persuaded Time-Life TV to put a fortune into this *Ascent of Man* show", he said, "So it had better be damn good."

For some time, it had been whispered up and down the corridors of Kensington House that *Civilisation*, written and hosted by the art historian Kenneth Clark, would be the most expensive and expansive non-fiction project that the BBC had ever undertaken. It was being created, under the fatherly eye of producer Michael Gill, just a few doors down from where I had been working for the last eighteen months.

"*Civilisation,*" said Aubrey, as if he had discovered both the concept and the word, "looks at mankind's history through the lens of art. What we're now planning is a companion series, which will look at the world through the lens of science. What makes you think, David, that you'd be a good member of the team that creates it?"

I cannot remember or even imagine how I replied to that question at the interview, coming as it did from someone who was one of the Archangels in the BBC heavens. I think I mumbled something about the travel I had done – not just Germany, but previous student jaunts to the Middle East, the USSR and India, and my time in the USA. I tried to come across as an eager striver, a jack-of-all-trades who could turn his hand to whatever needed to be done.

"Yes, yes, but I've seen that bomb disposal story you did," said Adrian Malone, who would be my immediate boss. "That was real *film-making*. I liked that."

The fellow from Personnel shifted uneasily on his seat and looked at me as if I was a small insect. "But you must understand that the job-description is that of an assistant," he said. "You'd be there to assist. Don't think you'd be directing or producing. Not for a minute. Dear me, no."

Two weeks later, Adrian Malone came up to me in the BBC Club bar – always the place to find people at lunchtime in the 1970's. He lowered his voice, looked around conspiratorially, and winked at me like a pirate.

"I'm not supposed to tell you this, but you've got the job. Well done. What's your poison? Have a pint." I was stunned, but I took the beer.

"Bollocks to all this stuff about not directing," he said. "They've given me such a small staff that we'll all be doing everything, if we're ever going to make this thing. Cheers!"

Within a few weeks, I had transferred my meager BBC possessions to a new desk in Science and Features Department, and, feeling like the junior cabin boy, met the crew of the Jolly Roger.

Top of the pole and presenter of the series was Professor Jacob Bronowski: a twinkly-eyed Polish Jew, who had escaped to London just in time to avoid death at the hands of the Nazis. He had worked at the highest level for the British government during WWII, won international prizes in mathematics, physics and biology, was renowned for his poetry, had starred for years in a radio program called *The Brains Trust*, and was currently a senior member of the Salk Institute in La Jolla, California. Plus, he was a legendary raconteur, who had worked with Adrian Malone on two previous films, one on Leonardo da Vinci: they got on well together.

Adrian, the Executive Producer and much else, was a Celt through and through: warm, funny, generous, poetic, tough, pugnacious, loyal, independent – and demanding most of those things from people who worked for him. He was one of my principal mentors in film and television – and in life generally, I suppose. He was quick to anger, but quick to laugh and quick to forgive. Of course, he could be morose and glum – that was the opposite side of the Celtic coin. But the Irish in him soon twinkled through again. He was a fine leader of men – and women, too – and we would have followed him anywhere. What am I saying? We *had* to follow him anywhere, and we were so short-staffed that there were many places we had to go alone. The mountains of Afghanistan, anyone?

Dick Gilling was the second-in-command, as Senior Producer: a very dear man, and still a good friend. Unflappable, pipe-smoking, already deeply experienced in making science

documentaries, he was the Yin to Adrian's Yang. When we sat round, dreaming ᴜ
scenes, new techniques, new approaches to the story of science, going crazy with aᴌ
wonderful possibilities, Dick would smile gently, suck on his pipe, turn to Adrian aᴌ
say:

"Steady on, Ade. We might not have the budget to do *that.*"

They knew they worked well as a team, and called themselves Launder and Gilliatt, after
two legendary comedy film producers at the old Ealing Studios.

Creative star of the production team was undoubtedly the producer-director Mick
Jackson. He had bright orange hair, combed over a prematurely balding head; he wore
outrageous "art-student" clothes; he had an infectious laugh and a better capacity to tell
jokes and see the funny side of things than anyone I knew, before I met James Burke. He
was also a really talented artist and draftsman, who could rough out an idea into
storyboards long before we had it made up by the BBC's design department. Many of his
frame-by-frame analyses of how we could achieve special effects – a decade before
computer graphics came of age – were a key part of the show's success.

There were several other key players: David Paterson, a science producer from BBC Radio,
who really did know his Einstein from his Heisenberg; Josephine Marquand, a leggy
academic blue-stocking who was our ace researcher; Jane Callander, who organized us
all; Philippa Copp, who was the secretary, and therefore even lower than me on the totem
pole. She was very young and very sweet, and Jacob Bronowski (or "Bruno" as he liked to
be called) enjoyed having her sit on his knee while she took dictation. This was nearly 50
years ago, but even then it seemed a bit risqué.

The first month was entirely devoted to slicing up the subject matter. Bruno had been
involved in several films and dozens of radio programs, so he knew roughly how much –
or rather, how little – content you could squeeze into an hour. And we had "only" thirteen
hours at our disposal. Being in that big production office for a month, taking notes, asking
questions, making the occasional suggestion: it was like studying for the science degree
I had never received. It was an incredible opportunity.

"Program One," said Bruno magisterially, "has to be about man: what makes him unique
from the other animals. Just that, no more and no less."

Again, you'll notice that the word was always Man back in the nineteen seventies: The
Ascent of *Man.* It never occurred to anyone on the team, even the women, to ask what
happened to the "fairer sex," as women were then often called. History was still seen,
even by enlightened liberals, as the history of Man.

So Program One would start in Africa, and list the developing skills of humanity: the
lifetime of development from fetus to old age, hand-eye co-ordination (lots of special
effects for Mick Jackson to design), the opposable thumb, the skill of the hunt. Its high
point would be a sequence in one of the caves, where mankind had drawn and painted
the animals he was hunting, 25,000 years ago.

I was lucky enough to film that sequence with Bruno, in the Altamira caves of Northern
Spain. We got special permission from Generalissimo Franco's government, and were the

to film there, before it was permanently closed to visitors: the humidity
nvading the cave, and the lights necessary to see the magical bison and
n the ceiling were destroying the art. Bruno's key point about the images
abled men to imagine and predict the future of the hunt:

set men apart: foresight and imagination."

Bruno decided, would take us from hunting and gathering to the
domestication of animals. The researchers came up with several options, and Adrian
decided that we would follow one of the twice-yearly trans-humance migrations of the
Bakhtiari people in Iran, to take their flocks up the Zagros mountains to the high pastures
in the summer. That was one of the sequences I would also be fated to do, with Adrian
and our loyal camera crew: it was no picnic.

Program Three would be about settled agricultural communities and writing: the
emergence of cities and the development of organized war. And so it went on… There
were certain programs that Bruno insisted on, right from the beginning: one was on
Newton and Einstein: for him, these were the two towering geniuses of science, the two
men who had revealed the mechanisms of the universe more deeply and clearly than any
others. Another was the final program: this, he insisted, would be mostly about the
future: what were our hopes and fears? What values, at least in the West, should we hold
most dear? Much of the filming was done with his own grandchildren at his spacious
home near the beach in La Jolla, basking in the soft autumn sun of California. It was an
inspiring and deeply optimistic conclusion to the series.

But what would be the style and feel of the series? Adrian was very clear from the very
start: "No boring shots!" he'd shout at us.

The principal cameramen were Nat Crosby and John Else – two of the best the BBC had.
They took part in various meetings to discuss what was possible in the field. We wanted
to create a project that was both exciting and yet timeless: a classic that was stylish.

"No dreary three-quarter angle exteriors", said Adrian. "And I do not want lazy zooms to
reveal whatever it is. I want good prime lenses, and I want a 200-millimetre lens for
spectacular long-shots."

The most important question was how we could achieve what we wanted by using 16-
millimeter film. It is hard to remember now that all those early BBC documentary and
wildlife series were shot on ten-minute rolls of film, which were incredibly expensive to
buy, ship and process, and were also very, very heavy to schlep around in bulk. We simply
could not afford to waste film, particularly if we were away in Iran, or Japan, or Easter
Island. Yes, really, Dick Gilling even went to Easter Island for *The Ascent of Man*, to film
the dead eyes of those weird statues: a culture that literally died of solitude and left us
memorial stones to their own demise.

And so we set out: usually six of us – producer/director, assistant producer, cameraman,
camera assistant (to be always "in the bag," changing the roll of film in the camera
magazine, so that no light could spoil it), sound man, and lighting man. We could not
afford to carry big dollies and tracks, so we picked them up locally, together with extra
lights, and the people to operate them if absolutely necessary. I have far too many

memories of the fantastic locations we filmed, to describe many in detail. A few are particularly vivid, however.

Imagine yourself in deepest rural Japan: Dick Gilling, the producer, and I are filming a sequence about the invention of steel. But we are not in any factory: we are crouched in a misty pine forest, with menacing Samurai warriors galloping past. Each horseman brandishes an impressive steel sword. The next day, we were to film one of the last few people on earth who could make a fine sword the traditional way – by heating and re-heating iron to prodigious temperatures and then folding and re-folding the melted metal in upon itself. This man was a living National Treasure of Japan, at least seventy years old: in the film, his impassive face is unblinking as he wields the bright orange and yellow metal. Steel of this quality was invented in Japan, and the secret of how to make it took hundreds of years to reach the west.

And now cut to the same evening, after the first day's filming is finished: we are back at the Ryokan – the traditional inn where we are staying. The Samurai are local men from the area to the east of the city of Sendai – dreadfully damaged a few years ago by a tsunami and the collapse of the Fukushima nuclear plant. The men turn out to be dentists, accountants, artists, 'salary men' – but they are all from local Samurai families. Their ancestors had worn these original, fearsome clothes and armor only two hundred years before, and now they have donned them specially for our filming. They re-create mock battles several times a year, to keep the Samurai knowledge alive, they tell us. It is an honor for them to show us their prowess.

Everyone (cast, interpreter, film crew and the local Mayor included), is now in the steaming communal baths, wearing wooden slippers, sitting on low stools, totally naked, being soaped, lathered and washed by elderly women. This everyday Ryokan ritual will be followed by a traditional Japanese meal, eaten with chopsticks while squatting on the floor, swallowed down with ample sake (warm rice wine). And then bed: on a thin mattress on the floor, behind translucent paper tatami walls. The real thing: this is Japan!

The following morning, after a breakfast consisting mainly of seaweed and fish, John Else, the cameraman, took me to one side.

"David," he said, "I'm sure it's a great honor to be treated like this, the traditional way, but me and the lads have been having a talk, and we got no sleep last night, and we can't eat the food, frankly. So, would you mind if we checked into a regular motel? We saw one on the edge of town as we came back from filming, and they said that they'd got rooms, so we booked some for tonight."

We could hardly refuse them: we needed a crew who had slept and eaten properly. So, the second night, Dick Gilling and I were the only foreign guests at the Ryokan. The following morning, we met the crew outside. They looked red-faced and sheepish.

"What's up?" asked Dick Gilling.

The crew showed us the bill: it added up to almost $10,000 for the four rooms (in 1970 dollars!). We showed it to our translator, who did his best not to laugh. It turned out that the "regular motel" the crew had stayed in was a Love Hotel, which charged for each room by the hour.

"Oh, that's why there was so much coming and going during the night," said John Else. "All that laughter and giggling and car doors slamming. We got a worse night's sleep than we did at the Ryokan."

It all ended happily enough. The local Mayor was aghast that the crew had been tricked into paying by the hour. The community would lose face if this was allowed, so he went to see the owner, and half an hour later, the entire bill had been canceled. Phew!

∎∎

From the ridiculous to the sublime: we are in the gorgeous Alhambra Palace, at Granada in Southern Spain. Adrian Malone and I are filming after hours, when the public has disappeared. We and the crew are with Jacob Bronowski in the private bathroom of the harem – an area no longer open to regular visitors. The night is warm, and all we can hear is the splashing of the myriad fountains in the baths and the surrounding courtyards. The Spanish lighting crew, directed by our BBC Gaffer, have done a wonderful job transforming a magical place into something even more mysterious.

Why are we here? So that Bruno can talk about geometry.

"Imagine," he says to camera, "these baths filled with gorgeous women, at their ease, padding around barefoot. From the balcony, through peepholes in the stonework, the Sultan can observe the ladies, and decide who pleases him the most, and who will join him in his bed that night."

Bruno smiled, an impish twinkle in his eye.

"But what do we find on the walls? Not the mildly erotic paintings or sculptures which the Romans or Greeks would surely have put here, but the most complex and intriguing geometric shapes."

He then proceeded to show how the wall tiles were composed of thousands of interlocking triangles, and triangles within triangles, and curved, "windswept" triangles.

"Representing the human form was forbidden to Islam," he explained. "So instead, they covered the walls with elegant mathematical puzzles – the highest art of abstraction. And not just any abstraction: the ratio of the sides of the triangles reflect knowledge of Pythagoras. You can rotate the triangles in any one of a number of groups, and they all return elegantly to the same place."

Then Bruno pulls his Coup de Théâtre: he takes from his pocket a velvet pouch of crystals, all about an inch cubed – except that only one of them (iron pyrites) is an actual cube.

"Nature works like this: mathematically. Each of these different crystals is a defined mathematical shape: six-sided, eight-sided, look…" The camera cuts to a close-up of the twinkling gems. "The Muslim scholars knew that, and so special was this knowledge to them that they adorned the walls – yes, even the harem bathroom – with tiles that testify to that knowledge."

I was sent to Afghanistan by myself, initially, to set up some tricky arrangements for *The Ascent of Man*. Adrian Malone was going to follow me out to Kabul with a camera team, to direct the shooting and share the glory, if we were successful. But first, I had to conjure up a spectacular location scene.

The year was 1972. It was to be the end of an era of relative peace and quiet in that war-torn country. The King, Zahir Khan, had reigned since 1933, and there were already signs of tribal and religious restlessness. The King had done his best to start introducing a measure of Western-style democracy, but basically the entire country was stuck in a medieval time warp.

There was just one western-style hotel in Kabul: the Intercontinental. It was twelve stories high, and nothing was taller in the whole city, except for the minarets of the principal mosques. It offered that splendid rarity, a bar, which is the chief reason that the wealthier westerners flocked to it. The less wealthy were mostly students and hippies on the trail from Europe, journeying across the deserts of Asia, to the enlightening swamis and gurus of India.

Bronowski was very clear in his own mind that a critical turning point in mankind's development had been the domestication of the horse, in central Asia. Cows, sheep, goats, dogs and cats provided food, companionship, guards and rodent extermination. But horses provided speed of communication, and the opportunity to wage war on a grand scale. Bruno pointed to the half-man, half-horse of Greek mythology: it was hard to comprehend the impact of this new "Blitzkrieg" technology, at the root of the success of Genghis Khan and many a conqueror from Asia.

Our research had discovered that there were still many fine horses in Asia, and nowhere better to find them than Afghanistan, where, it was rumored, the ancient game of Buzkashi was still played. Two teams of up to twenty men on horseback play an ancient form of polo, using a goat carcass as the "ball" and hooked wooden sticks (like long hockey sticks), hardened from years of use, to scoop up the goat. The pitch or playing area is a loosely defined rectangle up to a mile long and quarter of a mile wide. The idea is to gallop up to an opponent, then, using brilliant horsemanship and no-holds-barred swordplay with your stick, to wrangle the goat out of your opponent's grip and charge down towards the "goal" line.

I was bemused, on the morning after my arrival in Kabul, to receive two extra items on my breakfast tray, in my bedroom. I was still befuddled by jetlag, but they were both very clear. One was an imperious invitation to dinner, that same night, at the British Embassy. The other was a copy of the local English daily newspaper, the Kabul Times, published as a propaganda exercise by the Afghan Government, since no Western newspapers or television were available.

The newspaper had two large headlines, given equal space, side by side on the front page. One read: "First ever close-up pictures of Mars obtained by spaceship", together with one such picture. The other read "BBC producer arrives to make film about Afghanistan," complete with an equally large picture of me: it was a head-and-shoulders passport photo, never the most flattering angle. Each, apparently, had a similar news value, given the positioning and column inches.

I could not believe how the newspaper had found the photo, or why it was remotely interested in me or in our project, which it completely misunderstood. But I soon discovered that Kabul was a very small city. The pro-Western government wanted to proclaim the importance of Afghanistan in the eyes of the British media. The article suggested that our camera team would be taking pictures of everything from the hydro-electric plant to the folk-dancing contests. The photo was one that I had sent with my visa application months beforehand.

That night, I was entertained in the large and ornate British Embassy, by the equally large and ornate Ambassador. I told him and his wife and retinue about *The Ascent of Man*. Servants in impressive colonial outfits glided in and out with the Mulligatawny soup. The year could have been 1840, sometime around the First Afghan War, though that (like all other subsequent wars in Afghanistan, it seems), turned out badly for the British.

After dinner, one of the consular officials glided up to me, brandy in hand, and gently enquired what we were *really* there to film.

"You'll be in the north, of course, near the Russian border", he said. "We'd like to know a lot more about what's going on up there."

He explained that the Americans had already built a black-top metaled road from east to west, linking Iran with Pakistan via Afghanistan, but that HMG (Her Majesty's Government) had information that the Russians were planning to construct one from north to south, which would allow them free passage through Afghanistan to the Indian Ocean. The Russians had always coveted the idea of a port on the Indian Ocean.

At the BBC, I had been given very firm instructions to rebuff any request for assistance from "consular officials" or Second Attachés with unspecified duties: they would probably be representing the interests of MI6, not the BBC, and ne'er the twain should meet. I politely said that I would keep my eyes peeled, however, and let him know later if I ran across anything suspicious.

A few days later, after visits to the Afghan Tourist Authority, the Interior Ministry, and a translation service, I set off with all the necessary permits, two ad hoc assistants and a driver in a Toyota Landcruiser, for the far north of the country. Our destination was a legendary caravanserai and tribal headquarters, the sprawling city of Mazar-i-Sharif.

The journey took at least fourteen hours. A winding dirt road led up over an 8000-foot pass, through the high mountains in the center of the country. We passed and briefly detoured to look at the astonishing Buddhas of Bamiyan: these two sixth century Colossi were literally carved into the mountain. Each one was as tall as a many-storied building. They were both dynamited and utterly destroyed by the Taliban government in March 2001, after being declared religious idols, and contrary to the spirit of Islam.

The whole region beyond the mountains is an extraordinary mix of cultures: northwards lie the unending flat semi-desert steppes of what was then the Soviet Union. One of the loops of the famous Silk Road passes through, on its way east to Samarkand and China. Hellenistic ruins abound. The town itself is named after the very beautiful blue mosque at its heart.

In the streets of 1972, barely a single motor vehicle could be seen. The taxis were all horse-drawn cabs, vintage 1900: some polished, glittering and prosperous; others dusty, decrepit and hauled by tired old nags on the brink of death. On one trip through town, we saw a horse that had just died, and collapsed between the shafts of the cab it was pulling. It was surrounded by a crowd of children, waiting solemnly for whatever would happen next. Giant carts, laden with furniture, hay or whatever, creaked past, drawn by teams of bullocks. Most of the inhabitants were Uzbeks, Tajiks and Turkmen, with deeply lined and tanned faces; most wore traditional garb. There was hardly a western face, a T-shirt or a tourist to be seen.

We were to be the guests of a princely family, it turned out: their traditional house, built round courtyards and fountains, was a miniature Alhambra, and I was regally entertained. On my first full day with the family, I was taken out back to the farmyard, to look at the chickens: which one did I fancy? I realized that whichever one I pointed to was going to be my lunch. Was it polite to pick something modestly sized, thin and scrawny or large and proud? Having made my selection – at ten in the morning – I was taken inside, to lounge on vast cushions in the proper pasha fashion, and to discuss what we wanted to film, and how it could be arranged.

As we talked, we could all hear the process of the chicken being chased, caught and strangled in the courtyard, though we could see none of the activity. It started off like the soundtrack to a Looney Tunes cartoon, as half-a-dozen houseboys played tag with the surprisingly agile chicken. It ended like an episode of The Godfather a little later. Throughout, I had to make pleasant conversation with my hosts. It did not increase my appetite. But then the chicken had to be plucked, cleaned and roasted. Lunch was not served till 3 o'clock, by which time we had planned the entire filming and exhausted every last piece of small talk that I could think of.

The plan was to form two Buzkashi teams from two different branches of the large tribal family, who had cheerfully competed since time immemorial. I had been authorized by the BBC to offer a special prize to the winners, which I had brought with me: a handsome glass paperweight, with "BBC World Service" engraved upon it. This was seen as a very excellent trophy by my hosts, thank goodness. They were fiercely handsome and proud men, and told me that they would enjoy the contest, and that the winner would treasure the spoils, however modest.

It was still possible to telegraph London, back in the balmy days of 1972. There was barely a phone in Mazar-i-Sharif, and calling Kabul was a nightmare, so a telegram had to suffice. I sent word to the London team that all was in order, and the event would take place. In due course, I received a telegraphic reply: Adrian and the camera crew were on the way.

Meanwhile, what was to be done? Could we film from on horseback, I wondered? I went and inspected horses and tried to look knowledgeable. The BBC had taught me to ride, so as to film for *The Ascent of Man*, and that had already been useful in Iran, when we documented the annual Bakhtiari migration across the Zagros mountains, but these Afghan horses were huge. I explained that what we really needed was some sort of camera car, to film the breakneck speed of the horses, during the game. Much discussion ensued, and we went to inspect what vehicles were available. Suddenly, one afternoon, I spotted an old Citroen 2CV Deux Chevaux: with its springy elastic suspension, and its roll-top roof, it would be ideal. Nicely ironic, I felt: a "Two Horses" Citroen, to film the magnificent Arab steeds of central Asia.

My hosts roared with laughter. Why not use one of their latest-model Toyota Landcruisers, with a sunroof, rather than this shabby old thing? I explained that the Citroen's suspension was perfect for the almost-but-not-quite-flat terrain of the steppes, where they would play the game. They bargained on my behalf for the 2CV and came back with a very good deal.

"How many days have we hired it for?" I asked.

"You just bought it," they explained, laughing again. "You'll have to take it back with you on British Airways."

For men whose pleasure was a rearing Arab steed, such a dinky little car was a joke, but it did its job with huge success when we filmed. And when we'd finished, I gave it back to my hosts, as a humble "thank you" for their help.

There were other details to see to, but time started to drag, while we waited for the BBC crew to arrive. It was then that our hosts amiably offered me a hubble-bubble pipe of my own, and the largest cake of hashish I had ever seen or dreamed about. It is well known that the Taliban have always funded their operations by the cultivation and sale of the opium poppy, but my God! The strength and excellence of this hash, smoked while lying with my hosts on luxurious silk and velvet cushions in the evenings, helped me to understand why Islam takes a dim view of alcohol. Who needs gin when you have got this stuff?

With two days still to go before the arrival of the crew in Mazar-i-Sharif, the princes (as I called them) suggested we should fill the time with an all-day picnic and duck shoot on the "nearby" Oxus river. Now called the Amu Darya, it marks, very roughly, the border between Afghanistan and the Soviet Union. Luckily, shooting was the one sport I had more or less mastered at my boarding school, so I responded with some enthusiasm. It was agreed: a big picnic would be prepared, and we would set out for the Oxus at dawn the following day.

Of course, it was blistering hot, even by 8 a.m. I had had images of the Oxus as a mighty flow, cascading through the semi-desert. No such luck. The river was nearly dry, with small ponds here and there, where duck were apparently to be found. A suitable base was selected by my hosts, and we pitched camp. Out came the guns: a large selection of weaponry, much of it dating, like most of the country, from the 1840's or earlier. I did not fancy some elderly shotgun exploding in my face, so I chose a First World War Lee-Enfield, and, with sun hats firmly on heads – colonial-era solar topees would have been even better – we advanced into duck country.

What happened next was like a scene from a movie, but certainly not the movie I had gone there to make. After we had taken a few pot-shots and missed, we moved our base a few hundred yards north to a better position. Soon, we saw a small dust storm approaching us. Within moments, we had been surrounded by three Russian military vehicles, and a number of serious-looking soldiers in camouflage fatigues jumped down from the trucks. An officer climbed out of a Russian jeep and spoke to one of our hosts. Communication was obviously not easy: none of us spoke Russian; the Russians seemed to speak no Pushtun or Uzbek. Our hosts tried Arabic. Then I said something in English, and the Russian officer turned to me.

"Your papers," he said, and held out his hand.

I had left my passport back at the house of our hosts and was only able to give him my BBC identity card, with my picture on it: in the circumstances, not very helpful at all. How could we pretend we were simple tourists, out for a bit of fun with a shooting party, when one of us was a western journalist? The fact that we had a small armory of old guns, and my hosts sported expensive Leica and Nikon cameras, did not help.

There ensued a shouting match – in broken English – between the Afghans and the Russians.

"Do you know who I am?" was the gist of our hosts' angry approach. "We have a guest from Britain here, we are a private party, we are entitled to do what we like. We are proud Afghans. We spit on you Russians..." and so on.

The Russian officer shrugged. "You are in Russia," he said. "You have entered illegally. You are under arrest."

This led to apoplexy on the part of our Afghan hosts, who promised fearful vengeance in the face of this travesty. They were related to the King, they shouted. Heads would roll.

The fact is that the border is very ill defined along the northern edge of Afghanistan. The River Oxus splits into many slow-moving tributaries and disappears beneath the sand much of the time. There are virtually no landmarks, and certainly no fence, no signs or roads to let you know where you are. We had indeed wandered into Russia, it would seem.

"Get into the truck," the Russian ordered most of us.

He agreed to take the senior Afghan with him in his car, to check out who we really were and what we were doing. I protested that my Embassy knew all about my filming project, that we were here as guests of the Afghan government, that Her Britannic Majesty would take a very dim view of all this. After all, that is what it says inside every British passport, does it not? But the Russian was unmoved. So we were bundled into the truck.

After about half an hour of bumping and lurching across the riverbed of the Oxus, we arrived at a small Russian encampment. A few cinderblock huts shimmered in the heat of the noonday sun. We were herded into a virtually empty hut, and there we were left in the stifling heat. No water, no food was offered. No toilet seemed to be available. It was twenty years before the invention of the cellphone. We were utterly stranded, and no-one knew where we were.

After a couple of hours, the situation started to seem rather serious. There was virtually no activity in the camp. Our small group was stranded in Nowheresville, deep in Central Asia. One of the Afghans, realizing it was time to pray, got down on his knees.

"Allah Akbar!" he chanted. He was immediately joined by the other Afghans.

Luckily, I had memorized some small part of the prayer when filming earlier in Iran, so I was able to put on a modest show of emulating their worship. I think this impressed them, if only a little. It certainly helped calm me down: we would face this like a band of brothers, I told myself, wiping the sweat from my brow.

Sometime towards evening, the Russian officer returned.

"You may go," he said curtly.

What had happened? No explanation was offered. A truck full of Russian soldiers accompanied us for some miles, past the place where our camp had been, and some distance further south, till we were met by the drivers and cars we had been forced to abandon earlier in the day. There, the Russians stopped and turned. The officer saluted the senior Afghan prince (it was indeed a prince, I later learned) and disappeared, with his troops, back into the dust of the steppe.

The Afghans treated the whole episode with great hilarity and told Adrian Malone and the camera team all about it, when they arrived from Kabul the following day.

"What the hell did you think you were doing?" Adrian asked me. "What kind of headline would it make? 'BBC Producer on Duck-Hunting Picnic Triggers International Incident?'"

My Afghan hosts rallied round me, however, and praised my coolness under fire, and said I was a good Muslim and altogether a blood brother for life. And screw the Russians, for good measure.

"Well, at least you've made some friends," said Adrian.

Happily, the success of the filming the next day made up for the imbroglio with the Russians. The two teams of horsemen, clad in the garb of Genghis Khan, fought a mighty battle of Buzkashi. They thundered across the steppes like a Mongol horde, fearsome in their traditional headgear and black beards, scooping up the goat carcass with their inverted-umbrella shaped sticks. Our tiny 2CV camera car roared along in front of them, criss-crossed amongst them, and was nearly trampled flat on more than one occasion.

Suddenly, without warning, the game ended. It was entirely unclear who had won, or how many goals or touchdowns or whatever had been scored, or even who had been playing on which side. But apparently, honor had been done, a winner had been declared and both men and horses were proud but exhausted. There was a final ceremony in the setting sun, as both teams dismounted and bowed low to each other, providing us with phenomenal footage... and then it was party time.

I mentioned before that the upper classes in Afghanistan do not let a small thing like the prohibition of alcohol get between them and a good time. After everyone had washed and changed and got the dust out of their hair, the entire BBC team was ushered into a tent, where Belshazzar's feast was laid out. Sultry women served us, their faces masked by black silk, as we lay back on cushions. Oil lamps lit the scene: the cameraman was bitterly disappointed that there was not enough light for him to film, but our hosts said that it was just as well: this way, we could all relax, and it was considered bad form to mix work and pleasure.

They offered us every delicacy of Central Asia: goat and lamb dishes, rice with saffron and raisins, honeyed drinks and piles of exotic fruit. We all ate with our hands, scooping mounds of delicious stew into our mouths with wheat pancakes, like the Indian chapatti. Then there was dancing: our servers enchanted us with elegance and extraordinarily erotic moves: no cheap belly-dancing here. And finally, there was a hubble-bubble for everybody, full of eastern promise and powerful intoxicants. The crew was astonished. It was clear that there was no way they could refuse this final demonstration of hospitality.

I am very glad to say that we had no more filming to do. Although the hash was strong and plentiful, it gave none of us a hangover, when we woke the next morning. We just moved at one-tenth the normal speed. We slowly packed up our gear, ready for the journey back to Kabul and London. I made an expedition into the bazaar with one of our hosts, and bought the most beautiful small carpet, which is beneath my feet as I write this. My host haggled the price down to little more than the cost of a horse-drawn taxi-ride, to my embarrassment, but then threw the vendor an extra 100-dihram bill as we left. He had made his point: he was the big guy, the carpet-seller was not.

As a final gesture, the senior prince gave both Adrian and myself a gorgeously elegant and colorful robe, beautifully lined and embroidered. These were normally worn on special occasions by the most senior men of the Pushtun people. Whenever Mohammed Karzai (premier of Afghanistan for a decade in the early twenty-first century) appeared in public or at the United Nations, he wore an identical robe. I still have mine, and I very much treasure it. True, it has appeared in many a Christmas charade with my children over the years, and I am always urged to use it as a bathrobe, but it is far too precious for that.

We were also each given a cake of best Mazar-i-Sharif hash, the size of a Frisbee, beautifully presented in a cardboard box, as if it was a box of chocolates. Once we were back in Kabul at the Intercontinental, Adrian Malone called a meeting.

"There's no way we can take this stuff back to the UK," he said. "Imagine the headlines: 'BBC Crew Smuggling Drugs on Million-Pound Documentary Series.'"

Adrian was always worried about negative press coverage. What he said was plainly good sense, but the question remained: what should we do with the stuff? We were not even sure that it was legal to carry it around in Kabul.

"You can each find your own way to get rid of it," said Adrian. "I'm going to leave mine in the drawer beside the bed, like a Gideon Bible. Good luck to whoever finds it."

Personally, I awoke at dawn the next morning, as the Muezzin called the faithful to prayer from a dozen mosques across the city. It was a beautiful day – a perfect sunrise. I went out onto the balcony of my fifth-floor room, and flung the cake of hash like a Frisbee, far out into the hotel's lush tropical garden. With luck, a gardener's boy would find it, and see it as a gift from Allah. More likely, a large flock of tropical birds would get very stoned indeed over the next few weeks.

There was one final punch line. The British Ambassador invited us all to an informal buffet dinner on our last evening in Kabul, together with a couple of junior ministers in the Afghan government, and assorted box-wallahs and camp followers. It was generally agreed that the filming had been a great success and would lead to peace in our time between our two great nations, blah blah blah.

Confidentially, I was able to tell the story of our brief incarceration by the Russians to the Chief Spook, who had cornered me on our arrival. He smiled, the same way John Le Carré's Smiley smiled, as played by Alec Guinness.

"Yes, we know all about that," he said. "How do you think you got released so soon? We had a word with a couple of people in the right place. But the whole thing has confirmed our suspicions. The entire Oxus area is crawling with Russians. They're hatching some plan or other."

He was right. Not long after *The Ascent of Man* was completed, the Russians invaded Afghanistan. That was the start of a nightmare war that would help to unwind the old Soviet Union. The Afghans have never been successfully conquered by anyone – a situation that continues today. But on a personal level, I think my parents were amused and even proud that I too had played some tiny part in working with the British Secret Services: the Great Game was still afoot, in central Asia.

∎∎∎

The Ascent of Man was a turning point in my life. Not only did it offer a series of astonishing and exotic experiences, but it introduced me to the whole history of Western philosophy and discovery. It was, as Jacob Bronowski was fond of saying, "no accident" that this was so: it was what he intended his entire audience to learn and enjoy.

I want to finish my reminiscences of this remarkable project by recalling a short trip I made, with Bronowski and a small camera team of three. We had almost come to the end of our location filming budget, and were trying to plug holes in some episodes, where there was too much talk and too little action. Bruno felt that we had not given due weight to the majesty of the Earth itself, in all its diversity. We needed to remind the viewer that humanity – and physicists and mathematicians in particular, he felt – needed to be a little more humble, in the face of the mysteries of nature. Where could we go, to make this point?

During my graduate student year in the US in 1967-8, I had taken a highly surreal trip to Iceland, to meet my English girlfriend Hazel "half way", as I have already mentioned. I suddenly remembered flying over a spectacular landscape of ice and snow, mixed with volcanic fire and smoke.

"How about Iceland?" I said in a production meeting. "I'll bring my slides in tomorrow: there's no need to recce or scout it. I did that five years ago."

Bruno was captivated by the idea: he insisted on going along on the trip. He wanted to walk through a lava field, and to trigger a geyser by dropping a bar of soap down the hole. It is true: this frequently works. He wanted to walk on black sand beaches, with towering snow-covered peaks behind him. And so he did, and what he said on camera was marvelous: spontaneous, unscripted, full of childlike wonder at the majesty of the planet, and the paucity of our understanding of how it all really works.

There was a bonus, too: while already in Iceland, I introduced him to Thingvellir. Little known outside the country, this is probably the oldest fixed seat of democracy in the northern lands. It is a small circular amphitheatre. Here, every year for the last 1000 years, when the snow has melted, the landholders of Iceland get together to hold a parliament, and vote on various measures, to keep their windswept culture alive and well.

Once again, Bruno's eyes twinkled.

"This is how we shall open the last program," he said. "It's perfect. It's not so pompous as an ancient Greek site. And they've never had slaves in Iceland. Men and women have always been part of the governance of the island. They're an independent race – and look what they've done. Read those stirring sagas – they're the product of a real democracy. This is a template for humanity."

There and then, he sat and scribbled a couple of notes on a scrap of paper he had in his pocket, walked around the modest site, and told the cameraman that he was ready to do his piece to camera. It was word perfect, and ad-libbed, as usual.

Thinking back, it is astonishing that the place was empty, that there was no fence guarding it, no entrance fee to pay or permit to be obtained. It allowed us all to be entirely spontaneous, and that, for me, is part of the magic of *The Ascent of Man*. There were no script editors or layers of bureaucracy: Bruno said what he wished, where he wished, when he wished.

Even at Auschwitz, where he warned against the takeover of science by evil governments, he was utterly genuine. It was entirely his idea to step into the pond, where the ashes of the cremated dead had been poured, and to scoop up a handful of mud, with tears in his eyes. He had escaped to London, but many of his relatives had died in Auschwitz. He looked at the mud in his hands:

"We have to touch people" were his final words in this episode.

Jacob Bronowski died in 1974, less than a year after the completion of *The Ascent of Man*, which was first transmitted in Britain in 1973. He was only sixty-six, when he had a sudden heart attack in New York. At the US premiere of the series, Bruno's widow Rita said bitterly that it was his work on the series that had killed him. Taking him to all those godforsaken places like the African desert and the gaunt ice-floes of Iceland had been too much for him. Well, that is not how I saw it, or (I believe) how he saw it. Bruno loved every minute of those adventures: it was he who proposed most of them. Right to the end, there was no stopping him. If he could go somewhere extraordinary and explain the world just a little bit better, there was no finer work to be done, he felt.

That childlike twinkle in the eye is something I shall never forget. Now that I am older than he ever was, I understand more fully what he stood for, and how he shaped my life. It was Bruno and Adrian Malone who really made me into a real filmmaker. To both of them, a heartfelt thank you.

4.   FROM SCIENCE TO RELIGION

At the conclusion of production on *The Ascent of Man*, we all had a big party, at which Bruno held court and generously thanked every member of the team for the effort they had put into the production. Just eight of us had pulled off a thirteen-part series on the history of western civilization, seen through the lens of science. What is more, we were more or less on budget and on time, which, if you know anything about complex television production, was a miracle.

It would be several months before the series aired in the UK, and a year before it premiered on PBS (the Public Television network) in the United States, but early viewings by the press and invited audiences suggested that we might have a hit on our hands. Inevitably, we all felt far too pleased with ourselves, and could hardly imagine what exciting prospects lay ahead for us at the BBC.

So it was rather a shock when I was called to the office of the Head of Science and Features, Robert Reid, for my six-monthly interview. He was a dour and modest man, but, as Winston Churchill said about Prime Minister Clement Attlee, I thought he had much to be modest about. He took a sternly reductionist view of science, and a narrow view of the remit of his department. I think he believed that *The Ascent of Man* was a self-indulgent luxury on the part of the BBC: a thirteen-part gallivant around the world, trading on Bronowski's reputation and only occasionally of interest to real scientists. So he looked at me with some disfavor and opened my personnel file as if he needed tongs to touch it.

"What you need," he said, "is to come down to earth."

He reminded me that I was technically only a Grade MP2 Junior Assistant Producer, whatever work I had been performing over the last two years.

"I think you need to do a stint on *Tomorrow's World* and learn what it's like to work on highly focused stories in the provinces, on a small budget."

He may have been right. I was getting a bit too big for my boots. But, in my view, *Tomorrow's World* was a byword for tedium. Long train rides to gaunt cities like Newcastle and Stoke-on-Trent beckoned, to file a none too fascinating report on a young chap called Dyson, who had developed a new wheelbarrow with a spherical wheel, or perhaps a breathless description of a breakthrough in the treatment of athlete's foot. I was aghast and left the room with as much grace as possible. I promptly went and asked advice from Adrian Malone.

Adrian had always been a rebel himself, and came up with a good solution: why not apply for a job in an entirely different department, preferably at a level and at a pay scale substantially higher than MP2? If Bob Reid had taken against me, there was no future in Science and Features, while he was still at the helm. So I did.

The BBC had a policy of internally advertising all new job opportunities on large noticeboards, in every BBC building. So I scanned the vast range of possibilities. Remember, the organization then had more than twenty thousand employees, and someone was always moving, retiring or (very rarely) being fired. I looked at openings in the Stationery Stores at Ware, fifty miles north of London: no. Openings in Children's Programs: no... and the Sports Department: double no...! Then I saw one in Religious Programs. Hmm...

A job was advertised at the giddy heights of Grade MP5, for a 'young producer with original ideas, to work with the department on creating a new, topically relevant series, which will deal with moral, ethical, social and religious issues.'

But... could I see joining the Religious Department? I had been born a Catholic, assumed a Church of England identity at the age of five, and had attended a rigorously Anglican boarding school, but I was not on close terms with God, and church-going played no part in my life, except of course at Easter and Christmas, when the hymns and carols offered an exhilarating sing-along for all the family.

Then it occurred to me that I had nothing to lose by applying and being turned down. If I got the job, it meant a huge increase in pay, by BBC standards: almost £5,000 pounds (USD $10,000, back then) per year. And if I was lucky, what better way to rub Bob Reid's nose in the dirt? To think of leaping directly from Grade MP2 to MP5 was an unheard-of piece of bureaucratic chutzpah in the BBC, and to jump ship from Science into Religion would be to thumb my nose at everything Bob Reid held dear. So, of course, I promptly applied.

At the interview for the job, I was faced by three white males, once again: the BBC's Head of Religion, a smoothly bland John Lang – (think Smiley's People and the Head of MI6 once again); the Head of Religious Programs (TV), a puckish former priest called Oliver Hunkin, who was to be my salvation, as you will see; and finally a standard issue BBC bureaucrat from Personnel Department. I was informed that the job meant producing the live 6 p.m. Sunday program on the national BBC-1 channel, which was earmarked by custom for specifically religious material. Remarkably, the department was hiring Britain's most famous news and current affairs on-camera host, Robin Day, to present the programs.

"Do you think," I was asked, "that you have what it takes to tackle such a task?"

Well, I was only twenty-six at the time of the interview, and I suppose that my youth and inexperience helped me to brazen it out. I told the panel that I felt entirely ready to shoulder the burden. After all, had not I directed and produced a couple of programs in studio for the very serious *Germany 1870-1970* series? Did not I read the newspapers? Had not I coped with the whims of Jacob Bronowski?

I left the interview convinced that I had no chance whatever of being selected. Much later, Oliver Hunkin told me that he had gone to bat for me, in the discussions that followed the interviews. He wanted to take a risk and hire a new broom to sweep out some of the cobwebs from his department. I also suspected, from his surreptitious smirk, that John

Lang quite fancied me too, in one way or another, though he was too sophisticated a mandarin to make it obvious.

Two weeks later, I was offered the job: in the early summer of 1973, I was told that I would become the youngest Grade MP5 Producer in BBC Television. I was suddenly panic-stricken. How in hell's name was I going to be able to do this? It was live TV, nationally transmitted at 6pm! Be careful what you wish for, indeed...

I was given a big office, by the standards of BBC Kensington House, where most producers had rabbit hutches. I was given an experienced PA, who would help me not to commit any unconscionable mistakes early on, and there were three empty desks, which I had to fill, by selecting suitable people from the staff, plus a freelance researcher. How on earth would I know where to start?

At lunchtime on my second day, the door opened, and a striking blonde strode into my office.

"I'm Catherine Jay. I hear you got the big Religion job. Congratulations," she said, with no introductory small-talk. "What you're going to need is someone just like me, who knows all about news and current affairs, and has worked for the Religious Department too. I'm a researcher."

Unfortunately, however, it appeared that she was not personally available, since she was under contract to another program at the time.

"Don't worry," she said. "I'll have someone here to see you tomorrow morning, who really is just like me. She'll be ideal." And with that, she swept out of the office.

True to her word, someone did arrive the next morning – someone who did indeed look very much like her. It was her identical twin sister, Helen: also blonde, leggy, and wholly convinced that I need look no further for assistance. These were the then-famous Jay twins, daughters of the Labour Party Minister, the Right Honourable Douglas Jay, M.P.

Ever since they had gone (together, of course) to Britain's brand-new Sussex University in 1963, they had been lionized by the press. Countless pictures of them wearing tiny miniskirts and high boots had graced the pages of the tabloid newspapers. Their exploits and boyfriends were the talk of the town. Indeed, Helen told me, she had been partying in Dublin with the playboy Dominic Elwes and a gang of rich, well connected chums just the day before. Sister Catherine had called and told her to jump on the last plane of the evening and hightail it to London, to get this job.

There was, of course, a formal process to be observed, but it was clear in Helen's mind that there was no question about it: she would be offered the position. I asked Oliver Hunkin, my Head of Department, about Helen. He gave me the thumbs-up, and a knowing smile.

"I know both the twins," said Vernon Sproxton, a veteran religious producer and ex-Baptist minister, when we had a drink in the bar later. "You've got the best of the two."

So, without my playing any significant role, it was decided. How could I foresee that this famous blonde would become my first wife?

To give me practice, so to speak, the first show that Helen helped me produce was a bland affair called *A Chance To Meet*. This had been a staple of Religious Programs (TV) for many years and was hardly revolutionary. A serious-minded celebrity – a member of the government, a well-known classical actor or whoever – was invited to the studio every week, to be quizzed by a polite and carefully-vetted studio audience.

The celebrity guests had to have some sort of religious belief or interest in the Big Issues of the day, although, since the Religious Programs department was independent of the established Church, they did not have to have any definite personal faith. It was all just an excuse to have a nice chat about values and ethics, rather than God, the universe and such things. The host was an avuncular, moon-faced fellow called Cliff Michelmore, whom I already knew. He had hosted the two *So You Think You're a Good Husband/Wife* shows I had directed in the General Features department. Michelmore had once been a star in Current Affairs TV, on the legendary *Tonight* show, but by now had largely been put out to pasture among the vicars.

To be fair, some of our guests were certainly headline-grabbing and definitely touched on Current Affairs. The most memorable was the Right Honourable Enoch Powell, M.P., the Conservative ex-minister most famous for his apocalyptic 'Rivers of Blood' speech, about the future terrors of mass immigration. His fierce intellect shone through his gimlet eyes, and Uncle Cliff Michelmore was no match for him in the studio discussion. But the short biographical film we made, to introduce him at the head of the program, revealed a gentler, more intellectual man than most people would have imagined. He was a classical scholar, fond of quoting Virgil and Livy. He liked making dry jokes and enjoyed clever puns. But his shoes were always immaculately polished, his tie perfectly straight, his suit smelling slightly of mothballs. The idea of Enoch Powell ever relaxing was hard to imagine.

The one striking feature of *A Chance to Meet* to me was that the show went out live. It started at exactly 6 p.m. on a Sunday night (the so-called "God Slot") and had to finish at exactly 6.27 and 30 seconds. Cliff was an old hand at the knack of wrapping things up on time. Just in case he lost track of the clock, he had an earpiece, so that we could cue him from the director's gallery. Whenever I talked to him through the earpiece, suggesting a new line of questioning perhaps, he very pointedly took his earpiece out on camera. He was not going to take instruction from a young lad thirty years his junior.

Our floor manager, out in the studio, was Joan Marsden, known to everyone as 'Mother.' She had been a floor manager since the early days of television in the UK: she had dealt with prime ministers, visiting heads of state, rock stars – everyone. She had a stern face and an even sterner manner. Even the cameramen seemed afraid of her.

As luck would have it, however, she had been a theatre stage manager before she moved to TV in 1950. Indeed, she had stage-managed the London West End show *The Happiest Days of Your Life* – in which my *real* mother had played a character role for eighteen months in 1948-49.

When I invited my parents to join the audience for one of the episodes of *A Chance to Meet*, my real mother met the BBC's 'Mother' for the first time in more than twenty years: it was a touching scene. Afterwards, Joan Marsden came up to me and said that, whatever I did at the BBC – in studio at least – she would look after me with special care. I am certainly grateful: there were some scary events to come, in my next two years.

In late October, Helen and I had our first meeting with the redoubtable Robin Day, later to be knighted for his services to television. He was certainly the closest equivalent the BBC had to America's Walter Cronkite. He, like Joan Marsden, was stern-faced, though (like Joan) his face concealed a warm and friendly heart. Robin knew the Jay twins and was quite happy to work with a new young producer, provided we all did exactly what he told us to do.

It turned out that Robin had had one of his fairly frequent arguments with the Head of Current Affairs (TV), and had stormed out of his office, refusing to continue being the anchorman of the BBC's most important news analysis show, *Panorama*. Behind the scenes, Oliver Hunkin had been angling to land a real heavy-hitter, to chair a much more beefy, issues-driven program for the God Slot. Now was the moment, and Robin was raring to go. He had a great idea for a controversial show, which would poke his former masters in Current Affairs in the eye, and still (nominally) be "religious" enough for the Sunday timeslot.

I cannot say that I contributed more than ten percent of the creative ideas to the show that Robin had devised: *The Sunday Debate*. It was ninety percent his idea, and he had been planning it for months, behind the scenes. The idea was simplicity itself: it was a three-part, Oxford-style debate.

What was clever was this: Part One, which was transmitted live on the first Sunday, put the argument *for* a point of view: 'The death penalty should be banned immediately' for example. That part went out live and could be wholly biased in favor of the motion. This was a novelty, because the BBC normally required that any program on a contentious subject should be politically 'balanced' within the timeslot it filled. But we were allowed to balance it by broadcasting Part Two, a week later, which put the opposing point of view.

In both parts, there would be cross-questioning from the other side (the opposition) and from two judge-like 'assessors' who sat next to Robin Day throughout. But – for the death penalty, say – the anti-hanging brigade could have a field day in Part One, and could call up to three witnesses to buttress their case from personal experience. The results were both thought-provoking and highly emotive. For the normally placid God Slot, this was a revolution.

That same evening, after a break, we taped Part Two – the exact mirror-image of the first program. The pro-capital punishment lobby, represented by two stars of politics or the law, supported by their witnesses, pitched their case in opposition, and were duly cross-questioned. That show went out on tape the following Sunday.

The cleverest element was the third program. In Parts One and Two, Robin had asked the public to write in – yes, actual letters and post-cards, long before the Internet – and give their views. The best, most interesting and sometimes most provocative and weird people would be invited to come to the studio for Part Three, to help decide who had made the best case. Then the judges, sitting as assessors on either side of Robin, would give their judgment: which case had been argued most persuasively?

These assessors were all VIPs: Robin's address book included ex-Prime Ministers, bishops, famous Lords and Ladies, best-selling writers, Oxford intellectual stars, senior judges – all the great and the good in the land, it seemed. Many of them seemed to be members of the Reform Club, a none-too-stuffy hideout of very bright people, where Robin, of course, was a member himself.

So, we had really contentious subjects: hanging, abortion, communism, the wickedness of finance, the role of the Queen, homosexuality, the right to strike, immigration, you name it. It was a great format for allowing an argument to be developed in depth and with passion, public involvement, and the thrill of 'live' television. People could and sometimes did make fatal mistakes on camera, which spiced up the program no end.

There was one other brilliant idea, which, of course, was also Robin's. At his urging, the premiere show of the series was transmitted live between Christmas and New Year's Eve.

"Nothing ever happens then," said Robin. "All the important guests will have time on their hands, they'll be sick of turkey and Christmas pud, they'll be happy to come along and have a good argument. And the newspapers will have no news to print, so we'll get the front pages. Wait and see."

He was entirely correct. We got extraordinary news coverage for the first debate, on the death penalty. One of our star debaters was Sir Reginald Maudling. He had just stepped down from his position of Home Secretary – in charge of the law on prisons and capital punishment – after accusations of improper business dealings.

"Maudling Changes his Mind on Hanging", screamed the front-page headlines of the *Daily Mirror*.

"Who's for the Chop now?" screamed the *Sun*.

More serious newspapers ran columns on their news pages, on their television review pages, and in both the Op Ed and Editorial sections. We got unprecedented audience numbers, which grew and grew with every debate in the first series. Remember, this was still very much the era of "Appointment Television." What else was there to do on a winter Sunday at 6 p.m.? (Except go to church, I suppose). There were, at the time, only two other national TV channels in Britain (both of which were also obliged to observe the God Slot) and there were no local stations, and of course no internet.

When the last program of the series concluded, Robin came to Helen's house in Fulham (just a few miles south of the BBC's Lime Grove Studios) with armfuls of champagne. 'Mother' and the rest of the team, as well as a few favorite audience members and star guests, joined us for a party to remember. Robin could not stop telling everyone that he had had bigger audiences and more press coverage for this show than he had got for years for *Panorama*, the BBC's flagship News and Current Affairs show. I am not sure that this was true, but it was good to hear it from the great man himself.

Behind the scenes, I was near meltdown with stress. Remember, these shows were live. As Producer, the buck stopped with me. However much I could claim that some idea had been Robin's fault, or Helen's, or that we had just had some of the bad luck that can happen on a live program, I could not stop worrying about the shows. It did not help that they went out live on a Sunday evening, so there was no weekend to relax. I think I just slept all day on Mondays.

Then the sad but perhaps inevitable thing happened: I started spending so little time with my girl-friend Hazel, and so much time with Helen, that I began to fall for her blonde attractions. Blinded by fame, exhausted by work, on a high from all the national attention, I fell into bed and started an affair with a Jay Twin.

●●●

Hazel was stunned by the news, when I told her. We had been together for five years, apart from my US student adventure. We were living together happily in the wonderful Queensway flat and we were such good friends. How could I have done such a thing, out of the blue?

I asked myself the same question. Was I mad? But the die was cast.

I moved out of the flat temporarily, and Hazel, after a few weeks in shock, went to Australia to join her sister Mary. There, she met her loyal husband-to-be, a kindly eye-surgeon called Andrew. It took some years to rebuild the fences, but eventually Hazel and I became the close friends that we still are. I think that is amazing. It is totally due to Hazel's kindness and forgiveness.

Back at the BBC, Helen and I did a second series of *The Sunday Debate* the following winter, but nothing quite replaced the sensation of terror and glee, which I had experienced during the first season. We got lots more headlines, and some angry letters to the editor in the fustier, dustier broadsheet newspapers, but that only increased the reputation of the show. I suddenly got afflicted, as impatient twenty-eight-year-olds will, with the 'been there, done that' syndrome. More fun, in my opinion, would be to try something of my own devising – and so began the catastrophe which was *The Michael Bentine Show*.

During the summer, when the big shows were 'rested', the BBC was open to original ideas for short series, which would fill the slots. Half the audience was on vacation anyway, so why not experiment a little? That is what I suggested, when I proposed a talk and entertainment show (still for Religious Programs, Television, of course) that would take 'a light-hearted look' at various thoughtful but not too serious subjects. Doom-laden words, 'light-hearted.' Were we trying to be funny? Or just pleasantly ineffectual? We never quite worked that out.

Bentine had been a big star in his day: one of the original members of the famous BBC Radio *Goon Show*, he had gone on to create a zany and highly successful prime time TV series called *It's a Square World*, which ran for years, and a strange, unsettling show for children called *Potty Time*, which perhaps should have warned me that he might be one card short of a full deck. He wrote most of his own scripts, impersonated various characters, and had all sorts of unusual and silly props constructed. To take just one example, he created a complex model of a flea circus, where he appeared to make automated fleas dive into tiny swimming pools at his command.

Bentine was also good at parodying people like Robin Day: he could put on a very straight face, wear an enormous bow tie, and give a spoof news bulletin, with appropriate cutaways to archive film of weird events. The problem was, he was not just acting crazy. He was crazy for real, as I was to find out.

I had always suspected, from the occasional newspaper feature, that Bentine had a serious side. I thought he might be the perfect host for this 'light-hearted' summer project. So I went to have lunch with him and his fragrant wife in their spacious house in Esher, a leafy London suburb surrounded by golf courses.

That day, he must have been taking his medications, because he was the soul of rationality. He thought that charity was a great subject for a pilot show: he reckoned that people gave money to all sorts of odd and shady organizations they knew nothing about. We could film people soliciting for a fraudulent charity, he could do a couple of sketches about pompous do-gooders, he could interview some senior Oxfam official and find out what was really going on. We could have fun and make a couple of serious points. Why not?

Back at the BBC, Oliver Hunkin gave me just enough rope and budget with which to hang myself. We pre-filmed various scenes, some of which featured a young comedy writer and performer called Chris Langham, who was later to become rather famous, for both good and bad reasons. We eventually had some quite funny material in the can. We set up the studio and waited for Bentine to send us his part of the script. It never arrived.

"Don't worry," said Bentine on the phone, a little too cheerily. "I always ad lib my shows. I don't work with scripts. I do what seems funny or interesting at the time."

This should have rung a huge warning bell, but I was a young producer, still wet behind the ears. I felt I could walk on water, now that I had worked with Robin Day and Jacob Bronowski, to say nothing of Hitler's old mates. So we went to the studio on the recording day without a script. Unthinkable!

Luckily, 'Mother' had been allocated as Floor Manager again. I think she liked working at weekends. When she heard we had no script for the studio portions of the show, she rolled her eyes.

"David, what on earth do you think you are doing? You're going to let Michael Bentine do whatever he likes?" she demanded. "Ye gods, we'll be here till midnight. Thank God we're not going out live on *this* one."

Mother was right to be worried. The audience streamed in, apparently under the impression that this was going to be a comedy show, not a 'light-hearted' look at some serious subject. Michael was, of course, late, and came in with reams of paper, covered in odd notes and scribbles, of ideas he was "thinking" of doing during the show. I looked at them and was desperate. They did not amount to anything useful or comprehensible at all, as far as I could see.

All went well at first, when Michael warmed up the audience. This is the bit we should have taped. He knew how to go up to old ladies and be charming and cheeky. He had endless old vaudeville jokes to crack. Being of Peruvian origin, he saw no harm in parodying Latin American peasants with their sombreros, three-hour siestas and recalcitrant donkeys. He used to put on a great spoof Latino accent – like something out of an animated Looney Tunes cartoon.

"I think you're right," when uttered by Bentine with a big shrug of the shoulders, a roll of the eyes and a loony smile, became a guttural "I hhhheeeeeeeenk you raaaahhhhht!" The audience loved it, though today it would be considered politically incorrect beyond measure, even for a Peruvian.

And then we started the show, and Michael's inner bigot was revealed. To say that his political views were right wing would be a terrible understatement. He could easily have landed the job of Genghis Khan's Press Attaché. He accused the Oxfam people of being closet socialists. He derided audience members for giving to various causes that were close to their hearts. He was openly rude to a mild Dominican brother who had given his life for the poor. He was as obnoxious as it was possible to imagine, and worst of all, he was not at all funny. He was not even 'light-hearted.' Not once.

We went on taping, hoping that there were bits and pieces we could splice together, knowing in our hearts that the whole thing was a disaster. Thank God, indeed, that it was not live. Eventually, the audience was obviously as bored and fed up as we were. 'Mother' had Michael do a wrap-up to the program, and we barely got enough applause to cover the end credits.

My boss, Oliver Hunkin, had been watching all this, from up in the director's gallery, at a discreet distance. He said he had seen me looking as if I was trying to decide which form of suicide to commit.

"Never mind, David," he said kindly. "I don't think we'll proceed to the editing room with this one. You can't win them all. I'll call Bentine's agent in the morning and suggest that it would be better for us all – him included – if we make no mention of this afternoon's events."

Oh Blessed Hunkin, wherever you are, thank you!

There was a fly in the ointment, however. I still had to produce six shows, on the remaining budget. And who would host them? Someone suggested Harold Williamson, a charming regular interviewer on the *Man Alive* social issues series, and he jumped at the chance of hosting a show of his own. We could use the comedy sequences we had filmed for the Bentine version of the show, because Chris Langham was the star of these, not Bentine. Perhaps all was not lost...

On Sunday 14 July of 1974, re-titled *Through the Looking Glass,* the program was launched on BBC-1 in the "God Slot," at 6.15. Astonishingly, the *Sunday Times's* highly regarded *Pick of the Day* chose our show as the most promising new show of the week.

"I'd put my money on Harold Williamson," said the critic, choosing our modest effort over far more splashy efforts by André Previn and film expert Roger Graef. "[The program] takes a quizzical look at some cherished beliefs. To prove how gullible we are, producer David Kennard invented SUCA – the Society for Urging Charitable Action, and filmed the public being suckers, willingly giving money to it in the street. Why do people give? Are the reasons as pure as we'd like to think?"

Somehow, Oliver Hunkin said, mixing his metaphors with customary relish, we had pulled victory from the jaws of defeat – by the skin of our teeth. And yes, the show's script was generally better than that.

■■■

Nonetheless, I was at a low ebb. News of my catastrophic attempt to bring humor to religion with Mr. Bentine was all round BBC's Kensington House within twenty-four hours. Not many shows that make it to a studio, with an invited audience and a well-known host, are entirely scrapped. Many were the veteran producers, who were none-too-secretly delighted that this new whizz-kid Kennard had fallen so spectacularly on his face.

On the personal front, things were hardly plain sailing either. My romantic liaison with Helen had proved to be an on-again-off-again phenomenon. Michael Bentine was hardly her cup of tea. There were long periods when we did not see each other, and then something (lust, for my part, I'm sure), brought us back together. One of these reconciliations centered round a very cheeky idea that was probably Helen's. Why couldn't we do a one-off version of *A Chance to Meet*, but without Uncle Cliff Michelmore, and featuring one of the most prominent people in the realm: Prime Minister Edward Heath?

All this was unfolding during the catastrophic economic events of the Three-day Week. After the Arab oil embargo of 1973, Britain's energy situation was so grim that Heath had had to declare a limited working week, so that scarce energy supplies for factories could be shared fairly. The coal miners were determined to do their best to make the situation worse, by 'going slow.' The lights were going out all over England.

Ted Heath was a mystery wrapped in an enigma, further wrapped in a conundrum, as Winston Churchill might have put it. Heath was known as 'a confirmed bachelor', which back then was usually newspaper code for being gay, but in fact he seemed entirely sexless. He spoke with an odd, classless accent, using unemotional, almost autistic, phraseology. His laughter seemed wholly artificial, as if a robot had been programmed to demonstrate a rictus and heave its shoulders whenever anything reputedly 'funny' was said. He had two known hobbies. One was sailing: he owned and captained a trim yacht named Morning Cloud, with a complement of trim young men to do the active physical things like coil a rope, shin up the mast, belay his marlinspike or whatever.

His other hobby – at least, his other publicly-recognized hobby – was the key to Helen and I getting *Inside Number Ten*, as the two-part program was eventually called. Number Ten means Number 10, Downing Street, where traditionally the Prime Ministers of Great Britain have their London home as well as their offices. But Helen and I were paid by Religious Programs (TV), so what business did we have in Downing Street?

As it happens, one of our guests on Robin Day's *Sunday Debate* had been the Bishop of Oxford, an immensely likeable and intelligent man, who had expressed an interest in what it was, exactly, that motivated Heath. It was known that the Prime Minister loved playing the church organ and enjoyed choral music. Was there a Christian heart beating beneath his soulless exterior?

Helen approached Heath's PR people, through channels which I still do not understand. Actually, it was probably through a distant relative of her enormous political family: she had twenty-four first cousins, one of whom later became a senior minister for the Conservatives, while her father and uncle were still Socialist grandees. Anyway, it was decided by the great and the good that, beset by bad public relations from the Three-day Week and other government mishaps, a cozy quasi-Christian chat in front of a flickering artificial fire inside Number 10, Downing Street might be just the ticket.

What is more, it would not be that beetle-browed, bow-tied heavy hitter Robin Day who would be asking the questions, but the benevolent, laid back Bishop of Oxford. So the Prime Minister agreed. This, it has to be said, was another coup for Religious Programs, because the News and Current Affairs people were *never* usually allowed behind that famous front door. They had to wait in the rain, and ask visitors and ministers their opinion, as they dashed out into their waiting limousines.

When the big day came, we were allowed into Number 10 through a very heavily guarded back entrance. This was the era of IRA bombings and other atrocities in London. It turned out that every person on the crew had been 'positively vetted' by MI5: best friends and grandparents contacted, backgrounds thoroughly investigated. I learned that I was already in an 'OK: to be trusted' file because I had apparently been vetted twice before – once when I had applied from Oxford for a job at the United Kingdom Atomic Energy Authority, and once when I had been approached in Kabul (while working on *The Ascent of Man*) and asked to do a little light spying for Britain on the Russian frontier.

We immediately learned that the modest, good-taste Georgian façade of Number 10 is just that: a façade. Behind that famous door lies a small hallway, so that it still looks small-scale, reassuring and cozy from the outside, when the front door is briefly open. Then there is another door, behind which the whole thing opens up into a multi-story office block, with aides and assistants running everywhere. There are a couple of traditional eighteenth-century-style rooms which are maintained, so that VIP visitors can feel they are in a home of some sort, and the Prime Minister has a modest private apartment somewhere up under the roof, but the rest is a highly efficient modern workspace.

We were told exactly where to put our cameras, and how to light the scene so that the Prime Minister's jowls would not be too prominent. The Bishop was taken off for make-up: "a little light powdering," he was reassured: no rouge, no lipstick. The PM was going to be made up by his own people, and I have to say that the first impression, when he walked into the room, was that of a pantomime dame in a large dark suit.

When everything was set, the two men sat down opposite each other. They could not have made a more different impression: the artificially beaming PM, exuding robotic bonhomie, and the lean, austere but genuinely kindly Bishop, waiting to question him.

The spin-doctors had insisted on seeing all the questions in advance, but the Bishop had cannily intervened, and reserved the right to ask supplementary questions. Quite rightly, he had explained that a topic of conversation should be followed to its natural conclusion. This was intended, after all, to be a fireside chat, not a ruthless cut-and-parry cross-examination. Heath's people had reluctantly agreed but reserved the right to veto or edit anything that they or the PM really regretted or objected to.

And so it began: a wonderful game of cat and mouse. The Bishop started with Heath's favorite childhood memories. No psychologist could have done it better. Heath described his lower-middle-class upbringing with what almost amounted to real affection. He talked about having tea and cutting up white bread into "toast soldiers" to dip into his soft-boiled egg. He talked about trips to the beach with a bucket and spade. His family lived at Number 54, Albion Road, Broadstairs, an address which no novelist could have bettered. Broadstairs is a traditional historic seaside town on the Kent Coast, made famous by Charles Dickens, whose prominent house still overlooks the small pier and funfair. The Bishop got Heath to reveal the sober-sided but profoundly unimaginative values that he had imbibed, along with the bracing sea air.

Heath explained how he got a scholarship to Oxford University, and it was there that he seems to have made the decision to eliminate the down-market Kentish elements in his accent. He adopted a uniquely curious way of speaking, the butt of parody till his death. He said "now" as if it was spelled "neow." It was most odd, particularly in England, where the way you talk – your accent, your vocabulary, your phraseology – immediately places you both geographically and on the social scale. Heath's diction simply did not compute. Indeed, it was almost a computerized voice.

"Who is he *really*?" people would ask us. And nobody knew.

The Bishop got as close as anyone could do, I think, to revealing the real man. Heath was self-conscious and socially timid. He had never married. He had apparently never had a sustained emotional relationship with anybody. There was always the suspicion that he had been a little too keen on the choirboys, when younger, but a police enquiry in 2015 – when Britain was overwhelmed with accusations of pedophilia in high places in the 1970's – found no evidence.

Heath found his pleasures, it seemed, in music, and specially organ music. He really did play the church organ remarkably well, and this, he said, had brought him closer to God than anything else. He did not need to play in public, or at church services: he just loved to play the thing – to make these tremendous sounds, alone, up there in the organ loft. He seemed genuinely interested when I told him, after the taping, that my grandfather had designed organs for a living.

Heath was a clever man in many ways, but we got the sensation that he had been driven to the highest position in the land not by ambition alone, nor even by scheming, and certainly not by cultivating profound friendships, which he seemed unable to do. The Bishop virtually got him to admit that he had simply wanted to prove that a little boy from 54, Albion Road, Broadstairs could make it to the top, and win.

The sad thing, of course, was that he did not win. He was thrown out by a cabal of Conservative ministers, who replaced him with... Margaret Thatcher. Be careful what you wish for, indeed.

● ●

By this stage, I was starting to chafe at the limited opportunities offered by "talking head" television and hankered for the fun and freedom of distant locations and film cameras. I could not get the memories of *The Ascent of Man* out of my head. So I politely asked Oliver Hunkin, my boss, whether I could propose a topic for a one-hour film for the God Slot – a real 16-millimeter movie, on celluloid. It would be the first sixty-minute film I had directed and produced all by myself. Miraculously, Hunkin agreed. And then I told him the subject I'd like to tackle: Islam.

In the early to mid-1970's, BBC Religious Programs meant Christianity above all else. From time to time, the Chief Rabbi would be allowed to appear, and occasional late-night references would be made to Buddhist meditation and spirituality. But BBC's Religious Department still largely meant the Church of England – the Queen's religion, and indeed the established religion of the state. What was good enough for Her Majesty was good enough for the public, wasn't it? But Hunkin was game to try something new. As far as he knew, his department had never done a full-length film about Islam before.

Hunkin warned me against trying to do a historical portmanteau, which sought to explain all about the religion. He was right: I still had romantic memories of the Blue Mosque in Mazar-i-Sharif, and the multiple magical minarets and turquoise domes of Isfahan, in Iran. The exotic allure, which had been so important in establishing the power of Islam when making *The Ascent of Man*, was not what was needed for a film made in Britain.

It was Helen who suggested that we might make a great film by focusing on women's role in Islam, and in particular the Muslim families who had recently arrived in northern England from Pakistan, to work with their families in the textile mills. Newspaper reports had suggested that cities like Bradford and Huddersfield were being completely transformed. Was Enoch Powell right? Would we find 'Rivers of Blood'?

My family essentially hails from London or else from the county of Kent, that bit of Britain down at the bottom right-hand corner, just twenty-some miles from France. I had traveled to Japan, Israel, the US, the Caribbean, and all over Europe. I had visited the south-west of England, for idyllic childhood holidays on the coast with my cousins Helen and Diana. But I had only once or twice been more than ten miles north of Oxford, in England, and that was to visit the family of my former girlfriend, Hazel, in Stoke-on-Trent.

There is an old saying in southern England that 'The North begins at Watford,' a suburb of London that is at the end of a long tube line. It is a bit like Croydon, where I grew up, but north of the metropolis. It is where the dreary rows of houses finally peter out and some semblance of greenery can be seen: the celebrated Green Belt, which prevents London from spilling out all over south-east England.

The North was utterly alien territory to me. They spoke in funny accents up there. They ate food which I could not bear to contemplate. Many of them, I was told, had a healthy disregard for Londoners, who they saw as snooty and soft – far too full of themselves, and to be ignored or despised whenever possible. Could I make a good film about people who were going to be as foreign, in some respects, as any I had ever met?

Helen and I checked into a soulless modern hotel on the edge of Huddersfield in August 1974. Yes, we shared a room – for budgetary purposes only of course. On the TV, the news was dominated by the collapse of the Nixon presidency. Fifteen years later, I met Richard Nixon and directed an interview with him (see Chapter 14), but for now it was just a gloomy backdrop to a gloomy place. Outside, a steady rain descended on the gray and brown city. Welcome to The North.

The heart-breaking center of our story was that Pakistani families, who had immigrated from rural villages in South Asia, were happy to let their children have the free schooling Britain offered, but with one caveat. As soon as the girls neared puberty, they were withdrawn from school and put into purdah. In many cases, they were never seen again. Home-schooled in special houses, many of which doubled as informal mosques, they were never allowed out, even in burqas. As soon as possible, they would be sent back to their villages in Pakistan and forced to become the third or fourth wife of some toothless fifty-year-old.

Today, there is nothing much new about this story, but back in the 1970's it caused an outcry. Anti-immigration feelings were running high and local people felt that "Pakis", as they were rudely called, were taking their jobs. Ironically, within twenty years, all those jobs in the textile mills had disappeared – off-shored to China – leaving the Pakistanis as jobless as the locals. But in 1974, people were looking for any excuse to create trouble and chase the Pakis out of town.

Our film might well have poured oil on the flames, but luckily, Oliver Hunkin reminded me that there were other Muslims in Britain, even if they were not numerous. The chief mosque in the UK was in Woking, an unlikely location, being a commuter community to the south of London. The imam was a gracious man, and a very good speaker. He shared the plans for the construction of a beautiful new mosque in the heart of London, in Regent's Park: we were able to film the start of its construction. Best of all, he introduced us to other, more worldly Muslims than the villagers who made up the Huddersfield community.

But the film was still a tear-jerker. We watched as ten-year-old girls, both Pakistani and English, mingled and played in the schoolyard. We heard their accents: identical northern English slang, with not a care or a racial slur among them. And then we watched as the Pakistani girls were led away at puberty, to lead their sheltered life, far from the playground or the hurly-burly of British life.

My film editor, Paul Carter, who had also worked on *The Ascent of Man*, warned me that the choice of narrator was going to be crucial. A hard, journalistic voice would give the impression that we were trying to stir up trouble, or to create a sensation. We needed someone compassionate, knowledgeable, and if possible famous.

"Oh, not some Shakespearean actor," I remember saying. "God save us from that."

"I know just the guy," said Paul Carter. "He's my next-door neighbor, more or less, and I know him rather well." He refused to tell me who it was, until he had asked him if he was interested. Two days later, he told me: it was David Attenborough.

"What?" I said.

I could not believe it. Attenborough was a legend, even by 1974. When I was still in my first year at Hurstpierpoint Junior School in 1956, I had won a school prize, and asked for a book by Attenborough called *Zoo Quest for a Dragon*: back then, he was just starting to make a name for himself on black-and-white television. Our family had just purchased its first TV set, and I was mesmerized by this young man, striding into the jungle with a team from the London Zoo, hunting down specimens of the giant iguanas known as Komodo Dragons.

"David wants to see the film first," explained Paul, "But he loves the idea. You'd be giving him a job. He says he needs something to do."

I was astonished. In a career that had already been stellar, Attenborough had just stepped down as Managing Director of BBC Television, to go back to program making. He was the man who, along with Aubrey Singer, had initially commissioned *The Ascent of Man*. He was known to be fair and friendly as well as brilliant. And he had that warm, thoughtful, compassionate voice we needed.

Paul gave him a copy of the almost-finished film and got the thumbs-up. David Attenborough would be pleased and proud to narrate this film. I could not believe my good luck: this would guarantee us attention from the critics, and from the rest of the BBC as well. I told Paul that I would make all the arrangements: David wanted to do the recording on a Sunday, so I would book a BBC car to pick him up from his house in Richmond.

"No, no," said Paul. "He'll come by bus." Cue more disbelief from me. "That's David all over," said Paul. "The 65 bus passes his door, and it passes Ealing Studios too, where we'll do the recording. Taking the bus is what he'll want to do, I promise you. I know him."

Cut to a street in West London, in the pouring rain, on a winter Sunday. I am standing by a bus stop, as the occasional car passes. It is around 2 p.m., when David is due to arrive. There are no cellphones back then, of course, to check on his progress. Is this all a great hoax? Then, round the corner comes a red double-decker bus: the 65. It pulls up, and out steps the famous man, who promptly unfurls his umbrella.

"What a day," he says, as we struggle through the rain and past the studio gate. "Just as well we're not planning to do any pieces to camera."

By the time we had dried off over a nice cup of tea in the recording studio, I felt like we were old friends.

"It's a nice film," said David. "I hope you don't mind, but I've penciled in a couple of changes in the script."

My heart sank. We would obviously have to re-edit the film: the maestro was going to show us how it was done, the proper way. But it turned out that the changes were tiny: a few words and phrases here and there.

"I like to say things my way if I can," he explained. "It makes it more personal."

In a few minutes, we were ready. David sat in the booth and adjusted his headphones. "I haven't narrated a film for ages," he said. "I can't wait. I've had enough of all that management baloney. This is where the real work gets done."

The red light went on and he delivered a virtually fault-free delivery of the whole script – in one pass. It was a perfect performance. It radiated empathy, while still keeping a slight journalistic edge. Before I realized it, the session was over. All the cues had timed out perfectly.

David agreed to have a second cup of tea, to prepare himself for the rain outside, and then he was off, back to the bus stop. "I've really enjoyed it," he said. "Thank you. You've got me back into filmmaking. It was just what I needed." We shook hands, he got onto the bus, and within moments he was on his way home.

At the time of writing, David Attenborough is still going strong, at the age of ninety-something – still writing and narrating the miraculous string of natural history documentaries he has created: seventy years of creativity, with a brief pause for senior management in the middle. More than ever, he is one of my heroes. People sometimes tell me that my own voice sounds a bit like his, when I narrate a documentary. They could not give me a nicer compliment.

••

The Attenborough experience was a great note to end on. I had spent enough time in Religious Programs. I didn't really fit in. In the final analysis, I couldn't pretend to a faith I didn't have. So... where would I go next? I went back to the Appointment Boards and scanned them closely. I found nothing that appealed to me. And then a minor miracle happened. I was approached by my old friends and colleagues, Adrian Malone, Dick Gilling and Mick Jackson.

"How about coming back to Science Features?" they asked. "All will be forgiven: Bob Reid's gone. We've got a new Head of Department, Phil Daly."

"Yes, but what are you planning to do?" I asked.

"We're cooking up a new 13-part series to follow *The Ascent of Man*," said Adrian, smiling mischievously. "It'll feature the American economist John Kenneth Galbraith. Would you like to join us? Put the old team back together?"

Would I like to join them? Was the Pope a Catholic? Well, having been a Religious Producer, I knew he was, so I joined them.

••

5. THE GREAT GALBRAITH FIASCO

Adrian Malone, seeking to follow up Bronowski's epic with another blockbuster series, had persuaded the BBC's management to attempt a history of western social and economic thought. It being the mid-1970's, with a Labour Party government in power in the UK, a natural choice seemed to be the liberal economist John Kenneth Galbraith. The working title for the project was *The Age of Uncertainty.*

John Kenneth Galbraith was a giant of a man, both literally and figuratively. He stood six foot four or five inches tall – the tallest onscreen presenter I have ever worked with, alongside Brian Swimme and John Cleese. I am six foot one myself, so it is a nice change to have someone to look up to, in every way. And being thin and somewhat gaunt, and having a long face like Lincoln, Galbraith was a formidable presence. Cameramen had to lengthen their tripod legs and stand on wooden boxes to get the lens parallel to his eyes.

His close friends and contemporaries called him "Ken", but he was so formidable that it seemed like "JKG" and he liked that. He told us that he distrusted anyone (outside Harvard) who called him "Professor Galbraith" – even the lowliest minion. He had no time for toadies and forelock-tuggers.

Happily, however formidable he looked and sounded, Galbraith had a kindly disposition and a wonderful sense of humor. The merest hint of witty repartee, or a cutting description of some right-wing trope or conservative politician's foolishness, would crack his lined face into a huge grin, followed by series of hearty chuckles.

He was known to most Americans as the sparring partner of the right-wing commentator William F. Buckley in a talk-show on Public Television, and to the literary world as the writer of a steady stream of books and articles on economics and social science. He had a brilliant turn of phrase and a piercing wit, which made his writing on such dry subjects a real pleasure. He probably coined more original witticisms and one-line truths in these fields than any other American in the twentieth century. To take just two examples:

"Economists do not make predictions because they know what will happen," he liked to say. "They just do it because they're asked to."

Or, put another way, (my favorite): "The only function of economic forecasting is to make astrology look respectable."

Of his own work, he was happy to tell witty, self-deprecating stories.

"I was once asked to write a popular paperback about the causes of the Depression in the 1930's," he told us, "So I did. And later, just to find out whether it was indeed popular, I asked for a copy of it at a bookshop in Boston's Logan Airport. The sales assistant was astonished: 'Are you crazy?' she said. 'You don't think we'd carry a book called *The Great Crash* at an airport, do you?'"

Galbraith's career had been impressive: among other highlights, a professorship at Harvard, a senior post in the federal government during World War II, helping set prices for commodities vital to the war effort, and an ambassadorship to New Delhi at a crucial moment in the early 1960's, when India and China threatened to go to war over Tibet. He was a good friend of President John F. Kennedy, took phone calls from the White House during the crisis, and intervened personally with Prime Minister Nehru to avoid a catastrophic confrontation with China.

So this was the colossus, with whom we were selected to make a rip-roaring, as-popular-as-possible thirteen-part series about economic and social history. Well, where do you start? How can you make this particular subject matter in any way "popular"?

The initial weeks were spent in long discussions in a big office in the BBC's Kensington House, which by now had become my second home. It was good to be back working with Adrian Malone, Dick Gilling and Mick Jackson again: no more sanctimonious discussions with the fading flowers of Religious Programmes (TV). We could enjoy bad jokes and share the good ones with JKG.

Galbraith insisted that he would write essays on various subjects, and then we would be free to devise original and amusing ways to illustrate and complement and reorganize and edit them. He would talk to camera for no more than half the time, he promised. Since he often talked very slowly, for rhetorical effect, this was just as well, but it led to one of the profound problems with the series: each film would roar along with visuals and music of one sort or another, and then come to a near-grinding halt when JKG started talking to camera. However witty his script, the more long-winded he was, the more we filmmakers felt we had to accelerate the pace of editing in the other sequences. This, ultimately, did not lead to a satisfactory result.

The early days were great fun, as they often are on long film projects. Galbraith checked off a list of topics he wanted to cover. These included Marxism, John Maynard Keynes, the modern corporation, and the military-industrial complex. He would also have a crack at explaining money, and how it worked. As a former ambassador to India, he proposed to do a show about developing countries, which we eventually called *Land and the People*. Then, he insisted on lampooning the culture of the American rich from the 1880's to the First World War. After much discussion, we also agreed that the series would have to start in the 18th century, and deal with Adam Smith and the birth of economics, the "dismal science", though it didn't seem a very exciting way to open a TV series.

Finally, Galbraith suggested that we should round off the whole shebang with some sort of VIP summit meeting, to discuss the future of the planet, or at least of its politics and economics. He knew everyone from Lee Kwan Yew, Premier of Singapore to the famous Henry Kissinger, and reckoned he could get them all to come up to his country house in Vermont, "if there's enough to drink up there."

When JKG had left to return to Boston and his day job as Emeritus Professor of Economics at Harvard, we all sat round and drew straws, or made bids, for which programs we fancied producing or directing. I knew I would love to create *The Big Corporation*, partly because I had been to business school in the US, and partly because Galbraith had said some wonderfully funny things about corporate life. The military-industrial complex fascinated me too, though I had to arm-wrestle Mick Jackson for that one.

Mick took an immediate fancy to the film which would describe and display the affluent society of the nineteenth century robber barons and the mansions of Newport, Rhode Island. Dick Gilling, ever the kindly colleague, was willing to tackle the drier subjects: Adam Smith, Karl Marx and John Maynard Keynes. Adrian would be in charge of things generally, and elected to helm the last program, where we had to gather the great and the good of the world: a challenge which Adrian thought was thoroughly appropriate to his talents.

But what was the style we could develop, to illustrate social and economic thought? Obviously, there was stock footage to help us for much of the twentieth century, and photos for the nineteenth, but we all felt that this was a boring solution. In the 1970's, shaped by exposure to Monty Python's Flying Circus, we could not allow ourselves to be *boring*, could we? We were "creatives," in the language of advertising agencies. So we had to create as hard as we could...

After the release of the series, some of the less generous critics compared the films to a head-on collision between Monty Python and a Further Education series, supervised by an American professor who appeared to be running at half speed, when he spoke. There was, I am afraid, some truth in this.

Each program presented its own problems. One of the first that I ran into was that no real-life American corporation would even think about being associated with John Kenneth Galbraith. His previous critiques had been too barbed. I journeyed from one corporate HQ to another, to hear the same story. IBM flew me specially from New York's La Guardia airport to their private airstrip in Armonk, NY, to tell me politely to go to hell. So, what were we to do?

After a lot of string-pulling, the Dutch electrical giant Philips allowed us to film their operations and interview their top brass. They had some of the requisite qualities: an international reach, a large, boring company town (Eindhoven, in Holland), myriads of committees and gray men in suits, special corporate terminology that was gobbledygook to outsiders, and the occasional splash of color like their own brass band and soccer team. But this was not what Galbraith really wanted. He needed a US target that he could thoroughly eviscerate.

"The salary of the chief executive of a large corporation is not a market award for achievement," he wrote. "It is frequently in the nature of a warm personal gesture by the individual to himself."

His script was full of such *bon mots*, some of which he coined specially for our series, others being lifted from his previous work.

"Meetings are indispensable when you do not actually want to achieve anything," he explained. No wonder he was not welcome in the corporate boardrooms of America.

I suggested that we might invent a fictitious corporation – one we could be entirely rude about, because it did not exist. And we could be funny, too: there could be jokes. My colleague Mick Jackson was delighted by the idea; Dick Gilling, as ever, was a little more cautious; Adrian said that it all depended on what JKG thought of it. Happily, Galbraith was delighted.

After lively debate, we called it "UGE" (because it was, indeed, huge): United Global Enterprises. Back in the mid-1970's, it was the fashion to develop large, sprawling multi-nationals with fingers in every pie: ITT was a classic example, and so, to an extent, was IBM. So we decided that UGE would operate in twenty-eight countries, and have interests ranging from aerospace to soft drinks.

I had some of the greatest fun of my creative life, inventing the complex back-story of UGE with Ken Galbraith. He wrote the early chapters himself. Recalling his own Scottish ancestry – his forbears had emigrated to Canada in the mid nineteenth century – he invented the greedy but penny-pinching McGlow family. These rapacious capitalists, he imagined, had established themselves in the crooked end of the Chicago meat business in the 1860's. In competition with the Swift and Armor companies, they supplied American troops with canned corned beef throughout the Spanish American War. The cans contained little more than time-expired gristle and intestines, and, Galbraith recounted, "were responsible for more American fatalities than the Spanish artillery."

Along with the beef came a line of dubious hot dogs, "known affectionately as Glow-worms," said Galbraith. "They had no discernible trace of any nutritious content."

But the miracle product, which made the McGlows' first fortune, was an all-purpose oil called Ugol, which I am happy to say that I invented. The formula for Ugol, so our story went, was a tightly guarded secret, but it was a world-wide hit, because it fulfilled every function that could be demanded of an oil. Within the film, we created half-a-dozen false advertising breaks, featuring Ugol. We showed it being used as a hair oil, a sunscreen, a laxative, a motor oil, a cooking oil, a cough mixture, a household lubricant and the finest solution for a baby's diaper rash. We invented merry jingles to accompany the advertisements: "You know best – let Ugol do the rest!" and "Ugol? You betcha!"

UGE had also spread its tentacles into aerospace during World War II, Galbraith explained, and now ran flights almost exclusively to the capital cities of right-wing dictatorships. The mythical UgeAir became thoroughly believable when we filmed its logo applied to the tailfin of a full-sized Boeing 727 at Amsterdam airport. Of course, there was also a busy check-in desk, with comely female staff, plus matching tickets and baggage tags. UgeAir emphasized its high standards of service. Its motto was: "UgeAir – Serves You Right!" Let me send a belated thank you to the real-life KLM airline, which lent us the facilities. Like Philips, it was a Dutch company with a sense of humor.

UGE's soft drinks division had also prospered in World War II. The first allied supply trucks into Paris in 1944 were, according to Galbraith, carrying nothing but crates of Uge-Ola. We duly plastered a downtown Paris metro station and a passing train with Uge-Ola hoardings ("*Ooh là là, Uge-Ola! Que ça fait du bien!*"). We filmed hapless customers apparently drinking the repellent soft drink wherever in the world we were filming: on the pistes of the Swiss Alps, in a Singapore market and outside a Brooklyn warehouse.

Wherever in the world any of my colleagues was filming, I asked him to include a shot of someone using one of UGE's products. Perhaps my favorite was a black female short-order chef in Carmel, California, manipulating some plump, suggestive Glow-Worm sausages on a griddle, saying to the camera with twinkling eyes, "I don't need to know where they come from, honey, I just know that they're tasty and they're UGE."

Back in London, in the largest of the BBC's Ealing Studios, we constructed the top three floors of a putative UGE headquarters in Manhattan, surrounded by dry-ice clouds, through which the senior executive suites could poke. The 'building' had see-through walls, so that the cameras, on giant cranes, could sweep in and out of individual offices and eavesdrop on the fatuous scripted meetings going on.

"Gentlemen", went one line, "We need fresh new ideas that have stood the test of time." It was a pronouncement that would be uttered in all seriousness by a senior executive of GTE (now Verizon), when he turned down the opportunity to fund *The Messengers*, one of our series concepts, seven years later.

For the UGE show alone, we had a cast of a dozen actors, including the famous Sam Wanamaker, who went on to found the replica of Shakespeare's Globe Theatre in London. He played the Chairman of UGE's board and was very impressive: Galbraith's excellent script was full of corporate-speak of the dreariest type.

Meanwhile, to one side of the building, Galbraith stood on an observation platform, as if on the balcony of a nearby skyscraper, making sardonic comments from time to time. He recalled a New Yorker cartoon, of a father and child in a park, looking up at a statue featuring a cluster of dreary-looking bronze individuals.

"There are no great men anymore," the father is explaining to his son. "Only great committees."

The second program for which I had responsibilities as producer as well as director was entitled *The Rise and Fall of Money*. JKG got so involved with writing the initial essay on which this show was based that he found he had written an entire book. It was separately published as *Money: Whence it Came, Where it Went*. I was glad about this, because it was pretty dense, impenetrable stuff. We needed something lighter.

So Galbraith reframed the Money film to be more of a history of monetary shenanigans, from the South Sea Bubble of the 1720's to the unreliable frontier banks of the US in the 1830's. He poured scorn on the efforts of US governments to keep to the Gold Standard in the 1920's. He relished the stupidity (as he saw it) of monetarists like his contemporary, the celebrated Milton Friedman.

You will get some idea of the tone of the program from the fact that the set for this show in Ealing Studios was a cheesy carnival fairground. Galbraith prowled around brightly lit sideshows, where people were robbed of their cash, screamed with delight on a carousel and rode a roller-coaster car, which bobbed up and down, representing the greed-fear-greed-fear cycles of the stock market. You may well have deduced by now that this mordant, satirical treatment of economic history was going to provoke strong reactions in due course.

An altogether more serious program, *The Fatal Competition*, investigated the "military-industrial complex", a phrase coined by Eisenhower in his final speech as President. This was a subject dear to JKG's heart. He echoed Eisenhower, warning of the unstoppable growth of militarism, gobbling up more and more of the earth's resources.

Here, too, we had a studio set, but it was full of dark shadows and sinister doorways: *Dr. Strangelove* meets *The Cabinet of Dr. Caligari*. At Mick Jackson's urging, we made full-sized mannequins of people in key positions in the early years of the Cold War. I still have the rubber head of Allen Dulles, Director of the CIA and brother of Eisenhower's Secretary of State, the sinister John Foster Dulles: it sits on a shelf in the room containing my Bad Taste Collection – the fruit of fifty years of collecting weird stuff from locations around the world.

The Fatal Competition boasted some spectacular real-life locations, too. At Davies-Monthan airbase in Arizona, literally hundreds – perhaps thousands – of mothballed jet fighters and bombers had been stored in the hot, dry conditions of the desert. We did endless tracking shots and fly-pasts of the vast host of hardware that the US taxpayers had funded. I have no idea why the Defense Department let us film this: it was a shocking display of excess.

Better still, we got permission to film inside 'Iron Mountain', the NORAD (North American Air Defense) HQ in the heart of the Rocky Mountains. I could not believe it when I heard that the permit had arrived at the BBC's New York office. They were going to let a British crew into the belly of the beast? To film the screens where they tracked all incoming and outgoing missiles, planes and who knows what? We were ecstatic, but thought it better not to push our luck by requesting that Galbraith should come in with us. His wry wit and piercing satire might not have gone down too well with the crisply turned-out officers who supervised our shoot.

A final bonus was to film the nearby Air Force Academy chapel: it was just the way a screenwriter would have imagined. It looked like part of a space station. It had stained glass windows with abstract shapes that reminded the visitor (at least, they reminded *this* visitor) of missiles and bombs. To hear the manly Air Force Choir sing out in praise of Jesus, and to lay this sound track over the rows of mothballed bombers at Davies-Monthan, brought goose-bumps to my skin.

Meanwhile, on the East Coast, in the grotesquely huge mansions of Newport, RI, Mick Jackson was having a whale of a time, using life-size photo blow-ups of the original owners of the houses, together with staff: whole banquet halls of two-dimensional overfed socialites, together with soundtracks of inane chatter (recorded at real parties) and music from a string quartet. The famous casino at Monte Carlo got the same treatment. Thinking back, it is remarkable how easy it was to get into such remarkable locations for filming, if you muttered the magic spell "BBC." Why, we had even gained access (for *The Ascent of Man*) to the Vatican archives and inspected the divorce papers of Henry VIII and the transcript of the trial of Galileo Galilei.

The final show had to be the capper. JKG had set in motion a series of invitations to some of the world's movers and shakers. He invited them to "a casual weekend" at his farmhouse at Newfane, Vermont – a small burg of some two hundred and fifty souls at that time. The VIPs would all come in for a couple of nights, we'd have a celebration dinner at the ancient Newfane Inn, we'd cover the action with a number of different cameras, and we'd cut the best of the chatter together, to make a thoughtful discussion about the future in that Age of Uncertainty, the 1970's.

I picked the short straw (well, as it turned out, the best straw), and was given the responsibility of setting all this up. To be blunt, it was the most daunting professional task I had ever faced – far worse than coping with British celebrity guests on *The Sunday Debate*, or Prime Minister Heath in 10, Downing Street. I went up to Newfane and asked for a meeting with the Sheriff and the owner of the six-bedroomed Newfane Inn. I explained my idea to them, over a couple of beers.

"Holy Smoke!" is what the Sheriff would have said in a G-rated family movie.

"Sheesh!" is what the Manager of the Hotel would have said. A transcript of our actual conversation would have been more robust, and probably unprintable.

"You must be joking!" was the consensus. But then I told them that the invitations had already gone out.

"Oh my God…" was the response.

The main concern was security, even back in the balmy days of 1975-76.

"We're going to have the FBI crawling all over us," said the Sheriff. "This place is impossible to police at the best of times. There are so many lanes and byways and forest and… oh my God!"

But it went ahead: Lee Kwan Yew, Henry Kissinger and British government minister Shirley Williams came trooping in, each with police motorcycle accompaniment, plus a fleet of black cars, and a squadron of FBI men in black, all talking into their lapels. The FBI guys were very unhappy about us filming them, but we had so many cameras, and there were so many of them, that we got some exceptionally good action-movie material.

Overhead, helicopters roared, spoiling the sound. We got in touch with our FBI contacts and said that this was unacceptable, because we could not film with this level of noise. The choppers were finally grounded, much to the displeasure of the men in black, who instructed us to tell them the moment we took a break, so that they could go back up and see whether the Russians or the IRA or Milton Friedman's gang were advancing through the woods.

And so, finally, the shows were shot and finished. They were certainly unique. Mixing *Verité* hand-held documentary style with comedy scripts, Summit Meetings with wacky animation and cardboard cut-out historical figures… Why not? We felt we had gone beyond the call of duty and good taste to pump some life into politics, sociology and economics, and the result?

Hmm…

To say that the reviews in Britain were "mixed" is to put it kindly. There were a few brave critics who really liked Galbraith's humor and seemed to understand the need for actors, dummies, fairgrounds and photo-blowups. There were others who found it all too exhausting, although many thought it was "original": this was, of course, damning with faint praise. Many British critics did not like being lectured by John Kenneth Galbraith, with his "slow American drawl", even if we had had him sitting placidly in a studio chair. Nancy Banks-Smith, the legendary critic for the London "Guardian" newspaper, was the one who called it a "creative traffic accident."

But that was nothing to the reaction in the US. The show was scheduled to be transmitted nationally on PBS through the Los Angeles entry station, KCET. From time to time, an absurdly young-looking producer from LA (Greg Andorfer, with whom I was later destined to work on *Cosmos*) had come over to London to visit us. He must have taken some scary reports back with him. In due course, Phil Daly, the BBC's Head of Science and Features (our boss) was approached by Chuck Allen, head honcho at KCET, in something of a panic: how could he put this stuff on the air? Nationally? On Public Television? Daly reminded him that the BBC had creative control, per the contract, so he could basically take a long walk off a short pier, as the saying went back in the 70's. Allen said that it was not only the creative issue: the whole project smelled of – that dreaded word – socialism.

We did indeed have a socialist government in the UK at the time (see below – the Wedding Scene), and Galbraith's political views were well known, so what did KCET expect? From what I heard later, the whole of the LA Public Television station went into lock-down three-alarm crisis status, when they saw the final shows. They were obliged to put the shows out, but what could they do to take some of the sting out of them – to purge them of socialism?

Each of the "hours" was in fact about fifty minutes long: this was a time-honored BBC tradition, which allowed them to sell their shows to commercial TV networks around the world, which could cram in a few minutes of advertising here and there. The customary thing to do, on American Public Television, was to have a host at the top and tail of such programs, who would introduce them and prepare people for any strange British accents and folkways, and finally (at the end) explain what had just happened, for the hard of thinking.

In this case, however, a different solution was found. KCET produced their own eight-minute "rebuttals", which were tacked onto the end of each episode of *The Age of Uncertainty*. In these, an American studio guest (a different one each week) would carefully explain that Galbraith was, in fact, entirely wrong about everything the audience had just seen. There was nothing wrong with Andrew Carnegie's wealth; Karl Marx was a knave and a villain; the military industrial complex was a very good thing; money was an extremely useful invention, and the right sort of people had more of it than the wrong sort of people. As for the corporation, it was the last, best and final work of man and God.

The effect of all this was doubly ludicrous. Some critics in the US indulged our Pythonesque caricatures. Many of them, indeed, found Galbraith entirely acceptable politically, though they bemoaned the British compulsion to have grotesque scenes intrude upon strictly academic studies like economics. But the worst thing, critics agreed, was for Public Television to put the programs into national distribution and then take the last ten minutes to announce that the previous fifty minutes had been a pack of lies.

In retrospect, I have to admit, the project was in many ways a fully-fledged disaster. "A waste of a million pounds", one British newspaper put it. Thank God they did not know it had cost rather more than that. Professionally, it could have been a fiasco for all of us directors and producers. It does not figure very prominently in my CV, though I am very fond of many of the shows.

The series was never repeated in the US, and never went to VHS tape (or later, DVD) for public purchase. It is almost impossible to find. The library at UC Berkeley has a copy, but you can only watch it in a darkened room under supervision, and no iPhones are allowed in the room with you. I have a few episodes, pirated from very bad copies of other copies online. An economics professor from Finland wrote to me a few years ago, saying he'd "give anything" for a copy of the series. He had tried every department of the BBC, to no effect. He was told that the master tapes had "probably been wiped." And so, indeed, they have. George Orwell would have been proud. But you can still find the accompanying book online.

· ·

Just in case you have been missing the backstory element to this book, one of the most important events in my life took place while all this Galbraith malarkey was going on: I got married for the first time.

Helen Jay and I had worked together much of the time when I was in the Religious Department. But when I gratefully jumped ship, back to Science and Features, her contract came to an end – both with the BBC and with me, it turned out. We tried to keep together, but she had her house in Fulham and I had my shared flat in Queensway, and we probably needed a break from each other.

At Christmas 1974, I went to spend Christmas with my parents at their modest home in Winslow, just a few miles from Bletchley Park, where my mother had worked in the war. It was a treat to go home and get looked after: the three of us played games, ate turkey and gave each other many silly presents – a family habit to this day. But when I returned to the cold Beaumanor Mansions flat in Queensway, to find everyone else still away with family or friends for the holidays, I felt very lonely. I didn't even have a television set to keep me company, because I had lent it to Helen some time before, and it was still at her house.

I blame that TV for everything that happened subsequently. I called Helen, and happened to find her in.

"Did you have a good Christmas?" I asked her, just to be polite.

She had spent it at her twin sister's large Hampstead house, amongst countless Jay cousins, infants, aunties and grannies. It all sounded very exhausting, compared to our modest family event.

"Could I come and pick up my TV?" I asked, with no other thought in my mind than having some form of amusement. I thought I was coming down with flu, and the upcoming New Year seemed very bleak.

You can probably guess what happened. I drove over to Helen's place, in the rain. It was a dismal British winter's evening, so I stayed for a glass of warming red wine. And then another one. And then another one, but this time it was upstairs. I did not go home. The TV stayed right where it was, in Helen's sitting room.

The scene that played out, that late December night in 1974, was remarkably similar to one that was to play out with my second wife-to-be, Lizzie, in the spring of 1986. In both cases, the ladies made it clear that we had had an on-again-off-again affair for long enough. There would be no more of "that sort of thing" unless I was serious about them, and my intentions were honorable. In other words, it would have to be wedding bells, or say goodbye forever.

In both cases, I suddenly realized that I really did love them, too. It was not only a case of missing "that sort of thing." To be honest, I *did* miss it, of course. Neither of my two highly attractive wives has been a champion in the kitchen, but, to put it delicately, once you have got them upstairs, there are few who can compare. How astonishing that I met both of them in exactly the same place: the first floor of BBC Kensington House, right by the entrance to Club bar on the first floor: one in 1973, and one in 1980. God moves in mysterious ways.

Immediately, Helen and I needed to tell our parents and family the good news. For Helen, this meant getting onto the bush telegraph and informing about a hundred and fifty people. For me, it was rather simpler: I drove straight back out to Winslow and told my mother and father.

"Oh my God!" my mother said, before she could stop herself.

I knew she had mixed views about Helen, and about my involvement with a huge, famous and influential family: as an actress, she had been around too many celebrities to imagine that they were all as lovely as they pretended to be. My dear father, Mick, was the supreme professional in this instance.

"Well, that's wonderful," he said, and opened the fridge.

He took out the bottle of champagne, which he always kept there "for emergencies." He popped the cork, and my mother pulled together "some little nibbles", as she used to call them.

The most obvious questions were the ones they had the good grace not to ask: why had not I told them a couple of days before, at Christmas? Had it all happened so suddenly? Was she pregnant?

"When's it going to be?" my mother asked, and when I said, "As soon as possible", I am sure they both thought that Helen *must* have been pregnant. But she was not – not that time.

I think we had settled on an approximate date – around March 20, the Spring Equinox – because it gave us just enough time to organize everything. It was also so soon that we could not change our minds. Eleven years later, exactly the same scenario would play out with me and Lizzie.

What happened in the following eleven weeks is a blur in my mind. Indeed, it was a blur in my mind back then, too. Helen had immediately taken charge (was I surprised?) and declared that she wanted the entire package: white wedding, bridesmaids, Anglican church service with organ, at least two hundred guests, a bridal list at the trendy Peter Jones store on Sloane Square, formal dress for guests (that meant morning suits, not just dinner jackets or tuxedos), decent food and plenty to drink, and an award-winning roster of speeches from the largest possible number of famous people we could muster. Oh yes, and the whole affair could, should and would happen in the Houses of Parliament. Any questions?

Amazingly enough, it ended up by happening, and it did not bankrupt us or anybody else. The key to this was that Helen's father was the Right Honourable Douglas Jay M.P., and as a Member of Parliament of high standing, he could get the keys to the door. Saint Catherine's Chapel, situated in the basement, literally under the House of Commons, is just about the oldest part of the Palace of Westminster: we could be married there. Happily, the Jay family included a retired vicar from faraway Suffolk, who could be brought out and dusted down, and would be happy to lead the service. The Parliamentary Members' Dining Room could be used for our feast, at no charge except for the catering.

Helen and I threw ourselves into organizing this as if it was a television production we were doing together. Her home became the base of operations: bridesmaids' dresses were farmed out to relatives to make, mend or alter. Running orders and guest lists were produced – long before computers, remember – and the fax was still in its infancy. BBC phones were used for all the long-distance calls to astonished aunts, uncles and distant cousins. On my side of the family, every single person I was connected to was given strict orders to attend: even then, the bride's side of the congregation outnumbered mine by about four to one. We balanced it out by putting all our general friends on my side of the aisle.

Then there was the question of the Best Man. That was my choice, of course: virtually the only thing I chose, out of the whole wedding. He had to be an old friend, who had known me a longish time, and knew Helen too. And… this was the Houses of Parliament, for goodness' sake. It had to be someone with presence, self-confidence, humor… Of course! It had to be my old Oxford chum, Nigel Rees. He was at the peak of his fame in the mid-70's, co-hosting the breakfast radio *Today* show and making humorous appearances on *The Burkiss Way*. He was a good public speaker. He would be the ideal MC – or rather, the perfect Best Man.

But who would give the speeches? Of course, Douglas, as father of the bride, had to speak, though the risk was that he would think he was addressing the House of Commons and drone on for hours. (He didn't, in the event. There wasn't time). Nigel Rees would do his best to embarrass me – the traditional role of the Best Man. But wait, what about Robin Day, the famous TV presenter, with whom Helen and I had worked so well? He was a legendary speaker – both witty and catty, and always right up to date with the news. Yes, we needed him. And then it turned out that Douglas Jay knew John Kenneth Galbraith very well, and JKG said he'd *love* to speak at our wedding. Great!

Wasn't that enough speeches, however? Helen wondered whether we could shoehorn in a couple more Jay family superstars. How about Jim Callaghan, later to be Prime Minister, but at that time merely Foreign Secretary? His daughter Margaret, later to be Labour Party Leader in the House of Lords, was married to Helen's brother Peter, later to be our Ambassador to the US. But even Helen acknowledged that she didn't want her father to be overshadowed. She felt that one Cabinet Minister was enough. So Jim Callaghan and his wife kindly attended the wedding, but just as ordinary guests, albeit in top hat and tails.

I thought we might have got enough speakers by now, but then my mother remembered her old friend Humphrey Tilling. Humphrey was one of several influential "uncles" I had had in my childhood: all showbiz friends of my mother, from the 1930's and 40's. He had been the head of EMI, the music company, and had held several other executive positions, but in retirement, he had developed a lucrative sideline in humorous after-dinner speaking.

Helen was reluctant: "Yes, but who _is_ he?" she asked.

"He's very funny," I said. "You'll be glad we had him."

And indeed we were. Although the speeches went on for over an hour, each one was funnier or cleverer than the last, or so it seemed. My cousin Diana, after the event, said:

"It felt like we'd come up to London and had a complete night out at the theatre."

When the big day dawned (and yes, Helen and I had slept in separate houses, as tradition demanded), we saw it was raining, and we then heard the news: the House of Commons catering staff had come out on strike. Forget about the food for tonight…

Thank God, the arrangements for the drink – red, white and sparkling wine in prodigious quantities – were separate, so we could be sure that we could get everyone thoroughly merry. But they had to eat _something._ Helen's family and friends swung into action: they needed to produce a picnic for two hundred people, and deliver it to the House of Commons kitchens by 3 p.m. And that is exactly what they did: sandwiches were made, bridge rolls were constructed, hot sausage rolls were rolled, bowlfuls of stuff were purchased ready-made from Marks and Spencer: around thirty of Helen's vast Rolodex of family and friends were directly involved in creating this impromptu feast. The final hurdle to be cleared was delivering the food past striking pickets with menacing signs at the gates of Westminster.

The London _Evening Standard_ got so excited by the whole event that they ran a half-page picture of Helen and myself getting into the car that took us to our "Honeymoon Hideaway." In the picture, I look completely drunk, with eyes glazed over and a stupid smile on my face. Helen looks like a porcelain doll, with so much make-up that it might have been a bad Hollywood face-lift.

"Jay Twin marries BBC Producer" was the headline. My family was barely mentioned in any of the newspaper stories, but the Jays, the Callaghans, the starry guest list and our array of speakers featured prominently.

Galbraith, in an interview, said that he thought that the economic activity that Helen and I would create – with plenty of children of course – would seriously improve Britain's balance of payments crisis. It was not at all clear whether the British press understood that this was a joke. Robin Day was widely quoted, after he had enjoyed a substantial amount of wine and not quite enough sandwiches, saying that he had "always been impressed by our performance on the studio floor." Robin always liked a bit of schoolboy smut.

But the twist that the Tory newspapers loved the most was that the Limousine Liberals and Champagne Socialists (meaning the Jay-Callaghan-Garnett-Bottomley family cohort) had chosen to break the strike by the workers at the House of Commons kitchen, just because it suited them. Ah, bless the British press. But at least we got the coverage.

Helen and I disappeared back to her house after it was all over: this was our very modest honeymoon hideaway for the first night. It felt as if we had just wrapped up a monster location-based production. It did not feel the way I thought a wedding ought to feel, but it was still, we decided, a great success – viewed as a production, anyway.

We then left for a week's holiday in England, in almost continuous rain. We spent three nights at the cozy Old Swan Inn in Minster Lovell, Oxfordshire, in the very same room where Prime Minister Harold Wilson had celebrated his honeymoon. I am not sure whether Helen had planned it that way, to give us a metaphorical laying-on-of-hands (as it were) from the Labour Party hierarchy, but I did not find it any more weird than getting married in the Palace of Westminster. Helen's fun-loving stepmother, Mary Jay (indeed, Lady Jay as she now is) later moved to a charming house right across the road from the Old Swan Inn.

We then moved on to the Hartland Quay Hotel, on the Devon-Cornwall border. This, I was to learn, was considered a sacred piece of England's coastline by the entire Jay family. If it was good enough for the legendary King Arthur, who is said to have frequented the nearby Tintagel Castle, then it was good enough for the Jays.

The Hartland Quay welcomed us with a Force Eight gale and lashing rain. The Victorian hotel, never much fun at the best of times, I imagine, was deeply gloomy. I think we were the only guests.

"We've only just opened for the season," said the manager-cum-receptionist.

I am convinced that John Cleese modeled *Fawlty Towers* on this establishment, rather than the one in Torquay he usually credits as his inspiration. We gritted our teeth, wrapped up in sou'westers and other fishermen's foul-weather gear, and struggled out along narrow cliff-edge paths, while the Atlantic Ocean beat itself furiously against jagged rocks five hundred feet below us.

This was to be the first of several holidays I took on this coast with Helen and – later – her father Douglas and her stepmother Mary. Almost every time, a sense of humor was necessary, to see the benefits of voluntarily spending time here, rather than (say) somewhere warm on the Mediterranean. On one occasion I remonstrated with Douglas, when he took us all down a sheer cliff to a beach that I described as "a quarry." I was looked on with disfavor for an hour or two. It showed "family spirit" to tough it out in north Cornwall. Besides which, it made the Isle of Wight – the traditional vacation paradise of Helen's mother's side of the family – seem like a pansy picnic in comparison.

● ●

To finish this part of the backstory, Helen and I settled into the first and most peaceful year of our marriage, based in her beautifully refurbished terrace house in Fulham. It was very comfortable, handy for the BBC, and just around the corner from an agreeably shabby riverside pub, which had not yet been gentrified. They sold cheap beer to a cross-section of ne'er-do-wells and offered such traditional delicacies as Pork Scratchings (don't ask), pickled onions and Scotch Eggs. The latter are hard-boiled eggs, half-pickled in brine and wrapped in a shell of breadcrumbs, with traces of minced beef.

"Yum!" I hear you cry. But remember, this was before the great cuisine revolution in London, and it was quite a stretch for a traditional English pub to offer you anything at all besides warm beer, tobacco smoke, peanuts and potato crisps.

Helen had made friends with a great couple, half a block away: Jane Mann, a glamorous designer and chef, and her bearded ragamuffin boyfriend, Ian Gaynor, who bought and sold all sorts of stuff, of doubtful provenance. We had supper with each other at least once a week and shared many a laugh. One evening, on a bet, Ian and I decided to get up at dawn the next day and take the train from London to Glasgow (four hundred and fifty miles) to see the Queen, who was apparently visiting her Scottish subjects. And so we did.

The train left London (Euston) at 6.30 a.m., and by the time we had gone fifty miles, the bar car was full of Scots, singing and quaffing, with empty beer cans rolling around the floor of the carriage as the express train barreled its way north. We arrived too late to see the Queen, simply wandering from bar to bar in her wake, shuffling through the red-white-and-blue confetti in the streets of Glasgow. In every pub we visited, someone bought us a drink, on the strength of our story that we had traveled almost five hundred miles, in order *not* to see the Queen. But we did get to ride on the old Glasgow Subway, while it was still operating trains that dated from 1896, and that made the trip worthwhile for me, if not necessarily for Ian.

In December 1976, our daughter Amanda was born, and that was perhaps the happiest time of our marriage. Helen turned out to be a wonderful mother, as much to her surprise as mine, I think. Christmas was magical in that little house, with a steady stream of Jay cousins, uncles and grandmas coming through, followed by more and more friends from the BBC and even the occasional member of my sparse family. But, alas, the happiness was not to last.

In the spring of 1977, Helen decided two things in her own mind: first, that she was determined to be a full-time mother, and second, that we needed a much grander house. From that moment on, she never made serious moves to go back to full-time work for the rest of her life. That is true so far, anyway – and since she is over seventy now, I doubt if she will break the habit of the last forty years.

I did not understand how serious she was about moving, until she presented me with a virtual *fait accompli.* She had found a six-bedroom house, not much more than a mile away (as the crow flies), at a price she felt we could afford. Four bedrooms, presumably, to be filled with more little Jays – plus one for us and one for the au pair we would surely need. She also got down to the task of becoming pregnant again, and eventually succeeded, giving birth to Juliet in January 1979.

The new house was a mile away in one sense, and light years away in another. Instead of working-class Fulham, this house was across the river, in nose-in-the-air Barnes. It was a very desirable semi-detached residence, with an orchard, no less, in its garden. Facing onto the playing fields of St Paul's School (one of London's classiest and oldest private schools), the house was "a snip", as the Estate Agent put it. The same elderly couple had lived in it for thirty or forty years. It was structurally sound, needed a bit of "refreshment", and was ours for £29,000. Even at 1979 prices, this was a deal. The house would probably sell today for around £2 million.

But I hated it. It was the epitome of bourgeois tedium, I felt. Its Edwardian bijou mock-Tudor frontage was anathema. It was cold. It felt like my grandparents' old house. It made me feel middle-aged already. It had lawns to mow and rose bushes to prune. It was too big, and unwelcoming. It had a very intrusive neighbor on one side, and an old woman on the other. The nosy neighbor introduced himself on the first day by leaning over the garden fence and saying:

"Hello, my name's Bob Schroter. Easy to remember. Just think of Scrotum. Ha ha ha!"

Worst of all, though, this truly felt like the suburbs, and, by a few hundred yards, it was South London again. Ever since I had left Croydon, I had sworn I would never go back south of the river.

Helen, of course, was right. The house was a great investment. It just needed work. And the work needed money. So the first thing to be sold was my brand new MGB sports car. A tinny old Renault 5 was purchased in its place, because you could get the baby's buggy in the back, and the balance was spent on home improvement. And so it went on. The builders arrived and made a very nice modern sunroom at the back, removing the unsightly storage tank for the heating oil and upgrading the central heating system. All very sensible. But was any of this my idea? No. And did I feel at all at home in this grand family pile? I am afraid not.

I had a sinking feeling in my stomach. This did not seem at all like a marriage of equals. In my gloomier moments, I felt I was being pressed into service in the onward march of the Jay family dynasty. It seemed that every Sunday, some of Helen's twenty-four first cousins or siblings would turn up unannounced at our house, with all their children in tow.

"Hello," they would chorus. "We were just passing, on our way back from our weekend in the country, and Tabitha needed a loo. And do you have any nappies (diapers)? We've run out. And while we're here, you couldn't put the kettle on, could you? We'd love a cup of tea."

Something inside me threatened to break. My spirit.

Over the past twenty-five years – particularly since Helen's second marriage (to Rupert Pennant-Rea) ended in divorce – I have been welcomed back with warmth and generosity by the Jay family and all their in-laws and "out-laws." I think "Outlaw" was a term coined by Margaret, Helen's sister-in-law, to describe those who had gone a step too far, by divorcing one of the Jays, as she and I both did. She proposed that we should all sport a special silk scarf (for the girls) and silk tie (for the boys), but the idea never took wing. Mary Jay claims it was her idea, since she was the first "outlaw," having taken Douglas away from his first wife, the redoubtable Peggy Jay. But, after all these years, who can tell?

I sometimes think the kindness shown to me by the Jays is because I am the "least worst" husband Helen has had so far: Rupert's flamboyant dalliances subsequently made headlines on the front page of Britain's national newspapers. He was Deputy Governor of the Bank of England when the excrement hit the air-conditioning – leading at least one daily scandal sheet to call his affair with a journalist "The Bonk of England" in three-inch-high type on the front page. The moral of this story: never have an affair with a journalist. They know how and where to dish the dirt.

The Jays are a remarkable group of highly talented people – all three or four living generations of them. Helen's family have shown nothing but kindness to me and my second wife, Lizzie. Mary Jay has remained a particularly good friend, who has visited us in California and shared many a festive bottle of wine. But I still feel that my relationship with the Jay family is improved by my being 5,000 miles away in California for most of the time. Seeing me is something special now – almost something to look forward to.

However, I am getting ahead of myself in the chronology...

6. JAMES BURKE'S CONNECTIONS

You either loved James Burke on camera, or you did not. There were two distinct camps, back in the 1970's, from the very start of Burke's career. Some people, including some old-school British TV critics, saw him as a stuck-up, fast-talking smarty-pants: an intellectual con man, in a sense. After all, they would huff, he had no proper scientific training, no doctorate in history, no formal research credentials. Yet here he was in prime time on BBC-TV, with an expensive ten-part series, telling the world about the unlikely connections between vastly different inventions in unrelated academic fields. How dare he?

Luckily, the majority of the British audience, and the vast majority of the American audience, could not get enough of him. He was quite young, fresh, funny and incredibly knowledgeable. He did most of his own research and came up with startlingly original ideas. And, as I was to find out by working with him for two years, he was caring, generous and genuinely witty. What was not to like?

Burke had first made his name as a TV news correspondent, based in Rome. His news reports suggested a perfect knowledge of Italian – both language and culture – and always contained some little firecracker of information: something you had not quite expected. He soon returned to England, to join the long-running but often dull studio-based series *Tomorrow's World*, which had almost snared me, after *The Ascent of Man*. He transformed the energy of the program. He leapt around the studio, unveiling technological novelties like a magician finding rabbits in a hat. He ad-libbed – imagine that! Viewing figures skyrocketed. Suddenly, there was a really popular science and technology show.

In due course, he was offered a limited series of his own, right in prime time: *The Burke Special*. With a large team of dedicated producers and assistants, he selected a different topic each week. In the BBC's largest studio (TC1 in the iconic circular Television Center), he presented an all-singing, all-dancing science-relevant circus – and he was the ringmaster. The topics ranged from gravity to violence, and the live audience never knew what would happen next. One time, Burke drove a full-sized army tank through the studio loading-bay, straight at the audience. There were loud bangs, light shows, sudden entrances of celebrity guests, from scientists to movie actors and rock stars. To cap it all, these amazing shows usually went out live.

To do such a complex show live is to skate on very thin ice: it only takes one stunt to go wrong, and the timings of the whole show are at risk. But James was such a showman, with such a gift of the gab, that he could rescue the situation with a joke and a quickly ad-libbed link line to introduce a stand-by piece of film, which would fill the hole, till the director sorted things out.

Needless to say, there were those both in and outside the BBC who had profound doubts about this formula. Fellows of the Royal Society, science teachers from dull schools in Wales, confused housewives – all wrote in to say they thought the BBC had gone mad, allowing James Burke's Flying Circus to be given prime time space. But the audiences – of over ten million, a staggering number for a science and technology show – told their own story.

How could James Burke cap that level of success? He was a natural teacher: he just loved explaining things. He was not going to be tempted into showbiz, as such: no lazy late-night Johnny Carson or David Letterman-type talk-shows, for sure. It turned out that he had been hatching a very big idea for some years and had been putting some highly original research together in his spare time.

He first approached Mick Jackson, my fellow-director on *The Ascent of Man* and *The Age of Uncertainty.* Mick had a well-deserved reputation for visual brilliance and a great sense of humor. They in turn approached me, because Mick understood my strengths and weaknesses, and knew that I had the necessary sense of humor and a taste for adventure. A team of three could do it, they reckoned, plus a good researcher (John Lynch) and a great Associate Producer, Hilary Henson, whom Mick would later marry. The BBC produces fine programs, but also doubles as a first-class dating agency and marriage bureau.

But what was James's new show, being developed under wraps? I was duly let into the secret, in a number of evening sessions, in the BBC Club bar (of course) and in darkened offices, after everyone else had gone home.

James explained that the history of science and development of technology was usually seen as a stately progression *within any given field* towards today's state of the art: chemistry led to better chemistry, developments in transportation led gradually to more advanced transport, medieval armaments led inexorably down a path to modern-day weapons, and so on.

But in fact, James explained, this was not how creativity and invention worked at all, *in any field.* This was just the way that lazy academics saw things, hidebound in their own disciplines. It was the way librarians saw things too, and the way their traditional Dewey Decimal system had been organized: chemistry books are in one section, transportation is on another set of shelves, military matters are all clustered together upstairs: each in a different silo. So it was also the way the history of science and invention was taught, which was largely why it was so incredibly boring for most people.

Instead, James introduced us to the work of a few radical thinkers like Lynn White, Emeritus Professor of History at UCLA, who became one of the three world-renowned experts who underpinned and validated our radical series, *Connections.* He had published several papers, which demonstrated that almost any discipline or area of technological expertise is only galvanized into radical improvement by developments in *an apparently unrelated field.* What is more, Burke proposed, this transmission of information is usually completely serendipitous. Put more simply, someone working in one field may hear, often purely by chance, of some clever new invention or development in a quite different field of endeavor.

"Wait a minute", he or she says, "I could use that idea."

And so they do. Sometimes it works for them, and sometimes it doesn't. But when it does, it transforms everything.

So James, Mick, John Lynch and I proceeded to cover the walls of a large office in Kensington House with pink, yellow and blue three-by-five cards (each one representing a technique or a technology), linked to each other with pieces of string. The room looked like an insane spider's web, as we added more good connections (white strings), and also some traditional links, which seemed weak or unconvincing (red strings). This was one of the wonderful advantages of the BBC in the 1970's: it had the self-confidence, and the confidence in its producers, to allow them to run with an idea for months, so as to prove that it might work.

"How was the automobile invented?" asked James.

Well, obviously, it had cylinders, with pistons inside: they came from steam engines. It needed petrol, or gas – yes? Not necessarily: steam cars and electric cars were quite successful in the late nineteenth century. Oil had been discovered by accident in Pennsylvania in the 1860's and was initially used to replace whale oil as the fuel of choice for oil lamps. But oil lamps were dirty and smoky, and rapidly supplanted by gas and then electric lighting. So, what else could people do with the oil? You could simply burn it, like coal, and produce steam, but... Was there a more efficient way to unlock the energy from this viscous, mucky fluid?

The breakthrough happened in Germany. One of the Benz family, engineers from Stuttgart, was visiting relatives in the city of Cologne, famous for its perfume production, still known in Europe as Eau de Cologne. At the opera one night, sitting in a box and no doubt waiting for some interminable Wagner piece to end, Mr. Benz observed his cousin spraying herself with perfume from a cut-glass bottle, with a pink rubber bulb attached, which the cousin gently squeezed, to make herself attractive to her beau.

"Hmm...," thought Mr. Benz. "An alcoholic substance, atomized into tiny particles of spray...?"

Then, so the story goes, he observed another opera patron, lighting a cigar with some sort of flint device. A lighter. In other words, a spark... Put that together with an atomized liquid and...? History does not record whether Mr. Benz shouted "Eureka!" and leaped out of the box onto the crowd below, but he certainly made haste to return to Stuttgart with his novel idea.

He had made a crucial connection: the way to use oil was to refine it, and to squirt it through a tiny hole, which would atomize the droplets, as it did with the perfume. Add a spark at the right moment, and you would get a controlled explosion. Put that device into a cylinder, and the explosion (carefully timed) would push a piston up and back down again. Have more than one piston doing the same thing to a different rhythm in another cylinder, and you'd have a gas (or petrol) engine purring along.

After many months of tinkering, the whole contraption worked. The first models of the final petrol-driven car were a huge success. They were named after the family's eldest daughter: her name was Mercedes.

Well, who would have guessed? The immediate antecedents of the successful gas-driven automobile were not the horse and cart, the railroad or the electric streetcar, which all preceded it, but the perfume spray and the cigar-lighter. Hurrah! Another amazing connection: another demonstration of the way creative thought actually works in practice.

Of course, we found dozens more. Think how miserable life in an early medieval village or castle must have been: cold and damp, even for the master and his wife. Most people huddled in a large single-roomed barn, with a fire in the middle, and smoke lazily escaping through a hole in the roof, which let in the rain and snow. To ensure some warmth, the animals (cows, pigs, dogs, chickens) all slept in the same room too. Think of the flatulence. Think of the noise. Think of the lack of privacy.

What led to the development of a comfortable home for Northern Europe's upper classes? It took hundreds of years before someone realized that the blacksmith's forge, where strong bellows and controlled updrafts with a specially created flue created a fire hot enough to melt metal, could be adapted for use in the home. You guessed it: the chimney. Small amounts of fuel could produce relatively cozy warmth in every room: even the bedroom.

Professor Lynn White suggested that this new privacy was what promoted the spread of medieval romantic poetry and tall tales of knightly valor.

"My Lord Came Back from the Wars Today, and Pleasured Me Thrice With His High Boots On" was a wonderful song to sing, provided that the action all happened behind a closed door in a private bedroom. If that song was sung when everybody (master and servant) all slept together, shivering among the cattle on an earthen floor, the proud boast of Pleasuring Thrice might not have been quite so believable. Too many witnesses would have sworn that one quick fumble under the blankets was all that transpired.

To enjoy all the stories, you need to read the original book of *Connections*, or watch the first series. There were two later series, produced by the Discovery Channel in the US, but many people feel that they were not as fresh as the original. I am biased, of course, because I had nothing to do with them, but I am very proud that I helped to create the first series.

The new head of BBC Science and Features, Phil Daly, green-lighted production of ten episodes, with a generous budget. The one caveat was that Mick and I, relative neophytes, should be supervised at a distance by our old boss and mentor, Adrian Malone. Adrian privately confided in us that he trusted us, and that we should do whatever seemed fun, provided that we stayed within the budget. He left us entirely alone. Little did I know that he had upcoming plans for himself in mind, and that his gaze was fixed on the United States.

So off we went: we had written nine program outlines and structures – not scripts. James hated scripts. On location, on the day, he would privately rehearse what he might say, and then virtually ad-lib the first take.

We would set up the camera, and film the rehearsal: it was often the best take of all, because James was fresh, and did his best to make all of us laugh or look astonished.

Veteran cameramen and time-honored sound guys would often crack up at some joke that James had inserted into a perfectly serious explanation of medieval armor, for instance. To make a hardened thirty-year professional in the BBC camera department laugh on location, specially during a take, is a miracle. It is a pain in the neck for the sound editor of course, to cut out the chuckles, but for us as directors, we knew we had pure gold in the can.

The added bonus about working for James was that he was as much fun off screen as on. He had an astonishingly large repertoire of off-color jokes, true (or fairly true) anecdotes, limericks and rhymes. Only Michael Tilson Thomas, the Musical Director and Principal Conductor of the San Francisco Symphony, with whom I worked thirty-five years later, could have equaled him – and more about that later.

We had set ourselves a huge task, on *Connections*. Our locations included Taiwan – to stand in for China, which was not yet open to outsiders yet (see Chapter 9 on The Heart of the Dragon). We visited Malaysia, to talk about the tropics and such essential items as quinine, the heart of a good gin and tonic and the first palliative for malaria. Then we filmed all over Britain, much of Europe and large chunks of the United States. Plus, unforgettably, Egypt.

In the first episode, the vast expanse of temples, tombs and lakes in and around the ancient city of Luxor on the Upper Nile served to explain how an early interconnected civilization depended on so many skills, which still exist in ancient form in rural Egypt: the ox-drawn plow, the irrigation system, the lateen-sailed boats.

I will never forget the thrill of being able to film in the heart of the preserved city of Luxor (ancient Thebes), when all the tourists had disappeared. We had the full run of the lighting effects created for the *Son et Lumière* displays at our disposal. James Burke scampered through the tall temple columns in the moonlight like a kid in a candy store, popping up here and there and finally being able to say:

"What the ancient Egyptians finally created was... THIS!" Cue dramatic music, and all the lights were switched on, to reveal the entire city, dramatically illuminated in reds, whites and blues. Wow!

The first half of the opening episode featured New York City. Mick Jackson brilliantly recreated a vast power outage which happened in the 1970's, and James described in minute detail why and how it happened: how one switch failed at one power station at Niagara Falls, cascading into a series of brown-outs across the whole of the North-east of America and part of Canada.

Suddenly, subway trains ground to a halt between stations, pilots could not see any landing lights at Kennedy Airport, hospital surgical operations were plunged into darkness as scalpels were cutting into flesh... Mick recreated all of this, and much more. The message: all of civilization is connected by very fragile threads.

We had many experts to help us along the way. Some came from the BBC: the stalwart and much-acclaimed John Horton of the BBC Special Effects Unit followed us around in a van, with all sorts of tricks up his sleeve. In the city of Troyes in eastern France, we recreated the horrors of the Black Death of the fourteenth century, which killed at least half the population of Europe – ironically, later creating an economic boom for those who survived, who were forced to invent whole new technologies to build up their cities again.

John Horton had several mock corpses and dozens of fake but convincing dead rats in his van, to decorate a medieval street where we had been allowed to film in Troyes. To spice things up, he had a small cage of live rats, too. We were allowed to paint white crosses on old doorways (signifying the presence of the plague), and the local Fire Department ensured that we had constant rain splashing down on the dismal street. Courtesy of John Horton, a few local volunteers put on ragged medieval costumes, which, I'm sure, had been used in Monty Python episodes, and slouched around, looking suitably woebegone.

Given our small budget, it was all quite convincing. The local daily newspaper had a page three headline announcing "BBC brings Black Death back to Troyes", which must have done wonders for their tourist trade.

As he had been on *The Ascent of Man* and *The Age of Uncertainty*, my friend and co-producer-director Mick Jackson was the wizard of low-cost special effects. James Burke wanted to talk about the magical ideas behind the construction of the Gothic Cathedrals of Europe – and how some masons and architects – anonymous to this day – were just a little too daring. A large part of the cathedral at Beauvais, north east of Paris, collapsed because the nave was just too wide. Not even the new gothic arch and flying buttresses could support it.

"How are we going to film a cathedral collapsing?" asked James.

We facetiously discussed the use of dynamite at Canterbury – so handy for our office, just down the road indeed. But then Mick came up with a solution. He would get John Horton's special-effects brigade to construct all sorts of separate bits of cathedral in beige-painted Styrofoam: pointed arches, bits of architrave, gargoyles, crosses and angelic sculptures, ruptured columns etc. Plus, we would need bags full of building dust. Then we would find some cheap studio space, and light it as if it were night-time. We would drop all the bits slowly, in batches, from a great height, and film them in slow motion as they hit the ground. Then we added the roar of an earthquake and an excerpt from the ever useful and quite over-the-top Carmina Burana, the musical equivalent of Hieronymous Bosch's apocalyptic paintings.

It worked rather well and convinced many in the audience – in those halcyon days before sophisticated computer graphics – that we really had destroyed some part of an ancient building.

Actually reconstructing living scenes from the past is a tricky business. The first rule is to avoid all hokey dialog – indeed, all speech, if possible. The audience is willing to suspend disbelief and go along with the idea that they are looking at archive film from 1356 or 1747, if there are not too many wide shots and the pace of editing is rapid and exciting, supported by the right sort of music.

Mick and I recreated dozens of scenes – from the colonial jungle culture of the far east (complete with a working elderly steam train, which I got to drive – whoopee!), and working English smithies and steelworks in Ironbridge and Sheffield. Mick arranged for a jousting scene with medieval horsemen near the site of the original Battle of Hastings in 1066. That was the last time England was invaded, and a key part was played by the stirrup, an invention which left the knight's hands free, so that he could stand and wield both a shield and a lance.

But perhaps my fondest memories are the great parties we had, all over the world, at the conclusion of filming in almost every location. The secret was that we always involved the local people. We could not pay them – the BBC does not have that kind of budget for documentaries – so we partied instead.

One particularly stupendous party was thrown for us by the City of Hoorn in Holland, at the conclusion of location shooting. This had involved half the town's population, dressed in seventeenth century gear. They had removed streetlights, modern signs, cars and everything else which said "1977." We were there to explain the brilliant invention of the star-shaped castle, the best remaining example of which can be found at Hoorn. For the history buffs: if you build a castle in the shape of a starfish, each wall can protect its neighboring wall, by firing through gun-slots at anyone trying to climb up. Can you imagine that? If not, do please see the series or buy the book: they are filled with many strange creations of the human mind.

Anyway, the good burghers of Hoorn had elected to throw a huge party for us to celebrate the filming. For obvious reasons, Sunday is always the best day to close off the streets and get local people to cease all activity and dress up for the cameras. So the people of Hoorn decided that Saturday night was the time to have fun. We thought it might be a little risky to party *before* the filming, but the practical Dutch said that they were not going to party *after* the filming, because the following day was Monday, when they would all turn back into sensible Dutch people, having to earn a living. So... Saturday night it was.

I had told the BBC cameraman, Tony Pierce-Roberts (now a star Director of Photography in Los Angeles), that he should make sure to arrive by car from England in good time on the Saturday, to scout the location with me, and then to enjoy the party before the Sunday filming. He unfortunately declined my offer and used his Saturday to film something else for someone else en route.

He arrived at our hotel in Hoorn on Saturday night, to find a bacchanalian scene: the local Tourist Office had booked and paid for all the rooms in the local historic inn: some for us – the BBC crew – and many for themselves and the great and the good of Hoorn. The Mayor and Chief of Police were there, and everyone had started drinking at 6 p.m. There was singing and dancing, and then more drinking. And did I mention the singing?

On location, I cannot quite decide which nation wins the trophy for drinking: the Dutch? The Russians? The Icelanders? The English? One day, for sure, it will become an Olympic sport. I have thoroughly enjoyed the qualifying rounds of this jolly pursuit, and I can assure you that the inhabitants of Hoorn in Holland would be some of the finalists in a global location drinking contest.

The scene that night was mind-boggling, from what little I remember. It included much scampering along upstairs corridors from bedroom to bedroom, as attractive VVV (Tourist Office) girls led their sisters and cousins in a grand game of Hunt the Slipper –

or indeed, hunting any and all intimate items of clothing. Ah, the 1970's: will we ever see their like again?

Tony Pierce-Roberts, arriving stone-cold sober at midnight, was shocked. The whole town was rocking, and most of the inhabitants seemed to be somewhere in this hotel – including Tony's crew members and of course the director/producer in charge: me.

I am sure TPR was extremely irritated that we were all drinking and partying the night before a complicated location shoot – not exactly professional behavior. I am equally sure he was irritated because he had effectively missed the party, by not arriving as early as I had suggested. But a few weeks later, the scurrilous London-based satirical magazine *Private Eye* ran a story about a "BBC Orgy", organized, it appeared, by that wayward producer, David Kennard.

"Is this the way the BBC Licence-payers' money should be spent?" was the tenor of the article, which painted lurid details of a scene from Gomorrah, if not exactly Sodom.

I wrote a reply to *Private Eye*, pointing out that every last penny of the cost had been borne by the generous citizens of Hoorn, but my letter was never printed, and the damage was done. My BBC personnel officer later called me in for "a word in my ear." He talked about "bringing the name of the corporation into disrepute", much as the headmaster of Hurstpierpoint College had done, sixteen years before, but there was no other punishment, happily.

The question is: how did *Private Eye* ever get to hear about this debauchery? Perish the thought that it could have been sour grapes from a cameraman, surely…

■■

7. CARL SAGAN'S COSMOS

Carl Sagan was one of the few academics to become an international celebrity and a legend in his own lifetime. Remarkably, he is still a household name, more than twenty-five years after his death.

In the late 1970's, he seemed to be everywhere. He published two bestselling books – real smash hits – *The Cosmic Connection* (about everything from the Big Bang to the emergence of life on earthlike planets) and *The Dragons of Eden* (about life, evolution and human beings' place in the story). He was a frequent guest on America's favorite late-night TV show, *Tonight with Johnny Carson*: this was where his famous catchphrase "billions and billions" (of stars) caught on. Carson would gently tease him, if he got too academic or abstruse, and he became the go-to popular spokesman for anything big in the world of science.

He was also, indeed, a practicing scientist, deeply involved in the Voyager space project at JPL, the Jet Propulsion Laboratory in Pasadena, CA. Plus, he was a tenured Professor and wildly popular teacher at Cornell University.

Of course, you cannot be popular with everybody all of the time. As we learned while working with him, several academics were a little sniffy about Carl's authenticity as an intellectual. But such are the groves of academe. Others bemoaned his occasional lack of modesty. But who could blame him, if he sometimes thought he could walk on water? The real test – the test which the production team on Cosmos went through with him – was how to work side by side with such a personality for over two years, without losing your cool or being sucked into the vortex of his ego.

▪▪

For me, the Cosmos adventure began with an early morning phone call to my bedroom in a luxury hotel in Taipei. I thought it was my wake-up call, because we were due to film with James Burke at a Taoist shrine for the BBC's *Connections* series.

Back in the late 1970's it was next to impossible to film in mainland China, so we had chosen Taiwan as a location, to help explain why the Chinese had invented gunpowder, printing, paper and the compass, and then never exploited them commercially.

But it was not a wake-up call – at least not in the traditional sense. It was my old BBC boss and friend Adrian Malone, calling from California, where (he explained) it was still yesterday, and he was in his new office. In my just-woken, befuddled state – ample Chinese hospitality the previous night had taken its toll – it took me a minute or two to realize that Adrian had tracked me down, just to ask me one simple question.

"When you've finished filming in Taiwan, could you go back to London the 'wrong way' round the world – across the Pacific via Los Angeles?"

Apparently, in grand cigar-puffing Hollywood Executive Producer style, he wanted to make me an offer I couldn't refuse. Well, the call from Hollywood is what every producer-director-writer is meant to dream about, so I promptly agreed. James Burke was typically very accommodating, we were almost finished with the filming for *Connections*, and most of the editing had been done too. Our jaunt to Taiwan had been an extra scene, written into the show when we realized we still had some travel money left. No-one leaves any unspent cash in a BBC budget!

But why had Adrian called me? He was determined to keep it a mystery on the phone. But the temptation was too great to refuse. I re-booked my ticket, flew via Tokyo and arrived at LAX, jet-lagged and bemused. I was promptly whisked to the brand-new KCET-TV studios on Sunset Boulevard – in a black limo, of course. Here, I was introduced to the twenty-strong production team, which had already been assembled to undertake *Cosmos*. Adrian told me that the budget was over $6 million – in 1978 dollars.

"It will be the most ambitious, most technically-advanced, most expensive, and most amazing documentary series ever made," said Adrian, who was not given to understatement. "Would you like to be co-Senior Producer, together with Geoffrey Haines-Styles, who's another Brit? There'll be plenty of chances to direct on location. And your salary will be three or four times what you're getting at the BBC."

"Golly" is probably what I said; something understated and rather British. "But what about my BBC job?"

"No problem", said Adrian. "The project is a co-production with the Beeb. They're putting in about 10% of the budget. I'll see to it that they give you a leave of absence, to look after their interests in the series. When we've finished, you can go back to good old Kensington House – if you want to. What have you got to lose?"

My mind was racing along other tracks, however. What about my marriage to Helen, and my little daughter Amanda, living in London? What about the little bump in Helen's tummy, who was going to become Juliet, my second daughter?

"No problem", said Adrian. "The project can pay for you to make frequent extended trips to London, to share footage with the BBC, and get advice from Paul Bonner." He was the new and very likeable Head of Science and Features TV.

"Plus, I'll put you in charge of all location filming in Europe", Adrian continued. "So you don't have to abandon the UK, and you'll have lots of time with your family and friends."

It turned out that the job had become available because Ben Shedd, the previous co-Senior Producer, had not seen eye-to-eye with Adrian, and was fired. This was not unusual. Adrian treasured absolute loyalty: his Celtic temper was easily aroused by people not pulling their weight or disagreeing with him in public. He was either your trusty friend or your sworn enemy – or so it often seemed. And Adrian very much wanted someone with my experience to join his team

After much discussion back in London – with Helen, with my parents and friends, and with the BBC – I agreed to give it a try. It wasn't quite what Helen had expected, since she had plans for building up a traditional family life in south-west London, but she agreed that it might be necessary for my career. She found the USA a rather strange place – particularly the West Coast – and never expected, I am sure, that I would fall in love with it. I was secretly very excited, and for a very good reason.

Just a month before Adrian's offer, I had been summoned to the BBC's holy of holies, their HQ in central London – Broadcasting House, known as "BH." There, I had had a meeting with J.P.Mullins – the inscrutable BBC mandarin who was one of the panel, which had selected me for my original traineeship at the BBC. I couldn't believe he was still in place, ten years later.

Mullins rather formally asked me to take a seat, then browsed through the papers in my personnel file. He looked up after a couple of minutes and drily announced that I'd "had a good run" in production, but should now be thinking of furthering my career by joining the senior management team in BH.

"To do what?" I asked.

"Well," he said, "We usually start people off behind the scenes, drafting letters for the Director General to sign and send. Delicate matters. Politically sensitive stuff. You'll learn a lot. It's a privilege. To be honest, it's an excellent way to the top, in the long run."

A stark choice confronted me: become one of the Suits, or stay with the Pirates in the Neverland of Production? Panicked by the thought of joining Smiley's People, I virtually ran from Mullins's office. I took the tube back to Shepherd's Bush, to my home in Kensington House and the wild and woolly world of documentaries.

That was the pivotal moment in my career – in my life, even. I might have applied the skills I'd learned at Business School and gone on to become a well-paid BBC bureaucrat. But I remembered what David Attenborough had told me: nothing in management compares with the thrill of creativity and exploration. No wonder, then, that the palm trees and kidney-shaped swimming pools of LA seemed so attractive. And that huge budget. And that salary… I was on the plane as soon as possible and was ushered into my new office on *Cosmos* on my birthday, September 7, 1978. Would you believe it, they had organized a huge welcome party for me. More than twenty people sang Happy Birthday, some of whom would become friends of mine to this day: Cheryl King, Judy Flannery, David Oyster …

•••

Just a few days later, I first met Carl Sagan, who had flown in from his office at Cornell University. He was accompanied by an entourage that would represent the heart of "his" team, throughout the production: Shirley Arden, his ever-loyal assistant; Ann Druyan, an attractive young poet and Carl's girlfriend; Gentry Lee, an engineer at the Jet Propulsion Laboratory; and Steve Soter, a brilliant post- doctoral student and researcher from Cornell. There was no sign of Mrs. Sagan, whom Carl had apparently left by the wayside quite recently.

For the next two years, the Sagan group, plus several of the extra staff they had recommended – including planetary illustrators like the brilliant Jon Lomberg and physicists like Dan Goldsmith – inhabited a completely separate suite of offices from the rest of us at KCET. It was immediately obvious that there would be two camps: Carl's team, and Adrian's team.

From the very start, it was unclear who had final executive responsibility for the series. Adrian was used to being the boss, while deferring graciously on purely intellectual points to his previous on-camera hosts and writers, Jacob Bronowski and J.K. Galbraith. But these two experts had been almost twice his age, and he was happy to defer to them as father figures. Carl and Adrian were much the same age and both were used to being totally in charge of any project they embarked on.

To add to the complications, the real bosses were PBS, the network that had green-lighted the series, and the management of KCET, the originating station in LA. Chuck Allen, a kindly but politically astute executive at KCET (whom I'd met during the Galbraith series), claimed that he had been the one who dreamed up the *Cosmos* series – to be hosted by Carl Sagan. He claimed that he had personally approached the oil company, Atlantic Richfield (based in LA) to secure the larger part of the funding. So he was in charge, too. And of course, his office was in yet another part of the building.

I realized that managing and creating this enormous project was not going to be easy for any of us. How can a ship sail straight, with three separate captains on the bridge? But the ship had already left port, and if I was to help pilot its difficult voyage, there was no time to be lost. At least I had the experience of three previous multi-part location-based series under my belt: almost everyone else (apart from Adrian) was a newbie. Help!

I looked at what passed for a schedule. It was a mess. Location scouting had already taken place, and there were some very vague outline program scripts, which kept changing on a daily basis. The deadline for completion was less than two years away. Hundreds of thousands had already been spent. No-one had done a critical path analysis of what needed to be done in what order. Help, again!

The first task was to clarify who was doing what. There were already three groups of producers and associate producers working on plans for the production: Location Filming, Special Effects, and Studio Production. The trouble was that we had no scripts to work with, for the thirteen hours of complex television that was envisioned. What am I saying? We did not even have any firm program outlines or treatments. Six months after the start of production, we were not at all sure which of Carl's ideas would make it into the final cut, and which would not.

Carl and Ann Druyan kept changing their mind about what they both *really* wanted to say, particularly when it came to location shooting. Ann, you will note, was an extension of Carl's mind, right from the start. Early on, before the panic set in, we would have very laid-back script meetings, at which Carl or Ann would come up with more-or-less spontaneous ideas, which they had hatched together in intimate moments. When I arrived, they had recently been on a romantic cruise together.

"Ooh, Carl", said Ann, "Do you remember how we stood on the deck at night and watched the pale reflection of the moon, dancing on the water?" She is a poet, you'll note. "Wouldn't that be a cool way of introducing the influence of the moon in the series?"

Carl's response was initially a thoughtful silence, then a deeply indulgent smile – this was one of Ann's precious ideas, after all. Then he simply said:

"That's beautiful, Annie."

"Wait a minute, Carl", said the ever-practical director, David Oyster. "There's no way that we can shoot that. Given the available lenses and 16-millimeter film technology, we couldn't do it. It's too dim, we wouldn't get an exposure out there." Another silence…

Then Carl broke the news that he really did not want to include Earth's moon in the series at all. He felt that it had got far too much exposure during the moon-landings of the previous ten years.

"We've discovered that our moon is arid and pretty dull," said Sagan. "What's more, you should all know that I'm not in favor of manned space exploration at all. It's a waste of time and money. It has just been a cold-war substitute – a way of getting one up on the Russians."

So: no human-interest stories about astronauts. No ripples in the water. No room for Annie's romantic moment. No moon. No consideration for the fact that the public seemed to have been incredibly excited, when that American flag was planted on our natural satellite, back in 1969. I was almost expecting Carl to claim (as others have done) that the Apollo missions had all been a hoax – a recreation staged in a Texas studio, to please a gullible public. But he stopped short of that.

The hours and days ticked past, as we talked. Carl had originally planned to spend only a few weeks working on each of the thirteen shows. He had hoped to fit his entire work for the series into a single year, already full of academic commitments and speaking engagements. I think he felt initially that the effort required would be only slightly greater than doing thirteen Johnny Carson studio shows.

By the end of 1978, it was clear that he had grossly underestimated the work involved, particularly if he wished to sign off on every detail. So he applied to Cornell for an immediate extra sabbatical year (extendible if required) and Cornell – thank God – agreed.

∙∙

It took at least three months to get the location shooting sorted out. In principle, Carl loved the thought of getting out of the lecture room, the laboratory and the studio. But would he enjoy the experience in practice, with all the uncomfortable travel, unpleasant weather and tedium of a film shoot? We all agreed that it was a good idea to have him on location in Europe: to describe Tycho Brahe and the early modern astronomers for example, or to explain Rutherford's description of the divisibility of the atom by actually sitting at the Cambridge University High Table where it was discussed. But what about the tougher locations, beyond Europe and the US?

Carl and Ann very much wanted to go to southern India, to introduce the many-armed god Shiva and explain the Hindu concept that there were endless cycles of creation and destruction in the universe. He also liked the idea of joining the crew of a sailing ship in Mexico's Sea of Cortes, to describe how whales communicated: we needed an underwater camera for that adventure. It was neither easy nor comfortable in such places, but Carl was a trooper and did not complain. If he had had the idea of shooting somewhere, then he was prepared to put up with the hardships that came with it. Of course, if it had been someone else's idea, every minor discomfort was cause for complaint.

I think, however, that Carl came to like location filming. It seemed relatively unhurried. He could afford to be human – even fallible. He suggested that I should shoot some touching scenes in a café in his old-fashioned childhood neighborhood in Brooklyn. He recalled the times when, aged six, he wistfully looked across the East River at the distant twinkling lights of Manhattan. To him, it was another universe, and the lights were like stars in the sky.

In addition to straight documentary, Adrian argued strongly for tastefully produced dramatic scenes, recreating past events and atmospheres. I was delighted to create and film a traditional nineteenth century steam-driven fairground scene in the English Cotswolds, with a crowd enjoying themselves in Victorian dress, to emphasize how very modern H.G. Wells' contemporary novel *The War of the Worlds* must have seemed. It envisioned a hostile race, observing us from a distant planet "as if we were curious specimens under a microscope." In that crowd were my parents, friends, Helen, Amanda and new-born Juliet.

Director Tom Weidlinger created a full-blown reconstruction of the French expedition led by Champollion, sailing up the Nile to the ancient city of Thebes – now called Luxor (where I had filmed James Burke, just two years before). Carl joined them, to explain how Egyptian hieroglyphs were deduced and deciphered, thanks to the Rosetta stone, which had identical information carved in three languages. He suggested that we should hope for a similar key to the puzzle of decoding future alien languages from other civilizations.

We all agreed, as we had done on *Connections*, that our dramatic scenes should not contain hokey dialog. Too many drama-documentaries have been ruined by scripts along the lines of:

"Good morning, Mr. Dickens, I hear you're working on a new story, to be called The Tale of Three Cities."

"Yes, but it's too damned long. I'll have to cut something..."

I eventually took overall responsibility for all the location shooting. David Oyster, Richard Wells, Tom Weidlinger, Janelle Balnicke, Cameron Beck and I sallied forth around the world, begging, borrowing and stealing as much of Carl's time as we could get, knowing that, if he liked the place where we were filming, he came across as warm, compassionate and wise, while still acknowledging that the place itself might be greater than he was. Carl at his very best, in other words.

••

Then, there was the studio. This was potentially the biggest bugbear of them all. KCET, a frequently poverty-stricken PBS station in spite of its stylish premises, had decreed that a sizeable chunk of the $6 million-dollar *Cosmos* budget should pay for a set of brand-new studio cameras, and a state-of-the-art lighting and sound kit to go with them. But what on earth were we going to shoot in a large studio? This was not a late-night Johnny Carson chat show, after all.

Perhaps the greatest process of collaboration on the project was the way that Carl and Adrian Malone developed the idea of creating a vast spaceship in the studio, in which Carl could appear to ride through the Universe and ponder the ineffable. Rob McCain, Judy Flannery and others proposed all sorts of details, which might make it less cheesy and more convincing: multiple windows, through which you could watch galaxies pass by, and rippling light effects on the translucent skin (or walls), which would give the impression of movement.

On film, to create exterior shots, the spaceship would be symbolized by a dandelion puffball, blown onto its cosmic journey by Carl in Episode One, as he stood on a Northern California clifftop. Successful ideas have many parents, but I think that Adrian Malone should take credit for that one.

Personally, I disliked the Studio Spaceship. It really did seem hokey, to me. It was a vast construction: the big KCET studio had originally been built to make silent movies in the 1920's, and scenes such as The Fall of Rome and Armageddon had apparently been shot there. Now, we would have this vast pseudo-spaceship, inhabited only by Carl, who had to look wistfully out of green-screen windows and pretend he was just leaving the Milky Way or skimming past Orion's belt. Worse still, to give him something to do, he was directed to pass his hands, like a magician about to cry "Abracadabra," over some fake illuminated crystals, as if this would steer the ship to infinity and beyond. That was Adrian's idea too.

Several critics, putting their general awe to one side, made merry about Carl's mute expressions, while he gazed in simulated wonder out of the fake "windows." Some thought he looked constipated. Some thought he looked like he had forgotten his next line and was waiting for a prompt. One satirical review (in Britain, needless to say) suggested that he looked as if he was trying to remember where he had left his car keys.

But – wonder of wonders – it finally worked, for many people at least. The childlike idea of being able to wander wherever you wished in the cosmos was in some ways bewitching. I have often asked myself why, on balance, the spaceship was not an embarrassment for the audience. I think it is partly because Carl's voice-over script never strayed totally into the sentimental. He became once again, in a way, that genuine six-year-old boy that he had been in Brooklyn. And there was one other element that really helped: the music.

It is not clear in my memory who first proposed the music of Vangelis. Certainly, our series was launched long before the movie *Chariots of Fire*, which made Vangelis a household name around the world. But there was something just right about it: tuneful but timeless, optimistic but wistful. That romantic mood fitted exactly with the zeitgeist of the late seventies. After all, in real life, we were sending Voyager spacecraft past the giant planets for the first time ever, sending back real-time images of violent storms on Jupiter, and Saturn's fairy rings. Space was really cool back then – a powerful antidote to the memories of the Vietnam War and the mid-70's fuel crisis. And *Cosmos* caught that spirit.

■■

The final production elements were the special effects, and these turned into a nightmare. *Cosmos* was produced before any kind of sophisticated 3-D computer animation existed. Pong and Pac-Man were pretty much state of the art, in the late 1970's.

At the same moment, George Lucas was throwing a vast amount of money at his early Star Wars films, but many of his effects relied on cleverly shot models. Previously, *2001: A Space Odyssey* had been the one to beat, but its celestial effects were relatively modest. How could we possibly achieve scientific accuracy – which Carl, of course, insisted on – and get the "Wow!" factor as well?

The solution is hard to imagine today. The production hired a vast warehouse, almost a hundred yards long, and entirely blacked it out: black paint, black drapes, not a chink of unwanted light. Then, dozens of glass paintings were made by a team of artists under Jon Lomberg's direction: each glass held the image of (say) a single layer of a galaxy. Each one was then placed a few meters in front of the last, and individually lit, from the side (to avoid reflections). Then, tracks were laid for the camera dolly. At the start of the shot, the camera would roll forward and go on rolling for almost a hundred yards. The final effect was that of literally traveling "through" the galaxy. It had never been done before, and it took many takes of each shot, to get it right.

There were still two problems, however. One was that, even though the camera was traveling a hundred yards, the shot would only last a maximum of about twenty seconds: any slower, and the bumps and glitches of the dolly would have been too obvious, or the shot too boring. So that is why we needed the Studio Spaceship: none of those spectacular shots could last very long, so we had to keep cutting away to something else, to get the impression of a seamless journey.

We would cut from the full-screen effect to the very wide shot of the studio, with the effect playing on the distant windshield of the spacecraft. Then we would cut to Carl's face in rapt attention, then to a close-up effect then to Carl's hands hovering over the crystal steering wheel, then back to the wide shot of the studio... That way, we had time enough for the music to soar, or for Carl's commentary to explain what we were looking at.

The other problem was cost. Sometime in 1979, it became clear that the money was running out all too fast in the Special Effects department. The senior bookkeeper, Jim Ross, started to shut his door and refuse to speak to Adrian Malone or myself. His second-in-command, Cherie Rardin (later Cheryl King, who still works for me as Business Manager, besides being a very good friend), would roll her eyes and dish out paychecks to the minions, hinting that they should be cashed ASAP, before the bank caught up with us.

The deathblow, financially, was when the company that had leased us the special effects warehouse went into bankruptcy. One morning, the crew arrived to find the doors padlocked, with security men outside. Inside was all our priceless space art. Federal Marshals were called, and broke the padlocks, to allow us to get our stuff out: hundreds of fragile glass paintings – not just a job for a couple of U-Haul trucks.

Then came the financial crisis meetings: cutbacks to the location budgets, various effects cut from the script, and KCET desperately trying to scrounge a few more dollars from the underwriters and the BBC. But these were not the only tensions.

By now, we were starting to edit the thirteen programs, in the basement at KCET. Adrian had brought across yet another Brit to Los Angeles, to be the Senior Editor: Jim Latham was a distinguished BBC professional, who had worked on two of our previous long series. He was also a rather quiet, reserved man, whose realistic and somewhat gloomy view of the whole situation led to his nickname, Eeyore. He certainly seemed like a fish out of water among the palm trees of LA. He set to work with a will, nonetheless.

"I just shut my eyes and think of England," he said, when asked how he coped with the tensions swirling round the project.

Little did we know that Jim was also setting aside some of the more hilarious bloopers from our footage, to make a satirical fifteen-minute film of his own, which he called "Program Fourteen." It was a well-guarded secret. Carl would have blown his top, if he had ever seen it. There were images of special effects going awry: a technician's head coming slowly into frame as we flew through a galaxy. There were shots of sets falling over. There were botched takes of crane shots with dozens of actors in Holland, panning to reveal the catering truck. Best of all, however, was the priceless collection of Carl's on-camera mistakes. Not just the lines he forgot – that happens to anyone – though they could be very funny. There were also the lines he muffed.

"The really, really important thing," he once said, in his most portentous voice, "is, er... um... wait a minute. Annie, what is the really important thing?" Great stuff for a blooper reel.

My favorites were the thirteen takes of Carl standing in the desert near Alexandria, Egypt, attempting to say: "Welcome to the Planet Earth!"

He had decided that, after the twenty-five-minute voyage in the Studio Spaceship, we should arrive at our blue planet, pass through some clouds, and dissolve to a shot which panned down to reveal Carl, standing like a monolithic statue in an ancient landscape, welcoming us "home" to Earth. But, try as he might, he could not make the sentence sound anything but very silly. He tried shifting the emphasis from one word to the other.

"Welcome to the planet EARTH..." No.

"WELCOME to the Planet Earth..." No.

"Welcome to the PLANET Earth..." Forget it.

Jim Latham cut all thirteen attempts into his satirical film, one every minute, amongst the other mishaps and producers' curse words. It was all very funny. It was passed from hand to hand, like an illegal Samizdat manuscript in Soviet Russia, for enjoyment at home by the staff. Alas, I do not think a single copy of it still exists, even on VHS.

Back in the real world, however, we all had to face reality, once the editing started in earnest. Carl frequently stated that he did not like the way the programs were coming together. He wanted new scenes shot. He wanted major ideas scrapped. One day, Ann Druyan and Carl, with their faithful acolyte Steve Soter, swept into our large conference room to meet the production crew, and declared the whole project an impending disaster, because we had not done exactly what Carl wanted in the first place. Adrian Malone's face became redder and redder. He looked like an Irish laborer, spoiling for a fight.

"I'm in charge of the artistic interpretation," he shouted at Carl. "This is not going to be some sort of ego-trip, and it is not going to be an academic lecture. It's going to be one of MY films – one of MY series, and they win awards!"

There was a dreadful silence. This explosion had been brewing for weeks. Carl was stunned. Nobody had ever spoken to him like that, I am sure: not even in Brooklyn, when he was six years old – in fact, *particularly* not in Brooklyn, where he had obviously been the apple of his mother's eye and could do no wrong.

"Come along, Annie," said Carl, standing up. "Steve!" he said, as if calling a dog. "I'm not standing for this." And they marched out of the room.

"Right," said Adrian to all of us, his production crew, who were staring at each other in disbelief. "We're going on strike!"

Adrian, it has to be said, had a short fuse when he was opposed by someone he had cause to distrust and resent. He had also learned some good union labor tactics at the BBC: remember, this was still the 1970's, when strikes seemed like daily events in the UK, and even occurred from time to time at the BBC.

Adrian demanded that the entire production team should "down tools", walk out and go home immediately, at 11a.m. He sent a message up to Chuck Allen, KCET's vice-president in charge of the production, saying that the situation was "unacceptable", and then he led us all out of the building. Such was his own charisma, that all of us followed him – except for Jim Ross and Cherie in the accounts office, who were not at all sure where their loyalties should lie.

"Shut the door, Cherie", said Jim. "It'll all blow over."

KCET's Chuck Allen had been showing signs of stress for some time before this confrontation. He would come into the production offices very early in the morning, before anyone was in, and riffle through the papers on everyone's desk, trying to find out "what's really going on." Judy Flannery found him doing this before dawn one day.

He would then send long, agitated memos to all concerned with the project, usually highlighted with yellow, green and orange markers, questioning every decision and making dire predictions about the shame that would cover all of us, if the project went off the rails. He was, I suppose, in an impossible situation: somewhere between a rock (Adrian Malone) and a hard place (Carl).

The strike lasted just one day. My colleague Geoffrey Haines-Styles felt no particular loyalty to Adrian, whereas I did, since he had been my mentor for many years. Geoff acted as a go-between in negotiations with Carl, Chuck Allen and the KCET board. Geoff could be rather a pompous, over-serious fellow, but he was a pragmatist.

"Let's just get this damned thing done," he said. "It has already consumed more than two years of my life."

The following day, a compromise was hammered out. Carl was in charge of the intellectual material and could veto artistic decisions if he felt very strongly about them, but only if the alternative was feasible, within the remaining budget.

By spring of 1980, a miracle was happening. We all started to view the first extended sequences, and then the first completed shows. Even with rough music-tracks and uncorrected color, they were very beautiful. The spaceship journey to Earth brought tears to many people's eyes. Carl, at his best, was compelling: knowledgeable, caring, even mildly amusing, when he wanted to be. He had learned a lot, during the production, about how to talk to the camera as if it was a friend. The shows felt authentic. We looked at each other with incredulity. We might just pull it off! And of course, the better the programs felt, the better the relationships between the entire team became.

I do not want to leave you with the impression that I disliked my time on Cosmos. For sure, it was stressful, but I have wonderful memories. Forty years later, I think back to the evening when I sat out on the verandah of a bungalow in southern India, watching the stars twinkle with Carl and Annie, talking about the meaning of life. I remember with great joy repeatedly visiting JPL, the Jet Propulsion Laboratory in Pasadena, near our studios: we saw and filmed the very first live pictures beamed to earth from the Voyager spacecraft as it flew past Jupiter: incredible color images, with Carl as excited as that six-year-old Brooklyn boy once again.

Carl loved to remind everyone that he and Ann had been invited to design the official plaque on the side of Voyager. This was apparently mankind's message to alien civilizations. It depicted images of the DNA spiral, of Earth's position in the Solar System, of musical notations from Bach and scientific formulae. It was meant to give any little green men it might meet some idea of who the creatures were, that had sent this contraption into the furthest reaches of space.

It also featured an outline of a naked man and woman, both lacking any specific genitals – because, after all, this was a national family-oriented project, and you can't have pornography floating round in space, can you? I often wondered how an alien civilization, if it ever stumbled across Voyager, would figure out exactly how we reproduced. By humming a tune from Bach, perhaps?

Finally, in the late summer of 1980, after a grueling few months, the project was finished, just in time for the inaugural launch event at the Griffith Park Observatory. Luminaries from Hollywood mixed with senior executives from Atlantic Richfield, the chief sponsor, and nabobs from Public Television.

Carl and Annie were there in their splendor, surrounded by a swarm of celebrities and journalists. Adrian Malone had found a tuxedo that just about fitted him and was settling down to an evening of serious drinking and schmoozing. Limos arrived, champagne flowed, and we all looked down on the lights of Los Angeles, twinkling like yellow stars all the way to the horizon. Inside the observatory, a huge screen and massive speakers showed off Episode One to its very best effect.

The next night, the show premiered nationally on the PBS network, to an audience of more than ten million. In 1980, there were still only four national networks (NBC, CBS, ABC and PBS), and no cable channels or internet. *Cosmos* was a huge national event. Carl was on the cover of both *Time* and *Newsweek* magazines. And the reviews, thank God, were really pretty good. Carl's more saccharine moments were not to everyone's taste, but the sheer size and magnificent vision of the project swept away most of the commentators.

The show went on to be seen in more than a hundred countries. There were *Cosmos* calendars, *Cosmos* T-shirts, *Cosmos* astrolabes sold by mail from the *Cosmos* Store, controlled entirely by Carl and Annie. The accompanying book has sold around one hundred million copies worldwide and is reputed to be the best-selling science book ever published, anywhere. Even in England, where people usually hate documentaries narrated or presented by Americans – I mean, what do *Americans* know about anything? – it was at least admired for its ambition.

Carl continued to stay in the limelight, increasingly focusing on the dangers of nuclear winter, if an unthinkable international atomic war were to unfold. As it happened, the world got increasingly worried about the opposite effect – global warming – if climate change were to run wild.

After Carl's untimely death in the 1990's, Ann Druyan continued to be his torchbearer, and eventually persuaded Fox TV to create a re-make of the series, presented by Neil DeGrasse Tyson, thirty-five years after the original. For Ann, this has been a lifetime's work, nobly carried out, keeping Carl's torch aflame.

One final thought, however, on a slightly less elevated note: Carl and Annie reaped almost all the royalties from this entire worldwide effort, and the production team, technicians and artists (to my knowledge) reaped none. Ah well, we should have had better agents. Or any agents at all... And who knew it would be such a blockbuster?

But then, we documentary-makers tell ourselves that we do it all for the love of our craft, do we not? I think we realize that we are extremely fortunate to have picked this as our craft, or even our career. It sure beats real life. And you don't have to wear a suit.

▪▪

8. FROM WALTER CRONKITE TO JOSEPH CAMPBELL

While visiting England and my family in the foggy, icy depths of January 1979, I stayed at a welcoming pub in the ancient Cotswold village of Coln St. Aldwyns. I was there to set up the *Cosmos* "H.G. Wells" scene for Episode Five, complete with the steam-driven fairground I've mentioned, which we were planning to shoot as soon as spring had arrived. Suddenly, in the bar, my name was called by the landlord: he shouted over the hubbub of the pub's regulars, enjoying their pints of nice warm beer at ten o'clock on a Tuesday night.

"Mr. Kennard? Mr. Kennard? Telephone call for you. It appears your wife is having a baby."

There was complete silence in the pub, and all eyes turned suspiciously towards me. Was I a negligent father, or what? Drinking pints in a pub while my wife was giving birth? I could not believe my ears. My wife Helen was expecting a second daughter, but she was not due for at least six weeks. I grabbed the phone: a nurse told me that Helen was having contractions and had been admitted to Charing Cross Hospital in West London.

Outside the pub, the roads were icy, and all ways out of Coln St. Aldwyns led up a steep hill, it seemed. My rental car had no chance of making it out of the village.

"We'll give him a push," suggested one of the regulars, after the situation had been much discussed by all present. "Bill, you got your tractor here?"

A red-faced local worthy stepped forward, wiping the foam of the beer from his mouth.

"Rental car, is it?" he asked. "Right-oh then. A couple of scrapes and dents won't matter. Get in!"

I hastily paid my bill, packed my bag and left, with the sound of cheers, laughter, applause and catcalls ringing in my ears. Bill was as good as his word: his tractor pushed me all the way up the hill. He gave me a cheery wave and left me to drive very, very slowly along what amounted to a skating rink, all the way to the A40, the main road to London.

I was just in time to be present at the birth of Juliet. Being significantly premature (certainly by the standards of 1979), she was popped into an incubator for the first few days, to make sure she could survive on her own. It was incredible to realize that I now had two daughters, Amanda and Juliet, and it brought a big issue right to the foreground: my family was in England. How could I possibly remain in America?

I had sincerely hoped that *Cosmos* would allow me to have my cake and eat it: to further my career, have fun, and still maintain my family ties. But, as each month went by, I felt myself being drawn further and further away from London.

For sure, return visits to London could provide fantastic fun: I remember to this day chasing Amanda through the Science Museum, when she was just two years old, and having her picture printed out onto a calendar by one of those new-fangled things, a computer. I remember, on another visit, how the plane from Los Angeles was diverted from London to Prestwick in Scotland because of fog. I then had to take a special, unheated train for the overnight run to London. I jumped onto the very first tube train of the morning, and walked home across Hammersmith Bridge in the fog, arriving at the Barnes house at 6 a.m. in the dark, like a burglar. There, I found Helen's Christmas tree lights glowing like a beacon of welcome. I still really felt that this was "home."

To be frank, however, the Barnes house never really appealed to me. Was it too big? Too bourgeois? Too traditional? Too cold – especially in the north-facing front bedroom? It always felt like 'Helen's House': she had found it, she had redesigned and rebuilt the back of it, she loved it. But it never seemed cozy, and I never found any room or any corner that I could call my own and hide away. We had a steady stream of nannies and au pairs and lodgers to help pay for the mortgage. There was no privacy, and with the constant visits from Helen's vast family, it felt more like a boarding house or a transit lounge between flights.

I am afraid to say that it always seemed to be a mess, too. I am not a very tidy person, but the kitchen would look like the aftermath of the Battle of the Somme much of the time. Finding and sterilizing Juliet's baby bottle under two days' worth of dishes was a daunting task.

Perhaps my student adventures in Bloomington or my filming adventures for the Galbraith series had given me too much of a taste for the USA. Perhaps the apartment in LA, with its heated swimming pool and bikini'd residents, was a little too enticing. But I cannot place the blame on anyone or anything but myself: I just fell out of love with marriage, domestic bliss, suburban London, the weather, the whole kit and caboodle – and eventually, with Helen too, I am afraid.

Finally, I realized that it was only sex and the children that held us together, and honestly, that was not quite enough. Of course, I always ached to see Amanda and Juliet. Later, they were able to visit me, coming unaccompanied on a giant 747, all the way to the US. But increasingly, the thought of being married in Barnes was like scraping my nails across a blackboard. I was a late developer, in my teens. So, too, in my adulthood: it turned out that I was not ready for marriage till I was forty.

We saw a marriage counselor, who was pleasant but (we both agreed) ineffective. Things went from bad to worse. The final straw was a short holiday that Helen and I and the children took in the Cotswolds at Easter in 1980. We decided to invite our best man Nigel Rees and his wife Sue to join us and, subconsciously, I suppose, to help keep the peace. We shared a quaint old rented house, and Helen and I never stopped arguing. It was an embarrassment for all concerned. Nigel and Sue left early. I think that was the moment when Helen and I both realized that the marriage was over. We started formal separation proceedings soon after.

So, what was I to do when *Cosmos* was over? I had various bits of furniture and possessions in LA, which I stored with a friend. The BBC had been adamant: when I finished my two-year 'attachment' to *Cosmos* – the longest attachment they had ever given anybody, it transpired – I was to return to London and await further orders. The penalty for not doing so was to forfeit my BBC pension and my good name for ever, they said.

I horse-traded and wriggled, and the BBC gave me six weeks off for good behavior – actually, for 'accrued holiday allowance.' Then they agreed that I could give in my notice and resign at Christmas. But, meanwhile, I had to sit at a desk in Kensington House, Shepherd's Bush, for six weeks and twiddle my thumbs and "try and make myself useful."

Well, of course, that meant that I spent most of my time chattering with film editors and other producer friends, trading scandalous stories about Carl Sagan for bits of BBC gossip that I had missed while away. And of course, the rest of my time was spent in the Kensington House Club bar...

On the very last evening of my very last day at the BBC, on December 18, 1980, the documentary film editors held their annual party in that bar. It was a famously louche event. Not only was there a no-holds-barred disco and soft lighting, but the editors showed their completely uncensored annual blooper reel. They offered their guests half an hour or more of the choicest and most libelous moments, which had been cut out of BBC programs during the previous year.

There were images of government ministers saying "Oh bugger!" and much worse, celebrities in a studio circus show slipping and sliding in elephant shit, famous presenters losing their wigs in a high wind, every sort of hilarious misfortune that can happen in TV production. Jim Latham had even managed to sneak a couple of extracts from the *Cosmos* "Program Fourteen" into the reel, to complete the merry picture by having Carl Sagan make a fool of himself, to much ribald and drunken applause.

Five minutes after the screening of the blooper reel, as the disco music was starting, I met the person who would eventually become my second wife. At that instant of course, and for the next five and a half years, she was Liz Ross, a highly attractive blonde in tight jeans, who was sitting at the bar, commiserating with a couple of girlfriends about a boyfriend she had just dumped.

"Would you like a dance?" I said – nothing if not an original chat-up line. "I'm David Kennard."

"Yes, I know," she said. "I spotted you five or six years ago, but you went off and married Helen Jay."

As we danced, I realized that this was almost exactly the spot where I had met Helen – also a highly attractive blonde in tight jeans – in 1973. My office in Religious Programmes (TV) had been right across the corridor. And now...? Another blonde stunner? Ah, the magic of BBC's Kensington House bar!

"This is my very last evening at the BBC," I said to Liz, to make myself sound special and also, perhaps, a little deserving of sympathy – and even a little bit more than sympathy, perhaps...

"Shall we go and have dinner?" I asked – still not winning points for originality.

We got our hats and coats and dived out into the cold, dark streets of Shepherd's Bush. My memory is that we walked half a mile to a romantic bistro in Holland Park Avenue, called (appropriately) *La Pomme d'Amour*, but Lizzie remembers it being the place next door. Whichever it was, we both seemed smitten with each other, and when I suggested she might like to "come back to my place for a coffee" (small talk obviously not being my forte), she surprisingly said yes.

This placed me in a bit of a quandary. Since I was no longer *persona grata* in the family home, I had been camping in my friend Alasdair Clayre's house, in St. John's Wood. It was Alasdair who had offered me the job recording factory workers and boatmen, back in my Oxford days, and we had remained friends. Having had several liaisons and break-ups in his own adventurous life, he understood the problem of being separated from a wife and effectively homeless in London. So he had kindly offered me a bed, a chair and a chest-of-drawers in his huge, cold, empty, unremodeled Victorian pile in northwest London.

When English people say a house is cold, they really mean it's very, very cold. and often very, very damp. There was no heating of any kind in Alasdair's house. The warmest you could get was to sit in the hottest of water in an old enamel tub in the bathroom – itself a greenhouse-like appendage at the side of the house. Or else go down to the kitchen, boil a kettle and sit in the steam. This was the nirvana to which I had invited my newfound friend Liz Ross, soon to be called Lizzie for the rest of her life.

If she had been sensible, or a little less relaxed from the alcohol, I'm sure she would have immediately canceled the date, or insisted that we went back to her place, a comfortable, centrally heated flat she owned five miles away in Acton. But, brave girl, she took her chances in 23, Alma Square, St. John's Wood. To spare your blushes, gentle reader, I will leave the story there, except to say that there is one infallible way that nature has devised, for two people to keep each other warm. It worked, and it worked all night long.

The next day, we both went our different ways. Lizzie had arrangements with friends and family, and I went straight to the country to meet up with Helen and the girls for a Christmas carol service (!). My head was in a whirl. Until the previous night, I would have said that my established girlfriend was Janelle Balnicke, the good-looking and intelligent Associate Producer on *Cosmos*, who had accompanied me to the premiere gala in Los Angeles. But now?

•••

I spent Christmas partly with Helen, Amanda and Juliet, and partly with my parents out in the country town of Winslow, to which they had retired. I took long walks with my mother through the bleak English fields, along muddy footpaths, and talked about the future.

I was very confused. I had effectively left Helen, and my room in Alasdair Clayre's house was gaunt and virtually empty. So London was not an easy option, even though my young children were there. At the same time, I had started an affair in Los Angeles with Janelle Balnicke. What was I to do about that, now that Lizzie had entered my life with a bang, so to speak?

Early in the New Year, I needed to return to Los Angeles, to tie up various loose ends on *Cosmos* and look for work. After all, I had officially handed in my notice at the BBC, and they had only paid me up to Christmas. I also needed to tell Janelle that I had fallen in love with someone else. Since I had only been away three weeks, this came as quite a shock to her, and she was not pleased at all. Any idea of moving in with her, which had been an option only a month before, disappeared. I was officially sacked from my position as principal boyfriend.

I looked through the apartments-for-rent section of the Los Angeles Times and the free papers. Before the internet, it was the only way to do such things. I spied an intriguing five-line advertisement for one-bedroom apartments in a 'clothing optional' building, as the ad coyly put it. The location was not bad: Mount Washington, on the way to Pasadena. And the price was right. So I went to have a look.

My emotional state was pretty confused, of course. I can always claim that as an excuse. But actually, 4686 Woodside Drive was quite a remarkable institution. It was a fairly large apartment complex, inhabited entirely by nudists.

I was met at the outer gateway by a plump and friendly lady called Donna, wearing a tent-sized Hawaiian frock. As soon as we had entered the main concourse – with palm trees, swimming pool, hot tub, reclining chairs, bougainvillea – she cast off her garment and gave me a hearty welcome. We walked past several residents and their guests, of all shapes, colors and sizes – all totally and unabashedly naked. How unlike the home life of our own dear Queen, I thought.

The apartment was just what I needed. The living room was sunny and had a pleasant view over a park. Everyone I met on that first visit was scrupulously polite. But what would my friends think, if I joined a bunch of nudists? I had visions of the *Hollywood Reporter* running a story on "Cosmos Producer in the Buff" – as if they would have cared. I came to the conclusion that I did not have to invite anyone to my apartment, who might be offended by the rules and regulations of the place. So I signed on the dotted line, and 4686 became my new American address.

Lizzie and I had promised to get together as soon as practicable in the new year, but she was still working at the BBC, and had an Arts Features production to complete. Finally, she had accumulated a month's leave, and said she was very excited about coming to visit me in LA. Should I tell her about the strange customs of 4686? I decided not to. I did not want her to think that she was taking up with a crazy guy or a pervert.

In late spring, she arrived at Los Angeles International Airport – forever LAX in my memory – and I met her in my little Renault 5. It was a gorgeous evening: we drove back to Mount Washington on the scenic route, along Mulholland Drive. This runs east-west along the top of the hills which divide LA from the San Fernando valley to the north – home of the Valley Girls, a particularly vacuous species of suburban teenager who were much in the news at the time. The views were astonishing, and we avoided the traffic. There was no smog, for once.

I drove straight into the underground garage at the apartment complex and used the back stairs to get to my flat. As I had hoped, we met nobody. I had some food and wine ready, and Lizzie was exhausted after her long journey. We went to bed, delighted to be together again.

The following morning, over breakfast, I casually mentioned that the local custom was to swim and use the Jacuzzi without clothes on. So, would she care to have a splash, to wake her up?

She took it all in her stride and wore a light robe to get to the pool. We tumbled into the Jacuzzi first, where the bubbles protected her modesty to some extent. An affable black lady wished us both a very good morning, her sizeable breasts riding on top of the water like beach toys. Then Lizzie decided that the hot tub was a little too hot, stepped out and dived into the swimming pool, where she did a dozen lengths. Unfazed, she returned to get her towel.

"What a great place," she said, and slipped back into the hot tub.

I could hardly believe my good luck: perhaps she imagined that all of Los Angeles lived liked this? Or perhaps she was a wild girl at heart? Who knew?

We spent a blissful month together in California. First stop was San Diego, where we had a mutual ex-BBC friend – Stuart Harris and his partner Gayle Kidder. Poor Lizzie caught strep throat and had to go to the Emergency Room at great expense: she was seeing all sides of California life. Then we had a blissful two weeks, gently driving up the coast, making no reservations, stopping off at the weirdest places. At Los Alamos, a tiny hamlet on the old stagecoach road to the north, we took a room at a one hundred and twenty-year-old inn, shared a common dining table with a dozen other guests, and then found that they had a hot tub too. Once more, clothing was optional.

Later, we stayed in an old motel, perched on the cliffs near the extravagant Hearst Castle – which we visited, of course. It is certainly worth the detour, as the Michelin guide would say, but I won't tire you with a description here. Back in the motel, overlooking the Pacific, we both decided to tell each other our entire life story, and made a detailed list of all the people we had loved and left – all the encounters we could remember, even the one-night stands. I was very much in love: to find a girl who was so open, so unembarrassed about all her past experiences, seemed like a gift from heaven.

Our final destination was San Francisco. I had visited several times before – back in 1968 when a business school student, then in 1975 while filming for *The Age of Uncertainty*, and several times with Janelle Balnicke during *Cosmos*. But this time it felt different. To share it with someone you love is a magical experience. How could I ever have imagined that, six or seven years later, we would decide to live there together?

There were many tears at the airport, when I saw Lizzie off on the London-bound plane. And I was even more confused. Where did I want to live? California or the UK? To live 5000 miles away from Lizzie seemed really crazy. I drove back to Los Angeles as fast as

I could and faced the future. The immediate picture looked grim. I had no work, and not much money saved. What should I do?

Indiana University's Business School had taught me one thing: the usefulness of having a company, so that you could appear to be more than the sum of your parts. So I contacted an old girlfriend from Indiana, Agnes Siedlecki, who had moved to LA. She was now a lawyer and was happy to help me form a California Corporation, through which my income (when I had any) could be passed.

"This will help you to expense your outgoings", she explained with a wry smile, "to the maximum extent permissible by law, that is."

What to call the company? I had always been averse to using my own name in publicity, preferring to shelter behind the names of the famous and respected on-camera hosts I had worked with. So I was not going to call it David Kennard Associates. That would be a complete giveaway that it was really only me. I racked my brain to find the weirdest name possible and came up with Pantechnicon Productions.

Some older English people know what a pantechnicon is: it is a very British name for a large moving van. The name originates with a historic English company, founded two hundred years ago, which stored the furniture and possessions of colonial families, often for many years, while they went out to administer some part of the British Empire. This company required large moving vans, pulled by up to six horses. The vans had the name "The Pantechnicon" painted in large letters on the side, like enormous circus wagons.

"This is perfect", I thought to myself. "I don't know what productions I'll do, but I can toss them all into the van. And I do know that no-one else is going to have chosen the same name, here in America."

That was the problem. In the forty years of Pantechnicon's existence, I have had to explain how to pronounce the word many hundreds of times. It baffles everyone from bank tellers to police officers. It was deemed so unusual by the IRS that they picked us for a random tax audit in 2010 largely, it seemed, because such a bizarrely named company had to be hiding something. English friends appreciated the idea. American friends thought I must be berserk to trade under a name that was unpronounceable.

Slowly, the work trickled in. We won a contract to do a short film with an archaeologist called Vince Scully, out in New Mexico. There was also a famous Brooklyn (later Los Angeles) Dodgers baseball player with the same name, but they were not related. I did enjoy telling American friends that I was "working with Vince Scully", however.

During this uncertain period, I also kept in touch with James Burke, and spent some time helping him develop a new series called *The Day the Universe Changed.* We both wanted to do it together, outside the BBC, but never found the funding. He eventually went back into the BBC to create it with our former *Connections* researcher, John Lynch. I could not face giving up on the USA and returning to the BBC, so there was no work coming in from that direction.

I had also made friends, during the *Cosmos* years, with a delightful Irish American from Michigan called George Colburn. He lived in San Diego, like Stuart Harris, and ran an operation called *Courses by Newspaper* for the University of California's outreach division. He was always looking for good, strong PBS and BBC series, to turn into educational supplements for dozens of newspapers across the US.

George had loved the *Connections* series, was astonished by its popularity, and had worked with James Burke and me to create course materials for community colleges and newspaper supplements. He had a big grant from the National Endowment for the Humanities to do this, and the results were impressive.

From what I have said so far, you might imagine that George Colburn was a stuffy academic. Well, true, he has a PhD in history, of which he is very proud, but his academic persona stops right there. Back in the 1980's, he was an unabashed fun lover. His girlfriend Mary Hellman was a delight. They threw legendary parties, centered on tequila-based cocktails and guacamole, which they made by picking avocados from a splendid old tree in their own backyard. During *Cosmos*, I would often take the train down to San Diego. They would meet me at the station and the fun would begin.

Since George was a PhD at a recognized university, and since he also co-owned a local weekly newspaper back in his native Michigan, I decided to approach him for advice about an ever more pressing issue: my work visa in the United States. KCET had sorted out a 1-year visa for me to work on *Cosmos*, claiming that I was a person of exceptional talent, and was indispensable to the project – and of course that I could walk on water and raise people from the dead for good measure. I had managed to get a one-year extension to that visa, but now the time was fast approaching when I would have to go back to the UK. After that, I'd have to rely on three-month tourist visas to return to the US – not a viable solution.

"Well," said George, ever the problem solver. "We've got to get you a Green Card. That means permanent residency – and I think I know how to do it."

The 'Green Card' is officially called an Alien Registration Card and looks much like a US driver's license. It allows the holder to come and go in and out of the United States indefinitely. Provided you pay your taxes to Uncle Sam and keep out of trouble with the police, it is the perfect solution, at least in the short to medium term. But it is also quite hard to obtain and can cost a fortune in lawyer's fees.

You need to demonstrate, once again, that you are a person of 'exceptional talent', and are indispensable not just to a project, but to a valid organization with long-term goals. Plus, of course, you have to be able to walk on water and raise people from the dead, just as if you were going for a year-by-year visa. I am only half joking. It seemed to be an impossible goal.

"No, it'll be easy enough," said George, ever the optimist. "First, we'll find a good immigration lawyer in LA: they get dozens of people into the US, to work in Hollywood. Second, we'll invent a TV project that's so important and prestigious that only you can do it. You've done *The Ascent of Man* and James Burke's *Connections* and Carl Sagan's *Cosmos*. We can claim that your experience is unique."

"Yes," I said, "But I don't just want another one-year visa. Who is going to commit to me indefinitely, to create this new project?"

"We'll create a new company," said George. "Or rather, I'll create one, because you mustn't officially know anything about it. Then I'll advertise for someone with your unique qualifications."

I was stunned.

"How much will the lawyer cost, for a start?" I asked. "And what will this super-important project be? And how do you create a company that sounds really convincing?"

"The name is the important thing," George insisted. "The image."

After a lot of discussion, George came up with NVC: National Video Communications Incorporated. Later, there was also an IVC: International Video Communications Inc. Both were incorporated in Michigan, where George co-owned a small local newspaper. The agreement was that he and a friend, the other owner of the newspaper, would be the founders of NVC. I would get shares later, when I had been hired. Already, this imaginary communications behemoth put my tiny Pantechnicon Productions in the shade.

Next, we had to dream up a grand project. This took a little longer, but we came up eventually with a multi-part TV series – plus book and all the extras – called *The Messengers*. This would describe the past, present and future of human communications: from the Neanderthal grunt to the telecommunications satellite. The internet, which we did not foresee, did not yet exist, of course.

George pulled all the strings at his disposal. He knew a retired Federal Communications Commissioner, an enjoyable, puckish character called Abbott Washburn, who agreed to back our plan. Abbott put George in touch with Walter Cronkite, at that time by far the most famous name in non-fiction television. Indeed, we later went to meet Cronkite at CBS, during the last week he was presenting the nightly news. 'Uncle Walter' agreed to help, by being a senior consultant to the project. This was akin to getting the Pope to baptize your baby.

Abbott also happened to know the eminent science-fiction writer Arthur C. Clarke personally – indeed, he seemed to know half the interesting people in the communications field. Clarke responded enthusiastically to our project: he said he would love to help create it.

"Good heavens" was my immediate response. "Only in America..."

Abbott himself promised to support George's new company, but he said that a few more prestigious names might help, to buttress my application for the Green Card.

"Who do you know, David?" asked George.

Dr Bronowski, alas, had passed away, and his widow Rita was still telling the world that it was his over-exertion on *The Ascent of Man* that had killed him. So no luck there. James Burke was English, so no help there either. I knew and had kept in touch with Lynn White, the Emeritus Professor of History at UCLA, who had underpinned *Connections* with his brilliance and advice. Was he eminent enough?

"Yes", said George, "He might be helpful. But what about Sagan?"

Alas, I had to explain that I was not likely to get a five-star rating from Carl. There had always been two camps on *Cosmos* – Sagan's gang versus Adrian Malone's gang – and I was irrevocably tarred with the Malone brush. Besides which, Carl had refused point blank to collaborate with George and UCSD to do a *Courses by Newspaper* version of *Cosmos*, wanting to retain all control of the project himself. So George Colburn was not keen on Carl either.

But what about John Kenneth Galbraith? We had always got along famously – why, he had even spoken wittily at my wedding. So I wrote to him and asked if he would support me in my application for a Green Card. I got an immediate and positive response from his long-standing assistant, Andrea.

"He'll send you a letter," she said. "It could be useful."

Galbraith, as I have mentioned, was not only an Emeritus Professor at Harvard. He had worked in a senior position in the US Government during World War Two, in charge of an office that set price controls for essential commodities. Thanks to his ongoing TV talk shows, arguing with the right-winger William Buckley, he had remained a famous public figure. He was a former US ambassador to India. *The Age of Uncertainty* was the least of his credits.

Two weeks later, we received a letter typed on the august business paper of Harvard University. It was magisterial in its focus and brevity.

"To whom it may concern," wrote Galbraith, "I have no doubt that if David Kennard were to pursue his career on the United States, he would make a substantial contribution not only to the nation's intellectual life, but also to its economic well-being. His projects will employ many people. His leadership will be significant. I have no hesitation in recommending him for permanent resident status."

I detected the delicious Galbraithian irony in his knowing over-statement of my talents. The Immigration and Naturalization Service, happily, did not. But even our immigration attorney, Larry Krakauer, was impressed. He looked at the sheaf of recommendations from Abbott Washburn, Professor Lynn White and JKG.

"This should be an open-and-shut case", he said. "Leave it to me."

In the interim, however, George Colburn had to advertise "my" job in suitable media outlets: *Variety* magazine, the *Hollywood Reporter* and a couple of nationally respected newspapers. He then had to interview several potential candidates, who could all claim to speak several languages, had worked on prestigious TV series and so on. It was scary how good some of them were. But finally, after a proper time for thought and due consideration, National Video Communications sent me a letter saying that I had been selected for the position. The doorway to the Green Card was open, and in a couple of months I duly received it.

My first task was to create the major series we had concocted, called *The Messengers.* I will describe this later, in Chapter 18, when I talk about working with Arthur C. Clarke – a brilliant, funny, likeable man who excelled in both science and fiction.

Meanwhile there were summers to enjoy with George. I spent riotous times in Michigan during the early 1980's, often helping to represent George's local newspaper on a float in the Horton Bay July the Fourth parade, with every conceivable amusement – drinking, partying, dressing up – before, during and after.

Then there were Michigan winter visits: with George and his friends, I would go cross-country skiing in the moonlight as part of a big group, with a rendezvous at a roaring campfire, where we would roast hot dogs and steaks. We went ice-fishing on Lake Charlevoix, a sizeable stretch of water which allowed dozens of Michiganders – all men, of course – to erect tiny hovels over holes in the ice, and then spend all night, pretending to fish while they got royally drunk.

We once made the mistake of leaving our hut, to visit other nearby hovels on the ice, and then were unable to locate our own home base. We nearly froze to death going round and round in circles, looking for the kerosene lamp and tiny hut that was ours. Simple pleasures, but great memories, and quite unlike anything I had ever encountered in Europe.

∎∎∎

But real paid work had to pay for all the shenanigans in Michigan, as well as contribute to my children's and ex-wife's upkeep in London, so I was alert to every opportunity. One of these was *The Heart of the Dragon* – see Chapter 9. The other was a California-based project featuring the renowned mythologist and teacher, Joseph Campbell.

Out of the blue, I got a call from Stuart Brown, a Jungian psychoanalyst who knew the power of myth and storytelling. Goodness knows, he has had enough stories to tell about his own life – but more about that later. He was working with Bill Free, a young producer who was a Campbell devotee. Bill had tragically lost his original co-producer in a location accident. There, but for the grace of God, go all of us, who venture out into the world to make documentary films. Bill was now being sustained by Stuart Brown's wisdom and life experience, but they needed to find an accredited director, who might help them bring their Joseph Campbell film to fruition.

Stuart and Bill had initially approached Adrian Malone, my old mentor, and offered him the job. But there had been a classic clash of the titans, when Campbell and Malone first met. Neither man was known for the small size of his ego. Campbell felt, with much justification, that he had deeply researched his subject, had popularized the study of myth, and was internationally respected. Adrian, for his part, could be a great editor of scripts and director of talent. However, he was determined, after the bruising wars with Carl Sagan, to have creative control, no matter what.

Their meeting was destined to failure. No-one who knew both men would have been surprised. They both had a strain of Irish stubbornness, charisma by the bucketful, a deep sense of their own self-worth, and the gift of the gab. which is either a delight or a pain in the neck, depending on how many glasses of Jameson's or Bushmills you have had.

So Stuart and Bill saw me as the next best thing: I had worked with Malone, Sagan and Bronowski, and I was still only thirty-something, so I might know my place. Stuart Brown could assume the position of resident graybeard, acknowledging Campbell's mastery of mythology, while himself pulling all the practical strings behind the scenes. So, it was decided: I was hired, and Pantechnicon Productions with me.

Joseph Campbell had spent a lifetime acquiring a fervent following, which he still has, many years after his death. He had been a Professor at Sarah Lawrence College and was legendary for his ability to charm young ladies into sitting, rapt in wonder, at his feet. He would re-tell tales of the knights of the Arthurian round table or the elegant mysteries of the Bhagavad Gita. He was famously adept at seducing an audience – particularly an audience of one – with twinkling eyes, witty asides and deep feeling.

There were those who disliked him. They took exception to the fact that he hated the three great monotheistic religions, largely because they had attempted to destroy the rich, fascinating, pantheistic world of native peoples – and indeed of Hindus, Medes, Persians, Greeks and Romans.

Some saw in Campbell's attitude a deep anti-Semitism, though I never experienced this directly. He simply hated the idea of a unitary God – Jahweh – who created and controlled the universe. Jews had invented this tyrant, he explained. Christians had added a layer of complexity, with their Holy Trinity, but at least were prone to bouts of romantic dreaming, such as the Holy Grail mythology. And as for Muslims, well... They did not even allow representation of the human form in their art and architecture. Where was mythology in Islam?

Joe had already been popularized by a series of interviews with the ever-present TV host Bill Moyers, on PBS. In a cozy studio, Bill had quizzed Joe about his beliefs and his work, with occasional cutaways to artwork from Japan, Africa, Medieval Europe or wherever. Frankly, I find this kind of program format intensely dull. There is no music, no drama, no sense of atmosphere or place. Bill Moyers and his wife and team had created, over many years, an interview factory, churning out dozens of similar shows with popular academic personalities. I respected Moyers for taking on tough subjects (his *Death and Dying* was inspirational), but his chuckling, avuncular approach seemed patronizing and dated.

We decided to create the exact opposite of a Moyers show. We would try to capture the romance of Joe by filming a long weekend at the famous Esalen Institute on the wild California coast at Big Sur. We'd invite a range of bright people – Rick Tarnas, Robert Bly and others – to question, challenge and joke with him. Stuart Brown – always in character – also decorated the room with several attractive women, ranging from late teens to subtle maturity, to ask questions, entertain Joe and provide a supportive audience.

The plan was to follow their days: from early morning, shrouded by fog, to delicious lunches, provided by Esalen's great cooks and extensive vegetable gardens; plus hikes into the redwood groves and trips to the rocky beach and the dramatic hot springs, halfway down the cliff face. Esalen itself was a mythic place, site of an ancient Native American ritual ground and hot springs. What better venue?

Then, in the evening, we would huddle round a crackling log fire, cameras still running, and listen to Joe tell stories – ancient epics and tall tales from around the world, rich in detail, peppered with jokes. He explained how George Lucas had worked with him, weaving strands from these ancient stories into the plots and characters of *Star Wars*. Basic stories, Joe explained, had similar structures all over the world: take the many versions of the life-quest for example, or the classic tales of boy meets girl, boy loses girl, boy wins girl back. From New Orleans to New Guinea, that one wows the crowds and always has, Joe maintained. So we invited the audience to sit still, and listen.

"Once upon a time," Joe would start, and everyone was hanging on his every word... What on earth could go wrong with this, as a film?

Well, two things went wrong: one in the short term, one in the long term. In the short term, an unwelcome event paid handsome dividends. The mother and father of winter storms hit the California Coast, after we had been there a day or two. Torrential rain triggered landslides on the coastal Highway 1, both to the north of Esalen and to the south. For several more days, we were essentially prisoners on the premises: a glorious fate, because it meant that we had more time to film and to deepen our enjoyment and understanding.

When the storm had done its worst, the poet Robert Bly, later to achieve wide fame as the author of *Iron Man*, clambered down over the rocks to the glistening beach with Joe. As the clouds cleared, our audience of lovely women were filmed in mythical surroundings: the newly returned sun had warmed the wings of a host of Monarch butterflies, beaten down by the rain. They flitted through the redwoods in their thousands, creating dreamlike scenes of paradise. Joe told more stories, and still more stories: he loved it, and so did everyone else.

What went wrong, for me, in the longer term was how the film turned out. At Esalen, we filmed – in real time – nearly a week with Joseph Campbell: an incredible privilege. Friendships were formed, the pace was relaxed, Joe was wonderfully open and witty on camera. It had the feel of a genuine retreat, an extraordinary life-experience, drawing on Joe's wisdom and insight with no sense of hurry. He took us into a mythic land – a land of dragons and medieval knights, of vision quests and dreadful curses, and Esalen, in all weathers, was the perfect location for such an otherworldly journey.

I very much wanted to keep the film structured as it had happened – as a linear experience, unfolding and revealing new riches, new surprises, fresh wonder and excitement as the week went on. But it was not to be. The editing had to be delayed, while final funds were raised, and I had to join my next big project, *The Heart of the Dragon* (see next chapter). In my absence, there was much discussion between Stuart Brown, the Executive Producer, Bill Free, whose project this originally was, and my former girlfriend and Associate Producer, Janelle Balnicke, who was part of the team.

Stuart decided that the most promising and best-selling way forward was to make the film into a biography of Joe Campbell, called *The Hero's Journey* – the title of one of his best-loved books. This meant more filming with Joe, by Janelle and Bill, in Hawaii. They added biographical details and more interviews with other people. What emerged, to me, was a capable but by no means very special sixty-minute film for PBS and distribution on VHS tape and (later) DVD.

I was very sad. I did not pull a hissy fit and ask to have my name taken off the credits. After all, the delay in completion meant that I simply had not been available, to be part of the discussions: that was my hard luck. But I remain convinced that the Esalen-only film would have been a mythic adventure in and of itself, rather than the workmanlike biopic, which was eventually produced.

■ ■

9. THE HEART OF THE DRAGON

Back in the good old days, long before affordable personal computers or email, there were phone calls, letters and that newfangled marvel, the fax machine. In the early 80's, faxes were still the new kid on the block. When they came through, as likely as not, a bell would ring, or a buzzer would sound, as it did on an old teleprinter. The fax would print out very slowly, onto slippery, heat-sensitive paper, which had a tendency to roll itself up into a small, scruffy scroll-shaped object, as if it were destined for archiving in the Alexandrian Library.

At the time, I was sharing an office in Palos Verdes, a pleasant coastal suburb of LA, with Alan Gabriel, an Australian businessman, and his business manager, Pat Russell. She had agreed to do the accounts and some secretarial work for me, too. Indeed, my modest desk was the world headquarters of my original company, Pantechnicon Productions Incorporated or PPI as we called it, to save time. Pat's favorite comment was that PPI was a "one man and a dog" company, which of course, she said, made her the dog, "but never the bitch."

One day down there in LaLaLand, a fax came through to the office, addressed to me. It was virtually unreadable, because it had been hand-written, not typed. And the handwriting was so bad that it could only belong to a practicing doctor or an Oxford professor.

"Do you know an Alison Clayte?" asked Pat.

It was her job, back in those halcyon days, to do such secretarial tasks as ripping and reading the faxes. Alison Clayte? I was baffled.

"Well, she says she wants you to go to China," said Pat, "At least, I think that's what she says."

I took one look at the handwriting and knew it was from my old Oxford friend, Alasdair Clayre. I had been renting one cold room from him in London for a couple of years – that room where Lizzie and I had first got to know each other. But Alasdair and I had not worked together since I was an undergraduate at Oxford. What new ploy was this? An offer to go to China?

I tried phoning Alasdair in London: no reply. Alasdair had always despised newfangled ideas like answering machines. I tried faxing him: no luck, because he had no fax machine. He must have sent his fax from a post office or an office-supply shop. But a few days later, an aerogramme plopped into my mailbox.

Do you remember aerogrammes? They were always pale blue, and made of the same, ultra-lightweight paper as airmail envelopes and writing paper, but they consisted of just one sheet, which could be folded several times and glued together, and could then be sent for even less postage than an air letter. Alasdair had hand-written this letter, too, but there was more detail, and it was easier to read when it had not been squeezed through the wires of a 5000-mile telephone cable from London.

The news was incredible. Alasdair had joined forces with the much-respected Peter Montagnon, a British TV producer who had helped to found and run the Open University – the first British institution of higher education open to mature adults. Montagnon, in turn, had been approached by two other producers: Nigel Houghton, a business-school type, and a very mysterious entrepreneur from Hong Kong called Patrick Lui. Together, they had formed a production company, with the backing of London businessman Stephen Keynes, a great nephew of the famous economist John Maynard Keynes. And in their pocket they had a magical, golden key: a key that promised to open up the gates of the People's Republic of China.

I call Patrick "mysterious" because he seemed at first to be the least charismatic and least influential person you could imagine. But he had his tentacles deep into the British regime in Hong Kong, as well as deep into China. He was a wheeler-dealer, a clever salesman of projects of every sort. He had the knack of being able to smell a deal, long before it was obvious what the deal might be. He was therefore a quintessential Hong Kong guy, through and through. It is because of him that the West first saw China revealed on film with any semblance of compassion and objectivity.

It appeared that Patrick Lui was related to a VIP in the Chinese People's Liberation Army. The PLA man had let Patrick know that the Chinese Government might be open to an approach from a small, fully independent western production company, to create the world's first comprehensive documentary series about China. The Beijing government had consistently rejected overtures from large, established producers like the BBC or CBS, no doubt concerned about western government spying, or about losing control of the project.

The chosen group would have permission to visit all parts of the vast country, which had been almost entirely closed to outsiders since the shutters came down, after the triumph of communism in 1949. However, under their new leader, Deng Xiao Ping, the Chinese apparently wanted to open up very cautiously to the West.

This was an astonishing development. Could we really trust that Patrick Lui's relative could fix up everything in China? We underestimated the political and economic power of the People's Liberation Army. They were not just a bunch of soldiers – no, make that "a vast horde of soldiers." As we were later to learn, they owned factories, even whole industries. They often provided a counterbalance to the stifling orthodoxy of the Central Communist Party in Beijing.

They were also hand-in-glove with Xin Hua, the Foreign Press Bureau. Together, they were tiptoeing towards the massive change, which was to transform China over the last forty years from the repressive control of Mao's Cultural Revolution to the glittering state capitalism of the China we know today. But the first steps were only baby steps, and we would have to agree to co-produce with the gargantuan CCTV: China Central Television, which entirely controlled electronic media and broadcasting in pre-internet China. How would *that* collaboration work out?

The first step, for me, was to return to London, to join this historic project. I thought that everything was going to work out brilliantly in my love life, too. I called Lizzie and invited her for lunch at Julie's, a restaurant we both liked, in the back streets of Holland Park.

"I'm back." I said. "Now we can resume where we left off. No more of this five-thousand-miles-apart stuff. I can be based in London."

"Well," she said, "That's unfortunate. I've just agreed to join five other people, to sail across the Atlantic and deliver a boat to the Caribbean. And from there my plan is to hitch a ride round the West Indies, and onwards through the Panama Canal to Los Angeles, and possibly right round the world."

Lizzie tells me now that she hoped I would say, "Oh my God, you can't do that," and get down on bended knee and ask her to stay in London and marry me. But there was one problem: under the tortuously slow-moving British divorce system, I was still going to be married to Helen for another couple of years, however much we were technically separated.

So I said, rather limply, "Oh no! What incredible bad luck", or something to that effect. "But what an exciting trip that will be for you!"

Lizzie promptly turned on her heel and made her final arrangements to sail across the Atlantic – which she did, in a forty-foot yacht. She has always been decisive, but I have to say that I was stunned. Somehow I had managed to screw up my relationship with both Lizzie and Janelle, and was left with… hard work, as compensation.

I turned my attention to the China project and reported for duty at the elegant eighteenth-century offices of the production company, in London's Fitzroy Square. There I met the team: the executive producer, Peter Montagnon, who would direct three of the ten films; the other director, Mischa Scorer (Peter Montagnon's choice, and a talented and witty man); the senior researcher Jung Chan – strikingly beautiful, and later to become famous as the author of the book *Wild Swans*; Nigel Houghton, who performed the role of business manager and would direct one film; Alasdair Clayre, who directed the research, corralled the eminent academic experts and wrote the book of the series; and Anne Rowe, the lovely, no-nonsense associate producer, whom Mischa Scorer later married.

I think there are many reasons why the films turned out to be as remarkable as they did. One of them was the personality of Peter Montagnon. A courteous but impish smile often hovered around his lips. He was a true mandarin – a senior bureaucrat who had honed his skills in the BBC and Open University: immensely diplomatic, always understated, very British but cunning as a fox. After many negotiations with the Chinese in Beijing, they paid him the ultimate compliment of calling him "inscrutable." Coming from a Chinese bureaucrat, that is praise indeed.

There was a rumor that Peter had spent time with the British security services too – and perhaps was still working for them under cover, but that was never proven. But he certainly struck me, as had John Lang many years before in Religious Programs (TV), as one of John Le Carré's inventions.

The essence of our approach, Montagnon told the Chinese, was not to make journalistic films, which would aim to dig up all the worst aspects of modern China. Nor was it to make propaganda films, which would suggest that everything in China smelt of roses.

"After all," said Peter to the Chinese, "You make your own very excellent propaganda films, and you don't need our help to do that."

The first key to success, he insisted, was that we would take the "middle way": we would film everyday Chinese life as it happened, and not go out of our way to pass editorial comments. Taking the Middle Way is a very Chinese expression. It is often how they like to deal with things. Confucius would have approved, and after the excesses of the Cultural Revolution, our hosts were pleased to accept this approach.

The second key to success was Alasdair Clayre's concept for the series. This was brilliant, because it appeared so modest and so unthreatening to the communist government, and yet would reveal many timeless underlying truths about Chinese culture.

Alasdair's idea was that each film would take an everyday Chinese activity – indeed, a universal human activity – and concentrate on how the Chinese did it, both in the 1980's and historically. So we would create films called Eating, Working, Learning, Marrying, Negotiating, Healing, Understanding and so on.

"Who could object to that?" said Peter Montagnon, with his enigmatic smile. "We'll just be flies on the wall, observing everything they choose to show us. And if they show us too many perfect, well-scrubbed stooges, we'll politely decline to film them, and ask to see real life."

The Chinese accepted the concept provisionally – subject to discussions in Beijing. Anne Rowe made travel arrangements and we all set out for Hong Kong. Still under British Rule, this became the standard way for us to enter China. It was like a cultural decompression tank – a halfway house between London and Beijing.

I had the great good fortune of having an old college friend living in Hong Kong: Jeremy Eccles and his Australian wife Kate. The first time we arrived, Jeremy met us at the old Kai Tak airport, in the heart of Kowloon. It had been a scary, bouncy descent in a Jumbo jet: the wings of the 747 seemed to be close enough to the apartments to whip the washing off the balconies, as it landed. The moment we emerged from customs, Jeremy's booming voice rang out.

"Hallo, David. Hallo everyone! Welcome to the Orient. This way, please!"

Jeremy was at least six foot three inches, a good foot taller than the sea of southern Chinese people surrounding him. He was the Director of the English-speaking radio service in Hong Kong, though with a voice as loud as his, he could almost have shouted the news out to the inhabitants, rather than use the radio. He had arranged government cars to take us to our hotel and was excited by the whole project.

When we got to the hotel, Patrick Lui was waiting for us. He was considerably less enthusiastic.

"You can't use British government cars," Patrick said. "The Chinese Government has eyes everywhere. This will have been noted. They'll think we're making a British propaganda film." He was probably right to be careful.

For two days, we got over jet lag and were given a crash course by Patrick about how to behave in China. He taught us simple phrases:

"Hallo. Thank you. Goodbye. My name is…, You are very kind," and of course, "What a great country China is - Zhōngguó shì yīgè wěidà de guójiā."

Also, inevitably, for the endless toasts and serial drunkenness at official banquets:

"Cheers and bottoms up! – Gan Bei!"

Patrick reminded us that most people in China outside central Beijing and Shanghai had not seen a "round-eye" for over thirty years. They would stare at us, follow us, tug at our clothes, or alternatively run away, thinking they had seen ghosts. We should be as calm, quiet and discreet as possible.

Each of us stepped onto the plane for Beijing, carrying a sheaf of research notes, and a new Sony Walkman, just bought in Hong Kong. These were truly revolutionary in 1982: they both recorded and played back cassettes with a 3-D sound quality that was previously unimaginable. We all used them, to play music during interminable train rides and bus journeys, and to make impromptu and wonderful sound recordings of all the places we went.

Arriving at Beijing was like stepping back forty years or more, to my earliest childhood memories: grim, grey, foggy, the air laden with coal dust. The streets were eerily silent: hundreds – no, thousands – of people on bicycles, occasional electric trolleybuses with their eerie whine, the shuffling of countless feet on the sidewalk. Almost everyone wore the standard dark blue or bottle green "Mao suit", usually ruffled and the worse for wear. Occasional people from ethnic minorities, probably in the capital for an official function, stood out self-consciously in colorful robes and pantaloons.

From time to time, a decrepit 1940's-style truck would lumber past, carrying coal or concrete slabs, pouring out black filth from its exhaust. Once or twice, with a motorcycle escort and a blare of horns, a curtained Russian-built limousine would whisk past us, containing some Party VIP or delegation. But mostly, it was bicycles, bicycles, bicycles. Never any perky ringing of bells: the riders somehow avoided each other in total silence.

We were destined to stay more than a week at the infamous Peking Hotel, which still sported the old western name for the capital city. Designed in the Stalinist style, this huge edifice was legendary for its lack of hospitality and dreadful food. Here, we had many meetings with our hosts, discussing the contents of the series and the itinerary for the research trip, which lay ahead of us.

"Your rooms will all have microphones hidden in them", said Patrick, when we went for a walk round the bleak hotel grounds. "So that our hosts can discover what we *really* think about everything. So will the dining-hall, the lounges and the meeting-rooms. Probably the toilets too."

He also warned us that the team from China Central Television would be composed fifty per cent of real, trained producers, cameramen and lighting techs, and fifty per cent of stooges, who were trusted party members.

"Some of them are interpreters, and some pretend to be lighting men or other technicians," said Patrick. "It's standard practice. It's to be expected. All you have to do is to ask the man to actually plug a light in, and you'll soon work out who is the real thing."

When we got down to the negotiations, it was laughably clear who were the stooges, and who was for real. The party hacks all had very shiny, squeaky black shoes, and spoke like a living propaganda pamphlet. One of them, Cheng Ba, was a Tibetan who had been only too pleased to join the invading Communists when they had taken over his country twenty years before. He was a bully, who often threatened us with dire consequences if we tried to film something behind his back. But at least he had a sense of humor, if only when drunk – which he took every opportunity to become, at every meal.

At the opposite extreme was one of our interpreters, Mr. Great Wall (as his name meant, in Chinese). He was the real thing. He was kind, studious, officially trained in languages, and an avid listener to the BBC World Service, which was a punishable offence. At every opportunity, he wanted to learn more colloquial English. On long journeys, I taught him every off-color limerick that I knew, and he wrote them all down in a small notebook. He got so good at telling them, complete with the right stresses and rhythms to highlight the joke, that he would crack us up, during filming, just by saying:

"There once was a Bishop of Birmingham..." Or, "In the Garden of Eden lay Adam..." He claimed he learned more English this way than a month of unauthorized listening to the BBC World Service.

The head of the Chinese team was Lau Lang. "Lau" is a term of reverence applied to someone who is older, wiser, and usually in charge. We could never figure out whether Mr. Lang was a senior Party member or not. He was very familiar with all shades of the English culture and temperament. He and Peter Montagnon would have smiling matches, when we were debating a particularly thorny issue, each trying to outdo the other in diplomacy and inscrutability.

I suspect that Lau Lang had ties to the Chinese secret services, though he later emigrated to northern California, where I met him several times. Perhaps he had escaped a system he had come to hate. Perhaps he was in deep cover. I could never figure it out, but in essence he was a warm and kindly man, who often supported us when local or regional Party bosses were aghast at something we wanted to film.

After a few days we had been driven crazy by the horrors of the Peking Hotel: cold food, surly waitresses, no bar, steaming hot rooms with windows that did not open, dark elevators designed for some Steven King movie... And then suddenly we were offered two days of outings, while our hosts booked the tickets and made the detailed arrangements for our epic research trip.

At that time, tourists were not allowed to go to China. Occasional academic and political visitors or groups were permitted, but that was all. So, when we went to see the Forbidden City, or Tian-an-men Square, or a small section of the Great Wall, we were virtually on our own. The effect was magical, particularly when we got out of the smog of Beijing. There were simple farmers in their fields, draft animals, occasional groups of Young Pioneers (think Hitler Youth crossed with the Boy Scouts) marching around singing songs, flying kites and holding big red banners – like some unbelievable 1940's propaganda film come suddenly to life. This was China: not Taiwan, not Hong Kong, but the real thing.

••

Our research trip took about five weeks and was one of the most exhausting and mind-blowing experiences of my life. We visited almost every corner of China, from the industrial north east to the desert oases of Turfan in the Muslim far west, from Szechuan in the mountainous south west to Xian – the old capital, slap bang in the middle of the country – and Guangzhou (Canton), near which the first New Economic Zone, harbinger of things to come, was being set up at Shenzhen.

We took eighteen-hour overnight train journeys, sometimes hauled by magnificent steam locomotives, with big red stars on the front. We sailed for a night and a day along the Yangtse River, through the Three Gorges – impossible today, because the river has been dammed. We saw the fishermen of Guilin, still using cormorants to catch fish – each with a string round its neck, to prevent them from swallowing the fish. We met ancient calligraphers and visited countless tractor factories. And that is where we had our first arguments with our hosts.

One night in Chengdu, about halfway through the trip, we told our minders and CCTV colleagues that we did not want to see any more specially staged fake "reality." Peter Montagnon was most definite.

"We much appreciate all the effort that you've made to accommodate us," he said, smiling. "But I think we've seen one too many factory with new whitewash and squeaky-clean floors."

"All Chinese factories are maintained to the highest standards," blustered our host, the Tibetan Cheng Ba.

"I think we've also seen too many 'typical' family homes with one-child families, new TVs and propaganda posters on the wall," Peter continued. "I'm not sure that these are entirely representative of general conditions in China. What we have seen from the windows of the train, during our journey, suggests otherwise."

There was silence for a few moments.

"Well, what do you want to see?" asked Lau Lang, ever the diplomat.

"We want to see police stations, mental institutions, workers' apartments, divorce courts, party meetings, coal mines – real life, in other words."

"That may not be possible," ventured Lau Lang.

"Well in that case, we'll need to cancel the rest of the trip," said Peter bravely. "I think we need to make some changes to our itinerary."

There was consternation in the Chinese ranks and no doubt some hurried calls to Beijing. But eventually we got what we wanted. No more perfect pencil-sharpener factories, and lots more out-of-the-way oddities and real people. I was astonished. Once we were far from hotel microphones, we endlessly discussed our hosts' willingness to change the picture they were showing us. Was it because they risked losing face over our dissatisfaction? Was it because Lau Lang realized how wrong things were going, and put his own career on the line by insisting on a greater documentary honesty? We never knew.

Suffice it to say that even Mr. Great Wall, by now our closest friend among the Chinese, was amazed by the change. When walking down the street, far from microphones and stooges, he told us that he had never seen or heard of some of the things we were now being shown.

"I was sent to the countryside during the recent Cultural Revolution," he said, "because I was an intellectual. Even there I did not see some of the things you are now being shown: poor people, sweatshops, bad parts of the cities."

It is to the credit of our hosts, I think, that they changed their plan as they did. We respected them for it, and our documentaries turned out kinder and more compassionate than they might have been.

∎∎

After our return to London, we had copious notes, Polaroid photos and sound recordings to sift through. Now we had to put them all together into a definitive list of films we wanted to make.

Each director (Peter, Mischa and myself) had to choose three of Alasdair's topics – which he had subtly modified, as we went round China, learning more and more. Nigel Houghton offered to produce the final film, pulling everything together and looking at China's future. That final program stood the test of time rather poorly. We had no idea how fast China's future would arrive. Even the film's director, business-savvy Nigel, never imagined that many of China's major cities would outstrip Hong Kong in just thirty years' time.

My films were to be *Eating, Working* and *Understanding*. The latter topic was one of the hardest films I have ever had to make. In fifty-two minutes, I had to explain how the Chinese understood the universe, both in the past and present.

A central concept of Chinese thought is the importance of the balance of Yin and Yang. Simply put, this means the balance of what is darker/damper/lower/more female/more passive on one hand, and what is brighter/drier/higher/more male/more active on the other hand. This proved hard to illustrate in Chinese life, until I was introduced to the principles of Chinese medicine by Alasdair and Jung Chan. I decided to make this film after I had made the other two: I might have begun to understand China a little better by then.

Once each director had sorted out the research notes and drafted an outline script or 'treatment' for his individual films, he went to China with his own film team, and had about six weeks to shoot each film. I had chosen Chris O'Dell as my cameraman: he had a good eye, a placid temper, a willingness to rough it and accept unusual situations, and – best of all – a ribald sense of humor which would help us survive in many of the laughter-free Chinese communist situations. The first film I had decided to do was *Eating*. It was a non-controversial subject and would take us all over China.

Eating was a glorious opportunity. There is not much the Chinese like to do more – particularly the Southern Chinese. There is an old riddle in China, our interpreter Mr. Great Wall told us:

"What would a northern family do with $10,000 (or 10,000 Yuan), if they won the lottery? And what would a southern family do?"

Mr. Great Wall loved collecting snippets of Chinese wisdom for us, and beamed at us owlishly, through his thick glasses.

"In the north", he said, "they'd spend it all on ugly brown furniture, to show off to the neighbors. In the south, they'd blow it all on a huge banquet, and invite the neighbors – also to show off." We all laughed. "It's true!" Mr Great Wall assured us. "In Beijing, they say that a southerner will eat anything with four legs except a table, and anything that flies except a plane."

And so it seemed to be. In Guangzhou – not far north of Hong Kong, up the Pearl River – we were solemnly taken to the Wild Animal Restaurant. The menu, a fancy affair in both Chinese and English, offered extraordinary dishes: "Dragon, Snake and Eagle" was just one. The camera crew was nonplussed.

"What's the dragon?" said the cameraman Chris O'Dell, whose idea of a good meal was fish and chips.

"It's probably pork and chicken, with a dramatic name", said Mr. Great Wall reassuringly.

"Wait a minute," said Dave Beauchamp, the lighting gaffer. "Look at page three. There's dog and cat on the list."

"Look at page four," said Chris. "There's eel and snake."

"There's monkey on page four," said Dave, not to be outdone. "And shark's fin soup and bear's paw. Are they for real, Mr. Great Wall?"

"Yes, I think those ones are real. They're meant to bring good health," said Mr. Great Wall. "They're both very expensive, but they like these dishes down here in the south."

Chris O'Dell and the crew were understandably queasy about trying most of this stuff. Was it ethical? Was it digestible? Was it disgusting? To please our hosts, we agreed to try a small variety of dishes, including some recognizable vegetable offerings, where there'd be no surprises. Or so we thought.

Chris took a generous helping of green beans, with hot sauce and some meaty pieces in a dark gravy. All went well at the start. We had got quite good at eating everything with chopsticks – apart from fried eggs, which always posed a problem. Then, suddenly, as Chris was about to put something into his mouth, I saw, in his chopsticks, what looked like a tiny human baby's hand.

"Stop!" I shouted "Wait!"

Chris dropped everything back into his bowl.

"What's that?!" I asked Mr. Great Wall.

He consulted the waiter and our hosts.

"I'm not sure what the English word is," he said. His pocket dictionary was no help. There was more discussion. Someone found a larger dictionary.

"What's this word?" he asked me, as if I'd know. "Arma...?"

Armageddon? That idea hardly helped. My stomach was telling me that we should go and find a noodle stall instead.

"No, no," said Great Wall. "I know the word! It's armadillo. Or, to be more accurate, I think it's a pangolin."

As soon as possible, we made our excuses and left.

"I noticed you didn't eat much," I said to Mr. Great Wall. He smiled.

"I just tell them I'm a Muslim, and it's against my religion," he said. "Religion is very helpful, whatever Mao said about it."

"That's interesting," I said. "Are you a Muslim, in fact?"

He smiled again: "I am when I need to be."

As I write and re-edit this scene during the great worldwide Coronavirus Pandemic of 2020, it is worth noting that Covid-19 is believed to have jumped across to humans in a wild animal market in the Chinese city of Wuhan, either from a pangolin or a bat. We were never allowed to film these markets, where dead meat is on offer side by side with a staggering array of live creatures. Perhaps the Chinese authorities had their own doubts about the wisdom of these arrangements, even 40 years ago.

• •

But in most of China, once we got outside the cities, the food was delicious. We were under no illusions: the country communes were offering us special banquets, a far cry from the average daily meal of the peasants. Our favorite was the spicy food of Szechuan, where complex cuisine has a 3,000-year history. The earth is rich with mud from the rivers, and the sub-tropical climate allows a wondrous variety of plants and animals to thrive year-round.

In one rural commune, we went to film the pigs, just before shooting a wedding banquet. One of the pigs had been killed for the feast earlier in the day, and we did not quite understand why we needed to take a battery lamp into a vast pigsty to film a row of pigs' bottoms, as they munched on their evening swill.

But the commune's leader had reason to be proud of them: the ditch into which their voluminous effluent ran was hooked up to a system of pipes and tubes, which emptied into a large and very smelly tank. From this, the methane gas was captured and piped back to the various buildings. The kitchen was lit by methane lamps. The slaughtered pig had been roasted by methane gas. The commune was self-sufficient in energy, thanks to the pigs.

The commune leader roared with laughter at our surprise, and said something to Mr. Great Wall, which he had to have repeated. I thought this was because he did not easily understand the local accent, but it turned out that he was simply embarrassed.

"Come on," said Chris O'Dell, "Tell us, what did he say?"

Mr Great Wall assumed his most serious face.

"He said: 'How would you like to be cooked by the farts of your own brothers?'"

"Sounds like the basis of a good limerick," said Chris.

"Yes, it certainly does," said Mr. Great Wall. "David, would you like to help me to invent it?"

The meal turned out to be delicious, and like all banquets, revolved around a steady stream of dishes, served one by one from the kitchen, and a steady stream of alcohol.

The standard practice in China – in 1982-3, and probably to this day – is to have three glasses placed in front of you, at any sort of formal meal. One is designed for beer – often the pretty good Tsing Tao, brewed in a German-built brewery in the North East. One is designed for the sickly-sweet plum wine, which goes quite well with many spicy dishes. The third is reserved for the lethal liquor, Mou Tai. These days, that is a brand name, and the generic liquor is called Bai Jiu, but most foreigners know it – and its fearsome reputation – as Mou Tai.

The effect of drinking Mou Tai, it has been said, is like putting your head gingerly into a dark closet, and then having a very large football-playing friend slam the door on it. It is not a subtle drink. It ranks up there with tequila as a killer. But banquet etiquette still insists that all three drinks must be both served and consumed in heroic quantities.

The ritual goes like this: you start off, before the first food has even arrived, with full glasses of beer, sweet wine and Mou Tai. The host of the banquet then proposes a toast, say, to "peace and understanding between our countries."

He then shouts "Gan Bei!" - Bottoms Up! - and drains his glass. Everyone is obliged to follow suit. But custom demands that, if any of the glasses of your neighbor (to the left) is empty, you must reach out for the relevant bottle and refill his glass. So you do.

But, in turn, the neighbor to *your* right, at the circular table, will have filled up *your* empty glass. And how do you thank him? Why of course! By toasting him, "Gan Bei!", and wishing him good health - and draining your glass again. Which, of course, is then promptly refilled by your neighbor to the left.

You do not have to be a rocket scientist to figure out that this certainly gets the banquet going with a bang. In fact, you are somewhere between pie-eyed and blotto before you have even picked up your chopsticks. But there are ways round it. One is to have only a sip from the glass. The other is not to respond in kind: if someone toasts you in Mou Tai, you are meant to respond with Mou Tai, but you can cheat and just have a sip of beer instead.

On a later occasion, while filming *Working* in the industrial city of Datong, up north in the frozen wastes of Inner Mongolia, we suspected that our coal-mining hosts had developed a sneakier way of cheating. For some reason, they did not seem to be getting drunk. They were hardly even jolly. We guessed that the small glass jugs of Mou Tai served to each of them were filled with water, not liquor. Nothing else could explain how placid they stayed, as they quaffed the transparent liquid. So one of our team, Dave Beauchamp, the lighting man, made his excuses to go to the toilet, and left the room.

He quickly ran back to the kitchen, and... we were right! There were two trays, one for the hosts and one for the guests. He switched the trays.

Next time the waiters came out with refills for our hosts, *they* got the potent stuff. After the next toast, they immediately realized what had happened, but they could not lose face by admitting it: after all, they were miners from a tough, northern city, and miners are proud of how much they can drink, aren't they? So they settled in manfully, to engage us in what turned out to be a full-scale drinking contest.

As a camera team, we earned the respect of the locals in Datong by beating them at their own game. I remember Dave Beauchamp singing dirty rugby songs late in the evening, and Chris O'Dell danced on the tables in a wild impromptu highland fling, but the miners sang and caroused as well, till, one by one, they fell by the wayside, tumbling slowly off their chairs like ventriloquists' dolls. The final event, if I remember correctly, was arm-wrestling, but by that stage we were all so far gone that our arms had the strength of a baby's.

That particular banquet finished somewhere near midnight, with everyone practically legless. The local VIPs all elected to stay in the same Government rest-house where we were billeted: there were no hotels in Datong. The VIPs had drivers, of course - nothing equal or egalitarian for Party members in China. But they must have felt they could not easily go home to their wives and explain things. So we all staggered up to our rooms.

Around 2.30 a.m., the fire alarm sounded: there was much banging of gongs and ringing of bells and knocking on doors and shouting in the corridors. Sleepy, still drunk or hung over, we crawled out of bed and mustered outside in the courtyard of the gaunt building: it was freezing. What had happened? Was the building on fire?

In fact, one of the local Party chiefs, ecstatic at being able to stay in the comparative luxury of the visitors' rest-house for the night, had drawn himself a large hot bath, stepped in, and promptly fallen asleep with the taps still running. The water had cascaded through the two floors beneath him, into the reception area, and fused the electricity supply for the entire building, starting a small fire in the transformer room.

The following morning, it was generally agreed that the schedule would be pushed back by three hours and that *no-one*, whether English or Chinese, would make any reference ever again to the events of the previous night. Since it happened almost forty ago, I feel I can finally break my promise, and tell the tale. Everyone concerned, I hope, has long since retired or gone to the Mou Tai bar in the sky.

••

Not all banquets are that bad – or that good. Of course, the mixture of all three types of alcohol makes this rigmarole even more lethal, but it is surprising how quickly you get used to it.

"Banquets are a favorite gift for government officials in China," Mr. Great Wall explained once, "because you consume all the evidence."

In view of the recent clampdown on luxury goods and public displays of wealth in China, I bet that is still the case, though the number of vintage Bordeaux wines consumed – usually served with Coca Cola to make them more palatable to the Chinese – appears to have declined.

Not all our *Eating* film was about banquets and high living, of course. We visited one of China's first entrepreneurs, a Mr. Li, who owned a large battery-chicken-farming operation in a third-floor walk-up flat in Guangzhou. This caused amazement for our Beijing-based party stooges, who were part of the team. Mr. Li was allowed to *own* these chickens? Crates of them, stacked to the ceiling in almost every room in his family's modest flat? And he did not mind admitting he made a *profit* from doing so? There was much shaking of heads: how different were party rules down here in the feckless south!

The major question for us as filmmakers was how Mr. Li and at least ten of his family managed to co-exist with at least five hundred chickens in a smallish flat. And what about the neighbors? The noise, filth and stench were overpowering. Mr Li was an engaging fellow, with an entrepreneur's easy smile. He rubbed his thumb and forefinger together in the international sign for "money."

"How did you get permission?" I asked him on camera.

Thumb and forefinger were rubbed together.

"And what do the neighbors think?"

Thumb and forefinger again.

"And are you making money?"

At this, he simply laughed.

"We open up our second operation in my cousin's apartment next month", he said. "And we are a very large family."

Even the kindly, tolerant Mr. Great Wall was shocked, when we drove away after filming.

"This is no longer a very fair society, you know," he said primly. "One of his relatives must be a Party VIP. Or in the army. He must be making a very large amount of money indeed..."

His voice tailed off, as we drove slowly past the throngs of bedraggled urban peasantry. We had been given a first glimpse of the ensuing thirty-five years: the huge increase in China's wealth, led by brave chancers like Mr. Li, with a little help from his well-placed friends.

■■■

In the *Working* film, I wanted to show China at its most Soviet. For the first ten years of Mao's reign, China had received large amounts of money, know-how and equipment from the USSR, and in the 1980's, large state-owned industries dominated the mining, oil, power-generation, construction and heavy-machinery sectors.

Strangely enough, it was my Uncle Dick Relph, my mother's brother, who gave me the idea of filming in Datong. He, like me, was a lover of trains: he built his own model steam locomotives, which he ran on an extensive layout that filled the attic of his country home in Cornwall, on England's south-west coast. He subscribed to arcane railroaders' journals from around the world. He had been interviewed at length for a Japanese railway magazine. He knew enough to tell me:

"Ask to film in Datong. It's the last place on earth where they make steam engines in a factory: one per day rolls off the production lines. I'm sure they'll be proud to show you."

When I made my request in Beijing, there was some hemming and hawing. Our CCTV friends knew that the future was in diesel and electric trains. But Datong was a genuine worker's city, in the traditional communist mold. It was a mining center too: huge quantities of coal were gouged out of the ground. It was a staunchly Soviet enterprise, in the mold of Marx, Lenin and Stalin. How could they refuse?

It was always a childhood dream of mine to drive a steam locomotive, and I had achieved this dream once or twice before. In Malaysia with James Burke, I had been left in charge of a splendid and sizeable British-built engine, while our special train trundled down from the jungle highlands – until I ran over a bicycle parked in the middle of the tracks, and the engineer thought I had killed someone. (I hadn't.)

But to visit a locomotive factory? And to get the chance (maybe) to test-drive a brand-new engine, fresh from the factory? And to meet the impressive women who – for the most part – built these long-distance freight-hauling behemoths? Paradise has many forms, and Datong was one of them for me, though with its grim mountainous location at the gateway to Mongolia, surrounded by coal tips, who would have thought it?

It was everything I had hoped for. I got to drive a factory-fresh locomotive, and to race neck and neck, at a sedate 30 m.p.h., with a double-headed freight train on the parallel track. We even had a spectacular sunset. Bliss! We opened the *Working* film with these images, though we were careful to cut out the pictures of me at the controls.

Amazingly, they went on making these giant 2-8-2 Type JS locomotives in Datong till 1999. Twenty years later, they were the last steam trains on earth in everyday revenue service. Just seven of them remained, hauling wagons at a bleak coal-mine called Sandaoling, in the middle of the Gobi desert in distant Xinjiang province. An endangered species indeed.

These are particularly vivid memories for me, because we were welcomed like heroes in Datong. The people of this down-at-heel city were not used to VIP visitors of any sort, let alone foreigners. Their coalminers had everything that British miners traditionally used to have: brass bands, male-voice choirs, good cheer and – as described above – an ability to put away large quantities of alcohol in the twinkling of an eye.

Down the mines was a trip back in time. I had visited mines once or twice in England, and even been old enough to see pit ponies still at work in Nottinghamshire in the early 1960's. But Datong's mines – even the most modern – were obviously old and dangerous. We had to use miner's lamps and battery lights to film down there: using 16-millimeter film did not give you much of an exposure. They were too scared of sparks, igniting the coal dust, to let us use our own kit.

And there was one grim, unexpected extra: in fact, it was probably the reason that the Party authorities had allowed us to film in Datong at all. There was a small, ramshackle museum, perched on a hillside, which we were invited to film. It commemorated the Second World War, which for China had lasted from 1937 to 1945. In particular it documented the Japanese behavior during that conflict.

The museum building covered the entrance to a disused mine. As your eyes got used to the gloom inside the building, you stood by the railings and looked down into the jaws of hell: the mine was filled to the brim with skeletons.

During the Japanese occupation of north-east China, they had used the local population like disposable tissues. Young men and women were forced to work eighteen-hour days down the mines, to dig out the coal to power Japan's war machine. When they flagged – and long before they died – they were thrown down old mineshafts like so much garbage. When cholera struck the camps, they went on working, but often only lasted a few weeks before being thrown down the pit.

No-one knows how many Chinese died in this fashion. Trainloads of unskilled workers were constantly brought in to fill the ranks and fulfill the quotas. Literally hundreds of thousands died at Datong, and that was just one mining town. It is no surprise that the Chinese have little love for the Japanese, to this day. They have never received any reparations. They have never even had an apology.

● ●

Finally, there was the *Understanding* film to be made: the last of the three I produced and directed. After several months in the country, talking to people of all sorts from university professors to humble peasants, I had started to have a slight idea of what the Chinese mind-map was. Although communism was front and center in the cerebellum, much older, more Confucian ways of thought persisted, in the attitudes to society, family, duty, patience, and the sheer sense of time.

This was the Middle Kingdom, after all. As Jung Chan and Alasdair Clayre helped me realize, this where civilization had started, in the Chinese view. Outsiders had always been seen as barbarians. China was the center not only of the world, but of the universe. Their ideas about cosmic energies dated from time immemorial.

The Communist Party had wisely not tried to uproot these belief systems entirely. Side by side with modern western medicine in one hospital, they practiced traditional medicine in another. Both facilities we filmed – in Henan province, as it happens – were clean, well lit, and well equipped. If you tend to doubt whether Chinese traditional medicine is anything more than hocus pocus – think "eye of toad" from Shakespeare's witches scene in *Macbeth* – you should watch an operation on the cornea of the eye performed with no other anesthetic than two acupuncture needles. You should review the long-term history of success achieved by the Chinese, using herbs and roots to tackle chronic disease.

Indeed, this is the conclusion to which we came, and which many modern Chinese commentators support: if you have an acute crisis – say you are in a car accident – then go to the Western hospital. If you have a chronic condition – cancer, diabetes, heart problems – then start at the traditional medicine hospital.

But, as I learned, the same philosophy of Yin and Yang, and the life force Qi, undergirds all traditional Chinese approaches to life. Everything is part of an ecosystem that must be kept in balance. Whether it is the traditional morning exercise, or Qi Gong, or the swordplay of the monks at the famous Shao Lin Temple, which we filmed, balance is the key concept.

That is why, we were told, the Chinese are so very apprehensive about revolutions and political upheavals: they bring massive blood, sweat and tears, but above all, they disturb the balance of society and of the universe. How long these beliefs will survive China's twenty-first century self-confidence, economic success and international adventurism, we shall see.

● ●

All good things must, regrettably, come to an end. At the conclusion of our final film trip in China, my friend Jeremy Eccles threw a party for us, on the top deck of a traditional double-deck Hong Kong tram, which he had chartered. I was transported back to my childhood in Croydon, but instead of the drab streets of South London passing the windows of the tram, there were the brightest neon signs, the loudest cacophony of music and the largest swarm of people.

"Just tell the driver where you want to go," Jeremy suggested, "And he'll take us wherever they've got tracks to run on."

So we trundled up the side streets of Happy Valley, past the race-track and fancy apartments, past the narrow alleys and food stalls in Western Market, teeming with people. We clanged our bell as loudly as possible and the conductor tried to keep regular passengers off our chartered tramcar.

Downstairs was a full bar and buffet. Upstairs were about twenty Europeans – the film crew and Jeremy's friends and relations – plus a couple of Xin Hua newsmen and Patrick Lui's closest allies. We shouted, we sang, we drank, we patted balloons through the open windows of the tram onto the heads of the crowds below…

I wonder what they thought? "Bloody Brits!" probably. But in fifteen years' time, Hong Kong was due to pass back into Chinese hands, and an era would be over. The British camera crew told me later that they were really quite nostalgic for the "real China" they had left for the last time: the simple, earthy China of the early 1980's. What they would make of China today, goodness knows.

When we returned to London, we had a major brainstorming session, to pull the series together before the final editing. This meeting produced the definitive title for the series. Our working title, *The Chinese* had been just a placeholder. But it was pedestrian. These people deserved better, we felt. Out of the blue, I suggested *The Heart of the Dragon*, and even our brilliant but reticent researcher, Jung Chang, approved. In both senses of the word, she felt, we had touched the very heart of China. And she knew what she was talking about. She went on to write the worldwide best-seller, *Wild Swans.*

The films took a long time to edit. The book of the series took an even longer time to write. Alasdair Clayre, tasked with the job of writing the book, and distilling everything we had learned, became quieter and, in retrospect, more and more stressed. We all felt the weight of the responsibility: we were making the first ever full-length documentaries permitted to be filmed by foreigners in China since 1949. We had to get them right.

But Alasdair felt the pressure more than any of us knew. The printed word has a permanence and a certain authority, even if our book was an illustrated TV tie-in. The cloak of Alasdair's All Souls' College fellowship weighed heavily on his shoulders. Would the notoriously sniffy academics turn up their noses at his efforts?

I remember saying Happy Christmas to him, just before going home to spend a week in the country with my parents. He seemed anxious, distant, sad. I asked him what he was doing for Christmas: surely not staying in his big, cold London house? He said he thought that his mother was coming to stay.

In early January of 1984, just a few weeks before the launch of the book and the premiere of *The Heart of the Dragon* on Britain's new Channel 4 TV, Alasdair threw himself under a London tube train at Kentish Town station, just a couple of miles from where I was born. I am sure there were personal reasons as well, but we were all in shock, grief-stricken that our project had literally killed him. But I thought I was closer to him than anyone else. I had been sharing his house with him, as well as an office. I knew that he was lonely and had not been in a significant relationship since divorcing his wife Felicity Bryan in 1980.

It turned out that his mother had come to visit him, because she, too, had been concerned about his state of mind. But one day, she went out shopping and while she was away, he went for a long walk, ending up at Kentish Town.

I should have known that something was seriously wrong, shouldn't I? How could I have reached out to him? The questions still haunt me. They threw a long shadow over the launch of the series.

The project was duly dedicated to Alasdair. If only he could have seen the reception his work received. *The Heart of the Dragon* won the International Emmy for the world's best documentary series of the year, was excerpted on NBC in the US, and presented on PBS by Robin McNeil and Jim Lehrer. It was seen around the world – and even on CCTV's Channel 1 in China, where they ran the pictures and music uncut, but put a rather different narration over the top. I feel the series is a fitting monument to my dear, much-missed friend Alasdair Clayre.

10. THE WEST OF THE IMAGINATION

During the more than two years it took to make *The Heart of the Dragon*, I had often left China and returned to Los Angeles, rather than going immediately back to London. I still had a pied-à-terre in LA, thanks to my business manager Pat Russell, and was trying to develop new projects, which would allow me to spend more time in California. Also, my new American Green Card (the Resident Alien status) did not allow me to be out of the country for more than six months at a time.

I had also been juggling a complicated love life. For some time, after Lizzie had fired me and gone sailing round half the world, I took up with Janelle Balnicke again, and shared her pretty little duplex in a wooded avenue in South Pasadena, to the east of LA. Everything I had enjoyed during Cosmos was still there – the kidney-shaped swimming pool out back, her neighbor and former "Cosmonaut" Susan Stribling, a dozen shared friends – and Janelle.

For five years, things were on again and off again, so to speak, between Janelle and Lizzie. Both suspected that I was having my cake and eating it, and both of them threw me out at least twice. "Who do you really love?" was a line in the script both sides of the Atlantic, and to be honest, I did not really know, until I made the final decision in 1986, but that comes later.

The first stage of Pantechnicon Productions' one big project happened while I was still deeply involved in *The Heart of the Dragon.* The Head of National Production at KERA, the Dallas PBS station, was the elegant and witty Pat Perini. She had met me at one of the big, dull Public Television program fairs in the early 80's. She was very pleased to hire me and some of the Cosmos team, to create a short pilot film about the history of the American West, as portrayed by the artists who had painted and photographed it. She wanted lots of drama – real, dramatized scenes, shot in the original locations from the Mississippi to the California coast.

Perini had been offered a development grant from the unlikely-sounding Nelda C. Stark Foundation of Orange, Texas, and promptly hired PPI to make a short teaser film. I had limited time available, with my work on *The Heart of the Dragon*, so I asked Janelle – now an excellent producer and production manager in her own right – if she could help. She was happy to take the reins. Born in Lincoln, Nebraska, this was *her* story, she felt.

But we both acknowledged that we would need someone else, with more experience of scripting, editing and directing dramatic sequences. My mind immediately flew to David Oyster and Richard Wells, good friends who had done sterling service in this capacity on *Cosmos*. But the director who had pulled off some of the most complex and demanding historical scenes for *Cosmos*, with a fanatical eye for detail, was Tom Weidlinger.

Weidlinger is up there in the pantheon of gods who are significantly taller than me – J.K.Galbraith, Brian Swimme and John Cleese among them. He has never been accused of a surfeit of modesty, or troubled by much self-doubt, but he has remarkable talents, and he was available and interested in the subject. So we hired him, and he and Janelle set about creating a short sizzle reel, which, much to my astonishment, did the trick.

Just as I was concluding my work on *The Heart of the Dragon* and wondering where the next money was coming from, to support my ex-wife and Amanda and Juliet, Pat Perini sent me the news. The Nelda C. Stark Foundation had put up two-thirds of the budget for the series: a substantial $1.6 million. Having no idea where she could raise the remaining $800,000, Pat had driven out to Orange, Texas, to see Nelda personally and get some advice.

Orange, TX is a very small town, one hundred and ten miles east of Houston. Even today, it has less than twenty thousand inhabitants, and in the 1980's it was barely a blemish on the map. The one notable feature was the Stark Museum of Art, which housed one of America's foremost collections of paintings depicting the development of the American West. Pat was shown into Nelda's elegant sitting room-cum-office, and explained her plight: where to find the rest of the budget?

As Pat told it, the elderly Nelda reached for her purse, said "Never mind about that, honey," and promptly wrote out a check to KERA-TV for the remaining eight hundred thousand dollars. Bells rang, lights flashed, and we were green-lighted to go, as fast as possible – before Nelda changed her mind. Pantechnicon Productions hired real offices for the first time – a fancy suite in a small building near Santa Monica – and Tom Weidlinger, Janelle, Pat Russell and I dived into the subject matter and started learning.

It has to be said that much of the art of the American West is an acquired taste, particularly for a Brit like me. The bronze cowboys of Frederick Remington, the folksy saloon paintings of Charlie Russell – they all feel suspiciously like kitsch. The pale imitators of Remington and Russell are even worse.

Of course, there are also the magnificent landscapes by Albert Bierstadt, the early paintings of the Mandan people by George Catlin, and much else of great beauty and universal value. More recently, of course, there is the photographer Ansell Adams, the provocative Georgia O'Keefe and a raft of highly original Native American painters. So there was obviously work to do, to sort the wheat from the chaff.

To bolster the authenticity of her project, Pat Perini had enlisted the support of her former teacher, an Emeritus Professor in the American Studies Program at the University of Texas at Austin: William H. "Bill" Goetzmann. He, in turn, was later assisted in writing of the book of the series by his son, William N. Goetzmann: two for the price of one, and just as well, because Goetzmann Senior later came down with serious heart trouble. Whether this was exacerbated by his stormy relationship with the production team, I have never been sure.

Bill G was convinced that he was not only the world's expert on Western American Art, but a TV star in the making. He made it perfectly clear from the start that he expected to bestride all the significant locations in the American West like some latter-day Sagan, pointing at the marks of the wagon wheels on the Oregon Trail, sunning himself in Bent's Fort, wagging his finger in disapproval at the debauchery of San Francisco's 'Barbary Coast'.

Unfortunately, the entire production team agreed that Bill G did not have what it took to be a charismatic on-camera host. His owlish demeanor, his academic phraseology, his need to use five words where one was enough: what can I say? Pat Perini found herself facing a potential crisis, very similar to the one we were to face fifteen years later on *The Promise of Play*. Bill G threatened to go to Nelda C. Stark and tell her personally that the films were being hijacked by a bunch of Los Angeles philistines who cared nothing for the details of history, and had no appreciation for the subtleties of Western Art. Worse still, one of them was a Brit!

A compromise was reached: the films would be made at a length of fifty minutes, suitable for export to commercial television networks around the world. They would then be able to insert a couple of commercial breaks, to round them out to an hour. This happened to the series later, with great success, when it ran on Britain's national Channel 4, which had premiered *The Heart of the Dragon*.

The remaining seven minutes – to make the show up to a PBS hour – consisted of Professor Goetzmann being interviewed in a studio at KERA-TV, giving academic notes and asides. With his moment in the limelight guaranteed, he acknowledged that his own voice might be bettered by a professional narrator, so Tom Weidlinger suggested we should hire the veteran actor James Whitmore, who gave the story a nice, gritty edge. He had played just enough cowboys in his career to know how films about the West *should* sound.

So we were free to make some spectacular movies, based on outdoor locations, shot in gorgeous 16-millimeter film. These were the last films I made, which were actually shot on celluloid: by 1985 it was already punishingly expensive to shoot ten-minute rolls of Kodak stock and ship them back to labs for processing. But, when I look at the movies now, I am so glad we refused to countenance the early video that was then available. The shots of the Mississippi at dawn, Yosemite at sunset, cattle ranching in Montana – they were in many ways the equal of the paintings that they sought to emulate.

Tom Weidlinger produced and directed Episodes One through Four, covering the period (approximately) 1800 to 1910. He re-staged scenes featuring Lotta Crabtree, the teenage songbird who wowed the miners in the 1849 California gold-rush. He recreated the heady atmosphere of the early stagecoaches and gold towns in Columbia, CA. He persuaded the State Penitentiary in Montana to lend us half a dozen genuine cowboys, herding the State's cattle, out in the wild lands of 'Big Sky Country.' He organized compelling scenes, featuring the great trek west with the Conestoga wagons, when many of the weaker colonists –particularly the children – died and were buried right there on the trail.

What a fantastic contrast this was from working on *The Heart of the Dragon*! This time, we were employing actors, writing dialog based on historic records, digging into the history and mythology of what would become (in 2002) my adopted country. And how fabulous was the territory! No wonder the painters, photographers and (later) filmmakers fell in love with the subject.

I had seen Yellowstone National Park when I traveled out west in 1968, as a student at Indiana University: the magical, other-worldly colors of the sulfur ponds, the roar of the geysers. We learned that the photos and paintings of Yellowstone caused such astonishment back in nineteenth century Washington DC that they triggered a call for Yellowstone to be made the world's first National Park – forever off-limits to construction or destruction.

I duly produced Film Number Five, about the West in popular culture: Ned Buntline's theatre melodramas, reducing the West to Cowboys and Indians, and introducing the bad guys with the black hats; Buffalo Bill's Wild West Show, which toured worldwide and entranced Britain's elderly Queen Victoria; *The Great Train Robbery* of 1903 – the world's first multi-scene movie drama, ostensibly a Western, but filmed entirely in New Jersey – and all the ensuing films and TV programming.

Finally, Janelle Balnicke produced Film Number Six. A passionate advocate of Native American art, and of Georgia O'Keefe and the emerging women artists in a field previously dominated by men, Janelle gave a thoughtful spin to the way Western art was developing in the mid twentieth century. Her film featured dreamscapes, visions and challenging color palettes that told of a world we all now recognize: the myth of the golden west, where the sun is always setting in a magical blaze of light. Underpinning it, as today, was the tragic story of what had really happened to the Native American nations.

Essentially, Goetzmann argued, the "West of the Imagination" had been developed partly by accident – because surveyors, map-makers, artists and others had been employed, often by the government, to chart the vast new territories the US acquired from Mexico, and had faithfully recorded what they saw. Partly, however, it had been developed cynically as a business strategy by railroad tycoons, who wanted to sell the West as a glorious destination for investment and development. And partly, it was the inevitable product of "Manifest Destiny" – the nineteenth century belief that it was God's plan to give the white man this new paradise.

Most significantly, Goetzmann proposed that this "West of the Imagination" became the dominant new mythology of the United States. After the Civil War, said Goetzmann, the story of the pilgrims, Betsy Ross and the Founding Fathers with their powdered wigs had lost traction as a mythic tale, on which to build a nation. A new myth was needed, and a glorified, sanitized view of the West was what provided it. The US has liked to see itself as the Cowboy in the White Hat ever since.

This was an idea particularly easy to accept when we made the shows, during the presidency of Ronald Reagan, himself an erstwhile screen cowboy. However, it is a myth that endured, right through the era of the Marlboro Man and into George W. Bush's ill-advised US foreign policy adventures in the Middle East in the current century. It is hard to tell how much longer US exceptionalism will stand the test of time, but no better national myth has yet been forthcoming.

Back at the ranch – Pantechnicon's spiffy new offices in Santa Monica, CA – I also had to act as Senior Producer of the whole series, constantly worried by how fast the budget was disappearing. Tom Weidlinger was a perfectionist: almost every action shot had to be re-shot a dozen times, at toe-curling cost. Back in the cutting room, the same slow, deliberate detailed work created havoc with our schedules. Then Bill Goetzmann would arrive from Texas and demand re-cuts of almost everything. Happily, we had artistic control, so these instructions were taken with a liberal pinch of salt. But it was all taking too much time and too much of our budget.

The comptroller at KERA-TV in Dallas had installed, at the very start of the project, a computerized link between our offices and his, so that he could have real-time financial information downloaded onto his computer. This was revolutionary: the year was 1984. We had what was called a "modem" and an IBM 360 computer, complete with a rudimentary screen with green letters and numerals, which counted each dollar as it was spent. When it was time to do a monthly "download" (a new word back then), friends, colleagues and clients used to come to our offices and marvel at this futuristic phenomenon. It took many hours overnight to send all the information, but the machine looked like a prop from Star Trek, to all who saw it in action.

The grim reality, however, was that we were running out of money fast. And that meant, as I realized in the nick of time, that we would have to finish the sound, music and post-production in London, where everything was cheaper. But did I really want to be back in London, however nice it would be to see Amanda and Juliet more frequently?

■■■

11. FOUNDING InCA AND FINDING LIZZIE

It was early in 1985 that a friend drove me to Los Angeles airport to catch a London flight and, upon arrival, ironically said: "Welcome home, David."

He was right: I was so accustomed to the ten or eleven-hour flight to and from London, that the airport, plus the transatlantic flight and the corner seat at the front of the rear cabin had come to seem like home. Whenever London seemed dull and grey, there was LA to look forward to. Six weeks later, when LA seemed hot, dusty and superficial, there were my children, family and friends in London to retreat to. The plastic food and friendly chatter with the air crew had become a normal part of my existence. Several times a year, I simply migrated, like the Bakhtiari in Iran – except that I did not take the sheep with me (see Chapter 3, *The Ascent of Man*).

But this was no way to run my life in the long term – at least if I wanted to stay sane. I still felt more British than American, and missed my daughters Amanda and Juliet more and more, as they got older. They had visited me in the US, of course. The first time, they had traveled by themselves and arrived at Detroit airport like a couple of little refugees, aged 6 and 8, with name tags round their necks. I had taken them up to George Colburn's house in Northern Michigan, for sailing, swimming and cycling round Mackinac Island. They had visited me in California and done everything that LA had to offer to seven and nine-year-old kids: Disneyland, Six Flags Magic Mountain, Knott's Berry Farm, "boogie-board" body surfing, Universal Studios. But their home was still in Barnes, five thousand miles away.

In 1982, I had bought a nice hundred-year-old "mansion" flat in London, in the leafier part of Maida Vale, two or three miles north of Marble Arch. Helen had generously moved to a smaller house in Barnes, to release some capital and help me to purchase it. Our two daughters each had a room to themselves, when they visited. To furnish it, I had rescued several artifacts from the old Beaumanor Mansions flat that I had shared with Hazel, including the pinball machine and my precious and ever-growing Bad Taste Collection.

This consisted of bits and pieces I had picked up on location, all over the world: fake mule-dung cigarettes from cowboy country ("Not a Fart in a Carload"), hair-raising Chinese medicines made from bull's penis and monkey glands, genuine Australian money pouches made from kangaroo scrotum – you name it, I still have it, down in the basement of our house in Mill Valley, CA. Deep in the basement, says Lizzie, is where it all belongs.

More seriously, I knew that what I really needed was a production base in London: something to give me a professional anchor there. But I was well out of the loop at the BBC, and had no contacts at Channel 4, the newly founded national home of independent TV production. They had premiered *The Heart of the Dragon*, but it was not my production company that had created it. They planned to show *The West of the Imagination*, but this was considered an American import.

So I started to talk to a group of BBC Science and Features producers who were in the process of leaving the Corporation and going independent. It was a big step for them: no more guaranteed production, no more monthly salaries, no further increase in pension, no BBC Club, in which to exchange gossip and eye up the talent.

Two of them, the ringleaders perhaps, had already formed their own small company on the side, to make short industrial films, to supplement their BBC income. Willie Woollard was a well-known face on television, from the weekly science magazine show, *Tomorrow's World*. His partner Chris Haws could charm the spots off a leopard, and had collaborated with Woollard in making short industrial films. They had demonstrated that life outside the BBC was possible.

They had named their modest operation Sky Films, which was unfortunate, because a certain Rupert Murdoch had just started a rather bigger outfit called Sky. His lawyers politely suggested that Woollard and Haws should cease and desist. So if we were all going to form a new and bigger company, we needed a new name, as impressive and anodyne as possible – a name that suggested a vast production operation, with its eye set on distant horizons of vast profitability: something a little like the National Video Communications Incorporated that George Colburn had created in Michigan.

We eventually chose the name "Independent Communications Associates Ltd," and planned to have it known as ICA. But unfortunately there was already an organization known as ICA in London: the Institute of Contemporary Arts. So Chris Haws suggested inserting a small "n" into the logo, and we became InCA Productions. A little later, I rolled the American operations of Pantechnicon into a new US subsidiary of InCA, to add extra heft and output to the operation. Most people in San Francisco still think that "InCA" stands for "In California" and compliment me for the witty name, but it is just a happy coincidence that it worked out that way.

Veteran producer Karl Sabbagh joined us from the BBC Science and Features Unit, Lynn Gambles (the only woman) joined us from BBC Drama, and the much respected anthropologist Andre Singer abandoned a very good job with Granada TV's *World in Action* to become the only "InCAnaut" to join from commercial television. We were set!

We hired impressive and eye-wateringly expensive offices in Great Pulteney Street, near Piccadilly Circus. We nailed down the first two commissions from Channel 4 (including a three-part series on nuclear energy) plus some nice little earners in the non-broadcast field from the Ford Motor Company. We were properly busy.

It is feast or famine in the world of independent production. For once, it was time for a feast. While still busy completing *The West of the Imagination* (which we re-badged under the InCA banner), I was offered a producing and directing role on a new and prestigious series: *The Buried Mirror*. The Executive Producer was the legendary Michael Gill, who had created the landmark *Civilisation* series with Sir Kenneth Clark. His new project promised exotic travel throughout Iberia and the Spanish speaking countries of the Americas. How could I turn it down?

At the very same time, InCA had attracted the attention of an independent producer called Luc Cuyvers, who headed up the Mare Nostrum Foundation in Annapolis, MD, and was developing a huge international documentary project called *The Blue Revolution*. He liked the combined scientific and international experience that InCA offered. Could we work with him too?

There is a well-known analogy for the situation I was in: I was like a dog between four trees. I did not know which leg to raise. All I knew was that, if I tried to lift all four, I would fall flat on my stomach. I had too many options. Strangely enough, for once, the same was true for my social life. I had been having my cake and eating it quite comfortably for a year or two. I am not very proud of this episode in my life, but I was thirty-nine, a dangerous age for someone who, like Peter Pan, thought he could stay young forever.

In Los Angeles, my affair with Janelle Balnicke was history; we were working together on *The West of the Imagination*, but that was all. Her emotional needs were apparently being met elsewhere. Instead, when in LA, I was happily going out, on a rather casual basis, with a psychotherapist called Ann, who was at least a foot shorter than me, and not really my type at all. She was quite dark, with black hair and a fast sports car – an old, noisy and terrifyingly fast Alfa Romeo sedan, which promised to collapse into a pile of rust at any moment. However, she had a great sense of humor and a sexual appetite that was almost as fast, noisy and demanding as the Alfa.

In London, I had also met a kind, beautiful and intelligent woman called Lizzie Bingley. She was a highly respected acupuncturist, with a well-heeled private clientele and a significant following among those who understood the subject. We had met while naked in a hot tub at a New Year's Eve party (yes, a hot tub in London!) and she was astonished to meet the person who had produced and directed the *Understanding* film in *The Heart of the Dragon* series.

I believe that Lizzie Bingley truly fell in love with me. Alas, although I was fond of her, I could not reciprocate. She was generous, intelligent and kind, but she did not light my fire. I could not see any long-term future for us.

"She's too kind for you, David," said my elder stepsister Pamela on one occasion, and she may have been right. I was hooked on my own ego, living life at an unsustainable pace on two continents, thinking only of myself and the wonderful if exhausting time I was having.

It was at this high point – or embarrassing mess – in my life that I turned forty. I decided to throw a big party in London and hire a decent-sized boat on the River Thames, to entertain at least fifty people. We would have a buffet and live music, and everyone would be asked to come in fancy dress: nautical gear, naval uniforms or, at the very least, in red, white and blue. As it happened, the date, September 7, 1985, coincided with a big festival in London, so the boat trip (to Greenwich Maritime Museum and back) would be rounded off by a cracking firework display, which I could jokingly pretend had been put on for my benefit.

And so it came to pass. I got on board the boat early with a couple of friends, to put up some balloons and festive bunting, and we pulled up at Charing Cross Pier, in the heart of London, to see fifty friends and family on the dock, all arrayed in party gear, in the brilliant sunshine. Best of all, my ex-wife Helen was there with my daughters – bygones were bygones – and, a bonus extra, two former girlfriends had turned up as well.

You may notice that two names were missing from the list: Janelle Balnicke was in Los Angeles and had no interest in joining the festivity. Lizzie Ross, whom I had invited for old times' sake, had not replied to the invitation at all. A mutual friend told me she was dating a famous architect and designer and had no wish to see me any longer.

The party went well enough. The weather was kind. The fireworks were splendid. But all too soon, I was back on the plane to California. I remember flying over the icy wastes of Greenland, looking out of the window of the plane, asking myself what direction I wanted my life to go. London? LA? Both? Something utterly different? I was pretty confused.

Just a few months later, the situation escalated into utter chaos. I found myself involved in a massive emotional car-crash, involving many of the characters from my present and my past.

Janelle had come to London to help with the final post-production on *The West of the Imagination.* She decided that she should try living with me one more time at my Maida Vale flat, to see if we could make something work. Lizzie Bingley was properly shocked. She gave me an ultimatum: "It's her or me." Ann called from Los Angeles to say that she had booked a week's massage retreat at the Esalen Institute for us both, starting in a few weeks' time. And finally, my first wife, Helen, announced that she had fallen in love with Rupert Pennant-Rea, then Editor of *The Economist*, and intended to marry him rather soon.

What on earth should I do? Admit my two-timing (three-timing!) to all concerned? Go into hiding? We had almost completed the last of the post-production and sound mixing on *The West of the Imagination,* so I was soon to be free from immediate tasks, but… free to do what?

I remember standing in my Maida Vale flat, truly puzzled by what my next move should be, when I saw the light on my telephone answering machine blinking: a message. I nearly switched it to automatic erase, because I had decided to lie low and hope the emotional whirlwinds would blow over. But – and this is one of those important moments in life – I pressed PLAY on the machine.

I was astonished: the message was from Lizzie Ross. She had not contacted me for two years. If you remember, she had not even bothered to reply to my invitation to the boat party. Yet here she was, cool as a cucumber, saying casually:

"I was just wondering how you were doing."

She had left a number – not the number of her old Acton flat, several miles from the center of London, but a 727 number, from trendy Notting Hill. I immediately jumped to the conclusion that she had moved in with her famous architect boyfriend and was simply calling me to alert me to her good fortune. Perhaps she even wanted to rub my nose in the dirt, for not having scooped her up when she had been available. Well, I felt, it was not as if I needed another female ingredient in the rich stew of my social life.

But something stopped me from erasing the message. Why had she called at that moment? Was it pure coincidence? Or fate? Or did she know something about the whole situation? And if so, how much did she know?

What Lizzie had discovered, I later learned, was that my ex-wife Helen was re-marrying. Lizzie had always felt that I would not be truly emotionally free until and unless this happened. And she was right: I was profoundly relieved that there would finally be someone else to look after Helen, emotionally as well as financially.

So I phoned Lizzie back, and left a similarly casual message on *her* answering machine. Eventually, we agreed to meet for lunch the following Monday at an Italian restaurant just up the road from the InCA offices in central London. After all, what is the least "significant" arrangement you can make, to meet someone for an hour or two? That's right, Monday lunch. I knew things would be quiet at the restaurant: I had not even booked a table.

The name of the restaurant was the Andrea Doria – not in itself remarkable, unless you know that the Andrea Doria was an Italian liner, which had sunk after a collision in the Atlantic with the loss of 46 lives, *exactly thirty years beforehand.* Neither of us knew this at the time, but in retrospect, it was a bit like two Brits meeting in Rome for an emotional reunion at a pub called The Titanic.

I arrived early. I had put on some fairly smart clothes: being a TV producer, this meant a nice jacket, open-necked shirt and stylish jeans. Nothing too fancy, you understand. I did not want to look as if I was trying too hard. For some reason, the manager greeted me as if he knew all along that I had been coming, and what this was all about. He ushered me up to a completely empty dining room on the second floor, and brought some roses to the table, chattering about the "Bella Signora." A few minutes later, he ushered Lizzie upstairs, and escorted her to the table as if she was the Queen of Sheba.

I have to say, she looked gorgeous, and I was instantly smitten – more smitten than I had ever been before. We looked into each other's eyes, we kissed each other on the cheeks, we were soon holding hands. I am sure we had wine to drink, and I am sure we ate something, but I cannot remember a thing about the lunch, except for Lizzie's radiant face, and the laughter and smiles we shared as we each told our story of the last two years apart. After lunch, not wanting to go back to work, we wandered around Liberty's, the stylish store on Regent Street, mooning at each other and still holding hands.

Within a day or two, we had made the decision, entirely in secret: we would get married as soon as possible. We would rush down and tell her parents face-to-face in Sevenoaks, at their home just outside London. We would then rush and tell my parents face-to-face in their London flat. And then we would jump on a plane at dawn from London's Gatwick Airport and fly to Crete for a one-week pre-marital honeymoon, to celebrate what we were doing.

When Lizzie's family heard the news, they were stunned. Her brother Tim thought it was a practical joke. After all, they had not heard anything about me for more than two years, and a lot of water, so to speak, had flowed under Lizzie's bridge during that time. And now we were suddenly marrying? In eight weeks' time?

My parents, bless them, were more pragmatic. My mother hugged me tight and told me (this time genuinely, she later admitted) that she was so happy. There was no exhibition of surprise. My father, just as he had done when I told him I was marrying Helen eleven years earlier, immediately went to find a bottle of cold champagne: it is a Kennard family tradition at times of extreme joy or stress, I think. There is always a bottle of champagne at the back of the fridge, just in case.

On the way to Gatwick Airport, in the train, I wrote brief letters to all the women with whom I had gone out in the previous few months. I cannot remember what I said. I hope it was gentlemanly and reasonably polite. I am sure that it included the word "sorry" at least once. But I wanted to burn every single one of my bridges with past loves: this time, I prayed, my marriage would be forever.

Helen and Rupert Pennant-Rea were married the same week as Lizzie and I. They even came to our wedding, which was nice for my daughters, as well as for Lizzie and me. We celebrated in fine style on the lawns of the leafy Hurlingham Club in West London, and enjoyed champagne with friends, relations and the five other founders of InCA, all of whom turned out in their very best bib and tucker. Amanda and Juliet turned cartwheels under the trees, in their pretty bridesmaids' dresses. They were 8 and 10 years old and getting taller by the minute.

We even managed to get married in the eyes of the Lord, too. Adrian Benjamin, an old friend from Oxford, director of the centennial production of *Alice in Wonderland* (in which I had played the Duck in the Pool of Tears – appropriately), had become a most impressively bearded vicar. He looked like a Greek Orthodox Archbishop. He gave us a blessing, an absolution from sin, and an abbreviated marriage service, right there at the Hurlingham Club. A few years later, he baptized our son James.

• •

For all those who know this part of the story, there is one crucial detail missing: I got married with my left leg in a very large plaster cast. And why so, you may ask? Because I slipped on the steps of a pornographic pottery shop in Portugal.

And with that, let me return to the story of the films I had been trying to make. You may remember that I had recently been approached by the producer Michael Gill. He was the epitome of the English gentleman: kind, thoughtful, deeply intelligent, always willing to listen to the views of others. He very much wanted to create a landmark series on Iberian culture and had succeeded in persuading the Smithsonian Institution in Washington DC to give him a very generous development grant for the series. His working title was *The Buried Mirror*, a poetic and mysterious reference to the many cultures, which contributed to the Spanish and Portuguese empires.

The host, writer and star of the series was to be Carlos Fuentes, who was Michael's equal in all the social graces, besides being a superb novelist and poet, and a former Mexican Ambassador to the USA. They were very similar physically: tall but elegant, with big, brainy heads, square and candid faces, slightly graying hair and the most charming of smiles. Standing together, they looked almost too good to be true. They brought to mind the world of Dirk Bogarde, of David Niven, of elegant lunches on flower-decked patios, of literary evenings with fine wine, lovely ladies and witty banter.

Michael asked me to join him and Fuentes, with a couple of other producers, on a leisurely ramble round Spain and Portugal. We would scout historic locations and draft the outline script of the series. It sounded too good to be true. My colleagues seemed quite happy for me to take a sabbatical month or two off from InCA, to join Michael's team. I had settled on the date of July 12 to marry Lizzie, and there was plenty of time before that, to do the trip. So off we went.

Lisbon is a splendid place to start such a tour. Devastated by an earthquake in 1755, the city was entirely rebuilt. To this day, the center is completely intact: an eighteenth-century grid of elegant streets, with beautifully proportioned buildings in pastel colors, mostly a delicious buttery yellow. Remnants of the past, like the old castle and many rebuilt churches, dot the seven hills on which the city is built.

To my great pleasure, tiny four-wheeled trams, painted to match the buildings in yellow and white, ascend vertiginous slopes on narrow-gauged track, crowded with tourists and locals alike. Clanging their bells, wheels squealing on the tight curves, they pass within a whisker of people sitting at open-air cafés, taking a coffee or munching on a feast of Bacalau, the dried cod which the Portuguese for some reason find so appealing.

But Lisbon was only the start of our pilgrimage: there was the ancient university city of Coimbra, to the north, and many another castle or vista connected with Henry the Navigator or some other grandee from Portugal's colonial past. Our driver-cum-interpreter was a very amusing companion, and suggested one day, after lunch, that we should stop at a row of unusual shops in a provincial city called Caldas da Rainha.

"You'll want to buy some souvenirs", he warned us. We doubted that. But we were wrong.

Wikipedia primly suggests the following:

> *"If you're looking for a souvenir of Caldas, you should buy some of the famous local ceramic pottery. The factory of Raphael Bordallo Pinheiro produces useful and decorative pieces. For those who enjoy naughtier mementos, Caldas is noted for its ceramic phalluses, which like the real thing come in various sizes and shapes and can be found all over town."*

The modern city was founded in the fifteenth century by Queen Leonor, who traveled past a group of peasants, bathing in pools of foul-smelling sulfurous waters beside the road. They told her that the waters cured all sorts of ills. What they did not tell her was that, since Roman times, the hot springs had had the reputation of increasing virility in men – and also of persuading even the most virtuous of ladies to accept what was suddenly on offer.

Our guide suggested that, at the very least, I should take a ceramic bottle of the spring-water home, to give me pep and vim on my honeymoon night. And perhaps I might be amused to have a souvenir or two?

This was too good an opportunity to miss. I needed something amusing to give to our best man, Chris Haws, one of the co-founders of InCA. What better than a traditional present from Portugal, that seafaring nation? How about a ceramic lighthouse, atop some rocks and vegetation? When turned one hundred and eighty degrees, however, it became something very different: a crudely painted phallus, atop a couple of chunky testicles, with pubic hair in place of the seaweed.

I have a great weakness for bad taste. Indeed, I am quite proud of my informal museum of such items – not all of them sexually suggestive, I hasten to add. The Virgin Mary glow-in-the-dark protective bicycle clips from Northern Michigan are one of my favorite items. But this little shop in Portugal was too much. It was so ordinary, so matter-of-fact. And its merchandise was sublime.

It was run by an elderly couple, whose family had obviously been peddling salacious tat for generations, if not since Roman times. There were little clay soccer players, wearing the shirts and shorts of all Europe's best-known teams: if you pulled a string behind their backs, a giant penis poked out through their shorts. There were all sorts of mugs, which contained a selection of hidden wieners and willies: the unsuspecting drinker, given a full cup of coffee, would need to take only two or three sips, before the offending organ poked its head above the beverage. What a treasure trove!

Everyone bought something at the shop – even Michael Gill – but I bought a bagful. There would be presents for the bridesmaids as well as the best man, and there would be one of each item for me, too. The entire collection cost me less than twenty dollars, and I left the shop with my colleagues, laughing and chattering with pleasure. And then, while talking of course, and not looking where I was going, I slipped on the three ancient, polished stone steps, and fell…

It was a miracle. My body reacted spontaneously, twisting and protecting my precious purchases. I sat on the ground, still clutching my bag, and not a single piece of pornographic pottery had been broken.

"Are you alright, David?" asked Stephanie, the unit manager.

"Yes, I'm fine," I said cheerily, and then I tried to stand up. "Well, actually, I think I've sprained my ankle."

I was soon in agony. But the schedule was implacable: we had to fly to Madrid the following morning, where Lizzie was scheduled to meet us. So I struggled, limping, onwards. The next day, however, it was clearly more than a sprained ankle. I needed a wheelchair to get through the airports at both Lisbon and Madrid. As I was wheeled out of Customs, Lizzie took one look at my swollen leg and said: "We're going straight to the nearest hospital."

There, I was placed in the hands of a Taiwanese doctor who spoke no English and very little Spanish. We conversed in pidgin French, with much gesticulation: it was like playing an international game of charades. He x-rayed me, and it appeared that I had broken my fibula in two places, just above the ankle.

"We must operate immediately," he mimed, looking serious.

Lizzie and I looked at each other. An operation in a Madrid hospital? Two weeks to recover – and postpone the wedding? Simply no way. So I hobbled back out to the airport, and within a few hours was in St Mary's, Paddington: a major teaching hospital, right in the center of London.

That night, they operated on my leg. When I woke from the general anesthetic in the morning, a bunch of senior doctors and students were standing round my bed, holding x-rays and shaking their heads glumly.

"I'm sorry," said the Senior Consultant Surgeon. "We're going to have to do the whole thing again. Your fibula was broken in two places, and it was reset last night, but in my opinion, they should have put metal plates in, to hold it all in place. So, we're going to schedule a second procedure. But it's dangerous to have two general anesthetics too close to each other, so you'll have to wait here for three days, and then we'll have another go. Sorry about that."

What could I say? "Try not to screw it up next time"?

The irritating thing was that I would now miss the official launch of the new InCA offices, a full-scale party to which I had invited many friends and relations. So, while much champagne was consumed in Great Pulteney Street, a few of my older and more faithful friends came on from the InCA party to the hospital, to bring me flowers, jokes and consolation. Lizzie welcomed them all, and we had our own mini-party in the hospital ward, doing our best to conceal the champagne being poured into plastic cups.

• •

Six weeks later, we were married, as described above, with my leg in a large cast. Chris Haws of InCA, our best man, virtually had his speech written for him. Remembering my more ambitious films, he looked at my bandaged leg and called it, of course, "the cast of thousands."

He also observed that Lizzie had obviously been trying to nail my feet to the floor, before we had even signed the register. And so on. But it was a beautiful day, and all four of our parents were still alive and well, and were able to be with us, together with many other friends and family. We even got some great wedding presents, which I found vaguely embarrassing, since many of them came from generous souls who had already given me presents the first time round, when I married Helen.

At about 5 p.m., Lizzie and I slipped away, to spend our first wedding night at the beautiful old Richmond Hill Hotel. Why there? Because it was on the way to the airport. The very next morning – so typical of my life – we were booked to fly on British Airways to Detroit, Michigan.

The next six weeks amounted to what Lizzie called wryly "a working honeymoon." Long before I re-met her, I had already committed to being in Michigan to prepare a new project with George Colburn; then to traveling on to Annapolis, Maryland, for a conference about a potential big InCA project on the oceans (*The Blue Revolution*); then to fly to Mexico, to join Carlos Fuentes, Michael Gill and his team to scout locations for *The Buried Mirror*, then finally to end up in Los Angeles, to tie up some business with Pat Russell and InCA USA. It is hard to believe the frenetic level of activity I had casually planned, but it was hard to cancel any of it, so Lizzie took two months off from her job at the BBC and gamely came along for the ride.

That explains why the second night of our marriage was spent in the sleaziest motel you can imagine – in Saginaw, Michigan. We had planned to drive straight on through from Detroit to Charlevoix, up in the north of the state – over 200 miles, with no freeways. However, the BA flight had been late, and at about 9 p.m., I was falling asleep at the wheel of the rental car.

"We've got to stop," said Lizzie, "Or we'll drive off the road and be killed." This was dramatic, but perfectly true.

The trouble was that, back in 1986, there were not many hotels to choose from in Saginaw: it was a grim, industrial town, churning out Chevrolets and GM trucks night and day. A roadside No-Tell Motel looked like our only option: it had a buzzing neon sign saying VACAN*Y. It cost twenty dollars a night. The proprietor looked at us in an old-fashioned way, as he gave us the room key.

"We're married!" Lizzie insisted, giving him our two passports – hers still with her maiden name. "In fact, we got married yesterday!"

The proprietor had obviously heard it all before. "Yeah, well, you pay in advance and you leave the room clean, OK?"

Lizzie went up a further five points in my estimation, when we saw the room. It had seen better days. In fact, it had probably seen everything a motel room has ever seen. But Lizzie did not run, screaming, back to the car.

"I'm not taking my clothes off," she declared. "We'll just sleep on top of the bedding for a few hours, and then be on our way to Charlevoix."

I remember having to find a coin-box phone – remember a time before cellphones? – to call George Colburn and explain what had happened. He told me that there was a welcoming committee still waiting at his house, to greet us, and they had been hitting the bottle quite substantially since 7 p.m., when we had planned to arrive.

"Can we do a Take Two tomorrow?" I pleaded. Bless him, George understood, and his friends were the type to need no encouragement to have a party two nights running.

We had a week in Michigan. The weather was perfect, the welcome from all the locals was incredibly warm, and the mosquitos seemed slightly smaller than usual. Lizzie swam, I paddled with my broken leg in the air, and we went boating on Lake Charlevoix. We were invited to drinks everywhere with George's friends, and for the first time in several weeks we really relaxed.

I had already learned how to use crutches to get around. I was really rather negligent about my cast and the healing bones inside. I decided to wrap it all up in plastic, so that

I could splash about properly in the water, and I neglected to ask whether I should, perhaps, be doing some physical therapy to help things heal. Twenty years later, these chickens came home to roost: my leg set at a strange angle, which triggered inflammation in the pelvis and eventually required an entire hip replacement. But that was far in the future.

In Annapolis, Maryland, we were given a further heroes' welcome by Luc Cuyvers and his co-producer Chris White. We spent the minimum amount of time discussing scripts for *The Blue Revolution* and the maximum amount of time eating soft-shelled crabs from the Chesapeake Bay. And then it was on to Mexico City, to meet up with Michael Gill, Carlos Fuentes and the *Buried Mirror* team.

Yes, you guessed it, there was yet another welcoming party. The combination of being recently married and hobbling around on crutches caused equal amounts of concern and hilarity among the hotel staff, the production crew and drivers all over Mexico. But the schedule had been planned long in advance and was both grueling and very exciting.

Rather like my first six-week trip round China, this trip was planned to reveal all aspects of Mexico: from the sophisticated to the deeply rural and poverty-stricken; from the Spanish colonial splendors to the vastly impressive pyramids and ruins of Chichen Itza and a dozen other pre-Columbian sites; from scary, brooding volcanoes to turquoise waterfalls and stunning beaches.

Carlos Fuentes was the most knowledgeable tour guide anyone could wish for. He was not with us all the time, but whenever we were scheduled to visit a location that he felt was not self-explanatory, or where he hoped to film a piece to camera when we had full funding, he would be there. In Guanajuato, he introduced us to what many say is the most beautiful colonial city in Mexico: founded in 1559, it owes its splendid architecture to the vast quantities of silver discovered there by the Spanish. It is also considered the birthplace of the Mexican independence movement. But Carlos wanted us to see something very different and completely unexpected.

The mummies of Guanajuato have, in the last thirty years, become a well-known tourist attraction. Back in 1986, before the city was declared a World Heritage Site by UNESCO, they were still just a local phenomenon. There are over a hundred bodies in this macabre collection, in caves and corridors under the ground. Something in the mineral content of the soil, coupled with the warm, dry climate of the city and perhaps also its altitude, led to their spontaneous mummification. There are newborn infants, men and women in their prime, and arthritic, elderly corpses: all still fully dressed, if a little timeworn. Local legend has it that they were all people who had been buried alive for one reason or another, but there is apparently no proof of that.

Carlos wanted to talk about the unique Mexican approach to death, and where better to do it than here, and in the municipal cemetery above the museum? The celebration of the Day of the Dead takes place on November 1 and 2. Today, this happens all over Latin America, but it started in Mexico. Why? It seems to owe as much to pre-Christian cultures as to Catholicism. The Aztecs were notoriously bloodthirsty in battle and in sacrificial ritual. Two of their twenty-day months were consecrated to the dead, and it seems to have been one long festival.

For the common people, death became something you laughed at. What other option was there? It was part of the natural cycle. As in so many cases, the Catholic Church connected previous pagan traditions to a holy day of its own. November 1 is All Saints' Day, when Catholics all over the world visit cemeteries to remember dead relatives and friends. But in Mexico? Things are a little different.

There are no black clothes, veils or discreet tears here. Whole families gather for two nights and a day, spreading out large and lavish feasts on their family graves, for the dead to enjoy with the living. The atmosphere is one of carnival: skeletons dressed in stylish party clothes join the living for the festival; large and small painted skulls carved out of sugar are enjoyed by adults and children alike. There is fancy dress, music and dancing.

Our pilgrimage round Mexico covered everything from the sublime to the ridiculous. Back in the 1980's, when we were there, the only way to approach Tulum, the archaeological site on the Atlantic Coast, was by small boat, which meant jumping out into the waves and wading ashore.

How could I do that with my leg in plaster? The local boatmen came up with an instant answer: I would be carried ashore, horizontally and fully dressed, by six of them, on their shoulders, as if they were carrying a coffin. I just had to stay rigid, like a corpse. It turns out that it is not easy to stay frozen into a horizontal position, while sweating boatmen manhandle you like a piece of meat. But I did so, more or less, though they were laughing so hard that they nearly dropped me into the waves, as they swung me off the boat. That is not a scene that I will easily forget.

And how was I going to scale the many pyramids, with my crutches? I decided to throw the crutches to one side and rush up the step-pyramids on all fours - or, rather, on all threes, since I realized I should not put much weight on a healing leg. Lizzie and the production team were aghast: what if I fell? But going up crabwise lowered my center of gravity, and after a Mexican lunch - which, of course, involved at least one Margarita and a couple of beers - I felt able to do anything. At the age of forty, I was having my second childhood.

Talking about Mexican lunches, I need to record that Montezuma's Revenge, the famous Aztec curse, struck as all, as we wended our way round the country. No-one was hit harder than Lizzie. For most of us, it was the all too familiar need to find a toilet every ninety minutes at best. At worst we had to be prepared to leap out of a minibus or car and perform profusely at a moment's notice, behind the nearest tree or advertisement hoarding. But for Lizzie, it was serious. She was in real pain, unable to eat anything but equally unable to throw up or pass it through to the other end of her system. What kind of honeymoon was this?

Doctors were called at various cities en route. One of them listened to her carefully from every angle through a stethoscope, before offering his diagnosis: the pain was heart disease, he said, but he could suggest no treatment. Lizzie explained that her pain was in her gut, and that her heart was several inches to the north of where the pain was. The doctor was quite offended to be told that his diagnosis was nonsense, and left the hotel in a huff, without even presenting a bill. Lizzie decided she should rest whenever possible and take liquids, but under no account drink the water, unless in the form of hot tea.

But all good things must come to an end, even stomach pain, and by the end of the trip, she was fine. Well, ninety percent fine, and very selective about what she would put in her mouth: freshly scrambled eggs were the only sure-fire selection, and even then she virtually stood over the cook, to make sure he had washed his hands thoroughly before preparing them.

From Olmecs to Aztecs, from Cortes to Pancho Villa and Zapata, we all felt we had done Mexico from top to bottom and east to west by the time we had finished. It was sad to say goodbye to Carlos Fuentes and the team, but Lizzie and I were very glad to fly on to Los Angeles and relax.

But what was waiting for us there? Of course – another party, set up by my friend and business manager Pat Russell, at the house we co-owned in Manhattan Beach. And who was waiting, there in the yard? All my friends from *Cosmos* – Richard Wells, David Oyster, "H.J." Brown the cameraman – and a stunning live rock band, fronted by Pat's daughter. Pat had organized wine, a huge buffet, and a tremendous welcome for my new bride. In spite of my broken leg, we danced till the sun went down and the neighbors started to complain about the music.

And then? Lizzie and I said goodbye to our guests and took off to visit a sexy nightclub, just a few miles north in Marina del Rey. Thirty years later, I still cannot believe that we had the energy to prolong the evening into the small hours of the following day.

"Why don't we live *here*?" I remember suggesting to my bride as we sat by the nightclub's swimming pool in the warm night air, a block or two from the Pacific Ocean. But Lizzie never really took to Los Angeles. She felt it was too spread out, too smoggy, and too much associated with my past life.

"Who'd want to bring up a child here?" she asked me.

I had no good answer. But, being English, and by instinct wanting to own property wherever possible, we started to look at houses of our own in Manhattan Beach. Maybe the quiet ocean-side community would isolate us from the roaring tumult, artificial glitter, traffic jams and constant smog of LA?

It was sheer luck that we had planned to stay a weekend with my dear friend Brendan O'Regan in the San Francisco Bay Area only a couple of weeks later. We flew up the coast to a warm welcome and a bottle of wine.

At 6 a.m., the morning after our arrival, Lizzie woke up, walked out onto Brendan's balcony in Sausalito, gazed at the fresh, sparkling bay in the first rays of the rising sun, and changed my life entirely.

"Wait," she said. "I've got an idea. Let's live HERE!"

PART TWO: MY SECOND LIFE

INTRODUCTION TO PART TWO

As I suggested at the start of the book, my life seems to split into two distinct halves: before and after moving to the USA. It was Lizzie who inspired me to live in America full time and to start a second family there. Eventually, in 2002, we would both become dual citizens of the US and the UK, along with our children Pippa and James. But it was back in 1986 that our lives had a new beginning.

We had married in London in July of that year, and immediately toured around the US and Mexico, paid for by two projects – *The Buried Mirror* and *The Blue Revolution*, as described at the end of Part One. We had ended up in Los Angeles, and then made a side-trip to the San Francisco Bay Area, to stay with a friend. One August morning in 1986, Lizzie had woken to see the sun rising over the beauty of the bay and said:

"Let's live here!"

Lizzie makes quick life decisions and is usually right about them. When we came to discuss the practicalities of choosing San Francisco over Los Angeles, she had all the answers at her fingertips.

"You've had far too many girlfriends in Los Angeles," she said, "and I don't want to keep bumping into them. We couldn't live there."

"Well, I don't want to start my second marriage like I started my first, back in west London," I responded. "Barnes in the rain. No thanks."

"Right," said Lizzie. "So that's why we need to start somewhere completely new: San Francisco. It will be an adventure for both of us." She can be very definite, once her mind is made up.

I knew that I was already beguiled by the golden west we had described in *The West of the Imagination*. I had grown to know and even appreciate Los Angeles, but San Francisco was alien territory in many ways. True, it had cable cars – and trams, indeed! It was a favorite destination for vacationers. It liked to call itself 'Everyone's Favorite City', but that always seemed to me like a hokey PR gambit. Could it ever be 'home' for me? Or for Lizzie?

I drew up a complete list of the people I knew in San Francisco. There were only three: John Lyddon, a fun-loving former boyfriend of Janelle Balnicke, who I'd met (with her) in 1979; Judy Flannery, one of the *Cosmos* team, a great producer and loyal friend; and of course Brendan O'Regan, one of my best friends, ever since we were both graduate students at Indiana University. It was on his balcony in Sausalito that Lizzie had had her epiphany. They were all charming and happy to welcome us. But, knowing just three people: was this enough?

To me, Northern California did seem full of energy and optimism. Everyone liked to say that it was a wellspring of creativity and hope – and a bohemian paradise. But what would Lizzie feel about California in the long run? Would she take to it? Would it be just a passing fancy? Or would she feel like a 'trailing spouse', dragged to a far-off place with no friends, no family, no work, just me? Would she be homesick and depressed? Would I?

Of course, as we agreed, we could simply try it out for a year or two. We still had the London flat. We could still go back and spend time with our families in England. I could see my parents, Amanda and Juliet, and my various in-laws, cousins and stepfamilies. Lizzie could visit her parents, both in remarkably good health, and see her brothers, nieces, nephews and her many friends. But could we actually start all over again, living five thousand miles away from our roots? Would we come to regret it?

There was one major drawback at the start: my office was in Los Angeles. My business manager, Pat Russell, was in Los Angeles. The entire movie business was based in Los Angeles. How could I create a successful film company in the San Francisco Bay Area?

Remember, this was before Pixar, before the explosive growth of Silicon Valley and the world of CD-ROMs, let alone video games. There were a few advertising agencies in San Francisco, which supported one film laboratory and a couple of sound studios. But that was all, as far as I knew – apart from Francis Ford Coppola's office and George Lucas's secretive Skywalker Ranch, many miles north of the city.

How could I survive as a serious filmmaker in San Francisco? Where would I find the talent and the staff? But being a newly wedded husband, desperate not to screw up a marriage a second time, I agreed to give San Francisco a year to prove itself. And as it happened, I was soon to discover a treasure trove of independent filmmakers, hiding in plain sight in and around the Bay Area.

Lizzie promptly gave up her job at the BBC, as I had done six years earlier, and planned to come out for a year to join me in California. It was to be a lonely time for her in many ways: she had no friends of her own and was not permitted to work in the US for the first two years after marrying me. This is a heartless rule, devised by the US Immigration and Naturalization Service, to ensure that any union is not simply a marriage of convenience, to get an "alien" into the country. But someone had to work, and that was me. What could I do to earn money, in the Bay Area?

■■

12. WE THE PEOPLE, WITH PETER JENNINGS

By sheer chance, I had been talking for some time to Beverley Ornstein, a thoroughly experienced and no-nonsense producer from KQED, the Public Television (PBS) station in San Francisco. She was happy to continue the conversation, and happier still that I was thinking of moving up the coast from LA. She had a great project up her sleeve, she told me, if she could just get it funded: *We the People*, a celebration of the Bicentennial of the Constitution of the US, with the Bill of Rights thrown in for good measure.

The added bonus was that she had persuaded Peter Jennings, the celebrated ABC-TV *World News Tonight* anchor, to take his first ever sabbatical from that show, to front the PBS series – but could she shake the money down from the tree? She was off to New York on a "red-eye" (overnight) flight in a few days, to bend the knee at another corporate headquarters.

To set all this in context, you have to understand the reality of life at a PBS station. Always begging, always organizing fund-drives and obliged to flatter the local philanthropists, most PBS stations cannot afford to have many producers on staff who could be called "thoroughly experienced."

Beverley was the exception: tough and two-fisted, she would not take any in-house bullshit from committees or limp-wristed managers. It was a lucky time for KQED: my old friend Judy Flannery was in charge of Arts programming – with lots of mold-breaking dance, music and experimental work to cover in the Bay Area. Head of news and current affairs was the shrewd Nat Katzman, standing up for his journalists and defending their right to create accurate and provocative programming.

Beverley was quite clear about how *We the People* would be done: she would hire some extra office space down the road, well away from the main building. That way, her new creative team would be isolated from the union-minded, defeatist rump of old-timers at the station, whose idea of a good time was to do the least possible work for the maximum pay. She would hire mostly new staff on short-term contracts, to produce the show. She would fight for our editorial independence. And she would phone me in less than a week, which she did.

"Are you available, David?" she asked me on the phone. "You'll be co-Senior Producer, in charge of producing and directing all the Peter Jennings pieces to camera. Could you start next month?"

"Beverley," I asked, "Have you got the money?"

She chuckled. "Oh yes indeed," she said, "but I can't tell you who it is yet. There's going to be an official announcement next week. But you can book your ticket."

It seemed too good to be true. Lizzie jumped at the possibility. I negotiated a job for Pat Russell on the project, doing research into archive photographs and movie footage, so that we could move Pantechnicon and InCA USA up to San Francisco, at least temporarily. We started looking for a one-year rental apartment in the city.

We found the perfect thing: a furnished two-bedroom flat in a quiet street just behind the U.S. Mint, on Upper Market Street. It was owned by a gay couple, who kept it immaculately clean. They were entranced by the idea of English newly-weds looking after their slice of paradise for a year, while they went and had exotic fun on Mykonos, or whichever Mediterranean island was *de rigeur* for the gay lifestyle at the time.

Lizzie and I could not believe it: here we were, a block from Upper Market Street, handy for trams downtown, in a cozy nest in – could it be true? – "everybody's favorite city."

We immediately invited an English friend of ours, Richard Dixey, to stay in our spare room. He was touring California, doing some sort of informal scientific research on psychology and health. He was coming to visit our mutual friend, Brendan. What could be more fun, to invite our first guest?

We realized just what we had let ourselves in for on the following Sunday. We had heard there was a Gay Pride procession that was due to pass along Upper Market Street, so we turned out with Richard to have a look. There were thousands of people on the streets, rainbow flags everywhere. It turned out that our flat was on the edge of the Castro neighborhood, already the epicenter of the world's gay revolution.

The procession started with a bang: stunt riding from Dykes on Bikes. Two dozen lesbian bikers performing amazing tricks, rearing up on their back wheel, exhausts roaring, the crowd going crazy with cheering and applause. And then came the marching bands, the Gay Men's Chorus chanting the anthems of the differently sexed, bevies of acrobats in tiny posing pouches, vast fluttering flags and banners, an open (ex-Blackpool!) tram carrying the City's mayor and other worthies, waving at the crowds, and in stark contrast, a string of floats registering the terrible toll that AIDS was then taking on the gay community, but all in all in a spirit of optimism and defiance that was a tonic to behold.

"My God," said Richard Dixey, who liked to think of himself as a man of the world, "I've never seen anything like it." And nor had we. This was San Francisco on steroids. What would it be like, to work here?

I turned up the next day at KQED, for my first day of work. There, I was introduced to an even bigger production crew than we had had on *Cosmos*, or so it seemed. To fit in with Peter Jennings' contract, and the approaching Bicentennial of the Constitution, we had to get everything created and complete – all four films – in nine months. All four films had to be in production side by side.

Beverley had clinched the funding by putting the arm-lock on Merrill Lynch, an investment bank. As often used to be the way with PBS projects, funding could be secured from companies who felt they had something to be embarrassed about or ashamed of. Why else had oil companies like Exxon Mobil been such fervent supporters of the network? Some said that PBS stood for the Petroleum Broadcasting Service.

Underwriting a PBS series could therefore be a public act of corporate contrition – something that John Kenneth Galbraith liked to laugh about, noting that none of them were sufficiently ashamed of their conduct to underwrite his series, *The Age of Uncertainty*. More practically, supporting PBS also got the company logo spread around in front of traditionally liberal voters, hopefully triggering the response: "these guys can't be all bad, eh?"

In this case, though I forget the particulars, Congress had found Merrill Lynch guilty of some sort of financial shenanigans, and part of the public "mea culpa," they had been advised by their lawyers, might be the funding of a feel-good, all-American PBS project. What better redemption than a series celebrating the birth of American constitutional rights? And, what is more, Merrill could hold special events all over the country in connection with the broadcasts. They organized "Ratification Balls," to be held on the calendar date when each state had individually ratified the constitution. This was PR gold.

The final cherry on the frosting was the active participation, in an advisory capacity, of the American Bar Association, to keep us legally watertight and to give the project the gravitas that it required. Beverley took an overnight plane to New York, the deal was signed with Merrill Lynch and the first check was written within a week, I believe. We were off to the races...

Because Beverley was determined not to have all the old and tired production timeservers of the TV station seconded to her mold-breaking blue-ribbon production, independent filmmakers had been drafted in from all over California.

"But why me?" I asked her.

"Because you've worked with so many famous big-name on-camera hosts. I'm sure you know how to handle them if they get difficult, David," she said. "And Peter's Canadian, so he's halfway to being a Brit, after all."

Many of the production team became good friends. Just as on *Cosmos*, when I acquired twenty friends immediately upon arrival, so too with *We the People* in San Francisco. Joan Saffa, for example, who had started as an editor at KQED and graduated to become a full producer, went on not just to be a friend, but to play a leading role with me on *The Heart of Healing, Amelia Earhart: the Final Hours, The Promise of Play* and *Keeping Score*. The list of Bay Area documentary stars on *We the People* was impressive. It included Bill Jersey, veteran producer of thought-provoking current affairs films, Rob Epstein, multi-award-winning filmmaker and many others. This was a first-class team. But what would the star be like?

When Peter Jennings first came to San Francisco for our project, he had not visited the city for more than thirty years. I was part of a small delegation that met him at the airport. As we drove through the streets to his discreet boutique hotel, he was astonished.

"I can't believe it," he said. "This is still a wooden city."

We reminded him that, in earthquake country, there were only two alternatives: build houses and smaller structures in wood and hope they would creak and sway in the ripples of a quake, or build with strong reinforced steel and concrete, and bolt the skyscrapers onto bedrock. And in all cases, you kept your fingers firmly crossed.

From the very start, Peter was completely professional. He approached the project as if he was still in the newsroom.

"Let's have no wigs – no actors pretending to be Washington, Jackson or Franklin, and no quill pens," he urged us. "What we have to do is to show people why the Constitution and the Bill of Rights are still relevant today."

This became our guiding principle. To what extent had the United States stayed faithful to its Constitution and Bill of Rights? Which were the amendments that had challenged them, and which had strengthened them? Why was the Dredd Scott decision of 1954 so important? How well were our search and seizure rights being protected? How was it that the US was the only nation on earth that regularly referred back to a written Constitution that was 200 years old? Not even the French did that.

On one occasion, Peter and I were working together on a piece of to-camera script, when he looked up at me and grinned.

"I think it's pretty funny," he said, "that Beverly hired you and me to do this: a Canuck and a Brit. Maybe they couldn't trust themselves to be entirely objective."

Preparing for each shoot, Peter's immense experience as a newsman came to the fore. He could absorb large quantities of detailed background from Bob Peck, the consultant lawyer assigned to our project by the American Bar Association. He would immediately tease out the key issues that were still relevant today. Then he would sit down at his trusty portable typewriter and bash out a near-perfect script, with one carbon copy. The first desk-top computers were already available, but Peter would have none of them.

"I get my inspiration by hitting the keys of my old Remington," he said. "This way, I have to think as I type, and I usually get it right first time."

But he virtually never used that first version. Being a newsman, he always loved to rewrite at the last minute. One evening, we were filming him driving up Riverside Drive and across Harlem in New York City. His piece to camera was about individual rights, as well as thorny Second Amendment gun issues. We tried a couple of takes, and he suddenly pulled over to the curb.

"This isn't working," he said. "I've got to rewrite."

He grabbed his old typewriter, stepped out of the car, and sat down on the curb. In the light of a streetlamp, he started to re-type.

I nearly had a heart attack on the spot. This was one of the least welcoming zones in Harlem – at least, if you were a small bunch of white guys with a TV camera. We had decided – no, correct that, Peter had insisted – that we would not have a police escort of any sort, so as not to draw attention to ourselves. At that precise moment, however, I prayed for a cop car to come cruising past.

A small group of black youths materialized out of the background and approached us in a non-committal way. As producer-director, I was responsible for whatever might happen to the crew – and to Peter. But he was not fazed for a moment.

"Hi," he said to the group of locals, "I'm just trying to get some script right."

One of the guys frowned in disbelief.

"Are you the guy on the evening news?" he asked.

"Yes," said Peter, getting up from his seat in the gutter. "I'm Peter Jennings. "Who are you?" All four of the Harlem group politely introduced themselves, and Peter shook them by the hand.

"Now, perhaps you can help me," he said. "Do you have a couple of minutes? I want to read you the script and see if you agree with me."

To my utter disbelief, Peter then rehearsed the script he had just re-written, by performing it to the guys from the 'hood.

"Does that sound right to you?" he asked. It was a piece that described individual rights and the necessary limitations on state power. The listeners concentrated, and when Peter had finished, they made a couple of very good suggestions.

"Yes, that's much better," Peter told them. "Thank you. That's what I'll say. So, if that's OK, we need to get on and finish this now."

He then proceeded to shake everyone's hand again, get back in the car with me and the crew, and drive off.

Over my shoulder, I saw our critics giving us a polite and cheery wave goodbye, without a hint of irony. Peter had managed the situation with effortless professionalism. He was as good as his word and incorporated the suggestions word for word into the new script, which was excellent. Much later, when my heartbeat had returned to its normal rate, I wondered how those four guys had described what had happened to friends or family:

"Oh yeah, that guy from the *World News Tonight* pulled over, and got us to edit his script for him." Who would have believed that story?

On another occasion, we were due to film with Peter in San Quentin Prison, on San Francisco Bay. From a distance it looks like a fine, classical piece of architecture in a most impressive waterside position. Up close, as you go through four separate entrance gates into temporary holding pens inside the fortress, it is pretty scary. There are a series of clanging doors and huge deadbolts being shut firmly behind you.

Everyone, Peter included, had to sign a release that stated that, if taken hostage while in the prison, neither the State of California nor the Federal Government would be prepared to negotiate your release.

Peter had insisted that he should be filmed in the heart of the prison, inside a multi-story block with cells filled with real prisoners. No namby-pamby long-shots of barbed wire and conning towers with guards stationed with machine guns: Peter said he needed to be right in and among the prisoners.

Twenty years later, I went back to San Quentin twice more, to support a remarkable film created by Joe de Francesco, featuring a performance by prisoners of the classic work *John Brown's Body*. The same conditions applied. But that first time, to be inside a massive cellblock, in the open area between three stories of walkways and prison cells, was unforgettable.

We had taken an iconic personality right into the jaws of hell, it seemed: Daniel in the lion's den. And how would we be able to keep the prisoners quiet, so that Peter could do his piece to camera? The corrections officers had reminded us that there was no way they could personally prevent catcalls, hoots, whistles, boos, banging of tin mugs on iron bars or whatever else.

Peter, as ever, was the height of cool. There was a slight lull in the habitual chatter and banging while we set up our camera and lights in the central area. Peter cleared his throat, and then said, in a calm, clear and fairly loud voice:

"Excuse me, could I have your attention for a few minutes, please? I'm Peter Jennings."

Suddenly, you could hear a pin drop.

"Thank you," said Peter to the entire building-full of inmates, none of whom he could see directly. "What I need to talk about is how the Constitution and the Bill of Rights protects *your* rights as much as it protects mine. In fact, it protects you more than me, because I'm a Canadian, and if I do wrong, they can just throw me out of the country."

This produced laughter, light applause and whistles from all sides.

"So I'd be grateful if you can let me have about five minutes silence, to say my piece to the camera, and then we can wrap things up."

There was, incredibly, five minutes of almost complete silence – in a block that must have been fifty yards long, and three floors high, containing hundreds of prisoners: not just the "trusties" but the lifers, the rapists, "the scum of the earth", as one of the prison staff charmingly described them.

At the end of his piece to camera, Peter chose to say, "It was remarkable at the time, and it's still remarkable today. This Constitution – and the Bill of Rights – is so solid, so fundamentally fit for purpose, that it has lasted two hundred years with only a handful of amendments, and it may last two hundred more. It protects everyone – every citizen, every person in this cellblock. Could any of the Founding Fathers have imagined that? It certainly makes you think."

There was a beat of two, and then one lone voice – one prisoner from some cell high up in the building – said, in a very clear and nicely ironic voice,

"Well, it certainly made *ME* think, Peter."

The whole place erupted in laughter and applause, and – to do him credit – Peter joined in, laughing heartily.

"Yes, well, thank you and goodnight!" he said in his *World News Tonight* voice, provoking more laughter.

We got out safely, and, miraculously, Peter had done his piece to camera in one take. I think he knew that we had been lucky. The chances of us getting a usable second take, after the laughter, would have been zero. You could not do a piece to camera with cellmates banging tin cups on the iron railings.

The series, *We the People*, had a large audience on PBS and was repeated many times. Merrill Lynch, sniffing success in the air, committed a big advertising budget to the project. Press packs were presented in expensive blue folders, as if they were legal briefs, tied in red ribbon. Peter was a tireless promoter of the project. His day job at ABC's *World News Tonight* resumed, of course, but we were all proud that he had secured a leave of absence to do our project. He subsequently went on to do one or two further PBS projects, most notably on the tragedy of AIDS.

But a further tragedy was his own early death. I kept in contact with him and introduced him to a fascinating potential project about the writing of the early Christian gospels. Called *The Four Witnesses*, written by Robin Griffith Jones, chaplain of my old Oxford college, it was a detective story that asked how and why the many other gospels of the time had been suppressed. Peter, a practicing Christian, was fascinated, and even persuaded ABC to produce its own Easter special on the dramatic life of Saint Paul. But the longer series was not to be.

For twenty-two years, Jennings had hosted ABC's *World News Tonight*. In 2005, he died from complications connected to lung cancer, at the tragically early age of sixty-seven. I have never met or worked with a nicer man: generous to a fault, always encouraging those younger and less experienced than himself, always a stickler for hard work and accuracy, he was one of a handful of great newsmen who followed in the footsteps of Ed Murrow and Walter Cronkite. But he was also probably the kindest of them all – and I did meet both Cronkite (in connection with *The Messengers* in the early 80's) and Tom Brokaw (who hosted the NBC Special based on *The Heart of the Dragon*).

• •

13. FREQUENT FLIER: TAHITI TO MAIDA VALE

We the People had offered Lizzie and me nearly a year's free trial of living in the San Francisco Bay Area, and it had passed the test with flying colors. It became home for us for the next thirty years or more. But it took a good long time before it really *felt* like home in any way. Of course, we were living in a place unlike anywhere else in America, or indeed the world. Whether in the city – some of the time – or across the Golden Gate Bridge in the picturesque woodland of Marin County, it just seemed too special – even magical – to be real. It was Wonderland.

We discovered both natural and man-made wonders. We stumbled across the best English country pub west of Ireland: the Pelican Inn at Muir Beach. We realized that you could avoid the San Francisco fogs by driving fifteen miles in any direction, where it was almost unfailingly sunny for nine months of the year. We figured out that it took not much over three hours to drive to the ski slopes at Squaw Valley, or the semi-desert lands of the California interior, or the dramatic coastline of Big Sur.

But were we ready to commit totally to the United States? Not quite yet. We needed at least one big self-indulgent celebration of our marriage and of our freedom from our old ways of thinking.

So Lizzie and I decided to take a glorious break and have the real honeymoon we had never really had in Michigan, Annapolis and Mexico. That was an amazing trip, but we had never been alone, away from George Colburn, Carlos Fuentes or Michael Gill for longer than twelve hours at a time. Where could we go that was utterly new to us, and really fascinating? Looking west from San Francisco, the Pacific beckoned: all those islands, all those exotic adventures we could have... The problem was, unless we had a project to pay for it, we really could not afford to disappear for a couple of months on an extended vacation.

Fortune smiled, in the most unexpected way. Luc Cuyvers, the Belgian producer with whom we had stayed and briefly worked in Annapolis a year before, had received some funding and needed some research done, prior to moving into full production. His project, *The Blue Revolution,* required an InCA volunteer to go to the Great Barrier Reef in North-Eastern Australia, then to Hawaii, and finally to join him in Japan to set up some locations.

Well, how about us? In California, we were a lot closer than anyone based at InCA's London office. And if we played our cards right, we could work in Tahiti as well. And of course, to get to Japan from North-Eastern Australia, the best way – both going out and coming back – was via Hawaii... The makings of an astonishing trip were all lining up.

Within a month, we found ourselves on a jet, bound for Pape'ete, the capital city of the Tahitian Islands. Tahiti was then, and still is, a French territory. The main points of call for cruise ships – the capital, plus Bora Bora – were already, back in the 1980's, somewhat spoiled by the detritus and thick-headedness of international visitors. But Moorea island was still largely unspoiled, and the more distant islands were a revelation.

We started with a week in a simple beach hut on Moorea. We had not considered the weather: it was the rainy season, and boy, did it rain – but usually only for a few hours each day. There were no other tourists to be seen. Lizzie did topless cartwheels on the wet grass by the beach; we snorkeled for hours on end, in a paradise of luminous fish, weaving through the coral. I don't think I have ever been more relaxed than I was that month. Apart from the date of our onward ticket to Sydney, we had no plans.

We decided that we should visit more remote islands. One, called Maupiti, could only be reached by a mail boat that sailed twice a week. This turned out to be a rusty old tub, which stank of diesel and unwashed bodies inside, so we slept on deck for the overnight passage, and watched the stars. Lizzie, who had sailed across the Atlantic years before, tried to point out the constellations, but the southern sky is very different than the one we knew. This was an adventure into a new planet.

On Maupiti, we stayed with a teacher, under a tin-roofed house: when it rained, you could hardly hear yourself think. We ate delicious, simply cooked seafood with the family. Knives and forks were unnecessary. They were astonished to discover an English couple who actually spoke French, and we talked long into the night.

One morning, the teacher asked us if we had any plans that day. Other than lying on the beach and swimming, of course, we did not. So he invited us out with his eldest son on his outrigger canoe.

"This is a special journey", he announced, "And we'd be honored if you accompanied us."

It was a perfect day. The ominous clouds of early morning had melted away, and the whole island felt newly washed and sparkling clean. The canoe was quite big, with a substantial outrigger, and had both a sail and an outboard motor. There was room enough for all four of us, as we motored off into the turquoise lagoon. It was blissful, but why was this trip so special?

After about ten minutes, the teacher threw the anchor overboard a couple of times, till he was satisfied we were firmly locked in one position, and then nodded to his son. The boy stripped off, and dived noiselessly into the water, swimming slowly away from us, looking down into the water, scanning from side to side.

"It's his birthday," said the teacher. "He's sixteen today. He's entitled to catch and kill a turtle for the first time – if he has the skill to do it."

We watched the tousle-haired boy circling gently round, about fifty yards from us – and then suddenly dive underwater. There was a frothing mass. We strained to see what on earth was going on.

"He has to catch it with his bare hands, and get it onto the boat all by himself, before he can kill it," said the teacher.

In the previous weeks, we had often encountered turtles in the lagoons: gentle, patient creatures, which can move very fast when they need to. This challenge was not going to be easy.

The boy wrestled the turtle back to the boat, but how was he going to maneuver it on board? He had to lift and flip it over the wooden gunwale – and this thing must have weighed forty pounds or more. The turtle was getting tired, but so was the boy. But the rules forbade his father (or us) from helping him. Finally, in a sudden burst of strength, he did it – but we now had forty pounds of angry turtle flapping around our feet in the canoe. The boy's father held out his hand and hauled his son aboard.

Promptly, the boy took a small knife from a belt he had been wearing, and without a word, cut the turtle's throat. His father caught the blood in a blue plastic bowl he had brought for the occasion. The deed was done – faultlessly, it appeared. The rite of passage had been observed. Lizzie and I were both in a state of shock: here was man versus nature, red in tooth and claw. But we knew we could not show what we felt.

"Happy Birthday" said the teacher to his son and hugged him.

"Joyeux Anniversaire," we joined in, and shook the boy by the hand.

"Now he's a man," said the teacher proudly, "And we will eat very well tonight!"

Indeed we did. Other friends and family came for the festivities that evening. Each indigenous adult on the islands of Tahiti is allowed to kill just one turtle a year – and no more – to help preserve the species. Turtles are strictly off limits to tourists. But your first turtle is the most important: it means you are a boy no longer.

There are so many memories from that trip to Tahiti that they would fill a whole book by themselves, so I shall let just a couple more slip in, and then we will travel on to Australia. On an even smaller island than Maupiti, we spent three nights by a tiny lagoon, staying in some thatched beach huts, trying to capture the tints of the sunsets in water colors and eating amazing gourmet food, cooked by a French woman who had emigrated, as she said, "to this forgotten lagoon – to the end of the world."

This islet had no electricity, with one exception: by the tiny jetty on the ocean side of the coral reef, there was an international telephone on a white pole, powered by a single solar panel, with a dish pointing upwards to some unseen satellite, far above. The French had installed it, only a few months before. Apart from the short-wave radio, this was the only contact with the outside world.

On a sudden whim, I pulled together all the local coins I had in my pocket and swam across the lagoon to the reef. I clambered up the rocks to the phone and read the instructions. Then I fed several large coins into the slot and tried to dial my mother in London – literally, the other side of the world. It took only about ten seconds for the call to go through. Suddenly, there was my mother's voice, as clear as if she was only a mile away.

"Where are you?" she said. "Are you alright?" She sounded worried for a moment. "Is Lizzie alright?"

I told her where we were– which was hard to believe – and said something about it feeling like a dream. Then I checked that *she* was OK too.

"I'm *fine*," she said, but then she always said that. "And Dad's fine too."

"I miss you," I said, "How are you?"

"We're really *fine*," she insisted. "It's been raining here, but the sun's out now. What's it like there?"

I described the scene that surrounded me, in a couple of brief sentences.

"Oh, David, that's so *wonderful*. What an incredible experience. Don't worry about us. I'm so glad you're having such a good time. All my love…"

And then the beeps came. My money had run out after only a couple of minutes, and we were cut off. I remember standing there in the hot sun and weeping like a small child, as the turquoise water lapped against the reef. I was so happy to be granted this magical adventure, but I so wished that my mother and father could somehow have shared it with us. It says a lot for their generosity of spirit that they never made me feel guilty for traveling to the other side of the world or having a wonderful time. Perhaps they, too, had had enough exciting adventures in their life that they never needed to begrudge me any of mine.

••

Just a week later, we were flying on to Australia: a brief stop in Sydney to get our bearings and to see Dick Gilling – a colleague and friend since the days of *The Ascent of Man* – and Jeremy Eccles – a friend since university days and the Hong Kong adventures on *The Heart of the Dragon* – and then we were flying north, over Queensland, to Cairns, the last sizeable town before the Daintree River, the northern jungle and the biggest reef on earth.

The Great Barrier Reef has been described by many people who are far more knowledgeable than I am, but I can tell you that the experience is without parallel. The best way out to the reef is on an express hydrofoil boat. Then you choose whether to scuba or snorkel. Nothing can prepare you for the vertiginous drop you experience when you come to the edge of the vivid coral, teeming with rainbow-colored fish, and then look down into the inky depths of the Pacific.

For a time, I swam with three manta rays, which accompanied me in a very friendly fashion. You cannot help seeing strange, dark shadows of even larger creatures, and your imagination runs wild: was that a dolphin? A shark? An octopus? A giant squid? Or just a distant human diver with an oxygen tank? The reef, so tragically endangered by global warming, is a must-see experience. If you ever have the chance, just go.

For this book, my final memory from our 'second honeymoon' trip will be from Japan. I had been there twice before - on *The Ascent of Man*, to film Samurai sword-makers and the gaunt relics of the atomic bombing of Hiroshima, and on *Cosmos*, to film a strange

Japanese fairy story about talking fish and princesses – evidence of the wonderful unearthliness of our planet's distant cultures. This time, however, it was all about fish. We were, after all, preparing locations for *The Blue Revolution,* a series about the world's oceans.

We met the Executive Producer, Luc Cuyvers, in Shimonoseki, a distant port town at the south-western tip of Honshu, Japan's main island. It is an important fishing port, and that is exactly what it smelt of: fish. In that respect alone it reminded me of Reykjavik (Iceland) and Grimsby (north-east England). Lizzie likes eating fish – indeed she now eats no meat – but seaweed soup for breakfast, together with odd, unrecognizable bits of squid and who knows what in the broth – that was a little much. But we slowly got used to it (well, sort of). Then, on our final evening, the good fishermen had prepared a surprise for us.

We were already used to eating sushi and sashimi, I am glad to say: there was plenty of that in Los Angeles, though it had hardly been seen yet in London. So we had enjoyed the various seafood dishes brought to the table by our hosts, and I particularly like Sake and Japanese beer, though Lizzie is less fond of both. Nonetheless, we were enjoying ourselves, along with Luc, when the last dish arrived. It was a whole fish on a large wooden platter.

The platter was banged down on the table, and the fish promptly leapt into the air. Its skin had been scored down the back from top to bottom, with crosscuts every couple of inches, but it was still alive. Somehow, it had been stunned before serving, but the bang of the platter on the table had brought it back to life. It flipped and flapped, and we looked on, aghast. Even Luc Cuyvers – who assumed a perfectly honed affectation of Belgian nonchalance at such events (think of Hercule Poirot) – was shocked. This really *was* sashimi: how could it be any fresher?

Luckily, they took the fish away again, to carve it up, and we three Europeans gratefully accepted another drink or three. The Japanese fishermen found the whole thing tremendously funny and clapped us on the back for being such good sports. This was a traditional ritual for visitors to their town. What fun. We took it in turns to drink each other's health, and there were a lot of locals at our table!

Somewhat relaxed, we returned to our Ryokan, the traditional inn where we were staying. Luc suggested that we calm our beating hearts and sweat out some of the alcohol by visiting the hot baths and having a soak.

"Yes, but it's after midnight," I said.

"No problem," said Luc. "They keep them open all night. It's a tradition."

"Yes, but what about Lizzie?" I asked. "She's not going to have much fun just going to the women's baths by herself."

"No, no," said Luc. "Lizzie, you can come to the men's baths, with us, if you don't mind stripping off. It's very dark in there. If the men see two guys with a girl, they'll presume she's a hooker, and that's considered OK. They do this all the time."

Lizzie was game for an adventure and not in the least embarrassed by the idea of stripping off. A long soak in a hot spring did sound like a very nice idea, after our adventures with the live fish.

"OK, Luc," I said, "But do you know which side is the women's bath, and which is the men's?"

Luke rolled his eyes at me. "David," he said, "I've been coming to Japan for years. I should know the Kanji symbols for 'Men' and 'Women' by now. It's the same sign you see on the toilets."

So we went back to our rooms to get our small white towels and our cotton Yakata robes, and met Luc outside what was apparently the men's bathhouse. We tiptoed in: the place was very large, very dark, and completely empty. We all stripped off and finally relaxed in the welcoming steam. What a great end to a great day! Except, it was not quite the end...

Five minutes later, two old ladies walked into the baths, slowly advanced towards us, talking to each other, glanced our way, and then gave a piercing scream. No, that is wrong, they gave a continuous series of piercing screams, pointing at us and shouting who knows what in Japanese.

"Oh God," said Luc, "We must have chosen the women's baths after all. Quick, let's get out of here before the management come. Or the police."

We leapt out of the pool, clutching our Yakatas and tiny towels as best we could, to preserve our modesty, and ran like hell past the two old ladies - still screaming and shouting something about foreign monsters - or so Luc said, when we asked him to translate later. Luckily, we could run faster than they could, and we disappeared into our rooms, shouting a final "Goodnight" to each other, and trying not to laugh too loudly.

When we checked out the next day, not a word was said, while payment was made and a taxi ordered. The clerk was impeccably polite. Perhaps the old ladies had been so overwhelmed that they had forgotten to complain? But no. As he handed us our receipts, the clerk said, with a hint of a smile:

"I am glad you were able to enjoy our hot springs together. Please come back and visit us again." Stylish people, the Japanese.

As it turned out, *The Blue Revolution* was one of the series, like *The Buried Mirror,* which I helped to prepare, research and write, but never got to produce (see Chapter 24). Luc Cuyvers did not get the full production money for another two or three years, and by then I was deeply involved with other films. I regret not contributing further, in some ways, but Lizzie and I had had a glorious second honeymoon, thanks to Luc's splendid international project.

‥‥‥

The four years between 1986 and 1990 were probably the most busy, confusing and exhilarating of our lives. Where would we like to live? Answer: basically San Francisco, if we could make a living there, but also London. And as for work? I would take anything I could get, to help keep InCA alive in both London and California. But could I really start and maintain a new business in Northern California, with the responsibility of paying staff? And where would the office be?

We threw ourselves into an orgy of real estate activity, as the British often do. We sold Lizzie's London flat and moved her stuff into my place in Maida Vale. We snapped up a large Victorian 'railroad apartment' on San Francisco's Clayton Street, in the Haight-Ashbury district. Over the next year, Lizzie refurbished it brilliantly: she now had a real task to accomplish, so life in San Francisco became more exciting for her.

The strangest thing, for both of us, was that our San Francisco apartment was virtually the same size and had almost exactly the same layout as the Maida Vale flat in London. One long railroad-like corridor led from front to back, with rooms opening off it.

Oddly enough, however, Clayton Street was the exact mirror image of Elgin Mansions. In London, if you got up to pee in the middle of the night, you turned right, went halfway down the long corridor, and turned right again into the bathroom. In San Francisco, you did exactly the same thing, but had to turn left twice, rather than turn right. It is remarkable that neither of us ever pee'd in the linen closet, in one flat or the other. Somehow it just seemed natural that we had stepped "through the looking glass" into a parallel mirror-universe, when we crossed the Atlantic. Things were just the same, but diametrically opposite.

Our most dreamlike experience in the Haight-Ashbury flat was the night we returned from Japan and our adventures with Luc Cuyvers. Jet-lagged beyond belief, having just crossed the Pacific via the international dateline and Hawaii, we went to bed as the sun went down. Sometime after midnight, we were woken by violent banging on our front door and cries of "Fire! Fire!"

We hastily threw on the first clothes that came to hand and stumbled out into the street: more than a hundred people were gathered there, as we watched smoke pouring from the upper floors of a building on the corner of the street, just a few doors away from us. Several fire engines were already on hand. Searchlights illuminated giant ladders and high-pressure hoses, being trained on the flames. They take fires very seriously in San Francisco, since the devastation of 1906.

"What's going on?" asked Lizzie groggily, stupefied by jetlag.

"Someone tried to light a fire in a fireplace that was blocked up," said our neighbor, Patricia Rowan, an elderly artist who lived in the flat above ours. "Stupid hippies, I expect, smoking something. All these buildings are wooden, you know. It only takes a few minutes, and the whole block could be on fire."

Lizzie and I looked at each other. Welcome to Haight-Ashbury, where the summer of love had turned to the winter of fire. Somehow, in our jetlagged state, it did not seem particularly surprising. Within half an hour, everything seemed under control, and we were all allowed back into our homes. The following morning, we woke up at first light.

"Did I dream all that?" asked Lizzie, like Lewis Carroll's Alice, after her adventures. There was still a faint smell of smoke. "No, I can't have done."

For a time, Clayton Street was both office and home, while I slowly wound down our LA operation and sadly said goodbye to Pat Russell, who wanted to stay down south in Manhattan Beach, near her children. But I needed at least one other pair of hands in San Francisco, so I advertised for one in the local free newspaper.

The first and best person to apply was a bright young man called Michael O'Connell. I was interested to know how far he would have to commute, but it turned out that he lived literally next door. Only a thin wooden wall divided his building from ours on Clayton Street. This unlikely serendipity seemed to suggest even more strongly that San Francisco was an *Alice in Wonderland* world. Happily, it led to a twenty-year working relationship with Michael, and a friendship that continues to this day.

Then, to our great delight, Lizzie found she was pregnant. But she didn't like the idea of pushing a baby in a buggy through the discarded needles of the hippies and junkies who still dominated the Haight-Ashbury area. So we threw ourselves back into the real estate market, and found a small townhouse ten miles north of the Golden Gate Bridge in Mill Valley. Miller Terrace sat beside a stream and looked like an illustration in a child's picture book. We bought it, keeping the flat in the Haight as an office for another year.

So we had a base for InCA America's operations. But what about a complete team to work with? Who would do the business management tasks that Pat Russell had done in LA? Serendipity struck once more. By pure chance, in 1988, I bumped into Cherie Rardin, in the Safeway store, four hundred yards from our new house in Mill Valley. She had been the Unit Coordinator and business manager on *Cosmos*. She was not only good at her job but a great character. We had always got on well.

"What are you doing here?" we both asked each other. She had just moved north from LA, and was working at KQED, the PBS station which had produced *We The People*.

"Would you think of leaving, and becoming InCA's American business manager?" I asked.

"I'd love to," said Cherie. "And by the way, I go by the name of Cheryl King now. Cherie Rardin was my name two marriages ago." Ah yes, I thought, this is California, after all.

I found out that she hadn't changed, however: she was still the fun-lover and dancer she had always been, and still the hard worker and responsible manager she could be the rest of the time. At the time of writing this, she is still working with me part time, more than thirty years later.

∙∙

Meanwhile, Lizzie and I were still racing to and fro between London and California. She sat on the plane, heavily pregnant and very uncomfortable as we shuttled backwards and forwards across the Atlantic on British Airways.

Now in his eighties, my father's health was slowly declining. Luckily, I had managed to persuade my parents to move back from the remote country town of Winslow to an area just outside central London quaintly known as Swiss Cottage. It was halfway between Chalk Farm (and the flat in which I had been born) and our flat in Maida Vale. So I was able to see a lot of my father in his final years, for which I am profoundly grateful.

Till the very last, he was a source of kindness, wisdom and humor. He had actively encouraged me to make my new start in the US, when he might well have tugged at my heartstrings, wanting me to be near him in his final years. He, like my mother, was a wonderfully generous person. I felt closer and closer to them, and their deaths devastated me, when they happened. But first the good news...

Our son James was born on a drizzly day in November 1988, at the then-famous (and subsequently closed, alas) Queen Charlotte's Maternity Hospital in West London, where Amanda had been born, twelve years before. Lizzie was not yet sure about the idea of living in the US. She had no real friends of her own there and had been very lonely during the making of *We The People*: she was on her own, discovering the city, while I was – as so often – away having adventures making documentaries. We coined the phrase that – in a marriage – there is often someone who travels, and someone who is 'traveled against' – the one who stays at home.

Lizzie decided that she wanted her son to be British by birth. On 19 November, we welcomed him to the world. We took him home from the hospital to our Maida Vale flat and schlepped the vast pile of new cot, crib, buggies, squeaky toys, cute matinée jackets, nappies (a.k.a. diapers) and other baby kit up the three flights of stairs to the top floor. That is when it first occurred to us that owning a top-floor flat in a block with no elevator was not a very clever idea, if we were planning any long-term family life in London.

James was, like most newborns, a tiny person with scrunched-up features and miraculously complete and perfectly formed fingers, toes and other fiddly bits. He also had immensely powerful lungs. For the first six weeks of his life, unless he was actually on Lizzie's breast, he either slept or cried. He elected to do the crying most of the night. I tried to take the pressure off Lizzie by walking up and down the long 'railroad' corridor of our flat, patting his back, humming Winnie-the-Pooh songs, cradling him in the kitchen while searching for something to watch on British TV at 3 a.m. It never worked.

"Oh, he's just colicky," explained my mother, who'd only had the one child (me) and had always had live-in nanny care, since she was working on stage in the mid to late 1940's. "He'll get over it." And so he did, eventually, but he was never a good sleeper. Like me, he has a restless mind which finds going to sleep a boring process. To this day, he prefers to stay up into the wee small hours of the night.

That Christmas (1988), we took James to see my mother and father in their cozy flat on Christmas Day. I made sure to have my father hold him on his lap and took a photo of them both. Dad was already on an oxygen supply. He had lost one lung (and most of his duodenum) to cancer many years before. We all knew he did not have very long to live.

As I held up the camera, my father smiled and said, "I know what you're doing." And of course, he did: this was the only picture I was ever able to take of James with his paternal grandfather.

We didn't realize the monumental bureaucratic problem triggered by the arrival of James until two weeks later, when we returned with him to the US. We were stopped by the immigration officers at San Francisco Airport.

"Who is this?" they asked us, pointing at the tiny infant. "Does he have a passport? Is he listed on your passport?"

No, he did not, and no, he was not. What had we been thinking? We had registered his birth in London, but not given a thought to his passport status or nationality. There followed some of the most surreal hours I have ever experienced. We were all taken off to what felt like a Cold War interrogation room, somewhere in the bowels of the airport. Two Latino immigration officers came and went with volumes of forms to be filled in.

Their supervisor, a grim-faced charmer in full uniform with a braided military cap, grilled us: how could we have omitted to apply for a visa for the baby, before leaving England? Were we thinking of smuggling him in? How long was he staying? Would he qualify for his own Green Card? Luckily, we had brought his Birth Certificate with us in our carry-on baggage.

Eventually, after a lot of conferring between different grades of officials, the INS (Immigration and Naturalization Service) agreed to treat James as a "Landed Immigrant." They had no power to enter his name on our British passports, so he officially applied for residency all by himself – yes, at the tender age of six weeks. We did help him with the paperwork.

He then had to be photographed, according to the exacting norms of the INS, so that he could have his own authentic Green Card. The rules for such photos insist that the applicant must sit at a three-quarter angle, showing both eyes and one ear, staring into the camera, and that the face must fill half the frame on the photo.

Two Latino officials brought in an ancient box camera, a tripod and a light. They then proceeded to set up an impromptu studio in the room. It looked as if they were preparing to take a Daguerreotype in a nineteenth century studio. Meanwhile, I was given the job of holding James up from behind, like a glove puppet, to have his photo taken.

It was now starting to feel more like an old silent film comedy: Charlie Chaplin, perhaps, or Laurel and Hardy. However firmly I held James up, he flopped around like a rag doll: he was six weeks old, for goodness sake. He was physically unable to hold his head up, even if he had understood that this was required. The officials tried take after take, flash after flash, chattering away to each other in Spanish. Sometimes, James's head was not even in the frame. At the best of times, his head only filled about one eighth of the picture area, and as for showing one ear and staring into the camera – forget it! Eventually, all the hullabaloo and the flashing camera drove the little lad to tears, and then a thoroughly good bawling cry. Lizzie and I felt the same way.

Laurel and Hardy conferred, and went away with their camera, leaving us in limbo. We had no idea what would happen next. Were we free to go?

They eventually returned with a completed Green Card application in James's name. There was his photo: a tiny head in the bottom right hand corner of a one-inch square space. They made us fill out his details in the back of our passports. Then they duly stamped them, with the special relish that immigration officers reserve for stamping official documents, and said to James, without a trace of irony "Welcome to the United States", in a heavy Mexican accent.

Much to James' subsequent embarrassment, this was the Green Card he had to live with for the next ten years. As a piece of identification, it was a joke. But, as the key to residence in the US, it was priceless.

■■■

1989 was a year of constant personal turmoil. Just one month after we had immigrated with James, I heard that my father had died. I immediately returned to London, leaving Lizzie and James in the US: James was not allowed to travel until we had received his formal Green Card.

My mother was distraught: she and my father had been very close. But, as the consummate actress, her stiff upper lip barely trembled when she saw me. We hugged for a long time, without speaking. She threw herself into making arrangements for the cremation, and the modest party afterwards.

Peter and Pamela, Dad's son and daughter from his first marriage, arrived, with spouses. A small group of friends and relatives gathered with us at the Golders Green crematorium, and my father's body was consigned to the flames. I wept and wept, triggered by singing the beautiful hymn "Dear Lord and Father of Mankind." I can still remember, from my schooldays, that it is Hymn Number 383 in the English Hymnal. Its gentleness, its strength, its minor key, its alternating passages of fortissimo and pianissimo – I still tear up when I think of it – and when I think of my father. As the hymn says, "Forgive our foolish ways."

Immediately after the funeral, at Lizzie's insistence, I invited my mother to come out to California to spend at least a month with us – as Lizzie was later to invite *her* mother, after her own father died. My mother stayed with us in our little townhouse in Mill Valley, babysitting James and taking long walks around the town. This was her first time in America, and she found it both baffling and entrancing. She could not believe how kind everyone was to her, and she could barely believe the beauty of the surrounding scenery and the quirkiness of San Francisco.

Shortly before she went back to London, I took her up to a vista point on the Marin County side of the Golden Gate Bridge. It was sunny where we were. But it was also one of those magical mornings when fog shrouds the roadway on the bridge, but the tops of the two bridge supports poke out above the fog, and the distant city appears to float on the clouds, bathed in the morning sun.

"I think you've found it," she said, with tears in her eyes. "The place where the rainbow ends. The pot of gold. I think you'll be happy here."

I realized later what she really meant. She understood better than I did that she had lost her son to America forever, and she was both happy for me and sad at the prospect of her own future. I never really gave enough thought to how lonely she would be when she returned to London.

She and my father had been each other's best friends. She wasn't the type to join clubs or seek out casual friendships. For sure, she had two grandchildren to see and occasionally babysit – Amanda and Juliet – across the river in Helen's London house – an impressive pile in the posher part of Wandsworth. She was also, happily, quite friendly with Peggy Jay, Helen's mother, who lived up the hill in Hampstead. Her closest, oldest friend was Pat Bennett, was alive and well, but Pat still lived out in the country, in Winslow. My mother was also quite cordial with her neighbors. But she had never learned to drive, and just did not seem motivated to get out of London, or even out of her flat, except to do a bit of shopping.

I did not realize what a toll this loneliness was going to take on my mother's health, over the next three years. I was simply too wrapped up in myself and my own new family. I was too selfish to think carefully about her future. Only later did I taste the bitter fruit of regret.

· ·

To keep us afloat while I developed my own projects, I took a position as producer of a film in a series with the odd name of *Minidragons,* executive produced by Leo Eaton, another Brit. This was a PBS project that looked at the rising economies of the smaller countries in South-East Asia: Taiwan, Singapore, South Korea and – the one I picked – Hong Kong. This seemed an ideal choice for me, since I knew it well, from frequent visits during *The Heart of the Dragon.* But the official policy on this series was to have separate producers and directors, so I asked an old friend from LA, David Vassar, to do the directing.

By chance, I happened to be in London, staying in our Maida Vale flat, in October 1989. Very early in the morning of October 18 – about 1.15 a.m. – I was suddenly woken by the phone beside my bed. It was David Vassar, calling from LA. He was one of the very first people I knew who possessed a cellphone – back then, a giant brick of a thing, which he claimed was vital for a go-ahead director in LA.

"David?" he said, "Have you heard the news? There's been a massive earthquake in San Francisco. Freeways collapsed, everything. I just heard it on my car radio and pulled over on the freeway to let you know."

I felt a wave of ice-cold fear. Lizzie and James were in Mill Valley. I immediately phoned the landline in our California home. Miraculously, the call went through... Four rings, and then the answering machine kicked in:

"We can't take your call right now..."

I left a garbled message for Lizzie, put the phone down and thought hard. Apparently, the phone lines and electricity were still connected in Mill Valley, which had to be good news. But what else had happened? Who else could I call?

It happened that I had the business card of a realtor in Mill Valley, right there on the bedside table in London. We had been discussing the idea of selling the Maida Vale flat and buying a bigger place in the Bay Area. So I phoned the realty office. A bored-sounding receptionist answered the phone.

"What's going on?" I said.

"Nothing much," she replied. "How can I help you?"

"You've just had a huge earthquake," I said, as if explaining it to an idiot.

"Oh, is that what happened?" she said. "I just walked across the piazza, and I noticed the fountain had lost some water."

"Switch the TV on," I said, in those long-lost days before the internet. "I think it's a little more serious than that."

Twenty minutes later, Lizzie arrived home, to get my message. She called me to let me know that she and James were safe. Not long after, all lines between Europe and San Francisco were jammed solid, and I would not have been able to talk to her for more than a day, most likely. Thanks to David Vassar's timely action, I had been able to call within fifteen minutes of the event, when the phone lines were still open.

It later turned out that sixty-three people were killed and at least three thousand seven hundred injured in the Loma Prieta earthquake of 1989. A whole city block had collapsed and been consumed by fire in San Francisco and an elevated freeway had disintegrated across the Bay in Oakland. But so local and unpredictable are the effects of California's quakes that in Mill Valley, it had barely been noticed.

Lizzie had been in an exercise class, when she felt the room begin to sway and thought she was having a dizzy spell. She and the other women in the room, realizing what must be happening, crowded to the entrance hall, where they had all left their infants, gurgling contentedly in car-seats. All was well.

Subconsciously, I am sure that this natural disaster registered deeply with both Lizzie and me. We had been very lucky. Neither of us is religious or superstitious, so we never saw it as an omen, warning us against living on the edge of the Pacific "Rim of Fire." But it made us think. Ever since, each of California's disasters – particularly the recent wildfires – makes us think once again. But we just can't bring ourselves to leave. At least, not yet…

Knowing that my family was safe, I resumed my travels, which took me all the way round the planet via Hong Kong, and I returned to San Francisco about ten days later. I fell into Lizzie's arms, and we hugged harder than I could imagine. And then we hugged little eleven-month-old James. And then we went to bed. I may have been jetlagged out of my wits, but we made love like never before, to reaffirm the power of life and love. It is no accident, I am sure, that this weekend of lovemaking and affirmation led to the conception of our daughter Pippa: she was born the following July, exactly nine months later, in July 1990. She was our earthquake baby.

■■

We took Pippa back to England to be baptized, in August 1991: it was the last time that we set up a really big family event in the UK. We had done the same for James two years previously. On that occasion, my longtime friend the Reverend Adrian Benjamin, producer of the epic centennial production of *Alice in Wonderland* in Oxford, had performed the ceremony. He booked Saint Paul's, "The Actor's Church" in London's Covent Garden, to which he had the keys. A small congregation of family and friends watched the newly baptized James toot his plastic trumpet and piddle down his leg onto my expensive suit, thanks to a badly fastened "nappy" or diaper – my fault, of course.

Pippa, by contrast, was a model of decorum. Her christening took place in a one-thousand-year-old country church in the village of East Hagbourne, in Oxfordshire. As it had been for James, baptizing Pippa was more of a family custom than a need to affirm our personal beliefs. It just seemed a very English thing to do. We had often booked a quaint cottage next door to the church for holiday visits, and we knew some of the villagers – particularly the ebullient Robin Harries, our landlord, who had introduced us to the vicar.

It was a double celebration, because my mother also celebrated her eightieth birthday with us at the same weekend. She came to stay in the cottage and seemed remarkably fit and happy – and of course, as stylish as ever. It was a full-on family festivity, with Amanda and Juliet of course, and with my cousins and in-laws, stepsister Pamela and her family – Sarah, Peter and Adam – and many long-time friends, as well as members of Lizzie's family. And the sun shone throughout.

That afternoon, after the service and a suitably liquid lunch, we all played "See and Rescue" (a great Jay family hide-and-seek game) in the idyllic cottage garden and grounds of Robin Harries' house. We called it "Mr. McGregor's garden", because it reminded us all of the illustrations to Beatrix Potter's children's classic, Peter Rabbit. There were lots of good hiding places for the game.

"See and Rescue" had become the stock-in-trade family fun activity, whenever we had visitors. It involves hiding and trying to avoid being seen by whoever is "It" (the seeker), but it doesn't involve much running, so it can be played by both young and old. Whoever is "It" counts up to 50, to let everyone else hide. Then the hunter starts to look for them. She just has to point to anyone she has genuinely spotted and call out "Seen you Juliet" (or whoever has been discovered) and that person is thereby "captured" and obliged to return to the Home. What makes it fun is that, while the hunter is away, those who are still at liberty, and have not yet been spotted by the seeker, can surreptitiously creep up and touch-and-release those who have been seen and imprisoned in the Home. Bliss! Such fun, such laughter, for all ages. Even Lizzie enjoyed playing it, and she's not always a "games person."

Finally, there was a birthday cake for my mother, and presents, both for her and for the newly christened Pippa, in the cottage garden. It was so good to see all my children together, with both their grandmothers and Grandpa Ross as well as cousins, nephews and nieces. Both Lizzie and I were overwhelmed with nostalgia for the best of England. Our roots were here. It all seemed so real, so what were we doing in San Francisco? It was a thought which would trouble us many times in the next thirty years: which was our reality – England or its Looking Glass world, the USA? Which was the image in the distorting mirror?

That weekend was the last time that I saw my mother looking really well. I hugged her goodbye, as she joined her friend Pat Bennett for the car journey back to Winslow, never guessing what would happen in the next two years.

To my stunned disbelief, it was all downhill from then on. Until that magical day – the day she was eighty – she had never spent a night in hospital – not even to be born or to give birth to me, both of which she did at home. From that moment on, however, she seemed to have accepted that she had had a happy life, that her beloved husband Mick had passed on, and that her only child had settled on the other side of the planet. Perhaps she felt she could let go, or even give up. But I simply didn't understand this was happening until it was too late.

A year later, and after several more visits to London, Peggy Jay and Helen noticed that my mother had become forgetful and seemed less and less able to cope safely in her lonely London flat. Pat Bennett suggested that she should move back to a care home in Winslow, down the road from Pat's house. I duly helped her move. She had a bright and sunny room, overlooking contented cows, grazing in a Buckinghamshire field. But it never felt like home, I'm sure, even though Pat was nearby, and her memories of the town stretched back to her secret Bletchley Park work in World War II.

Shockingly fast – in less than two years – she lost her reason and succumbed to renal cancer. I was back in England, attending an alumni gathering at my old Oxford college, when I heard from Pat that things weren't looking good. I phoned Stoke Mandeville Hospital, and was told that she had been recently admitted and wasn't doing well. I drove the thirty miles to her bedside. I am glad to say that she recognized me. She looked haggard, but peaceful. The last thing I remember of her is the way she smiled at me from her bed, squeezed my hand gently as if to comfort me, and closed her eyes.

The next day, I was booked to return to San Francisco on British Airways. I had to make a decision. Maybe I made the wrong one. I thought she had some time left to live, and I needed to see my baby children. I got on the flight. Just before the door of the plane was closed, a BA official came on board to speak to me. My wonderful stepsister Pamela had tracked me down, to let me know that my mother had died overnight.

I was allowed to step off the plane and talk to Pamela on the phone. Amazingly, BA delayed the departure of the flight for a few minutes.

"David," said Pamela, "go back to your family. I'll see to all the arrangements. We'll make it a very small affair: a simple cremation. Then you can come back in a few weeks and we'll all give her a big send-off: a Memorial Service in Winslow Church. That's what she would have wanted."

Is this what I should have done? I still don't know. What would I feel if one of my children heard that I'd just died, and nonetheless got back on the plane and flew off to California? And I was my mother's only child. Dear Mother, dear "Beanie", as she liked to be called by her grandchildren, I'm sorry – so sorry.

I still miss her, just as much as I miss my father, Mick. They were so kind and understanding, and never more so than when I was between marriages. They had both been divorced and found happiness in their second marriage: they were always happy to listen and laugh or offer sound advice. I came to realize that they were much more than your average parents: they were two of the best friends and most joyful companions I could ever have wished for.

Rest in peace, Mother and Dad, wherever you are. I will always miss you.

■■■

14. DANGEROUS YEARS: FROM NIXON TO BUSH

With a new wife and two new children to support, it was more important than ever to bring in the bread. Helen's divorce lawyer, an old friend called Adam Maberley, had been gentle with me, at her suggestion. However, I was still obliged to support Amanda and Juliet, as well as James, Pippa and Lizzie – who was starting her undergraduate studies in psychology. She had never been given the chance by her parents to go to university, "being a girl, in the 1960's," as she explained. Elder brother Robert had followed his father into the shipping industry. Brother Tim had gone to Oxford. But little sister Lizzie, in spite of gaining excellent grades in 'A Levels' (national qualifications, preparatory to university), was only offered an executive-level secretarial training, complete with obligatory elbow-length white gloves. In America, I'm pleased to say, she was later awarded four degrees, including two Master's and a Doctorate.

Back in 1990, one way or another, I needed a constant stream of projects, either from InCA (see next chapter) or elsewhere, and I needed them urgently. Happily, as I floundered about in San Francisco, trying to get my own projects off the ground, the phone rang, as it often has at a crucial moment.

I had known George Colburn, my old friend from Michigan, for more than ten years when he called me with an unexpected proposal:

"How about working with me on a new film, celebrating Eisenhower's presidency?"

My immediate response was: "What? A political film about Ike? Why me? And for that matter, George, why you? You're a Democrat, for God's sake."

George had created the splendidly pompous-sounding National Video Communications Inc. in 1982, partly as a way to get me my Green Card, to allow me to live and work permanently in the US. We had worked together on several NVC projects, including a three-part PBS series called *The Communications Revolution* with Arthur C. Clarke, the world-famous science-fiction writer (see Chapter 17).

But at this stage, I really saw George more as a friend and fun lover than as a colleague. We had both conveniently been between marriages at the same time in the early 80's, and there was no end to the raunchy parties we had enjoyed in San Diego, Michigan and New York. He had a wonderful, funky vacation home in the woods of Northern Michigan, complete with sauna, near one of the many hundreds of local lakes. If those walls could speak, they would blush. As I have mentioned earlier, he also co-owned the local paper in Charlevoix, Michigan, which meant he could somewhat control the local gossip, back in those halcyon pre-social-media days.

George had invited me to help him represent this tiny newspaper at the Democratic National Convention in 1988, just for the fun of it. I could hardly believe that my Charlevoix Press pass entitled me to go virtually anywhere and do virtually anything at an American political convention. But wait a minute… that was a Democratic Party event. George was a Democrat through and through. What was he doing flirting with the Republicans, doing a film about Eisenhower?

It turned out that the crucial link in this piece of serendipity was Abbott Washburn, a former Federal Communications Commissioner, whom George had met during preparations for the Arthur C. Clarke series in 1982, and who had helped me to get my Green Card. Abbott moved in the grandest circles of Washington life. Some of his influential Republican friends had apparently suggested that it was about time someone did a good film about Ike – not seen as the military hero who beat the Nazis in Europe, but as a remarkable President.

I was fairly naïve about American politics, civics and history, never having been to high school in the US. I certainly knew about President Roosevelt, the Cuban Missile Crisis, the shooting of President Kennedy and the Vietnam War, but frankly, I knew nothing much about the period before 1960. The two things I knew about Eisenhower in the White House were that most people were fond of him – the "Ike" nickname from World war II had stuck – but that he had also had a reputation for being a little too relaxed. His adversaries called him a "Do Nothing" president: while our Cold War foe, the USSR, seemed to be increasing in power and prestige, Eisenhower seemed to be out on the golf course much of the time: out to lunch, in both senses of the phrase.

"George," I said, "Why on earth do you want to do this? And how do you suppose we'll ever get close enough to the corridors of power to make it happen and get the interviews we'll need?"

George was virtually rubbing his hands with glee. "Number one", he said, "We've got the money to do the show." That is often the most persuasive reason for doing a project. It makes you feel like a taxi for hire, but if the project is interesting, why not?

"And number two," said George, "Abbott Washburn knows all the right people. He can get us access to every living Republican president, and some of the greatest reporters who covered the White House beat in the 50's. Hey, he's even persuaded John Chancellor of NBC to front the show for us!"

I felt myself weakening. "But where's the money coming from, George?" I asked. "If it's from Republican sources, PBS will never accept the program. They would consider it propaganda – a whitewash. It'd break all their rules."

"Aha!" said George. "That's the beauty of it. It won't go to PBS. We'll get it onto cable TV, and we're targeting this new Discovery Channel."

I was amazed. This was 1988, and cable channels were still in their early childhood, if not their infancy. Just a couple of years before, John Hendricks, the founder of the Discovery Channel, had visited our new and spacious InCA Productions HQ, near Piccadilly Circus – in the heart of London – and sat on our kitchen counter, begging us to give him any spare stock footage we had, so that he could start making cheap documentaries. Was such a high-profile show, featuring a truckload of ex-Presidents and star journalists, going to be given to a media sideshow like Discovery?

To be fair, at least the Discovery Channel was doing its best to cultivate a serious image, back in 1988. Hendricks had announced that he intended to challenge PBS for supremacy in the non-fiction world. That is hard to credit today, when a typical cable show might feature Kim Kardashian's rear end, or be titled, I like to joke, *I was Hitler's Attack-Dog's Dentist.*

Anyway, the temptation was too great. Imagine the chance of actually meeting Ronald Reagan, or of shaking hands with Richard Nixon, or of directing an interview with George Bush in the White House: he had been Director of the CIA in the Eisenhower Years...

"Fine, George," I said. "Count me in. Let's make it an InCA-NVC co-production."

The work on the film lasted over two years and was interwoven with work on other shows that InCA was producing – *Things To Come*, mostly. That often happens in the life of a production, but in this case, scheduling the major interviews was not easy. In my memory, they stand out as a series of vignettes: unforgettable experiences that revealed both the personal and the professional sides of every Republican President then alive.

• •

To start at the top: the President in office at the time was George Bush Senior – the intelligent one. Getting into his calendar was certainly not a breeze, but Abbott Washburn and his Republican cronies eventually pulled it off in late 1989.

This was the second time I had been involved with the White House. Back in 1977, we were allowed to film the famous 'Hot Line' telephone in the Oval office, which linked the President of the United States to his opposite number in the Kremlin. The idea was that the President, as Commanding Officer of the US, could get straight through to Mr. Brezhnev and say:

"Hey, Leonid, is that really a nuclear missile you're launching towards us, or is it a speck of fly dirt on our radar screen?"

It was the culmination of a *Connections* episode, where James Burke traced the strange path of the ideas that had led to nuclear weapons. On that first occasion, with Mick Jackson directing, everyone thought that the President was far away, which is why our BBC crew had been allowed to spread their gear – lights, cables, dolly, tracks, cameras and whatnot – all over the floor of the Oval office, while we set up for "President Burke", as we were jokingly calling him that evening.

Suddenly, the door opened, and in walked Jimmy Carter.

"Oh," said everyone, in a typically British way. "Sorry."

There was a flurry of press attachés, while James tried to explain to the President why we were there, and then he flashed his big smile at the crew.

"Don't worry, you boys," he said, in his kindly Southern accent. "You go right ahead. I can find somewhere else to work."

This time however, with George H. W. Bush. things were more formal. There was tighter security, for one thing: our equipment was carefully checked, as was the background of each crew member. I was the single non-American in the team – my wife Lizzie and I did not take American citizenship till 2002 – so therefore I was the chief suspect, if any monkey business was being planned. It is probably just my imagination, but I was frisked with particular vigor, in my tight-fitting suit. Was I nervous? Yes, I was.

We had the comforting presence of John Chancellor with us: after Walter Cronkite, there was no more solid a rock to lean on. Already retired from regular assignments on NBC, he had a calming effect on us all – even on President Bush, when he finally arrived. The President had a severe cold, for which he apologized profusely as his face was being powdered, to avoid his forehead glinting in the lights.

By far the most interesting of the President's responses concerned his work at the CIA. He had been Director of the Agency only from 1976 to 1977, but he had started working for them full time as early as 1961. Most probably, he was recruited when much younger, in his college days at Yale, when he was a member of the secretive Skull and Bones Society. As a young man, he had moved to Houston, where he ran an oil drilling business, the Zapata Offshore Co., which was reputedly a CIA front company, with rigs conveniently located all over the world.

Obviously, President Bush was not going to talk about his early clandestine endeavors for our cameras, let alone his alleged connection with the Bay of Pigs operation under President Kennedy. But he was very willing to talk about Allen Dulles, the sinister presence who was Director of the CIA for most of the Eisenhower presidency.

"Eisenhower was never a Do-Nothing. He just knew how to delegate," was Bush's summation. "He knew he did not have to do everything by himself. That's what he had learned from the military in World War II: choose your generals carefully and then let them get on with it."

Whether or not Allen Dulles could be trusted to "get on with it" in any respectable or responsible way did not seem to be an issue.

"It worked," said Bush. "We never had World War III on Ike's watch."

At the end of the one-hour interview, President Bush graciously excused himself and signed a few autographs, insisting that he would have some photographs of the session sent on to us later.

"I've enjoyed it," he said, shaking all our hands. "though I have to say I still feel sick as a dog." He turned to me: "I canceled all my appointments today, apart from you Brits."

Since I was the only non-American in the room, I asked him what he meant by "appointments" in the plural..

"Well, I saw you guys in the morning, and this afternoon I'm having tea with Queen Elizabeth. She's in town and I think she's from your part of the world, isn't she?"

The most memorable interview we had, however, was probably the one with President Nixon. He had been Vice-President to Eisenhower for eight full years – all the way from 1952 to 1960, when he ran against John F. Kennedy for the presidency and only narrowly lost. Who could possibly have known Ike better than Tricky Dick?

The street address we had been given for the Nixon interview could have been chosen by a veteran undercover agent. It was in deep-cover territory: suburban New Jersey, at the end of a very ordinary strip-mall. A few Grecian-type urns, pseudo-Roman statuary and Doric columns had been tacked on as an afterthought, to give that end of the mall a little more 'style,' perhaps? There was no sign posted on the wall, or on the entrance-door. What could it have been? A shady lawyer's offices? An abortion clinic? A Mafia front? It was obviously there to protect someone who did not want much publicity.

Inside, all was bland. A conservatively dressed lady instructed us which room was to be used. When the cameraman asked if there was any alternative space, because the room was as dull as a brown envelope, he was told that this was the designated space, and there were no others available. So we set up and waited. And waited.

And then suddenly, there he was: Richard Nixon, in the flesh. He had sidled in like a ferret, without any announcement, without a noise. His face was so familiar, from all the agonizing days on television during the impeachment proceedings of 1974, that all we could do for a moment was to gape at him. Was he really a flesh-and-blood human being, not some villain from a melodrama?

In fact, he was highly professional. There was no sign of his six o'clock shadow – the dark, sinister jowls that reputedly had cost him the election in 1960. He chuckled as he was introduced. He had found a new role for himself: the misunderstood elder statesman.

His view of Ike was subtle and nuanced. As VP, Nixon had had to do most of the achingly dull international travel, to comfort our allies, broker the deals and keep the peace. He persuaded us all that Ike knew every move that was being made on the chessboard. Of course, there had been ugly moments: the sudden launch of the world's first satellite, Sputnik, by the Russians in 1957 had been a genuine surprise to everyone in the US government, he told us. Ike had seen to it that a number of butts had been severely kicked at the CIA.

But on balance, Nixon insisted, this had all been a good thing: it had persuaded America to pour vast new amounts of money into the so-called "Space Race," culminating in the landing on the moon a scant twelve years later.

At the conclusion of the interview, Nixon's professional mask slipped, and he reverted to type in the strangest way.

"Just a minute. Wait here," he told us, as we started wrapping up the gear. "I have something for you."

He disappeared for a couple of minutes, and then reappeared, carrying a cardboard box. He looked around the room in a paranoid fashion, as if checking the silverware, then opened the box and proceeded to set out six small, elegant cups and saucers with the Presidential Coat of Arms and his name "Richard M. Nixon" embossed on them.

"Well, thank you, Mr. President," we all murmured. "How very kind."

"How very strange", we all thought, "Does he think we're all English and therefore drink tea?"

"Keep them as a souvenir," said Nixon. "I've had so many people in here interviewing me, but they all steal something, so that they can get a piece of Richard Nixon. So now I give these things out, and the thieving has stopped."

•••

We had not expected much from President Gerald Ford, and we did not get much either. He had to be included, because he was one of the living Republican Presidents, and he had taken over from Nixon, after the latter resigned. But how well had he known Eisenhower? Hardly at all, it turned out. He was just an everyday congressman, rising to house minority leader for a few years. Sure, he was on committees dealing with foreign policy and the military, but how close did that get him to the President? Good grief, he had not even been elected as Vice-President. He had been drafted in after Spiro Agnew was thrown out for income tax evasion and bribery.

Duty-bound, however, we made the pilgrimage to Palm Springs. How typical was that: Gerry Ford retired, playing golf in Palm Springs? We met him at a typical Republican ranch-house. Remembering Ford's vast number of trips down steps, falls at public occasions and gaffes of every sort – immortalized by Chevy Chase on *Saturday Night Live* – we were tempted to ask him to walk along some complicated route to get to the interview chair, in case we could get something great for the blooper reel. But no such luck. He told us that President Eisenhower had been an inspiration for him, though he never looked inspired at any time during our interview. And that was that.

To try and light Ford's fuse, George Colburn enthusiastically tried to swap stories about Michigan with him. Hey, Jerry had grown up in Grand Rapids! And George had a house barely a hundred miles to the north of Grand Rapids! How about that? And Jerry had been a football hero at the University of Michigan. Go Wolverines! And Jerry had served Michigan wine in the White House! How great, eh? No response. No response at all. So we packed up our stuff and left.

•••

Our encounter with Ronald Reagan was in another league, however. It had been difficult to find a date that worked for him, and we realized later that he was beginning to suffer the effects of the Alzheimer's that would finally claim him as a victim. Some days, apparently, he was better than other days.

Suddenly, at very short notice, we were told that Reagan could see us. We were instructed to come to a penthouse suite of offices in Century City, Los Angeles – right at the business end of Showbiz. How perfect was that?

We set up the classic configuration for the interview: two upright but comfortable armchairs, diffused lighting – much kinder to older faces – individual microphones for interviewer and interviewee – and before we had even finished, Ronny Reagan bounced into the room.

What a difference between him and any of the other Presidents we had met! Bush was weighed down by a bad cold and the affairs of state, Ford could have been a plastic statuette for all the charisma he radiated, Nixon scuttled around the room like a rat, looking over his shoulder to see who was stealing what – but Reagan? He was a star.

Once an actor, always an actor of course, as my mother had reminded me. But here was a real professional. The first thing he did was to walk round the room, shaking everybody by the hand and asking their names, and thanking them for being there: every grip, clapper-loader and gaffer's assistant got the full-on charm offensive. Then he sat down and was powdered and prepped for the interview, exchanging pleasantries with John Chancellor.

"So what's the subject today, John?" he asked.

"The Eisenhower Presidency, Sir" came the reply.

"Oh good, said Reagan, with perfect timing. "I think I can remember more about *that* than I can remember about my *own* time in office."

The room erupted in spontaneous laughter, with Ronnie Reagan leading the laughs. At a stroke, he had dispelled any of our worries about his memory. The most moving point he made during the interview was that Eisenhower so impressed him that, by the time Ike stepped down from the presidency, Reagan had decided to throw away his ticket as a Democrat and join the Republicans.

This was an astonishing change of heart: Reagan had supported Roosevelt and the New Deal. He had served six terms as the President of the Screen Actors' Guild and presided over the Guild's first three strikes. He had called union membership "One of the most elemental of human rights." How could he cross the aisle so swiftly?

There is a famous story that Reagan said "I did not leave the Democratic Party. The party left me." He said, of John F. Kennedy, "Under that tousled boyish haircut is still the old Karl Marx." In our interview, President Reagan acknowledged:

"I just knew Eisenhower was the kind of man I could trust, and if the Republican Party was good enough for him, it was good enough for me."

During the two years of production, we amassed a gold-mine of great material. Editing it with George Colburn was one of the hardest production jobs I have ever had. It was not just a case of cutting it all down to an hour: it was a commercial hour. I had been used to PBS timings, with room for explanation and second opinions, but the cable channels insisted on commercial breaks every seven minutes, which meant a total running time of only 46 minutes, which seemed woefully inadequate, to do justice to all the good material we had.

But that's what we had to do. We added overly dramatic music at every 'junction' (cut to commercials) and great cold-war stock footage to boot. Our Republican patrons seemed pleased. The show finally aired on Discovery in the fall of 1991 and garnered a fair few warm reviews. Not from the *Los Angeles Times*, however:

> *"At its best, Dangerous Years shows a president working hard and failing to come to a human understanding with an enemy. At its worst, this bite-sized portrait does not even make time to include Eisenhower's swan-song warning against the military-industrial establishment, which he knew all too well."*

Well, you can't win 'em all. The *Times*' critic had not had a chance to be in the room with all those Presidents. But I do maintain that we should have had an hour and a half – two hours, perhaps – with such strong material. However, thirty years ago, documentary producers were limited by the 'slots' they could get on TV or cable. Today, you can self-release a film on the internet and make it as long as you like.

● ●

15. NANOTECHNOLOGY AND THINGS TO COME

The future has always intrigued me. Once again, the perennial eleven-year-old boy inside me shows his face: either curious or facetious. What will we live to see? Fully intelligent robots? Worldwide artificial intelligence systems, which will dominate the lives of the newly humbled Homo Sapiens? A cure to all disease, even that wiliest of killers, cancer, or the rise of new all-powerful super-viruses?

I vividly remember watching the first moon landing on television in 1969, sitting in Croydon, side by side with my grandmother. She had been born ninety years before: 1879. Imagine her world. When she was a girl, there were no cars, no air travel, no radio and barely any useful electricity. No-one knew what a virus was.

Futurists of the 1870's puzzled about how they would ever cope with the rapidly escalating quantities of manure dropped on the streets of London and New York: tens of thousands of horses dragged carts, vans, cabs, public buses and streetcars, and left their mark while doing so. Fifth Avenue was routinely covered in up to a foot of compacted horse shit. No-one foresaw that the electric streetcar and the petrol-driven motor would solve the problem within ten years.

But how on earth could we make documentary films about the future, when it did not yet exist? Well, we could interview luminaries like Arthur C. Clarke, which I had already done (see Chapter 20), or else – I thought – I could try to write some science fiction myself.

So in 1988, I took up my pen, quite literally, and started writing *Many Happy Returns* in longhand. What started out as a proposal for a five-part dramatic TV series about the years 2000 to 2100 turned into more of a book – or at least, a very detailed one-hundred-and-fifty-page book proposal.

It featured the entire life of a baby, born in the year 2000, who lived to be more than a hundred years old: she saw the start of the following century, in 2100, with all her faculties intact. Indeed, at the end of the final chapter, she longed for death, because the prospect of a quasi-eternal life was too awful. The final scene showed her holding the pill that would consign her to eternal oblivion – if she decided to take it.

She had been named Millennia by her doting parents, who saw the date of her birth, 1/1/2000, as remarkably auspicious. She married five times during her life, and, because she could afford a Birth License, was still producing children in her eighties. Genetic technology had kept her body young, but nothing could be done for her mind, which, though lucid, became wearied by the routines of existence.

Re-reading the manuscript today, I am struck by how much I got wrong – even in forecasting the period between 1989 and 2020 – and how little I got right, which was very little. It was the social, political and psychological issues, where I had my few insights. I did forecast the rise of radical Islam as a threat to western civilization, though I placed its impact in the 2020's. I foresaw some of the problems of a world in which more than half the population was over sixty: a gerontocracy was likely to be hugely conservative. I proposed a radical self-imposed sterilization program (or the choice not to have children), which most developed nations adopted by 2030. Political leaders became more like television personalities, overseeing a world of bread and circuses for the poor, and grand exclusive benefits for the rich. Does that sound familiar?

The defining event of the 2060's, in my book, was the massive eruption of Tombora, a volcano in Indonesia, which indeed had done something like that before. In 1815, it caused the largest volcanic eruption in recorded history. Krakatoa, its neighbor, also blew up in 1883, but with more famous but far less long-lasting results. The Tombora eruption caused global weather anomalies that included the phenomenon known as 'volcanic winter': 1816 became known as the 'Year without a Summer' (see Wikipedia) because of the effect on North American and European weather. Crops failed and livestock died in much of the Northern Hemisphere, resulting in the worst famine of the nineteenth century.

I asked myself what would happen to the advanced satellites and communications systems of the twenty-first century if such a thing happened again. Carl Sagan had been more concerned by the prospects of 'nuclear winter' than of global warming, but I realized that we did not have to wait for a nuclear holocaust, to screw up the technology-dependent world of the future.

On the broader technology front, I foresaw nothing much of consequence – or, at least, of consequence so far. I regret that I did not predict the internet or the world-wide web. If only I had, I might be rich right now. I did predict a world where many of Nikolai Tesla's early twentieth century inventions and imaginings had come to pass. I proposed that energy would be transmitted great distances by the beams of super-lasers rather than the ugly aerial cables of the grid. Tiny batteries, woven into every object we manufactured, would mean total freedom from centralized power generation, and therefore from government control as well. Cold fusion would finally be practicable, I hoped. (People have been hoping for that for most of the past half-century). But, all in all, I realized that my science fiction writing was not going to be imaginative enough to pass muster.

Pat Russell, my indomitable business manager and assistant in Los Angeles, typed out my 20,000-word book outline on an IBM Selectric typewriter – the one with the flying golf-ball, which in Pat's hands fairly flew across the pages. It was one of the last things she volunteered to do for me.

You will note, perhaps, that the book was not typed on a computer. The only computer we had in the late 80's was another IBM product: the one we had acquired in 1984, to do the accounts for *The West of the Imagination*. It was next to useless as a word-processor. It is ironic that my book proposal about the future was typed on the descendant of a nineteenth century machine. So there has never been a digital copy of the book. I just have a couple of typescripts, two inches think, bound like telephone directories.

To help me try to sell the book concept, or indeed the potential TV series, Karl Sabbagh, one of the co-founders of InCA, introduced me to the eminent London book agents, A.P. Watt. To my astonishment, they showed interest. Would I care to step by their offices when I was next in town? They felt that there was a market for imaginative fiction about the future.

When I sat nervously in their offices, they explained that they did not think I had the experience to pull off this feat by myself.

"Would you care to consider co-writing the book with one of our clients, Brian Aldiss?" they inquired.

At that point, I made a very stupid decision. Brian Aldiss was already a grand master of sci-fi: not quite up there with Isaac Asimov or Arthur C. Clarke perhaps, but certainly top of the second division, and a great fan of H.G. Wells. When I met with A.P. Watt, Aldiss was about sixty, and apparently looking for new inspiration and a possible collaborator.

But I said "No."

Why? Was I so convinced of my own brilliance? So full of piss and wind (as the Brits like to say) in my early forties? Did I think that I was going to become a star under my own steam? Probably all the above. At the very least, I was convinced that I could persuade someone to make a television series out of my manuscript. And there I was wrong.

Nothing ever happened to *Many Happy Returns*: no book, no TV series. I am sure that something interesting would have emerged, if I had worked with Brian Aldiss; at least, I would have learned a lot. But what still remained in my head were all sorts of thoughts about the future.

I had received a grant from the Corporation for Public Broadcasting to develop *Many Happy Returns*, and one of the things we had promised to do was to convene a panel of experts, for a two-day discussion about future scenarios. My colleague Karl Sabbagh came out from InCA's London office to join me. We welcomed a distinguished group of visionaries, both men and women, in a hilltop retreat overlooking Silicon Valley.

One of our experts was Eric Drexler. He was the quintessential uber-nerd, though that phrase had still not entered the lexicon in the late 80's. He had just written a book called *Engines of Creation*, in which he argued that molecular-level engineering was not only feasible, but inevitable. He did not coin the word 'nanotechnology,' but I believe he was the first to use it outside an academic paper.

At the event, we all discussed the predictions I was making in *Many Happy Returns*. The writer Howard Rheingold was particularly generous with his ideas, and I had to stand up to well-informed criticism of my proposals.

"That's just not physically possible," was the most damning of comments, but the book outline provoked an interesting discussion. I was pleased to hear that self-driving cars were generally acknowledged to be inevitable.

After our visionaries had gone home, Karl Sabbagh said:

"I think there's a very good film to be made about nanotechnology. I'm sure that we can find enough work that's going on, round the planet, at that microscopic level. Let me see if I can interest Channel 4 in London."

I thought that Karl was crazy: what on earth was available for us to film? But three months later – still long before email – he sent me a fax, saying that he had persuaded the commissioning editor of *Equinox*, Channel 4's science series: she was so intrigued that she had promised us the entire budget for a one-hour show.

The film was eventually called *Little by Little.* It was Karl's joke, recalling a deeply tedious and sentimental Victorian school-based novel, called *Eric, or Little by Little.* Eric Drexler was flattered but (like everyone else) slightly bemused by the title. But, amazingly, the film eventually won the International Science Film Festival's Jury Prize, which was presented to us in Paris by the President of Tokyo University. We were praised for "stimulating the scientific imagination with both insight and a sense of humor."

So, what did we eventually manage to film? Drexler's main contention was that we would soon be able to engineer simple molecular machines, which would be able to do many of the things that large machines do, including making endless copies of themselves. Indeed, Drexler's chief worry was that such tiny devices might run amok, making vast quantities of endlessly self-replicating microscopic stuff that would emerge as "gray goo", and would soon overwhelm us.

Drexler explained how the instructions for manufacturing molecular items, and then combining them, could be regulated by complex computer programs. He foresaw small neighborhood factories, with pressurized containers, much the size and shape of the stainless-steel vats in a winery. For our film, we duly shot diligent workers, appearing to take fully formed vacuum cleaners – still dripping from the fluid in which they had been suspended – out of the inspection hatch of a winery vat.

Smaller items could be cooked up at home, Drexler proposed. A machine about the size of a bread-maker or a toaster oven would turn out tailor-made gizmos, at the press of a button and the insertion of the right computer program. In fact, what Drexler had foreseen was the invention of 3-D printing (see Chapter 24), but on a molecular scale.

Serious scientists were prepared to be interviewed about these ideas. Some of the most compelling thoughts were shared by biochemists, who explained that DNA computers are a long-cherished hope for the future: the DNA in a single cell is a stunningly complex repository of information.

We were told that there is nothing impossible about training molecules to self-assemble: it happens everywhere in the universe, and not only in oxygen-driven life forms. But they self-assemble into patterns that have emerged from millions of years of evolution. What chance do we have of getting molecules to jump through hoops and join hands like circus performers, the way we want them to?

While we were making the film, we were approached by IBM's Almaden Laboratories, near San José, CA. Would we be interested in filming something that had never been filmed before? Well, of course we would. So off I went, down the coast from the InCA San

Francisco office with a cameraman. On arrival, we were asked to sign a non-disclosure agreement.

"When do you plan to release the film?" we were asked.

"I'm not sure," I said lamely. "It all depends on Channel 4 in London."

The laboratory's Chief Scientist and a senior PR person exchanged glances. The PR woman said:

"Well, when can you get a firm date for the UK transmission? We'd like it to be as soon as possible please – then we can decide when to announce this to the world."

Then she took us to a large scanning electron microscope.

"Have a look in there," she said.

On a screen, we saw a glimmering image. As our eyes got used to it, we made out the IBM logo, represented by dozens of tiny pinheads.

"Right. Good. Very interesting," I said, feeling that our journey to San José had been a complete waste of time.

"Thank you," I said, and turned, as if to leave.

"No, no, wait," said the Chief Scientist. "Each one of those dots is a single atom. This is the first time in the world, as far as we know, that anyone has managed to control individual atoms, and array them in a meaningful pattern."

I looked at the cameraman, and he started setting up the tripod. Nanotechnology was here already…

So, unexpectedly, *Little by Little* contained an amazing scoop. The IBM people were as good as their word. They announced their breakthrough to the world's press on the very day that the film premiered on Channel 4 in the UK. I think that this is what attracted the attention of the International Science Film Festival and won us the prize. I don't think it was Eric Drexler's charisma or our funny scenes with vacuum cleaners.

••

It was Britain's Channel 4, which also took a chance by backing a completely different show about the future, just a year later. This time, they helped us to fix up co-producers in France and Spain, to share the cost.

Things to Come was a very British enterprise: a humorous series of thirteen half hours about the future, mostly created by our team at InCA London. It was presented by two young hosts from a surreal studio set, full of bizarre objects and futuristic images. The finished shows had cutting-edge animation and strange sound effects and music, slicing and dicing the show into small story segments. The most original aspect of the series was

239

that you could never tell which of our "future" stories was intended to be likely or genuine and which was satirical nonsense: either a complete fiction, or a segment featuring an inventor who was a nutcase.

The French co-producers liked to film elegant stories about everyday life in the future. They dreamed up a smart home, in which the owners communicated with machines by talking: they anticipated Siri and Alexa twenty-five years before such things were commonplace. The Spanish contributions had a strong element of Salvador Dali: bizarre "intelligent landscapes" would – they said – hold folk memories and interact with us, as if they had a personality. This, of course, anticipated the currently burgeoning field of Augmented Reality.

My contributions, all filmed in California, relied on humor for effect. Are you surprised? I drew on the rich fund of quacks and crackpots, who have always flourished on the West Coast. To take one example: a fully functional company in the Bay Area offered cryonic embalming: the dead body of your relative or your cat could be preserved "forever." It would sit inside a tank full of cold, steaming liquid nitrogen, until such time as science had caught up, when it would be jump-started and revived, promising the possibility of eternal life. We filmed the bubbling retorts, and then came up with some bubbling retorts of our own.

"But surely you wouldn't *want* to be brought back to life, looking the way you did when you were eighty?" asked the cameraman.

The owner, an unsettling man with more than a hint of a down-market Baron Frankenstein about him, attempted to reassure us.

"You can choose to pass on, before you reach old age," he said, a gleam in his eye. "And we are sure that rejuvenation techniques will be far more effective in the future. Here is our catalog."

"Yes," we said, "But suppose the money runs out or the company goes bankrupt before the body can be usefully revived?" There was a pause.

"If money is the problem," said the Baron, "You can choose to have just your head preserved. That's much cheaper."

He took us to see some smaller stainless-steel vats, in which, he assured us, a couple of dozen heads were being iced down for the long haul.

"Would you like to book a canister for yourselves?" he asked.

Strangely enough, we declined his offer.

Elsewhere in the Bay Area, a former Southern Pacific railroad signalman had come up with "convincing proof" that, as he put it, "Gravity is a Push, not a Pull."

He had made a number of small magnetic devices and mechanical teaching aids, which he took round local schools, in the attempt to expose the dreadful fallacy that Sir Isaac Newton had foisted upon the world, three hundred and fifty years ago. He claimed that we adhered to the earth's surface because all the other heavenly bodies were pushing us down onto it, not because the earth attracted us.

"Yes," said the cameraman, Mike Anderson, "But in that case, when the sun rose in the morning, we'd all feel much heavier, specially round lunchtime, when it's right overhead."

Our inventor looked at him with beady eyes.

"Who says you don't?" he asked.

All these characters made for wonderful, zany stories, and much of the pleasure came from the editing process: how many unlikely ideas or characters could we cram into each episode? And would the audience enjoy the idea that they would never know, when each story began, whether it was "for real" or a spoof.

But, as the program's publicity said:

> *Many of today's inventions would have seemed like a joke, or like pure magic, just fifty years before they emerged.*

We had Arthur C. Clarke to thank for that thought, and it is demonstrably true. Today's iPhone would have seemed like science fiction in the early 1970's, when the world's cleverest small device was a Texas Instruments pocket calculator.

I have suggested that *Things to Come* was very British, in its desire to mingle the serious with the flippant, and thereby make a point about the unexpected sources of creativity. But the editing process was all too British as well. To play my part, I had to haul Lizzie and James back to London, for four dreary winter months in a small rented house in the suburb of Barnes, less than a mile from where I had lived when married to Helen. I commuted every day by bus and train to InCA's offices near Piccadilly Circus, and got more and more depressed with the reality of living back in London. It always seemed to be raining, or at least it did in my soul.

"No wonder you need a sense of humor to live here," I said to Lizzie.

But there was one compensation: I was able to see much more of my daughters, Amanda and Juliet, who turned 14 and 12 in the winter of 1990. Amanda had progressed to the Senior School at St. Paul's, and both girls seemed to love the mixture of hard academic work and highly competitive sport they were offered. It was wonderful to be able to go and watch them play, and then have them back for tea in our little rented house. But that pleasure was not to last.

When the editing was finished and *Things to Come* was complete, the money ran out. Lizzie and I gathered up all our bags and the various extra bits of baby stuff that we had bought for James, and made a pile in the hallway. It was huge. Undaunted, we called a black cab to take us to Heathrow Airport. When he arrived, the cabbie looked at all our stuff, and scratched his head.

"Blimey," he said. "Are you emigrating?"

I looked at Lizzie, and we both laughed.

"Yes," I said, "This time I think we finally are."

The cabbie managed to cram everything into the rear of the cab – beside us, or into the laughably small trunk, or onto the platform beside his seat.

"Hold on tight," he said. "We haven't forgotten the baby, have we?"

■■■

On our return to San Francisco, I tried my best to get an American version of *Things to Come* off the ground. The stories were entertaining, and the message that the future would be a crazy mixture of the unlikely and the unexpected seemed just right for the US market. I even risked the wrath of God by proposing that I should be the on-camera presenter, and we taped some pilot segments, with me wearing a tight suit and performing like a watered-down version of James Burke.

KQED, the local PBS affiliate station, put a lot of effort into selling the idea to corporate underwriters. We did not need much money, relatively speaking, because all the on-location stories were already in the can. We were convinced that one of the Silicon Valley companies would go for our quirky approach. Hewlett Packard, perhaps? Or Intel?

But these were not companies you would associate immediately with a sense of humor. They were full of men in short-sleeved shirts with pocket protectors. So, as you may have guessed, nobody took the bait. In the boardrooms of US companies – even high-tech ones – the future was not seen as funny: it was a religion, a faith, virtually a rock-solid belief. It mostly felt good and exciting in the 1990's, and if it posed any challenge, America (or possibly Japan) would confront and surmount it. Finding the future humorous was unacceptable, unless you were making a "wacky" cartoon like *The Jetsons*. And that show was only acceptable because it was for children: *The Flintstones* in reverse, nothing more.

I learned a lot about the US from this experience. Many Americans are uncomfortable with ambiguity, and they find a lot of British humor weird and out of place. If it is clearly labeled as "zany", like Monty Python, then it may be acceptable. Americans assume an indulgent smile, settle down with a beer, turn on their screens and let the Brits run around doing their crazy stuff.

"That's wild," people say, but I believe that, secretly, they have the sneaking suspicion that Brits truly are aliens, after all. Who needs Little Green Men when you've got the Pythons' Pet Shop Parrot sketch, or the Fish-slapping Song?

So, what *do* Americans like? And, particularly, what do educated Californians like? It turned out to be obvious: inspiring films that create joy and positive outcomes: optimistic stuff. So that is what we gave them in *The Heart of Healing*, and that is what I have been trying to give them ever since.

■■■

16. THE HEART OF HEALING:
AROUND THE WORLD IN 80 WEEKS

Who would have thought that a casual student friendship made in 1967 would bear spectacular fruit in an extraordinary project in the early 1990's?

I first met Brendan O'Regan at Indiana University (IU), when I was studying for a graduate business degree, and he was studying for a Master's in brain chemistry. I had started to realize that the world of spreadsheets and profit forecasts was not for me, and he was pretty fed up with his field too.

"If I have to cut the head off any more rats, I shall scream," he told me.

Like most of the foreign students at IU, we lived in the Graduate Residence Center, a dull row of cinderblock buildings that looked like a low-security prison. But the price was right, and we were both on scholarships, so why not? The great advantage was that it threw a wonderfully motley crew of young people together, from all over the world. Brendan was from Cork, in Southern Ireland. He had a great sense of humor and was always uncannily knowledgeable about the latest developments in science, technology and medicine.

During the year in Bloomington, apart from working at all three radio stations (see Chapter 1), I managed to travel the length and breadth of the US. Brendan and I begged rides off wealthier students, and got to Palm Beach for Christmas, staying with an Irish Monsignor from County Cork and a convent full of nuns. We hopped across to Kingston, Jamaica for New Year on a bargain basement flight. We flew down to New Orleans for Mardi Gras in a private plane, owned by a conveniently rich business school friend of mine. We took a bus up to Chicago, to see the Second City improv group develop the special brand of comedy that later spawned Saturday Night Live.

Best of all, three of us crossed the continent in a classic Ford Mustang – not much room for three lanky lads, let alone baggage. We took the northern route, through the South Dakota Badlands and the Yellowstone National Park, to reach that fabled city of light – San Francisco. We were one year late for the famous Summer of Love of 1967. But, let me assure you, there was still a lot of loving on offer. And yes, I am afraid I did inhale.

When I left Indiana to take up my job at the BBC in 1968, Brendan followed me to London, took a room in our shared Queensway flat, and went to work for the prestigious Architectural Association. Later, back in the US, he was invited to be chief assistant to the visionary scientist and designer Buckminster Fuller. Finally, he moved to the San Francisco Bay Area, where (see Chapter 12) he persuaded my new wife Lizzie and me to join him. He called it heaven on earth, but just why he called it that we were not to find out for some years.

Brendan, Lizzie and I were the closest of friends. We partied together, and he introduced us to many of the creative movers and shakers of San Francisco – many of whom he seemed to know well.

"You should meet Nion McEvoy," said Brendan. "His family own the San Francisco Chronicle, so he's in media, like you."

Lo and behold, a few weeks later, we joined Brendan and the McEvoys for dinner. It turned out that Nion had children the same age as ours, and we lived five blocks from each other in San Francisco. It has to be said that Nion lived five blocks uphill, in an altogether more select neighborhood, but, hey, we were just walking distance away. Brendan waved his magic wand and created a friendship, which continues to this day.

In 1991, Brendan found InCA an office in Sausalito, in an unpretentious block near a boatyard, just ten minutes' drive from our new Mill Valley house.

"I'd take it, if I were you. It's a nice area. And it's in the same road as my office in Sausalito," he explained on the phone. "That may be useful, as you'll see."

Brendan loved giving me mysterious hints. I asked him what he meant.

"I have an idea," he said. "I think I've got a perfect project for you. Shall we have breakfast tomorrow?"

Brendan had been working for a few years as Director of Research at an outfit called The Institute of Noetic Sciences (IONS). It was a name that he had had to explain many times during the next three years.

"No, not Poetic Science. Not Emetic Science. *Noetic Science,*" he'd say. "It's based on the Greek word Nous, meaning Mind." Who knew?

IONS was interested in knowledge of a special sort. It had been the idea of the astronaut Ed Mitchell, after he had witnessed the sight of Earth, hanging like a transcendent blue Christmas-tree bauble in the blackness of space. He believed that there was a lot more going on in the universe than traditional science would acknowledge. He also believed in the value of mankind's intuitive knowledge –things we just *feel* are true.

So, with Ed Mitchell, Willis Harman and a band of other inquiring minds, Brendan shook the money tree, and lo and behold, a pile of golden apples fell down, courtesy of a cluster of wealthy and some would say gullible philanthropists. They duly set up IONS, to investigate fringe areas of science, where others, perhaps fearful of their reputation, had been loath to tread.

IONS has pioneered some worthy and valuable research over the last forty-plus years it has been in existence. It has also dabbled in psychedelic drugs and psycho-kinetics – the ability to move objects at a distance, just by mentally focusing on them. It even promoted Uri Geller's fork-bending fad in the 1970's. Whenever the validity of an IONS project was challenged, the project leader would wink and tap his nose and say that DARPA and the Pentagon – and the Russians indeed – were very interested in this kind of thing.

Brendan robustly championed a more solid avenue of research, however: the mind-body connection in health: this was the basis of the great idea he had had for a major television series.

"Why don't we work together, to create a world-wide investigation of the many traditions which practice successful mind-body medicine?" he asked me, over breakfast at the traditional Blue Anchor café, a greasy spoon right beneath his office on Gate Five Road. "Something truly epic – a multi-part series, with a colorful book, educational modules, the full English breakfast, so to speak?"

"Surely you mean the full *Irish* breakfast," I said. "Sausages and all."

But he was very serious. I took hurried notes, as Brendan outlined some of the IONS research that he had been collecting and curating.

"Western psychology and medicine recognize many physical conditions that are affected by the state of someone's mind," he explained. "They're called psychosomatic diseases, and include asthma, allergies and many skin conditions. But it goes much further than that.

"Hypnotism has been proven to be helpful, in reducing the damage caused by third-degree burns. Shamans in Haiti appear to be able to forestall or even cure certain cancers in people, who are put into a state of trance. The secular medical authorities at Lourdes investigate all the apparently genuine 'miracle' cures, which the faithful ascribe to the intervention of the Virgin Mary. Some of them are inexplicable, medically – but they happened. There are many documented cases of remission from a variety of 'incurable cases' of cancer, when the patient practices meditation or guided imagery."

Brendan and IONS had been collecting such evidence for years, and the best evidence did not come from quack doctors in faraway places, but from fully accredited hospitals, here in the US.

"But, isn't that just the placebo effect?" I asked, still skeptical.

"Yes indeed," said Brendan, his eyes aglow. "But that's just the point. Think about it. That's the power of the mind in action. The placebo effect can make you better. If you're given a pill that's just chalk, by an authoritative doctor in a reputable hospital, it can be very effective. But how is that possible? The mind must have the power to heal the body by itself. The only question is: how can we trigger that healing effect in a reliable, systematic manner?"

I was hooked. Fascinating stuff, I thought – and the project offered the chance of lots more travel to far-flung places, meeting extraordinary people. Documentary-making can become a powerful drug by itself – and highly addictive. So I signed on. Within a couple of months, Brendan and IONS had charmed $100,000 out of the pockets of some benign philanthropists and board members – mostly from Laurance Rockefeller, I believe – and we were in business.

Before I describe some of our adventures in creating *The Heart of Healing*, I should reveal the tragic punch line to the story, because it made what happened later all the more poignant. It turned out, just before we were about to start full production, that Brendan fell ill. Lizzie and I thought we were close and intimate friends of his: he led us to believe that his "dis-ease" (as he called it) was just a passing problem. But it was not.

Brendan started to look really sick. We were told he had cancer. We wanted to help, but somehow there was always some excuse – some reason why he could not or would not see us. Then, out of the blue, we heard from a mutual friend that he was literally at death's door. I visited him by myself and saw the grim black patches of Karposi's Sarcoma all over his body. Within a week, he was dead.

Brendan had had AIDS. He had never told any of us about it. He was deeply ashamed, at one level, I suppose: a good Catholic boy should not have been secretly visiting San Francisco bath houses. He had never revealed to anyone but his (equally closeted) boyfriend that he was gay.

Stunningly, Brendan had personally gone to bat for the funds for our TV series on worldwide mind-body healing, largely because he thought it might reveal a psychological or mental strategy for beating the HIV virus. Alas, it did not. He died in 1992 and was given a beautiful send-off on a hill-top at the Unitarian Church in Tiburon, overlooking the San Francisco Bay. More than a hundred people were there. What a tragic loss of a lovely man. Rest in Peace, dear Brendan!

■■

Somehow, we had to soldier on without him, however. It was one of the toughest and most complex projects that I have ever produced, and also one of the most personally fulfilling. We all felt we were making the films as a memorial to Brendan, and I hope that they convey some of his hope, his humor, his intelligence and his imagination.

Right from the start, raising the funds for *The Heart of Healing* – the whole $2.5 million for the series, the book and accompanying educational materials – was a great deal more difficult than raising the development money.

IONS could pull strings at a number of foundations, most notably at the Fetzer Institute of Kalamazoo, in western Michigan. Founded by John Fetzer, a former broadcaster and Detroit Tigers baseball team owner, it promoted a spiritual view of life, and in the early 1990's it was deeply interested in the overlap between the spiritual, the humanistic and the scientific: the healing properties of the mind and spirit were of particular interest to them.

To seduce individuals and organizations to part with their money, Brendan and I had devised the most lavish and beautiful printed document that I have ever helped to create: a very large format non-glossy brochure, printed on stout parchment-like paper stock, with hand-drawn visuals that smacked of nineteenth-century engravings. It was colored throughout with subtle, faded shades of dark crimson, faded blue and olive green. It had something mysterious and almost Kabbalistic about it, and it certainly drew the eye. The title was *The Healing Mind.*

The Fetzer Foundation, which I later visited, sits in the middle of a forest on the edge of Kalamazoo, a rust-belt town where they used to make the big old classic Checker cabs. Employees glide around Fetzer's spacious premises like priests and acolytes of a well-endowed cult. They take their time to deliberate about everything from the color of their pencils to the shape of their hallways. Their Board pondered our project at great length and in great depth, we were told. They took many months to decide that *The Healing Mind* was not for them.

That was sad, but would have been quite acceptable, had it not been for the fact that the well-known PBS talk-show host Bill Moyers was on their Board. He had obviously recused himself from their decision, of course. Not to have done so would have been unethical. But a few months after their decision, he announced that he would be going into production on his own series, called – by a remarkable coincidence – *Healing and the Mind.* He had been interested in the field for years, apparently.

Being Bill Moyers, his series would consist largely of him interviewing experts in studio, with short cutaways to "b-roll" stories of patients and doctors on location. This was the standard Moyers format, which I find quite dull, so I was not too worried by the competition, except for one thing. PBS would not want two series running at the same time, on the same topic.

We did know that Moyers was well-informed about this kind of subject matter. He had been famous for interviewing the mythologist Joseph Campbell in the 1980's, at the time that I was filming Campbell with Stuart Brown (see Chapter 8): we had been competitors back then, too. This time, the parallels with our project seemed a little too obvious, but what could we do? There is no copyright on ideas, or even titles.

And then a remarkable thing happened. One of the IONS Board members invited a friend to stay the weekend with her in Belvedere, a wealthy enclave across the bay from San Francisco. The friend saw a copy of our large and exotic printed prospectus for *The Healing Mind,* sitting on a coffee table, and picked it up.

"This is just what we've been looking for!" he exclaimed. "May I take this back to Atlanta with me?"

The visitor was Marty Killeen, a producer at Ted Turner's brand-new cable TV network, TBS. They were looking for major documentary projects, and in particular for two-hour specials to run in prime time. Marty was not only a veteran producer, he was also a cancer survivor, who attributed his remission in large part to the role his mind had played, in aiding the healing process.

A week later, my phone rang at InCA: it was Joel Westbrook, Senior Executive Producer at WTBS.

"Would you care to step on a plane to Atlanta and discuss this new series?" asked Joel. "I hear you need $2.5 million. Does that include the book?"

By this stage, Brendan was already too ill to travel, so I went by myself. I met Marty and Joel, and we seemed to agree on everything. I told them about Bill Moyers' plans for a competing series.

"We'll blow him out the water," said Westbrook. "Like you say in the treatment, we'll shoot spectacular stories on location, all over the world: Haiti, Japan, China, Brazil, Africa: it'll be like Indiana Jones." And that's just what we did.

Our first order of business was to find a new title, since that nice Mr. Moyers had borrowed our original idea. Thinking back to our China series, *The Heart of the Dragon*, I suggested *The Heart of Healing*, and everyone loved it. We all agreed that the heart and soul had more to do with healing than that cold, calculating organ, the conscious mind.

The project was a co-production. The Institute for Noetic Sciences took control of the research, and of producing the book. Caryle Hirshberg, a good friend of Brendan's, was chosen as the chief researcher and book-writer, and the kindly Wink Franklin acted as my co-Executive Producer. The films were supported by the large database of case histories that Brendan had built up at IONS, and it was agreed that the book would be an all-color glossy affair, based largely on the visuals and the stories that we captured for the films, with a sprinkling of historical illustration. It was a highly productive and creative arrangement.

Watching the films again now, twenty-five years later, I am struck by how emotive they are. Some critics (including my friend Judy Flannery, from *Cosmos*) called them overly sentimental at the time, but I think this is unfair. They described and evoked really powerful emotions – healing emotions.

Take, for example, our story of Thanksgiving at Starcross, in far northern California. Here, a small community of Christian monks and nuns looked after small children who had been born with HIV and contracted AIDS, and had then been abandoned by their parents. Medically, the question was: why did these children fare so much better in a warm, loving environment than their peers in hospital? In human terms, it was blindingly obvious: the power of love can trump the power of medicine and even the power of disease, in many cases.

But to watch the children's faces, as they ate their turkey, laughing and singing, was to bring tears to the eyes of many a cynic, when the films aired. I remember returning to my own family on the afternoon of Thanksgiving Day, after filming that scene at Starcross. When I arrived home at dusk and saw James (aged 5) and Pippa (aged 3), waiting for me with Lizzie, ready to eat our own turkey, I just burst into tears.

The whole production team went through experiences like this. The indomitable Joan Saffa filmed the Shanghai Cancer Survivors' club, on retreat at a beautiful ornamental lake just outside the city: meditation, dance and Chinese herbs had triggered at least a temporary remission from the gravest cancers in every one of the club members. Traveling back to Shanghai on a train, they sang *Happy Birthday to You* to one of their members: it was the anniversary of her remission. They all engaged in bursts of "laughing therapy," to the amazement of the other passengers. Finally, there were beatific smiles all round, and not a dry eye in the house for those who watched the scene.

I filmed a remarkable story in Lourdes myself. You might not expect it, but the Catholic Church goes to great pains to explain away ninety-five percent of the "miraculous cures" that are said to happen there. The modern church is sensitive to accusations of superstition surrounding healing. They employ an independent secular medical council, to vet the hospital records of all who come to Lourdes and claim to have been healed by faith. If something does not add up – insufficient proof of the original disease, missing medical records, or whatever – they politely reject the case.

But roughly five percent of the cures at Lourdes are inexplicable in strictly medical terms. We interviewed an Italian man, who had been brought back from death's door, and had been cancer-free for two decades. His numerous metastatic tumors had started to shrivel, immediately after an ecstatic visit to Lourdes in the 1970's. We filmed twenty-five years' worth of his x-rays. We talked to doctors. You could take your pick: either God had intervened, or the man was hyper-suggestive and transformed by his ecstatic experience, or it was just a coincidence. Either way, the story triggered strong emotions in those who watched.

In fact, the dominating emotion in our production team, and in our eventual audience, turned out to be joy. I filmed the Candomblé ceremony on a beach some miles to the south of Sao Paulo, in Brazil. Here, you can find thousands of adherents of animist religions originating in Africa, which have been spiced with some of the ceremonies of Christianity.

In February, during their summer, worshippers of Candomblé spend three days without sleep on the beach, dancing themselves into trance-like states of exhaustion and – here is that word again – ecstasy. Then, at dawn on the third day, everyone puts on white and turquoise robes, and slowly moves into the ocean. They float little model boats that they have constructed out of palm leaves: each one contains a slip of paper, expressing their desire for healing and a description of their disease.

As the sun comes up over the rim of the Atlantic, they start singing and chanting. The camera pulls back to reveal that there are hundreds of people at this mass baptism, waist deep in the waves, chanting joyfully, their ecstatic faces warmed by the rising sun.

A conservative doctor at a teaching hospital in Sao Paolo was happy to be interviewed for our film.

"I have no idea how it works," he admitted. "But it certainly does seem to work. Our records show that the incidence of remission, of cancers and many other life-threatening diseases, is substantially higher among the followers of Candomblé."

He shrugged apologetically. "I wish I could publish a paper which explains the mechanism, but I can't," he said frankly. "It's just a fact of life round here. We thank God for their healing."

Once post-production started in earnest, I realized how important that music would be, in creating the right atmosphere for the films. I had the great good fortune to work, as on several subsequent projects, with the composer Ed Bogas. He was one in a million – a talented musician who would let me come into his studio and simply hum or whistle ideas I had had for certain film sequences. Then he would pick up the melody on his electric keyboard and develop it. Gradually, his three or four session musicians would join in, on drums, saxophone or whatever they had lying around. Within a couple of hours, we had created multiple versions of the music we would then use, to cut the picture. I was in heaven, having never been able to read or play a note of music.

"Hey," said Ed, his eyes twinkling. "They're all your ideas. You should take a composer credit." Seeing my disbelief, he went on: "OK. We'll share the composer credit. We'll get you signed up with BMI," (one of the world's two biggest music copyright organizations) "and we'll split the royalties."

That is exactly what happened. For many years I received modest checks from BMI, as the series (and two other films I did with Ed Bogas) were sold around the world. Even our accountant, Chuck Locati, was impressed.

"I didn't know you were musical," he said. I didn't tell him my secret.

■■

Joan Saffa and I were back in the cutting room, trying to knit the different *Heart of Healing* stories together into satisfying two-hour story arcs, when I had a phone call from Atlanta.

"David?" said a new voice. "My name's Pat Mitchell. I've just taken over from Joel Westbrook. I'm the new Executive Producer for the Turner Network. We need to discuss your project. I need to make some changes."

My heart sank. To be ordered to change direction, when you have filmed ninety per cent of the content of a show, is bad news. But there was worse to come.

"I think we need on an-camera host", said Ms. Mitchell. "And I've got just the person!" My heart sank further.

Pat was brisk and businesslike. "Do you know Jane Seymour?" she asked. "She's a friend of mine, and I think she'd be ideal."

I had imagined that, for once, we would be able to create a series of two-hour adventure films, where the storyline would be strong enough to carry the show. And now? We were being offered an English actress of a certain age, pretending to know about a subject she had probably barely thought about before. I felt that this was network television at its worst – pure Hollywood motivation. Of course, Hollywood is where Pat Mitchell had come from.

The next bad news was that, for her new pieces to camera, Jane Seymour insisted on being directed by her new husband. In turn, I insisted on being on the set, so that I could try to ensure that what Jane said was at least usable in the context of our films. I went down to her luxury house in Santa Barbara, north of LA, and found a feature-film-size crew. Her husband, I learned, had decided to use a gauze filter, to soften the definition of Ms. Seymour's face – and probably to conceal a couple of her facial lines. It made her look like a Penthouse magazine model, preparing to shoot a cheesecake shot in the 1970's. My heart was in my boots.

Jane's first line to camera was: "I'm not a doctor, I just play one on TV."

At this point, my heart got its hat and coat and left the room. La Belle Seymour was known at the time for her star turn in *Doctor Quinn, Medicine Woman*, a popular *telenovela* - as the Mexicans so aptly call them - about "the trials and adventures of a female doctor in a small Wild West town." Or so the official website describes it. It allowed Jane to wear period costume and act her heart out, surrounded by cowboys who seemed to say "darn it" and "dang" a lot. It was said to be a much-loved series - by people who liked that kind of thing.

So, Jane was spliced into the films. She interrupted the action approximately every twenty minutes. Her inclusion largely prevented any foreign sales of the series. But I realized that I did have a couple of things in common with her, when I came to record the narration for the films, some months later.

I flew back to LA, scripts in hand. The narration had been scrupulously timed to fit exact slots in the film. All the music and soundtracks were already in place. What would I do if she insisted on copious rewrites, right there in the recording studio? Our budget was fast running out.

It turned out that, when push came to shove, Jane was a real pro. She arrived on time, carrying her own copy of the script. She had made a couple of word changes here and there, which is the prerogative of any voice-over talent. But everything fitted, to the nearest half second. What is more, she usually got it right on the first take. Best of all, she was happy to do alternative takes - faster, slower, happier, more serious - as long as we had time left in the session. And - hooray! - she did not bring her husband with her this time.

We recorded the narration for all three films in one day, which is quite a feat. During the breaks, to rest her voice, she sipped juice and we chatted about our shared English background. She was a couple of years older than me, and had grown up in Wimbledon, less than ten miles from my childhood home in Croydon. Our backgrounds had been similar, and yet here we both were, out in California. The big difference was that she had made a ton of money and I had not, of course. Oh well. Documentary making is somewhere between a vocation and an obsession, and I had had my chance to join the commercial rat race when I lived in LA.

Pat Mitchell was no fool, it turned out. Indeed, she went on to become one of the grandees of television, winning a stream of awards for the advancement of women in the media. Because we had Jane Seymour in the films, TV Guide gave us a mention on the cover and an extensive article inside, with pictures: back in the early 90's, before the internet, this was gold dust.

But wait, there's more. Behind the scenes, Time Warner, the media conglomerate, was holding talks with a view to gobbling up Ted Turner's fledgling cable TV empire. *The Heart of Healing*, as one of Turner's many properties, was inspected by people from the Time-Life Video division, and they liked what they saw.

They made us an offer: how about re-cutting the Turner series? They proposed taking out Jane Seymour, adding new and unused material, which we had already filmed, and reissuing the project as eight separate videos, packaged with our glossy book of the series. I was over the moon: at last we could create the series the way I had wanted.

As luck would have it, we had cut the project on the Avid, the world's first digital editing system, introduced in August 1992. Indeed, for a few short weeks, InCA Productions owned more Avid systems (three) than any other video outfit in Northern California. We were lucky enough to have three top editors – Charlotte Grossman, Joe de Francesco and Blair Gershkow – in three separate suites, with machines that cost over $40,000 each, a fortune in those days.

Today, of course, greater editing power can be installed on the simplest laptop. But back then, we were pioneers. Using an analog system – with VHS tapes constantly shuttling backwards and forwards – we would have gone crazy, trying to edit what amounted to a six-hour film. Unpicking it all and repurposing it for Time-Life Video would have been impossible. But with Avid, retelling the stories a quite different way was a real pleasure, thanks to the skill of our editors.

The editing room is where a film is really created. You can write a dozen scripts, shoot a dozen locations, get a dozen great performances and do a dozen takes of each shot. But the film only finds its character and voice when it is stitched together.

The relationship between the Director and the Editor is crucial: the process is more like a dance than a linear stage-by-stage process. The Editor will take a fresh look at all the ingredients on offer and may recommend creating a subtly different film from the one the Director or Producer originally had in mind.

This, of course, can lead to some anguished confrontations, as well as some creative synthesis. Each editor has his or her own signature style, based on their personalities, interests and techniques. On *The Heart of Healing*, Charlotte Grossman was the coziest editor, if I may put it that way: she loved having company in her cutting room, chatting away as she tried out two or three versions of a scene, to see how she felt about them. She later went on to make her own excellent film, featuring women who spend years carefully creating multi-colored quilts. The film reflected to a tee her own companionable and careful way of working in video.

Joe de Francesco liked working alone, however: he would agonize about moving a single cut just a few frames earlier or later, and he often chose to work late into the night, all by himself in our empty offices. A former seminary student (like Michael Anderson, our excellent cameraman), he would wrestle with a sequence as if with the devil. The results of his efforts were spectacular – always slightly different from Charlotte's, but every bit as good.

Blair Gershkow, our third editor, was used to working fast and without much hands-on direction – the way he had worked for TV stations, with a 6 p.m. news deadline. Though he was always very professional and in many ways a technical wizard, I never got the impression that he was touched by the emotional depth of the material, and we had some interesting sessions with him, massaging and re-shaping his material. (Later, we'd work together again on *Keeping Score*).

In amazingly short order, we turned the three Turner 2-hour specials into eight 45-minute videos for Time Life. These are my favorite versions, because nothing gets in the way of the stories. Without Jane Seymour, talented though she may be, the films seem 'real' – full of genuine feeling and warmth. Watching them, some people have said, even seems to help their healing process. This is a kind thought, but it is indeed remarkable how watching the combination of a good documentary well told, with evocative music and subtle editing, can be a profoundly moving experience.

At the end of the project, we received several sets of both versions of the project. They were all on VHS tape: DVDs were not invented till 1995 and did not become popular until the twenty-first century. In 2000, Time Warner, having swallowed Turner Broadcasting, was itself swallowed by a fish that was even bigger – at least back then – AOL. Dozens of Turner shows were simply left on the shelf. *The Heart of Healing* was never re-released.

I did decide, however, that one person deserved to be given a complete set of *The Heart of Healing* in all its VHS versions, plus the book. That person was Bill Moyers, who had pipped us to the post with his project *Healing and the Mind*. I sent him a very large package and a very polite letter, inviting him to enjoy it all.

Within a week, I received the nicest possible personal letter – a page and a half long, with much flattery and congratulation – signed personally by Mr. Moyers.

"David," he wrote, as if he was an old friend, though we had never met. "I have always admired your work and cannot thank you enough for sharing this impressive project with me."

Such poise. Such style. Such sincerity. Or not, as the case may be.

■■■

17. PULLING OUT ALL THE STOPS: FROM PIPE ORGANS TO LEVI'S

By the end of production on *The Heart of Healing*, I was exhausted. We had created three two-hour specials for TBS Cable, and eight forty-five-minute versions for Time-Life Video, besides collaborating on the book. It had been a fascinating but grueling two-year haul. But for once, I had made some decent money while making the shows. I did not have to careen directly into the next production. In fact, I started to suspect that I was becoming jaded with continuous television production. *The Heart of Healing* was a high point. Now, I was tempted to find something else.

"Listen," said Lizzie. "You need a break. More important, I need a break."

The children, James and Pippa, were then four and two-and-a-half years old, respectively: cute and wonderful of course, but quite a handful. Also, Lizzie had started to study psychology, with a view to a totally new career outside television. She suggested that we should go somewhere far away and very quiet, so that we could have a gentle nervous breakdown in peace, by ourselves.

"Not England," she said, "Please, not England."

We knew that, however much we loved them, we would get completely embroiled in family, friends and the complications of the InCA London office, and neither of us would find the quiet we needed.

"But somewhere European: old towns, old stones, old buildings, old culture," I said, envisaging long siestas, and perhaps starting a completely new project.

"OK," said Lizzie, nothing daunted. "How about France? How about somewhere deep in the French countryside – down in the South West, near Albi and Toulouse, where we know people: Mike and Liney Simler."

We had visited them the previous summer. They had fled from advertising jobs in England years ago, and they had promised to find us a house to rent, should we ever be brave enough to make the break.

"They'll know the local schools," said Lizzie. "We can put the children into a village school, I'm sure. We've all got British passports, so we can live anywhere in the European Union. The kids can learn French, and we can have a six-month holiday – or maybe longer."

It sounded like paradise. To be honest, neither of us was completely convinced that we wanted to live in the US forever. Did we want our children to grow up as Americans? Did we want to leave the door open to a return to Europe, sometime fairly soon?

Advised by Mike and Liney, who assured us that there was a big British expatriate community in the Département of the Tarn, we sent photos of our children and a short application form to a local village school and made our plans. I placed the InCA San Francisco office in the hands of my loyal business manager, Cheryl King, and my compadre on *The Heart of Healing* series, Joan Saffa, with instructions to keep the home fires burning. We installed our friend and colleague, the young producer Michael O'Connell, to house-sit our modest house in Mill Valley.

Then we packed a mountain of suitcases and baby gear, to cover six months' freedom in Europe. Taking a taxi to San Francisco Airport, en route to London for a Christmas with all my children – Amanda and Juliet included – we felt a huge sense of relaxation and relief.

■■

Picture, if you will, the bleakest stretch of French countryside you can imagine, in the dead of winter. Now picture a ramshackle old farmhouse, built into the side of a hill – a very damp hill. The French family who owned it had decided to go to Istanbul for at least six months, so that the father could take an engineering job, and – as it turned out – the mother could get divorced from him. This was to be our home from January to June 1994: the tiny hamlet of Milhavet.

The house was either cold as the grave or hot as hell. The heating system was powered by an old oil-burning boiler that roared and grunted like a wild animal. It turned out that the only way to get the fuel to run it was to have it delivered by truck. But this was France. The imposing entrance gateway of the house was too narrow to allow any of the oil tankers to get through – with the exception of one single vehicle, based fifty miles away in Rodez. Did we panic? Yes, we did. But luckily, the dinky-sized truck reached us with new supplies just a day or two before we ran out of oil.

Then there was the car. Our deal with the French family included use of their family vehicle. To be fair, they had warned us that it was by no means new. They kept it in a hay barn that was an extension of the house. When we peeked inside the barn, we saw an elderly Volvo 240, a dull maroon color, slowly rusting in a corner. We coaxed it to life, and lurched and sputtered the ten miles to the nearest garage, to have it inspected. The garage mechanic laughed heartily when he spotted us: he knew this car and had been trying to keep it running for many years.

"*Ah, mais c'est foutue, cette voiture,*" he told us. *Foutue,* for non-French-speakers, can be translated by a similar English word beginning with F. "She is dead, or at least she is dying."

Being a Swedish car, we called her Princess Beatrice, and she had all the temperament of an old queen: I have worked with one or two, so I should know. After a few weeks of struggling with her in the cold weather, we put her back in the barn and bought a fairly new Volkswagen Golf with our credit card. Casually proffering a VISA card to buy a car was something new to me.

But the village school turned out to be a miracle. Three days after we arrived, at the end of the first week of January, we took Princess Beatrice and the children through the snow to discover a one-room schoolhouse, five miles from our farm. This was the only pre-school for the whole region, and it housed just ten children, one teacher and an assistant.

We had been asked to arrive late one morning, just two days after the start of term. All we could hear, on arrival, was the sound of children singing. We opened the door, the singing stopped, and everyone looked at us. Immediately, the teacher smiled and walked towards our children.

"*Bonjour, Pippa!*" she said, "*Bonjour, James! Bienvenue*! Welcome. Look – here are your desks."

On each of the two vacant desks, there was a photo: one was James's, one was Pippa's. So that is why they had wanted photos sent from the USA. There was also a drawing of a happy playgroup, made by children from the class, plus a posy of flowers and a small bar of chocolate. Immediately, the class broke out into a well-rehearsed song of welcome, and then applauded us as if we were royalty. James and Pippa were stunned: they couldn't believe their eyes and ears.

"Now, we'll all play a game," the teacher explained to us briskly. "I think it's better if you go now, so the children won't miss you. See you this afternoon at four o'clock."

We were amazed: no clinging from Pippa, who normally hated being without us. No pouting from James: they were gathered up into the whirl of activity as if they had been born into it. Lizzie and I backed off and drove into Albi. We were free! We celebrated by having lunch at a local bistro. Maybe these six months would turn out to be a vacation after all.

Within a few days, the children were speaking some French. They never once asked to miss school in the six months they were there. Pippa, with the other two and three-year-olds, took a nap on a blanket every afternoon after lunch. James climbed trees and tumbled around with the local farmers' children as if this was his regular life.

Talking about lunch, we were in for a big surprise. We were told that we did not have to provide a lunchbox, which seemed miraculous. But it took us some weeks to realize what a feast was provided, every day of the week. The first we knew of it was when our children complained about some pasta I had made for their supper and said that it was not as good as the school food. I could hardly believe that, so the next day Lizzie and I decided to drop in on the school at lunchtime, to see what was going on. At a single table, twelve little boys and girls were quietly eating their way through a three-course lunch: *salade niçoise*, roast chicken and two vegetables, and a wholesome but delicious cream dessert.

Apparently, every day, a van arrived from Albi, the nearest big town, with pre-made lunches, which just needed heating up and arranging on plates. This was done by a stern-looking farmer's wife from the neighborhood, who ruled the roost in the dining room, shouting "*Taisez-vous!*" ("Be quiet!") at the top of her voice, if there was the slightest sign of obstreperous behavior. Meanwhile the two teachers ate lunch off a white tablecloth in a separate and blissfully quiet staff room.

This was a scene that apparently happens all over France: free lunches, served on proper crockery with cutlery, for every schoolchild in the country. It is seen as part of their education – how to appreciate good French food and polite French table manners. No Coke and pizza here. I have to say that, ever since their time in France, Pippa and James have enjoyed all the diversity of French and many other cuisines. Oh yes, and they still speak excellent French.

The final cherry on the cake was to meet Guy Bonardi, a witty French video producer in Toulouse, an hour and a half to the south. He welcomed the idea of co-producing some short commercial films with me. We co-formed InCA France, and eventually produced several ten or twenty-minute videos. One featured a typical English family – yes, it was the Kennards, of course – enjoying a boating vacation on the Canal du Midi. Another was a hymn to the delicious and hugely fattening regional dish, the *cassoulet*, full of duck, sausage and broad beans. None of these videos represent the high point of my filmmaking career, but it was great fun to work with a French crew and keep my hand in, when it came to production.

••

Spring took a long time to come, in Milhavet. There were finally leaves on the trees and temperatures warm enough to enjoy the great outdoors by May 1st – Lizzie's birthday. We had a little party in and around our shabby farmhouse, with the Simlers, the children's teacher and other French and British friends we had made.

But what of the future? Should we return permanently to Europe, or try to make a serious living in California? Lizzie missed England more than I did, I think. But I was certainly missing my elder daughters, Juliet and Amanda.

Juliet had decided that she didn't want to follow obediently in the footsteps of her sister through St. Paul's School in London, so had applied to Marlborough College, a prestigious private boarding school in the rolling hills of Wiltshire. They had only just started taking girls in the Senior School and were interested in unusual candidates. I said to my first wife, Helen, that I couldn't possibly afford the fees of a boarding school, but Juliet solved the problem at a stroke.

She visited the school on an 'Open Day', wandered casually down to the track sports area and, wearing just her regular jeans and a T-shirt, leapt over the High Jump and immediately broke the school record for anyone her age, male or female. The Coach was so impressed that he offered her an Athletics Scholarship on the spot.

Amanda, meanwhile, almost 18, was considering Oxford and Cambridge, but finally settled on Bristol University for her undergraduate days. Eventually all three of my daughters went to Bristol, but more about that later.

In spite of bumpy times in the marriage between Helen and her second husband, Rupert Pennant-Rea (see the end of Chapter 5), both Amanda and Juliet seemed well able to stand on their own two feet and were charting their own futures with confidence and skill. They had also been coming to visit us in California from time to time, so I didn't feel as estranged from them as I might have done. Also, my mother and father had both died by now, so I felt less and less of a need to be in England.

Lizzie, however, was still deeply divided about where we should bring up our children. We visited several schools in England on our return from France. But we no longer owned the Maida Vale flat in London (which we'd sold after a disastrous winter flood a couple of years before), so we didn't have a base. Lizzie's parents were still alive, as were her two brothers Robert and Tim, though relations with them veered from cordial to stormy.

The deciding factor, however, was that InCA London was not doing well at all. Chris Haws, our Best Man, had assumed the role of Managing Director and effectively, over a couple of years, had run the company into the ground. We had high overheads and barely any TV commissions or other industrial film business. My credits, over the previous ten years, had been more resonant in the US than in the UK. There was simply no way that I could have taken over or earned a living as a Director/Producer, based in London in the mid 1990's.

Luckily, I had been spending some of my time in France emailing old friends in California. "Emailing?" I hear you say. Yes, astonishingly, the ramshackle farmhouse had a very slow internet dial-up connection, and this was the dawn of the internet – the era of AOL and "You've got mail."

Getting bored during long afternoons in the Milhavet farmhouse, I asked a few of my American friends if any of them was interested in joining me in a totally new venture. I realized I was bored with TV production, at least for the time being. Thinking back to Business School in Bloomington, and letting my mind wander into futuristic pastures, I devised various plans for an off-the-wall marketing company, which might be able to do many of the things that advertising agencies would not or could not do: special events, live virtual meetings linked by telephone or virtual reality, or sky-writing and zany public relations stunts. Why not?

To my great surprise and pleasure, two California friends took the bait: Bill Bennett, who was working as a Senior Vice-President of Hill & Knowlton, the big PR Company, and Jim Gollub, a Senior Researcher at SRI, the Stanford Research Institute. Like me, both were in their forties and had had their share of success, but both were quite ready to enjoy a mid-life crisis and head out to pastures new. They suggested that we should create a partnership or a Limited Liability Company and try to do something new in the marketing field. We came up with the name IDeA (similar to InCA), standing for Information Design Associates. Quite what we'd do, or where we'd raise some money, was unclear at the time, but it seemed to be just what I needed: a new start. Nothing ventured...

Lizzie and I sadly bade goodbye to rural France and England in mid-summer, when they were both at their best: green, lush, overflowing with the new fruit of the season. We have been back many times to that same area in France, and are still closely in touch with our expatriate British friends, Pippa and George Richmond-Brown. We keep promising ourselves that we'll retire and buy a little place there – or perhaps Italy or Portugal, or even Oxfordshire or Hampshire in England – but... a quarter of a century later, it has still not happened.

It did seem very strange to be back in San Francisco. Wooden buildings, rather than stone? The weird sound of American English? Easy living: too easy? Pleasant but somewhat shallow relationships, rather than the deep and necessary friendships that develop in the tougher world of Europe? And the pace of life, even in easy-going San Francisco, even in quiet Mill Valley, seemed scarily hectic, after the Milhavet farmhouse and the village school. But there was no time to be lost in random philosophizing: we had spent all our spare money on our French idyll, we were nearly broke, and we both needed work.

At this stage – and, financially, in the nick of time – two things happened. My old friend Judy Flannery – a tireless colleague on the *Cosmos* series, who had welcomed us with open arms to the Bay Area when we first moved there – brought InCA a most unusual documentary project: a feature on the American pipe organ in all its glory. The other stroke of good fortune was the chance, with Bill and Jim, to float a totally new company, and to return, for five tumultuous years, to my roots in international marketing, and finally put to use whatever I had learned at the Business School of Indiana University.

To take the film first: my grandfather (on my father's side), Francis T. Kennard, had been a well-regarded pipe organ designer and builder back in the day. For a few years, when I was six, seven and eight, our summer holidays consisted of a week in the faded seaside town of Folkestone with Granny and Grandpa, and then a week on the coast in Cornwall with my Uncle Dick, Aunt Daphne and two cousins, Helen and Diana.

The Folkestone visit was the tougher assignment. My grandparents were still very much living in the Victorian era. Their gloomy house was suitably full of big, ticking long-case "grandfather" clocks, each needing to be wound daily by Grandpa, who took this job very seriously. Every horse-hair-stuffed armchair was covered in a prim antimacassar, to avoid being besmirched by visitors with hair-oil. Their one bath, with realistic claw-foot legs, had an ancient and frightening gas water-heater above it, which had to be lit with matches and wheezed and bubbled ominously, while it raised the water from Setting 1 (Icy) to Setting 2 (Scalding). When I later saw illustrations of the Addams Family house, I recognized it immediately.

Granny Kennard wasn't used to having children around and viewed me with some suspicion. She liked to call me "Tom Noddy", which she found very humorous: only later did I discover that it was ancient slang for an idiot or a dunce. Thank you, Granny K! I hid out among the thickets of raspberry bushes in their rambling garden and ate as many as I could before I was sick.

The main activity in Folkestone, besides spending days with my parents on the nearby stony beaches and nearly freezing to death, was to visit churches, where Grandpa was working on their elderly organs. He was pleased to have company, I think. He would tune them, replace faulty parts, and generally take them for a test drive. I loved spending time up amongst the giant eight-foot, sixteen-foot and thirty-two-foot pipes as they roared and blared around me. He showed me how the stops worked, and how you played the massive instruments with two hands and two feet, all at once.

It was therefore a happy coincidence that Judy Flannery landed a pipe organ film for InCA to create. Through her arts community connections, she had heard that APOBA (the

American Pipe Organ Builders' Association) and the AGO (American Guild of Organists) wanted to celebrate the centennial of their organizations, and had collected sufficient funds from well-wishers to commission a Public Television one-hour film and several subsidiary versions for the trade.

I jumped at the chance, though it was eventually my friend and colleague Michael O'Connell who did most of the filming. We covered half a dozen individual stories, from classic church organs to organs in parks, department stores and cinemas. The latter were represented by the machine in the Paramount Theatre in Oakland, CA: a massive brute, which included a dozen special effects like train whistles and clanging bells, to accompany silent films: welcome to the Mighty Wurlitzer!

The most moving story came from South Carolina, where a community had saved up for twenty years, to afford a proper 'tracker' organ in their church – no electronic Hammond keyboard would satisfy them. Once it was complete, it was shipped in pieces from Chicago to the small township, which had ordered it. In procession, the church members each solemnly carried one of the new pipes into the church, with two strong men needed for the sixteen-foot pipes, and small children carrying the tiny piccolo pipes. The inauguration of the organ was a mighty celebration, full of tears and laughter: great emotive material for what might have been a rather dry, technical film.

The other big event of the mid 90's was Jim Gollub's revelation that our new baby, IDeA – the putative marketing company – had been offered the chance of a fat contract with a major advertising agency.

He used to travel to his regular job in San Francisco by ferry from Tiburon, and had struck up a friendship with another frequent commuter, Mick Feld, Head of Direct Marketing at a long-established agency, FCB, or Foote, Cone and Belding. We learned (from Mike Simler, who had worked there) that it was known to its more jaded employees as Foot-Sore and Bleeding. Perhaps in response to this calumny, the group was renamed True North a few years later: one of those completely senseless corporate names which came into fashion at that time. Of course, it was promptly dubbed "Going South" by the same group of cynical company time servers.

Mick Feld, unlike many of his colleagues, was a shrewd and witty operator. He was part of the family that had owned and run Barnum & Bailey's Traveling Circus, and he obviously found direct marketing pretty dull. It mostly consisted of creating junk mail. Mick was looking for new ideas, and – incredibly, for a long-term corporate employee – was genuinely open to them.

Jim explained the benefits that the IDeA team could bring him: a combination of original media, public relations and data analysis and feedback – something far more exciting than FCB's daily diet of print, radio, TV and direct marketing. Hey, we might even use this wondrous new medium the Internet, and the World Wide Web, whatever that was. Mick met with Bill, Jim and myself, and we tossed a lot of off-the-wall ideas around. Mick decided to go for it. FCB would invest $1.5 million in IDeA in return for half of our time over a three-year period and 11% of our stock.

We had struck a deal that was pretty much perfect, from my point of view. By agreeing to offer only half of our time to FCB, that left us the other half, for IDeA to cultivate new clients or for me to do my documentaries at InCA. We were given elegant offices in San Francisco's Levi Plaza, a campus-like environment on the edge of downtown and a stone's throw from the Embarcadero and San Francisco Bay.

With Mick Feld's support, we developed special events for clients like Clorox, the bleach manufacturers; Tower Records, now defunct; and Levi's, the jewel in FCB's crown. I was also sent to FCB's Head Office in Chicago to pitch Johnson & Johnson – makers of baby powder and a host of family-friendly products – on a series of wholesome rock concerts. Bill Bennett's contacts in the music world were helpful here. Best of all, we developed what I believe were the world's first interactive virtual reality kiosks as a pilot project for Levi's.

We used the fastest connections available in the late 90's – T1 lines – and the technical wizardry of NTT Docomo, a Japanese telecoms giant where Jim Gollub had connections. We devised an animated world, in which the user of the kiosk could fly through a virtual San Francisco and meet other users of the system, playing from other kiosks elsewhere, in the make-believe world that inventor Jaron Lanier had named "virtual reality."

These other users could be playing, in principle, from anywhere in the world. In our demonstration, they were either at the Levi's flagship store in San Francisco's Union Square or in Las Vegas, where T1 lines were also available. On screen, other people would appear like pawns on a game board, representing the grid plan of San Francisco's streets and surrounding areas. Their heads were superimposed on top of the animated pawns. A camera in the kiosk took video pictures and live sound from each player in real time. So you could say to a friend in, say, Las Vegas, "I'll meet you at the Golden Gate Bridge" and then both travel there onscreen in our virtual reality world, and meet and have a conversation. Imagine!

What on earth did that have to do with selling Levi's Jeans? Nothing, but that was not the point. In the last five years of the twentieth century, the first dot-com boom, novelty was everything. Levi's installed a permanent kiosk in their flagship store in San Francisco, to entice people into the shop. It was said to be very cool, and Mick Feld was very pleased.

Other clients were less adventurous. Clorox in particular stood out as a bastion of unimaginative marketing. The three of us agitated furiously to develop a "green policy" for them: their toxic chlorine-based products were already sounding and smelling like a bad old idea. Their Bay Area manufacturing plant was infamous in ecologically sensitive circles. How could we help them to project a greener image, or even develop a greener product?

Jack Boland, Mick Feld's boss, was adamant: we were forbidden to contact Clorox.

"Don't rock the boat," he said. "Clorox, like Johnson & Johnson and Levi's, have been our faithful clients since well before World War II. If they choose to advertise by simply saying 'Buy More Bleach', that's their privilege, and we're charging them plenty for it. They've contributed a great deal to FCB's bottom line over the years, and that's the main thing, isn't it?"

But time and tide wait for no man, as fortune cookies remind us. In 1999, the dot-com boom led rapidly to the dot-com bust. Novel, whimsical ideas like virtual reality kiosks were dead in the water. IDeA's contract with FCB – renamed True North by now – was not renewed. Within a few years, Jack Boland was offered a pink slip, Mick Feld had moved on, Tower records went bust, Levi's chose another agency and IDeA withered on the vine. Jim, Bill and I went back to our previous employment. Luckily, I had kept InCA going during the weird and wonderful life of IDeA.

Another era was dawning: the Millennium. What had seemed impossibly remote – the stuff of science fiction – when I was starting at the BBC was suddenly upon us: the year 2000.

Do you remember the furor and anxiety caused by "Y2K"? Many experts predicted that the western world would grind to a halt at midnight on 31 December 1999, because computer systems had not been programmed to cope with a year that ended with the digits 000. There were doom-mongers everywhere, it seemed. The end of a millennium, for goodness' sake! The more fervent Christians prepared for the rapture, and even anxious agnostics feared the worst.

Lizzie and I decided that we would take James and Pippa to Mexico for two weeks, to avoid the chaos – or at least to go somewhere that copes with chaos on a daily basis. We all dressed up as Space Aliens for a futuristic photo, had it made into a Christmas card, and sent it to friends and relations all over the world. They must have thought we were mad. Then we booked two weeks at the Club Med at Ixtapa in Mexico and flew south on Christmas Day, 1999.

Two weeks of swimming, sailing, drinking and wonderful children's activities eased our way into the twenty-first century. I lay on the beach, reading biographies of Picasso and the terrible twins, Monet and Manet. Steve Wynn, the casino mogul of Las Vegas, had given us $50,000 to develop a show on modern art. But that is another story: please see Chapter 19 and *The Promise of Play* for all the details – well, some of the details. One does not want to get on the wrong side of Mr. Wynn.

Y2K did not happen, of course. 9/11 happened instead. For a story about that, please jump forward to Chapter 20. But first, let me offer you Arthur C. Clarke, Amelia Earhart, and Jane Goodall.

• •

18. ARTHUR C. CLARKE:
MASTER OF THE IMAGINATION

To make this part of the story work, I will need to rewind the tape, to use a suitably twentieth-century metaphor.

I first worked with Arthur C. Clarke in 1983, on a three-part series called *The Communications Revolution*. I next worked with him in the year 2000, on a ninety-minute special – with a sixty-minute PBS version – called *2001: HAL's Legacy*. Both productions stay vividly in my mind, thanks to the extraordinary charm, charisma, humor and wisdom of Clarke himself.

Back in the early 80's, as I described in Chapter 8, I was thrashing around, trying to determine whether my future lay in the US or the UK. My partner in the grand-sounding National Video Communications, George Colburn, was energetically promoting the idea of a mega-series for PBS called *The Messengers*, which would describe the development of human communication across the ages, with a healthy side order of futurism about dedicated networks and what would later become the internet.

Our ally in promoting this grand project was former FCC Commissioner Abbott Washburn, whose address book was bursting with famous names, from Walter Cronkite to Arthur C. Clarke. From the very beginning, he persuaded both of them to play a key role in our project, if we could get the funding.

For good measure, Abbott also had a direct line to what was then the nation's second largest phone company. The first, by a wide margin, was the all-powerful "Ma Bell", the original AT&T. It is hard to remember a world without competing cellphone operations, and without the internet. But back then in the dark ages, AT&T's Bell System had a virtual monopoly, from coast to shining coast, except for a small patchwork quilt of regions across the US, where local telephone service was provided by GTE – General Telephone and Electric Corporation. Those engineers sure appreciated snappy, captivating titles for their companies.

Abbott knew the folks at GTE rather well. He told us that some of the GTE board were very interested in promoting their company to a wider audience. After all, they also had interests in Canada and the Caribbean, and were fed up with having sand kicked in their face by Ma Bell. So, what better vehicle for bringing GTE to the nation's consciousness than a huge series on Public Television, which GTE could sponsor? This strategy had worked for Atlantic Richfield, the company which had sponsored *Cosmos* on PBS: a smallish West Coast oil company had become a household name (ARCO) thanks to that project. So why not pull another rabbit out of the hat for General Telephone?

It needs to be said that GTE's general advertising at that time was dismal. A series of newspaper advertisements showed two guys chatting over a garden fence, with dialog that ran something like this:

"I hear there's a phone company that has fully automated connections across North America."

"Gee!"

"No, GTE!"

At some level, they must have realized that this sounded like a meme from the 1930's, and greater effort might be required. Should we ask them for the full five million dollars for the entire project, *The Messengers*? This seemed a little risky, so we proposed that they might stump up $100,000 for research, development of scripts, and the filming of a sizzle reel by George and myself.

"OK, you've got it," said Al Vibranz, their Senior VP of Marketing. "Nobody gets fired for investing $100k in a pilot project."

The check was processed within a month. George and I, with an ex-BBC film crew, booked our flights to the tropical island of Sri Lanka, off the southern coast of India, to meet and film Arthur C. Clarke.

Before we spend time with Arthur, however, I should pay off the story about GTE. When they finally saw the sizzle reel and the lavish marketing materials, they were impressed, but not entirely in a good way. The decision about the project led to a major argument at a board meeting, according to a later report by Al Vibranz, who was present.

The President of the company backed Al and the project, and said he was ready to write a $5 million check to have it produced, complete with educational materials, full publicity and all the bells and whistles. The Chairman of the company, by training and background an engineer, strongly disagreed with him.

"For goodness sake," said the Chairman, "Why would we want to support a project on human communication? We're a *telephone* company."

The President was overruled, and the project was dead, as far as GTE was concerned.

"Ah well," said Al Vibranz later, over a friendly dinner with George and myself, "I'm sorry it turned out this way. That's GTE for you. We're the kind of company that likes fresh new ideas that have stood the test of time."

It was exactly the same line we had invented for a sales executive of the fictional UGE Corporation in the Galbraith *Age of Uncertainty*. Life was, alas, imitating art.

Soon afterwards, Vibranz left GTE and took up a post as Director of the National Gallery of Art in Washington, DC, where I hope he was happier. Meanwhile, George and I had inherited full possession of some priceless material featuring Arthur C. Clarke. What should we do with it? Was there a chance that some other big corporation might step in and fill the funding gap? Abbott Washburn was not optimistic about opening another set of doors at such a high level.

So we decided that we would raise a small amount of additional funding from various sources, and produce a more modest three-part series of half-hour programs, featuring Clarke – partly interviewed by me, on camera, and partly on location all over Sri Lanka. This more modest series would be called *The Communications Revolution*, and would be divided into The Past, The Present and The Future – not a desperately creative structure, I must admit.

Arthur turned out to be a wonderful discovery. He was already a legend in his own lifetime – a science-fiction writer on a level with Isaac Asimov, his long-time friend, competitor and literary sparring partner. He was up there in the Pantheon of sci-fi gods, in my opinion, along with Jules Verne and H.G.Wells. Carl Sagan had taught me to respect science fiction writers, because their work had inspired many ideas that real-life scientists had put into practice. Carl himself had been entranced as a boy by Marvel comics and the adventures of John Carter in Barsoom, alias the planet Mars:

"Those stories are what made me determined to become an astronomer", Sagan had told us.

With Arthur C. Clarke, we had two for the price of one: a superb sci-fi writer and a respectable scientist as well. He had been the first to invent, describe and illustrate the concept of the geo-stationary satellite – in 1945, twelve years before the Russians put Sputnik, the first practical satellite, into earth orbit.

On meeting Arthur, you would have had no idea initially that he was such a genius. He was charmingly modest, like a favorite uncle. His Somerset burr was a wonderful surprise: not just an English accent, but a warm, rural, West Country one. He admitted that he had left his homeland as soon as the revenue from his book sales allowed him to.

"England's much too cold and wet." he said. "Any visitor from another planet would pick somewhere far warmer than England to live."

He had picked Sri Lanka, the former British colony of Ceylon, off the southern tip of India. It was famous for its tea, its Buddhist temples and its fabulous fishing, diving and snorkeling opportunities.

In the 1980's, Arthur was still diving, pulling on his gray wetsuit and adjusting his mask: he looked like an affable seal. He had a retinue of young boys, with whom he liked to dive. Unkind souls suggested that the company of young boys was particularly appealing to him, and that his underlying motivation for emigrating to Sri Lanka was this. But who cares? Arthur was deeply happy in Sri Lanka, where it seemed he was revered by everyone.

Unexpectedly, he loved hearing and telling mildly offensive jokes. He enthusiastically swapped limericks with me. It was he who first told me one of my favorites, a real tongue twister:

> *There once was a lynx-eyed detective,*
> *Who said "Is my eyesight defective?*
> *Has your east tit the least bit*
> *The best of your west tit,*
> *Or is it a trick of perspective?"*

Arthur's hospitality was genuine and copious. He was plainly enthusiastic about our project. He could not wait to get out on location.

For Episode One, "The Past", he took us to villages, where the ancient art of ululation was still practiced, as a means of communicating from one village to the next. It is a bit like yodeling, without the musical quality, but the sound can be heard up to three miles away. This was truly a prehistoric form of communication.

He then sent us up to the hill country, to discover Anuradhapura, one of the most magical Buddhist temples, with a vast white dome, where age-old rituals were practiced twenty-four hours a day against a background of lush jungle scenery. Sacrament and shamanic ritual, he maintained, had often been the most profound form of traditional human communication.

Arthur was enthusiastic and knowledgeable about every aspect of the subject. He was brilliant – but always down to earth, humorous and modest. I remember thinking that he was the polar opposite of Carl Sagan in many ways.

For "The Present", he took us to the vast satellite dish on the island: part of the international telecommunications network that had sprung up in the 1970's. Arthur had lobbied hard to get Sri Lanka chosen as the site of one of these giant dishes, and was proud of his success. The entire system was based on his original invention of the geo-stationary satellite, and there was a giant dish, virtually in his back garden. He spoke movingly about the astonishing changes he had seen in his own lifetime: a planet woven together by talk and coded messages: human communication in action, and a promise of world peace and understanding, as Arthur saw it.

For "The Future", he chose a deserted beach, which was a particular favorite of his. I sat on the sand with him, under a palm tree, looking out over the vastness of the Indian Ocean, while Arthur talked about computers and the first glimmering of what was to become the internet and, later, the World Wide Web. He foresaw the extraordinary impact of universal access to information: the possibilities of electronic libraries, accessible to everyone, and education that could lift the less fortunate and less gifted out of their traditional ignorance.

But even Arthur could not foresee tiny portable devices like the iPhone. He was still talking about mainframe computers, or at least about devices the size of HAL, the famous computer in Stanley Kubrick's film (based on Arthur's novel) *2001: A Space Odyssey*.

"Don't the computers of the future scare you?" I asked him.

"Not at all", said Arthur. "They'll be a different species. It doesn't bother me that a horse can run faster than I can, or that a duck can fly, and I can't. It'll be a pleasure to sit next to an intelligent computer and discuss the world.

"In fact," and here he gave me one of his trademark infectious grins, "I'd have a much more interesting afternoon chatting with such a computer than I would with most of the human beings I know." I just hoped he did not mean me.

Arthur's conclusion was remarkable: in evolutionary terms, he felt, humankind was just one step towards a planet ruled by artificial intelligences. Humans were necessary, to invent silicon-based minds in the first place, but sometime in the twenty-first or twenty-second century, A.I. would outpace us completely, and run everything far more efficiently and constructively than we do. For sure, they might keep a few hundred specimens of humanity around, much like we keep apes in a zoo, for experimental, educational or entertainment purposes, but that would be all. We are, he suggested, unwittingly inventing our own successors.

To put *The Communications Revolution* together, we needed more footage than we had been able to shoot in Sri Lanka, with the restricted time and budget that our development budget had allowed. That is why George Colburn persuaded me to appear on camera, for the first and only time, to introduce and host the three half-hour shows, and to fill in some of the details of the past, present and future that Arthur had not had time to deal with.

This was, indeed, a learning experience. When I look at those shows today, and see myself at age thirty-seven, with long hair and wearing a trendy pale gray suit with fashionably tight trousers, speaking to camera as if I was the world's expert on everything to do with human communications, I truly cringe.

Thanks to Abbott Washburn – again – we had unparalleled access to the Smithsonian's collection of historical artifacts. I was able to handle Samuel Morse's original handset of 1840 – the one on which he had first tapped out his Morse Code, across America's fledgling telegraph network. I stood on the roof of the Smithsonian, with the US Congress buildings in the background, and was filmed while pontificating about the effect of this device on world affairs in the nineteenth century. I stood next to a massive IBM mainframe computer in the Smithsonian's main hall, after the public had gone home, explaining the implications of machine intelligence.

I can make the excuse that I did this, because our minimal budget persuaded me that it was necessary. But secretly, after directing Jacob Bronowski, Carl Sagan and, particularly, James Burke – who was not an official expert on any subject – the devil of self-regard tempted me mightily. I think I believed that I could perform on camera as well as any of them, so why not? After all, I had Arthur C. Clarke's expertise to hide behind.

But in practice, I looked like a juvenile local TV presenter: someone who might have been doing the weather on some inconsequential station in the middle of nowhere. At Indiana University, we had invented such a station for a comedy sketch: WART, "the station that grows on you." I was not believable as a serious PBS presenter. I was terrible.

Nonetheless, the three shows were completed and duly distributed on Public Television: Arthur C. Clarke's name saw to that. They were used for educational purposes for years afterwards, but happily achieved neither prominence nor notoriety. David Kennard's moment on camera was widely ignored – and thank God for that. I made a resolution never to appear on camera again, though I have narrated several films.

"You sound rather like David Attenborough", I have been told occasionally, even by old friends like Nigel Rees in England.

But I have remained out of sight. That way, if the show is a success, I can take the credit, and if it is a failure, I can blame the person on screen. Not something to be proud of, but pretty much the truth.

· ·

I certainly never imagined I would meet or work with Arthur C. Clarke again. For sure, he remained sharp as a tack, and we kept in occasional friendly contact by fax, and later with the new invention of email, initially through AOL. "You've got mail" dominated the 90's. But Sri Lanka is the other side of the planet from San Francisco and Arthur hated to travel away from his beloved tropical island. So I, among many others, had to be satisfied with his witty email blasts, with running commentary on the great ideas and deep stupidities of the era.

Then, in 1999, David Stork arrived on the scene. He contacted me out of the blue, presenting himself as a complete renaissance man. He played in the Stanford University orchestra; he taught math and physics to doctoral students; he was the Chief Scientist in the US for Ricoh (makers of copying machines and much else); he knew a great deal about perspective, optics and the history of art; he had written a major university textbook and – above all else – he was a passionate fan of Clarke's *2001: A Space Odyssey.*

The year 2001 was just around the corner, yet nothing even approached the intelligence of HAL, the onboard computer that plays a leading and sinister role in *2001*. What fascinated Stork was why space travel had advanced significantly since the film was made, but computers had evolved so slowly.

"Why not? That's the key question I want to ask Arthur," said Stork.

He had conducted successful seminars on this subject, both to live audiences and online, and now reckoned it would make a great PBS documentary, with David Stork – no surprise – as the proposed on-camera host, like a latter-day Carl Sagan.

The good news was that Stork was in active contact with Clarke, who was very interested in the idea. Even better news was that the Alfred P. Sloan Foundation, which had paid for Stork's public seminars, had hinted that they were well disposed towards funding such a full-length film for PBS.

The bad news was that Warner Brothers and Stanley Kubrick told us that they would not allow any clips from the original film of *2001: A Space Odyssey* to be used, for any purpose whatsoever. This was a deal breaker, of course. How could we make our documentary without hearing the flat, mesmerizing voice of HAL 9000, the master computer, and seeing its sinister red eye, surveying the action?

In one of the most famous scenes, HAL locks Dave, one of the astronauts, out of the ship, where he has been doing some repairs. "Open the door, HAL," shouts Dave. "I'm sorry, Dave, I'm afraid I can't do that," HAL famously says, thereby consigning Dave to what seems like a certain death in space. No-one who has seen the film can forget HAL's chilling logic and complete absence of human emotion. The idea that an Artificial Intelligence may one day decide that a human astronaut's actions would compromise a mission, and that he should therefore be jettisoned as surplus to requirements – well, that is scary.

Who can forget the scene where Dave eventually exacts revenge on HAL by dismantling "his" memory banks? Back in the 1960's, when Arthur co-wrote the screenplay with Kubrick, that required Dave to enter the mainframe and slide out long racks of transistors, one by one. The computer dies a slow and almost tragic death. Typical of Arthur's brilliance as a writer – and of his sheer Englishness – he has HAL start to sing a traditional nineteenth century song, like an old person with increasing dementia, as he is dismantled.

"Daisy, Daisy, give me your answer, do! I'm half crazy, over the thought of you..."

The song slows down, till it becomes a deep bass, slow-motion growl, and then stops. HAL is finally "dead."

So it seemed a wonderful idea to follow David Stork's excellent outline for the film, which would start with a list of technical questions:

- What voices or images can a computer recognize, as we approach the real year 2001?
- What level of robotic controls can it manipulate?
- To what extent does every possible "thought" or action have to be pre-programmed?
- Is it possible for a computer to learn, much as we do, from experience?
- How could it predict or "imagine" future scenarios?
- And why, relative to HAL, are our computers still so dumb?

The film would also ask broader questions, involving neuroscience, ethics and even philosophy. Dan Dennett, the highly regarded philosopher, could help us develop core script points in what turned out to be a brilliant interview:

- What is a "thought"?
- What is intelligence, or logic?
- Why and how do we have a sense of "self" and of "other"?
- What does it mean to be human? Or humane?

Other superb contributions would come from Marvin Minsky, a veteran of MIT's Media Lab, and Stephen Pinker, whose work on the human brain and mind was both brilliant and accessible to ordinary people.

But there remained the fundamental problem about using clips from the film. The Sloan Foundation would not give us full production money until we had got a signed release from Warner Brothers, stating that we could use at least ten minutes of clips from the movie. David Stork and I made a long-distance phone call to Arthur in Sri Lanka, to ask his advice.

"Oh, good grief," said Arthur. "Leave it to me."

"But wait," Stork said, "There's more bad news. As you know, Stanley Kubrick recently passed away, and the people who run his estate are being even tougher than he was, about using clips from the film."

"Never mind," said Arthur with a chuckle. "As I said, leave it to me. Give me a week to sort it out. Bye bye." And the line went dead.

Miraculously, about a week later, I had a call from a senior lawyer at Warner Brothers. Permission had been granted for us to use ten minutes of material, provided we paid the customary residual fees to the actors, composers, musicians, Kubrick's estate and all the usual suspects. They refused to explain why the change of heart had taken place, but they drafted up a mercifully short agreement in double quick time and the matter was resolved within days. We called Arthur to give him the good news.

"Yes, I know," he said, with his mischievous chuckle.

"But how did you do it?" we chorused.

"Oh, it was quite easy," he said. "I just said that I'd never help them again with any publicity or promotional event for any film based on my books, if they didn't collaborate with us."

The Sloan Foundation wrote us the big check and, once again, I was bound for Sri Lanka on a series of planes, via London, together with a British film crew, our excellent associate producer and editor Michael O'Connell, who had worked with us for almost ten years by this time, and of course David Stork. Arthur gave us his customary five-star welcome in Colombo, and we were off to the races.

In the intervening fifteen years, he had aged, but not by much. Confined much of the time to a wheelchair, he was less excited about gallivanting around the island, but there was no need to do so. He gave us a series of brilliant interviews about the fundamental questions listed above, about the differences between the original book and the film, and the experience of working with Kubrick.

"I met my match with Stanley" he said. "He was even more determined to have his way than I was. He had this particular vision of the story, including the whole dream sequence at the end. I loved it. But I have to say that he did follow my instructions about HAL. That single, evil glowing red eye... He didn't change that."

It was Michael O'Connell who had the brilliant idea of asking Arthur to read whole passages from his original book. Arthur loved it. He selected a high-collared pale-gray coat – what used to be known as a Nehru jacket in the 1970's. It made him look like something between a Star Trek officer and a James Bond villain. Then he sat at his desk, with a large-print version of the book in front of him. The final touch was to have his favorite pet sitting on his lap: a one-eyed Chihuahua named Pepsi. (Yes, really.)

As he read the chilling story in his warm, English voice, he gently and slowly stroked the dog. It was a compelling image, and for some reason deeply sinister. We could have edited together an entire second film just focusing on Arthur, telling his original story.

My final memory of that second visit to Sri Lanka is the epic table tennis match that took place on our final evening. Arthur had mentioned that his only exercise, since walking had become difficult, was what he quaintly referred to as ping pong.

"I play as often as possible," he said. "I can beat anyone. I still can, even at my age."

David Stork's eyes glittered. He is lean and fit, and obviously could not resist a challenge.

"OK," said Stork. "Try me. Let's have a serious match."

I was mortified. To thank a host for his generous hospitality on the last night of your visit by thrashing him at table tennis did not seem a gentlemanly course of action. But Arthur surprised us all. He wheeled his chair into the games room, turned on the strip lights, and peeled off his shirt, revealing an old and shabby "wife-beater" underneath. That, Michael O'Connell assures me, is the popular description of the white sleeveless mesh under-vest that Arthur habitually wore.

Like Lazarus rising from the dead, Arthur miraculously got up from his wheelchair and stood, rock solid, with bat and ball in hand.

"Take off your jacket," he instructed Stork. "Be serious! Best of three games, OK?"

Within moments, Arthur had served a stunningly fast opening ball, which David Stork missed completely. The first three points were all Arthur's.

"I can see you know what you're doing," said David, brushing the hair out of his eyes and adopting a more serious stance.

"Get on with it," ordered Arthur. "Your serve."

Stork lost the first game by at least a couple of points. Arthur had made him run around a great deal, and he was visibly perspiring.

"Take your shirt off!" said Arthur. "You're in Sri Lanka, not Silicon Valley."

The second game was David's, but not by much. Michael O'Connell and I, mute spectators at this battle of the titans, were hoping against hope that the third and final game would go to Arthur. And so it turned out – but not until the score had reached 24-22.

"Good game," said Arthur, unflappable as usual. "Thank you. I don't get to play as often as I'd like these days."

David Stork was plainly surprised at his defeat and looked with new wonder at his hero. "One day you'll have a robot to play against," he said.

"Never mind," said Arthur. "I'll make sure it's got a random bug in its system, so I can still win from time to time."

Once we got home to California, we had to edit the film together. Although we had filmed some of the table tennis match, we all agreed that, though priceless, it should play no part in the final program. It is among many items in the InCA video vault, which may never see the light of day.

Eventually, we made two versions of the film – one with David Stork's pieces to camera, one without. The shorter one-hour version, crammed with excellent content, great interviews with experts, Arthur's extraordinary storytelling and haunting clips from the original film, ran on PBS in prime time for a couple of years, and was a great success. The longer version, which went into the technical details at a deeper level, and benefitted from Stork's lucid academic explanations, was widely distributed to universities across the US and abroad.

The ironic outcome, however, was that this film had a shorter shelf life than almost any other program I have made. David Stork had demonstrated that, as of the year 2001, computers were still virtually useless at facial recognition, autonomous decision-making or machine learning. The iPhone was still six years in the future. Google was in its infancy. Indeed, Stork decided to discuss Artificial Intelligence by featuring not Google, but an outfit called Ask Jeeves. In 2001, it appeared to be the best representative of a search engine, even though its answers to most of the queries were still curated by humans in 2001.

As you'll be well aware, computer intelligence has made giant strides in the last fifteen years. But – happily, perhaps – we are still some years away from inventing the real HAL. The worry is that, when its time comes, it will probably have invented itself.

I have absolutely no belief in an afterlife, be it heaven or hell. But it is nonetheless fun to think of Arthur C. Clarke, chuckling and rubbing his hands with pleasure, gazing down on us all with his unique combination of humanity, humor and technical imagination, as many of the futures he predicted come true, in one form or another.

■■■

19. AMELIA EARHART:
RECREATING THE FINAL FLIGHT

My encounters with Arthur C. Clarke spanned an eighteen-year period, between 1983 and 2001. But plenty of other exciting projects happened in between, and none more so than the adventure of reconstructing Amelia Earhart's last flight. Like so many other films described here, it was pure serendipity that it crossed my threshold. But then, as Arthur liked to remind his visitors, Serendip was an old name for Sri Lanka – a magical world where anything can happen. Who was to say that the whole world could not work the same way?

A sound recordist called Doug called me one morning in 1996 at my office at Foot, Cone and Belding. This was the advertising agency, which had offered a home to IDeA, the marketing company I had co-founded, during a period when I had gotten a little bored of making documentaries.

Doug claimed that he was hatching up an interesting idea for a film, featuring a flying boat and locations in the South Pacific. It seemed an unlikely idea. I would have put the phone down within seconds, if it was not for the fact that the owner of the flying boat was a wealthy and much respected Silicon Valley venture capitalist. Doug told me that the entrepreneur was intrigued by the idea of being featured in a film. All they needed was a production company, a producer and a director. Promptly, I suggested a lunch to discuss it. I had been praying for a really interesting new documentary to suggest itself and lo and behold – here it was.

Reid Dennis was a veteran. He had been personally investing in technology since 1952 and was a senior partner in a highly successful venture capital firm on Silicon Valley's legendary Sand Hill Road. He was also an enthusiastic collector of vintage cars and planes, and this is what had led Doug to meet him. Rich or poor, old or young, if you both enjoy counting the number of rivets on the wing of a Handley Page Halifax or the size of the carburetor in an Alvis Coupe, you have found a new friend.

Reid's original idea was to honor the Pan American 'Clippers' – giant flying boats, which used to take off from the water in San Francisco Bay. Beginning in 1936, they made their way, in a series of hops, across the Pacific Ocean to exotic destinations in what was then known as the Orient. Happily, Reid Dennis was not only a fully qualified pilot, he was the owner of a Grumman Albatross, strictly speaking not a flying boat but an amphibious plane. It, too, could take off and land either on water or on an airstrip. It dated from the early 1950's and had originally been commissioned by the US Coastguard.

Reid had restored the plane to a state of glory it had never known in its first life. Behind the cockpit was a luxurious cabin, with leather seats that could turn into beds, a bar, refrigerator and simple cooker, beautiful rugs and decorations. It was a flying palace in miniature, furnished in the best of taste.

To top it all off, the Grumman had a "Dutch door" at the back, the top half of which could be opened in flight. Since the plane was not pressurized and preferred to be flown at a leisurely 175 knots (about 200 m.p.h.), you could fly safely with the door open, and therefore, you could film from it with a good solid camera. You just had to remember not to stick your head out of the door, because 200 m.p.h., while slow for a plane, is fast for the human face.

We were soon well advanced with plans for making this trip to the South Pacific. The idea had developed significantly: we would also tell the story of the Pan Am Clippers' wartime heroics, supporting US troops in WWII, as they gradually retook the Pacific islands from the occupying Japanese. We would land the Grumman in colorful lagoons and look for local people who had been children and teenagers in World War II – people who might vividly remember the planes, the soldiers and the war.

Then, tragedy struck, or so it seemed. Reid called me one morning.

"I'm sorry, David," he said. "I've got to call the whole thing off."

I wondered what had happened. Had Reid's health suffered a grave setback? Had the Grumman crashed? Or had his investment company hit the rocks?

"No," said Reid, "I've been asked to join a Texas aviator called Linda Finch, who's planning a round-the-world trip, in an old Lockheed Electra. She'd love to have the reassurance of an amphibious plane flying alongside her, just in case she has to ditch in the ocean. No-one's ever flown a Grumman round the world before, so this would be a first for the record books. I'd like to do it."

"Why on earth is this woman making the flight?" I asked innocently.

"Oh," said Reid, "Next year, 1997, is the sixtieth anniversary of Amelia Earhart's final voyage: the one where she disappeared. She was trying to circumnavigate the globe for the first time. Linda Finch is recreating that journey. All being well, she'll complete the trip – from Oakland back to Oakland. Great idea, isn't it?"

"Reid," I said, trying not to sound over-excited. "It's more than that. It's a really terrific documentary movie." There was a brief silence on the other end of the phone. Then:

"My God! Of course. You're right." said Reid.

We arranged to meet at the Bohemian Club, San Francisco's most venerated gentleman's establishment, for lunch.

"By the way," said Reid as he met me at the entrance, "We're not allowed to talk business in the club. So, please be careful. Don't pull out a pen and paper or talk about money. But we can discuss the film, eh?"

By the time dessert was served, we were like two fifth graders describing adventure movies. It all seemed so possible: Linda Finch's expenses were being paid by Pratt & Whitney, the maker of the plane's original engines, as a publicity stunt. Reid could well afford to cover his own expenses, plus the cost of a film. But what *was* the cost of the film, he asked? I thought quickly and made a guess.

"One M," I said, "Give or take a bit."

Reid beamed. I had managed to convey the essentials without breaking the rules of the club.

"It's a deal," he said, and we made sure not to arouse suspicion by shaking hands on it.

■■■

How do you spend a million dollars on a documentary? Well, if you have to film in nineteen countries around the world across a two-month period, with three different teams of producer-directors and assistants on the ground, the answer is: very quickly.

Reid made meticulous plans for the trip, traveling to Texas and doing everything he could to collaborate with Linda Finch – even trying to become friends. Little did he realize that he was dealing with a two-fisted Texan, for whom everything – every little issue or decision – involved a fight to the finish. Finch had competed in many air shows and veteran airplane rallies. She had bought the shell of the old Lockheed for peanuts, personally raised the money from Pratt and Whitney, and rebuilt the plane from the ground up, with her own hands and the help of a couple of skilled mechanics. She was determined to be nobody's fool, and also to be the star of the show.

Whenever the project ran out of money, or whenever there was something new to pay for, she turned to Reid. I suspect that the only part of the whole venture to stay on budget was the film. Even before the start of the flight, Reid was thin-lipped when asked about Linda. After the trip, when everyone had made it safely back to the US, he finally broke his gentlemanly silence about her. Some of the things he called her could not be printed here.

He referred scathingly to her "day job" – running a small chain of nursing homes in Texas. Apparently, her company had been in trouble with the law on more than one occasion, and allegations of incompetence and neglect had been publicly aired. This was the spider who had lured Reid into her web.

I remember discussing all this with him, when we were editing the film. I said that her behavior reminded me of an off-color limerick. Reid was very keen to know how it ran. I told him:

There once was a hooker from Kew
Who filled up her privates with glue.
She said with a grin
"If they pay to get in,
They can pay to get out again too."

Reid laughed. "I'll remember that," he said. From then on, whenever he made presentations about the project to adult audiences, he would recite that limerick, making very sure to explain, as his lawyers had suggested, that it in no way directly described the attitude or actions of Ms. Finch.

Long before the start of the adventure, every stage of the flight had to be mapped out. The two planes were going to fly as one "flight." That meant that they would be counted as one plane, for the sake of takeoffs and landings, and for air-traffic control centers round the world. This was unusual, but not unprecedented. It depended on the skill of the pilots to keep the two planes very close to each other, without colliding in mid-air.

It also meant that we could get dramatic shots of the Lockheed Electra from the open half-door on the Grumman Albatross. The best shots of all depended on the Grumman being slightly higher than the Lockheed, so that you could see the earth two thousand feet below: this way, we got spectacular shots of the Lockheed flying over the vast estuary of the Amazon, the endless deserts of Arabia, and the islands and archipelagoes, set in the turquoise sea of Indonesia.

Linda and Reid had determined to follow Amelia Earhart's final route as closely as possible. The first quarter of the journey seemed to present no problems. From Oakland Airport, in San Francisco's Bay Area, Amelia had flown down to Burbank, near Los Angeles, to test the plane and all its systems, and to hold a glitzy press-conference, organized by her husband, a PR man, in true Hollywood style. Then she had flown in several stages cross-country to Florida, hopped through the Caribbean islands and made her way onwards to the north coast of Brazil. There were only rudimentary airstrips en route, and to this day some of them have barely been improved.

The first serious challenge, successfully accomplished, was the long ocean crossing from Fortaleza (in the top right-hand corner of Brazil) to Dakar in Senegal, West Africa. Here, Amelia's plane was met by a troupe of dancers and singers, chanting traditional and jazzed-up versions of their bewitching music. This was where things started to get really dream-like. We recreated the scene exactly, with Linda's plane surrounded by half-naked singers and drummers, celebrating in traditional costume, all happy to be filmed.

As luck would have it, one of InCA London's early partners, Richard Vaughan, had left with his Kenyan wife Jerusha to establish a highly successful InCA outpost in Nairobi in the early 1990's. InCA Africa took care of all the arrangements from Senegal to Luxor in Egypt.

Our problem in Africa was that, in 1937, Earhart had flown straight from Dakar due east across the continent to Luxor in Egypt: ancient Thebes. That presented no problem in 1937, apart from finding flattish places to land, and arranging for the occasional stash of aviation fuel. But in 1997, there were at least two wars or national uprisings in progress on that route: in Zaire (in 1937 still known as the Belgian Congo) and in the Sudan (previously known as Anglo-Egyptian Sudan). In 1937, angry Africans would have had little more than spears or ancient rifles to throw or shoot at a passing plane. In 1997, they had rocket-launchers.

Discretion was obviously going to be the better part of valor in Africa, so Linda and Reid flew round the northern edge of the continent, passing Morocco, Tunisia, Algeria and Libya. They then turned south at Cairo and followed the Nile down to Luxor. Even that would have been totally impossible in 2017. With ISIS and Al Qaeda groups everywhere on this route, and Libya a failed state, only an idiot would risk it today. Two precious old planes, lumbering past at an altitude of two thousand feet would present too tempting a target for any murderous mischief-maker.

On the production side, only one person accompanied Reed the whole way around the world: Michael Anderson, our intrepid cameraman. He was an old friend, who had shot many of the shows we had produced in San Francisco. He had a superb eye and, just as important, endless patience and kindness. He had to be away from his family for two months, to shoot our Amelia Earhart film.

For all the moments of excitement and the award-winning shots, there were hours of droning along at two hundred m.p.h. with nothing much to see, and it is almost a 25,000-mile journey, to circumnavigate the earth at the Equator. It was also a potentially dangerous undertaking. However well reconditioned or rebuilt, these were old planes. For sure, Reid and Linda carried GPS and other navigational aids that Amelia Earhart never had. Indeed, if they had been available, she would probably never have disappeared. But still, if one of the engines on one of our planes had died when crossing the open water, the chances of survival were slim, even in the Grumman. It could land on placid waters in a lagoon but would have crumpled up and sunk to the bottom if it tried to land on Atlantic waves.

The InCA production teams took it in turns, to direct and organize the filming. I started off, venturing as far as Tucson, AZ. There, I stepped off the Grumman with a batch of recorded videotapes, and Joan Saffa took my place, with a big bag of new tapes. She stayed with the plane till Fortaleza, Brazil. Mike Anderson crossed the Atlantic alone, to reduce the weight of the plane and save fuel. He did it without the benefit of a director shouting in his ear "Shoot this! Shoot that!" Quite a relief, I imagine.

In Dakar, InCA Africa took over, accompanying the plane round to Luxor, and taking another batch of tapes to be shipped back to San Francisco. The planes then flew on to Abu Dhabi, where I met them, and took off not just the exposed tapes but the main camera and tripod as well. There was a very good reason for this.

The Indian government had forbidden us to film over the India-Pakistan border, and the Pakistanis were none too keen on that idea either. But we had a fallback plan: in the Grumman was a secret compartment, concealed behind the elegant teak trimmings of the cabin. Here, we concealed a modest Panasonic consumer camera and a box of the latest invention – small-format DVCam tapes. This camera could record only half the number of video lines on each frame, so in principle it was only half as good. It also had a less than excellent lens. But it was small, it looked like an amateur camera (if found) and we had no other option

In Karachi, the planes were inspected by the Pakistani customs and border police: no camera was found. The transit papers were duly stamped, and the expedition could proceed. On arrival at Calcutta airport in India, the planes were again searched. Again, no camera was found: all good, so even more rubber stamping. The Indians do love rubber stamps and paperwork.

Meanwhile, I had flown on an Air India jet directly from Abu Dhabi to Calcutta with the main Arriflex camera and wooden professional tripod. I greeted Reid Dennis and Linda Finch with this equipment in my hands.

"Oh, I don't think we need those clumsy great things anymore," Mike Anderson joked. "We did perfectly fine with the Panasonic."

When the different versions of the film were finally edited together, the consumer-standard footage from the little camera stood up remarkably well side by side with the Arriflex material. Indeed, when the PBS show was premiered on a large theatre screen in San Francisco, only one person noticed the technical difference between the two images: Ray Dolby, the legendary founder of Dolby Labs, creator of the modern universe in motion picture sound.

"David, did I notice a little line-doubling, somewhere around Karachi and India?" he said to me casually, as he left after the screening. "Never mind. It's a very nice film." Thanks to Mike Anderson's skill with the Panasonic, and some skillful color correction, no-one else seemed to have spotted it.

Calcutta offered a welcome respite from the rigors of the journey. Joan Saffa had turned up again, to take over from me. She knew a well-manicured local family, who were members of Calcutta's most snooty Country Club. We all took tea there and watched the cricket. It felt more than a little like 1937. Meanwhile, Reid, Linda and Mike, Reid's co-pilot, relaxed in the Taj Hotel, enjoying every one of its five stars. The cockpits of the old planes are hot, uncomfortable and incredibly noisy. A nice long shower and a bed with soft white sheets provided a taste of heaven for all of them.

Personally, I enjoyed myself by recreating on film a tram journey that Amelia might have taken in 1937, through Calcutta's streets. I stepped down to the Dickensian headquarters of the Calcutta Tramways Company and negotiated the three-hour hire of one of their more elderly contraptions. Neither the trams nor the street scene appeared to have changed much in the 60 intervening years. Amelia recalled in her diary the teeming crowds, the noise, the smells and the colorful markets. Indeed, India had hardly changed at all in the 32 years since I'd first visited, on the COMEX student theatre tour.

The climax of the whole trip, and of the film, was the journey through the islands of the Western Pacific. Not only are they beautiful, they are full of beautiful people. The reception the team got in Papua New Guinea was the same welcome Amelia had received. What little archive film survives from her original trip comes largely from that stop in New Guinea. There was more singing, more dancing, more tribal costumes, but it all felt even more heartfelt and colorful than it had in Senegal.

Ahead lay the trickiest part of the trip – for Reid and Linda, but most of all for Amelia, sixty years before.

The first problem is that the distance between the islands becomes rapidly larger and larger. Back in 1937, Amelia had to cross the Pacific from Papua New Guinea in three hops: one to Howland Island, then another to Hawaii, then a final two-thousand-mile leap to Oakland, California.

The second problem is that Howland Island is only one mile long, and about five hundred yards wide. Given little more than a sextant and a compass to navigate with, how do you ever find an island that small? It is a speck in the ocean – truly a needle in a haystack.

Of course, Amelia had a radio, but unfortunately she had decided (for reasons of weight and space) to leave behind the long trailing aerial which would have made the radio really effective. Waiting for her at Howland Island was a US Navy ship: the US had constructed a simple runway on the uninhabited island, because Roosevelt's government was already anxious about Japanese naval activities in the area. Amelia was a symbol of American pluck, so she was thought to deserve all the help she could be given, as the first woman to fly round the world.

The US warship broadcast a constant stream of messages to Amelia, intended to guide her into Howland, but she was not able to hear them, because of the missing aerial. She broadcast increasingly tense messages to Howland, where they were heard with dawning horror. It became obvious that she was deaf to their instructions. So, what happened? Why and how did her plane disappear?

We made several versions of the Amelia Earhart film: the first – to be transmitted as soon as possible after the 1997 trip – was the one that featured Linda Finch. This was well-received, but we all knew that we hadn't cracked the central question of Amelia's disappearance.

Then, as luck would have it, less than a year later, Reid Dennis discovered an old, retired air navigator up in New England, who had known Fred Noonan, Amelia's navigator. He had just published a slim monograph, explaining what Fred Noonan would probably have done, and why Amelia Earhart might have refused to follow his advice. She was the skipper, after all: hers was the final word.

To understand what may well have happened, you need to see the film: it is still available on DVD: *The Final Hours: Amelia Earhart's Last Flight*. I won't go into the details here, because they'd need a chapter to themselves. However, I am proud to say that the Smithsonian Institution authenticated and co-produced this version of the film, and its experts state on camera that we put forward the most scientifically convincing explanation – so far – of what had happened. They believe that we effectively solved the mystery of Amelia Earhart's disappearance.

But I believe this is only part of the reason why our film has been replayed countless times on PBS, and has been bought by so many thousand people, only some of whom are history nuts or plane-spotters. Fundamentally, it is a very touching story: our images of the Lockheed flying over Howland Island, which has not had a working runway for seventy years, are very emotive. Linda, in a rare moment of grace, threw a wreath out of the window of her plane, in memory of Amelia.

Then, of course, there is the stunning photography in the film: thank you, Michael Anderson. Never have clouds and planes looked more gorgeous or more fragile. Then there is the music: I worked very closely with the composer Ed Bogas, to create the haunting score, which is mostly played by a single piano. The three themes Ed developed have echoes of Chopin, but are entirely original, and tug mightily on the heartstrings.

But the most moving elements of the film are the words of Amelia herself. From her teenage years on, she kept diaries, recording her love of flight, and of the thrilling danger involved. As a girl, she had taken a life-changing roller-coaster ride at a fair in St. Louis. She had watched barnstorming air displays in the 20's. She was determined to do as well or better than any man in the air.

In our film, Amelia's words are read by Kate Regan, who was one of our production staff at the time. Kate is a talented singer with a delivery that reminds me of Janis Joplin. She read the lines in a husky voice that was nothing like Amelia's, but somehow caught Amelia's spirit. In combination with the music and the dreamlike imagery of flying through the clouds, the effect is inspiring. I still weep, every time I see the final ten minutes of this film.

Making documentaries can be frustrating, worrying, expensive and occasionally downright boring. But I have to say that I am very, very proud of *The Final Hours: Amelia Earhart's Last Flight.* It was teamwork that created it, like the flights it depicts. Somehow, its combination of science, storytelling, adventure, laughter and grief adds up to a very powerful cocktail. If I had to stand in front of St. Peter tomorrow and say: "This is what I did when I was on earth, with a lot of help from my friends", I would be holding *The Final Hours*, along with *Beethoven's Eroica* from the *Keeping Score* series, *A Year in Burgundy* (my most recent favorite), and one each from *The Ascent of Man, The Heart of Healing, The Heart of the Dragon, Cosmos* and *Connections.*

20. PLAY, FUN AND CREATIVITY: JANE GOODALL AND COMPANY

I must admit that I have always been somewhat "young for my age", as one of my teachers put it in an early end-of-term school report. As an only child, I had to make up my own games, initially with my stuffed animals, and later with imaginary friends as much as with real ones. Poor, lonely little David? Well, not entirely. I spent a lot of time reading, drawing, and dreaming up gags, japes and jokes that I could play on other people, or entertain people with, when I did have company.

My great delight has always been in making people laugh. I tried my hand at comedy sketch writing at school and university, but what I wrote was not much good. My talent, such as it was, consisted of improvisation, preferably at moments when my words would cause the maximum mirth and – as a bonus – embarrassment.

At my boarding school, from age eleven, it was strictly forbidden to talk in the dormitories after "Lights Out", as I mentioned early in Part One of the book. Of course, everyone did talk, but for the most part they whispered and were never caught out by the roaming Duty Master, whose job was to police the corridors and try to nab boys who had dared to chatter in the dark. Sometimes, however, there were splendid extra amusements to be had: farting contests, for example, which are about as funny as anything imaginable, for an eleven-year-old boy. They were worth taking the risk.

The champion farter in our dormitory was a boy called Reeves. Only family names were used, at the school. First names, as I have said, would suggest an unwholesome intimacy. The farts of Reeves were impressive in many ways: they were loud and frequent, he could control the pitch of the sound they made, and they invariably stank, as a bonus. When baked beans had been on the supper menu, Reeves' productions were impressive. In the contest, other boys attempted to equal Reeves' accomplishments, without success. I had the idea of supplying a running commentary, akin to the sports reporter at a horse race:

"Well, we're waiting for Atlantic Gale, and there he is now…"

The combination of ad-libbed commentary and Reeves' serenade was a winner. The dormitory erupted in laughter, and in stormed George Hill, the Duty Master.

"Who was laughing?"

Everyone's hand went up.

"We were all laughing, sir."

"Well, what made you laugh?"

Reeves put his hand up: "Me, sir, I farted sir, I couldn't help it, sir."

"Well, what's so funny about that?" asked Mr. Hill, ill-advisedly.

There was more laughter.

"Shut up. Be QUIET", said Mr. Hill to the assembled company. He cannot have been more than twenty-four, and this was his first teaching job.

"Someone was talking, as well," said Mr. Hill. "Who was it? Own up, or the whole dormitory will be punished."

At this point, I put my hand up.

"Ah, Kennard," said Mr. Hill. "I might have guessed. Get up and come with me."

I followed him out of the room and into the corridor. He took off one of his leather slippers.

"Bend over," he said. He took a run at me and thrashed me six times. It wasn't the first occasion he had done this.

When I re-entered the dormitory on this occasion, I was given a round of applause, because I had been brave and not uttered a sound – not even a whimper – during the whacking. Stiff upper lips were appreciated back then. Hearing the applause, George Hill came flying back into the room, his temper flaring.

"Right, that does it," he said, "I am sick and tired of the Fifth Form Dormitory. You'll all be in detention this afternoon. No games, no activities. I shall see the Headmaster about this."

Suddenly, Kennard was no longer very popular. My trying to be funny had landed everybody in the soup. It happened again many times, during my school career and subsequently. I have recounted the episode of the satirical School Revue, which got me and two others expelled from Hurstpierpoint College several months early. The urge to be facetious and get a laugh at inappropriate moments has landed me in more trouble than anything else I have done in life. It still does, if I am bored during a business meeting, for example. I think I have ruined the chance of more than one funding deal for a television or film documentary, by not appearing to take the process seriously enough.

The answer, I realized when I was thirty, is to have kids of your own, and then enjoy being childish in their company. When my first child, Amanda, was two years old, I loved getting in the bath with her, in our London house, and playing the silliest games with bubbles and plastic toys. Often, we played so long that the water would start to get cold, and Amanda would be lifted out of the bath with her teeth chattering by her anxious mother, Helen. One time, Amanda laughed so hard that she moved her bowels right there in the bath. We were surrounded by tiny turds, and the more we tried to move away from them, the closer they floated towards us. Cue more hysterical laughter, from both of us. Cue entrance of irritated mother.

It was devastating, when I realized that my first marriage was breaking up. Although Helen was generous and compassionate when we negotiated the divorce settlement, I only had access to the children sporadically, because I was away in the US half the time. Playtime with them became a rare treat. So I threw myself into silly games by myself or with girlfriends in Los Angeles – dressing up in medieval costume at the Renaissance Fayre, and running fairground sideshows, using comic British accents. But it was not until I had children the second time, with Lizzie, that I truly realized what I had been missing.

James was born in 1988, and Pippa two years later. From the very beginning, I was deeply involved in their play: simple "peek-a-boo" games developed into building blocks and dressing up. Down in our basement, we developed an enormous model train set, with seven separate loops, bridges and mountains, and tiny buildings with lights inside. James would make the scenery. Pippa loved engineering spectacular train crashes.

Outdoors, we would go on great adventures to Muir Beach, twenty minutes from our Mill Valley house. There, we would paddle in the waves, hunt for crabs, build sandcastles, play beach cricket and have games of tag. It reminded me vividly of my childhood vacations in Cornwall, with cousins Helen and Diana – and it was only twenty minutes from my front door. I loved this wonderful opportunity to play. In 1999, when James and Pippa were eleven and nine respectively, they were at the peak of their playfulness, before puberty kicked in.

So it was incredible, when the phone rang, and a well-known voice said:

"Hi David. How would you like to do a film on play?"

It was the psychologist Stuart Brown, with whom I had worked on the Joseph Campbell film. You can imagine my joy. A film about playing! Perhaps, I thought, I could finally get to film Pippa and James playing, too.

••

Quite often, individual documentaries and whole series have come my way out of the blue. Just when I had been earnestly trying to raise funds for months – or even years – for my own film ideas, the phone would ring and someone would say,

"Hello, David. What are you working on at the moment?"

Then, with luck, the caller would invite me to collaborate on his or her own favorite project. If I was lucky, he would already have raised some or all of the money. If I was really lucky, it would be a subject that truly appealed to me.

Stuart had stayed in touch with me from time to time, ever since the completion of *The Hero's Journey*. After a professional indiscretion, he had been obliged to quit his day job as a psychiatrist in San Diego, and had moved north, to a woodsy house in the Carmel Valley, about thirty miles north of the Esalen Institute and Big Sur. Here, he invited Lizzie, me and our two children to stay and enjoy not only the main property, but also an enchanting and fully functional tree house, which was nirvana for the kids – and for me, of course.

Stuart was inherently playful: indeed, his amorous adventures in San Diego had emphasized that point a little too clearly. He loved to see our children play every sort of game around the property and enjoyed the way Lizzie and I got caught up in the fun of it all.

"I want to write a book about play," he told us. "About why we all need to find a way to play, and what happens to people who just can't be playful."

Stuart had been Head of the Department of Psychiatry at the University of Texas in Austin, when a crazy shooter had climbed the campus bell-tower and mown down a dozen people, some years before. Stuart had led the official investigation into the psychology of this man. He had concluded that the most striking factor in his psychology was an absolute inability to be playful. He could find no release from his demons in any kind of enjoyable activity. Stuart had concluded that play was an essential ingredient for developing a healthy human mind – not only in children, but throughout adult life.

"I've got some development funds," he said. "How about it? A series on play?"

I jumped at the idea, of course. What could be more fun? It was only when I put the phone down that I realized how difficult this might be. To analyze seriously what makes playing so enjoyable would be to risk killing the enjoyment entirely. I remembered one of the books I had in my library – *Rire: Phénomène Humain*, a dreadful French tome that approached the phenomenon of laughter from a Freudian viewpoint. In a nutshell, it seemed to suggest that laughter was an attenuated form of orgasm, but less messy. Exactly *why* different people found different things funny, or why they could or couldn't seek pleasure and release in play and laughter – these things had escaped the author's attention completely.

Stuart told me that he had already secured the services of a noted international authority on play, a professor from New Zealand called Brian Sutton-Smith. With the funds at his disposal, Stuart proposed that the three of us should spend time at his house in the Carmel Valley, and sketch the outline scripts for a short series for PBS.

"How great. What fun!" I said. Wrong!

Brian was not a modest man. He was at the pinnacle of an all too long career. His early academic papers had been published around fifty years previously, and he had elbowed his way to the top of the pile of academic experts worldwide, who could claim deep insight into playful behavior. It was not a large pile, however. Nor, frankly, was it distinguished by many piercing insights or much rigorous analysis, or so it seemed to me.

Much of Brian's work had been focused on flat-footed observation of children's behavior in playgrounds and schoolyards. He had observed the social etiquette of four-year-olds taking turns on the teeter-totter or chasing each other in games of tag. His latest published work was *The Ambiguity of Play*, which appeared to suggest that you often could not tell when someone was playing and when they were serious. Indeed, the player often could not tell which was which, either.

"If that's the case, then what's the point in studying it?" I remember asking Stuart. For once, I was not trying to be funny.

Our other problem was that Brian saw himself as a latter-day Sagan or Bronowski, holding forth at great length on camera about the minutiae of play, while kiddies romped around, out of focus, at a safe distance. This was not what Stuart Brown wanted and I certainly agreed with him. In a couple of camera tests, Brian demonstrated absolutely no charisma, plus an inability to remember lines, and a disconcerting, choppy style of speech which made his thoughts even less interesting than they might otherwise have been.

The problem was that Brian was a long-standing advisor to the Toy Manufacturers of America (TMA), and it was from this august body that we hoped to get the production funding for the series: about $1.5 million, no less. My friend and colleague Bill Bennett (co-founder of our ill-fated marketing company, IDeA) had a direct line to the TMA, from his time at the PR company, Hill & Knowlton.

The TMA is a trade body, which lobbies news sources, opinion makers and governments on behalf of major toy manufacturers like Mattel, arguing that replica guns are just fine for young boys, or that Barbie does not stereotype girls in the slightest. So we did not want to ruffle Brian's feathers too much, in case he complained to the TMA.

You might have thought that PBS regulations on self-dealing would have ruled out the toy manufacturers as underwriters of a series on play. But we argued that playfulness does not require toys. If we promised not to feature toys anywhere in the three one-hour films, would PBS green-light the TMA as our sponsor? After all, we said, we were going to concentrate on playfulness in adults, and the TMA's target was children.

After a week of deliberation, American Public Television, our distributor to the PBS network, agreed to accept the Toy Manufacturers as the funder, and the money started flowing. We had called our project *The Power of Play*, but the TMA promptly used that title for an advertising campaign, so we had to change it to *The Promise of Play*, which I think I preferred.

We pulled together a great production team, including the indomitable Joan Saffa, the excellent Michael O'Connell and two new faces I had never worked with before. Neysa Furey and Lisa Fraser were two bright young women with great creative ideas. Neysa was in her thirties and quite new to television production. Lisa was a seasoned producer, unashamedly Australian, from her strong accent to her broad sense of humor. Where Neysa seemed crisp, straightlaced and orderly, I hope Lisa will forgive me for saying that she was a happy mess: the inside of her car was a testament to every experience she had had during the previous two months. But both were brilliant in their own way, and we needed their diversity of talent. Best of all, we had Charlotte Grossman as Senior Editor.

Using all Stuart Brown's contacts and great new research done by the team, we reached out to a galaxy of different characters, some famous and some completely unknown, but all of whom recognized the importance of play in their adult life. They included Patch Adams, the clown who brought humor to people under stress, in poverty and in third-world countries; Steve Wynn, the casino magnate who had turned playfulness into a lucrative business; and Jane Goodall, who understood completely how and why primates play, and what that tells us about humans.

Of all these, Jane Goodall was the real revelation to me, personally. I have never met a nicer, kinder, more insightful woman. She was truly full of grace. In describing the antics of young chimpanzees, she would hoot and gibber, like one of the best. She could explain why adult chimps would tolerate cheeky behavior from their kids and even join in.

Jane had a twinkly eye for playful behavior in humans, too, and a small smile was never far from her lips. Indeed, she explained why many species – many more than we had once imagined – love to play: not only primates but dogs and dolphins, lions, some bird species, and even the occasional fish. The joy of randomized, apparently "purposeless" behavior was appealing to many animal brains, and not only in childhood. The brighter the brain, it seemed, the greater the urge (and the need) to play – to create and enjoy and learn from an alternative reality.

Steve Wynn operated on the other end of the play spectrum. He had turned play into a pile of money. When I met and filmed him, he co-owned and was running the vast and impressive Bellagio resort in Las Vegas. He was a gambler by nature.

"It's all play. You win some, you lose some", he told me.

He had started to collect the works of famous artists – Picasso, Monet, Manet – and opened a public gallery right next to the one-armed bandits and high-stakes card games. Critics were astonished and predicted that this would be an embarrassing flop: it was not. Steve Wynn was the first to bring the Cirque du Soleil to Vegas, and had commissioned an astonishingly playful and complex show, called "O": this was a play on words, since the French "Eau" means water. The entire show combined circus acts with fire and water on a stage, which was flooded and emptied in a dozen different patterns of light, flame and mirror effects.

Wynn maintained that business was a creative game, where you were always trying to outsmart your opponent. To be successful, he said, you could not take it too seriously. It was a high-stakes chess game. Just after we had filmed, he found himself in check, and then checkmate, when the jewel of his empire, Bellagio, was taken over by a competing company. But it only took him a year or two to come roaring back, twice as impressive, with his own Wynn resort.

"With a name like mine," he liked to say, "You can't afford to be a loser."

Somewhere else on the spectrum was Patch Adams, who was played by Robin Williams in a biopic some years later. Personally, I have never liked clowns. They terrified me when I was a child, and – for slightly different reasons, thanks to Stephen King – they still terrify me today. But we had to admit that Adams brought laughter and compassion to children and adults in third world countries, when he visited hospitals where there was not much else to laugh at. The story we filmed with him showed groups of women in El Salvador, faced with desperate poverty and disease, falling about with laughter at his antics, though neither side understood the spoken language of the other.

But the greatest joys of the series *The Promise of Play* were the countless scenes that featured ordinary people, not celebrities. We filmed Cheryl King, InCA's longest employee – my friend and trusted business manager for over thirty years, and a veteran of *Cosmos*

- as she jumped out of a plane for the first time and discovered the pleasures of skydiving. We visited New Orleans and documented a single, tight-knit community preparing a spectacular Mardi Gras float, as well as the final orgiastic parades and parties.

We saw how IDEO, the cutting-edge design company in Silicon Valley, used playful improvised drama techniques to help brainstorm new ideas. We set them the challenge of coming up with a device to amuse a dog, which had to spend all day cooped up in an apartment. We filmed the team in real time, sketching out the craziest ideas in the space of less than an hour of laughter and creativity. And yes, we did get to film James and Pippa at play – in the Exploratorium, San Francisco's ground-breaking hands-on science museum

Throughout the filming and initial editing, there were stories full of laughter and enjoyment, and really fascinating interviews with people who enjoyed playing in a dozen different ways and could explain the source of their joy. But how were we going to string all this together into three coherent films, each with its own message?

We might have hoped for some guidance from Brian Sutton-Smith, but he was quite unable to think in terms of a storyline or a film script. He lived in a world of dry academic papers and was uncomfortable about the whole emphasis on adult play. He gave us multiple interviews, and we desperately tried to stitch something interesting together from what he had said. I wrestled with this issue from early on in the production and shared my concerns with Stuart Brown. He had a couple of suggestions but kept veering off into the psychopathology of people who could *not* play.

It was our Australian producer, Lisa Fraser, who cracked the puzzle of how to structure the series. One day, in a routine production meeting, after we had reviewed some rough-cut stories in the editing suites, she said:

"How about this? I woke up last night with an idea…"

We sat and listened. It took her less than five minutes to explain it, and we instinctively knew that it was right, and that it would work.

Play, said Lisa, obviously had to be fun in and of itself. If it was seen as "useful", then it risked no longer being playful. But, from everything we had learned while filming, it seemed to have three separate underlying bonus benefits, whether for animals, children or adults:

- It was a great way to learn things – perhaps the very best way
- It revealed each individual's personality, from the way they chose to play
- It helped to bind individuals into communities, teams, or interest-groups

"So why don't we have the three films feature these benefits?" said Lisa, "And run them in that order?"

Stuart Brown was very happy with this structure for the series. Obviously, it reflected both child's play and adult play. It radiated out from the inner life of the individual to the communal life of the group. It was essentially a positive, constructive message that anyone could understand, and that no-one would quibble with. Except, of course, Brian Sutton-Smith.

As I have said, Brian, like Bill Goetzmann on *The West of the Imagination,* had expected to be the Carl Sagan of the series: a powerful on-camera presence, the intellectual author of the project, the decision-maker about the stories, the narrator of the voice-over, the whole kit and caboodle. He had proved himself unable to give us any constructive help under any of these categories. Even the narration finally had to be given to someone else: Brian's whining voice and pinched, New Zealand accent simply did not work, and in any case he refused to voice the words we needed to be said, to make the stories work. Instead, we invited Michael Pritchard to do the job. He was a local Bay Area stand-up comedian with an engaging voice, who was deeply involved in social justice issues. He did the job very nicely.

Brian was furious that his position had been usurped. He wreaked his revenge by contacting the Toy Manufacturers of America, our funders. He had been one of their consultants for years and now unloaded his venom. He refused to support a word of what our script was saying. As we heard later from a sympathetic employee at the TMA, he suggested that they should disown the series, and do their best to have it canceled on PBS.

Having already spent almost two million dollars on the project, however, the TMA were loath to scrap the shows entirely. Our distributor, American Public Television (APT, based in Boston) reminded them that funders were not permitted to intervene in or control the content. So what could they do? They decided to shoot themselves in the foot. They announced that they would withdraw all publicity funds for the project: that way, presumably, they hoped that no-one would hear about it and no-one would watch it.

Happily, APT took our side in the matter and provided very effective promotion to all the stations in the PBS network. Ninety-five percent of the stations (more than three hundred, nationally) ran the shows in good, family-friendly slots. The feedback was rewarding and refreshing. But when I think of the impact that the series might have had, with the kind of publicity money that the TMA, backed by Mattel, Lego and the rest, could have given it, I despair.

Brian Sutton-Smith has now passed on to a higher plane. He is doubtless tirelessly chronicling the play habits of the younger angels. I never found out quite what he did, for play, while on this earth: malevolently disrupting the plans and projects of others, perhaps? Defending his reputation in front of other academics, with wittily barbed ripostes? Whatever. He did not seem a playful man.

Many years later, I am happy to say, Stuart finally wrote his own book: *Play – How it Shapes the Brain, Opens the Imagination and invigorates the Soul,* which was published by Avery in 2009. He formed the non-profit Institute for Play, gave a successful TED talk, and is now acknowledged as a major expert on play in his own right. And, unlike BSS (known to our team as BS2, of course), he seems to have remained deeply playful. Bravo, Stuart!

• •

As a postscript, my connection with Jane Goodall continued for some years after *The Promise of Play*. It turned out that her home was originally in Bournemouth, a genteel resort on England's south coast. This is also where my stepsister Pamela has lived for much of her life, and where she has brought up four children and countless grandchildren. When Jane visited California and spoke at the Marine Mammal Center, just twenty-five minutes from our home in Marin County, we chatted nostalgically about Bournemouth in the 50's and 60's.

The Marine Mammal Center is a magical place, at the edge of the ocean, where volunteers look after baby seals and sea lions that have become injured or separated from their mothers. The plan is always to nurture them, but to keep them wild, so that they can be returned to their home in the Pacific. Jane met our own children, James and Pippa, at the Center. They were just the right age to appreciate who she was and what that meant. They had learned about the environment at school, and now, aged ten and twelve, they were meeting a goddess of the environmental movement, a true child of nature. Jane posed unselfconsciously for photos with the kids, with an arm round them both.

"Do you know what *Roots and Shoots* is?" she asked us. "It's an idea I had, many years ago. I thought to myself, 'Suppose we could create schools where an understanding of nature was at the center of the curriculum, particularly for elementary school children, K through Fifth Grade, in cities here in the US.'"

"Did you ever do anything about that?" I asked.

"Oh yes," said Jane. "It works wonderfully well. Come and see, when you're in New York."

A few months later, I took a camera team out to one of the toughest areas of the Bronx in NYC. In an old building, where once there had been a failed high school, stood three new academies, each one independent of control from the City School District. There was a Technology Academy (to teach skills which would lead to real practical jobs), a Business Academy, and a *Roots and Shoots* Academy.

Inside the latter, founded by Jane, were about a hundred and fifty children, from every culture and background imaginable. Everything they learned – Math, English, Science, Art, Language – was tied were all taken from the wild spaces in the neighborhood; the sciences were tied to everyday experience and the planetary forces that sustain us all.

"Most kids who live in cities never get outside them," Jane reminded us. "They don't get to see the real wonders of nature. So they don't relate to it. They don't care. What we have to do is to show them that nature is all around them and inside them, all the time. We have to plant seeds of understanding, seeds that will sprout into roots and shoots, or else we'll be raising generations who simply don't care about the future of the planet."

And there in the Bronx, as in dozens of other Roots and Shoots schools worldwide, it was happening. Who would have thought that soft-spoken Jane Goodall was such a force for change? The little film we made at her New York school was used by her organization for many years, and I am proud of that.

●●●

21. CHURCHILL'S GRANDDAUGHTER AND THE NEW YORK SCENE

In the summer of 2001, after much discussion, Lizzie and I decided to apply for American citizenship. Pippa had been born in California, but the rest of us, including James, had been born in England. We had Green Cards – permanent resident status – but were subject to detailed cross-questioning, every time we re-entered the United States.

"You guys should think about becoming one of us," said an immigration official at SFO Airport, in July of that year. Was it a veiled threat, or a pleasant invitation?

We had to admit that it was a difficult situation: Pippa had dual citizenship, but James, having been born in London, did not. This seemed unfair. Being younger than eighteen, he could not apply for US citizenship unless Lizzie and I did. So that made our decision easier. "Let's become American, as well as British!" we said. We filed the necessary papers and then forgot all about it for the time being.

On 7 September 2001, I celebrated my fifty-sixth birthday quietly at home, with Lizzie, James and Pippa. They were twelve and eleven respectively, and both had just transferred from the local *Lycée Français* (which followed the French school system) to a local Montessori school, Marin Horizon.

The problem with the *Lycée* was that the children's written and spoken French was now all but perfect, but their written English was abysmal. That was really not appropriate, we felt. Also, we had discovered that French teachers can be remarkably cruel to the children in their care. James, particularly, had trouble at the *Lycée*. Trying to figure out why, we learned from a speech expert that he had a hearing disorder, which made it hard for him to distinguish one voice from a myriad of others in a group situation. When they were all talking a mixture of French and English, that made it even more difficult. It was time for a change.

Marin Horizon School was literally walking distance from our house, in the peaceful semi-rural atmosphere of Homestead Valley, our neighborhood. The children settled in immediately, at the start of the fall semester. Everything seemed set fair, but in my briefcase was an air ticket to New York, dated 11 September 2001.

I had intended to have meetings in New York, to develop some new film projects, but on 8 September I was told that one of the key people I was due to meet was sick and would be unavailable. So I postponed the trip for one week and re-booked for 18 September.

If I had tried to fly the next day, on 9/11, I would never have reached New York. This, of course, was the terrifying day on which two planes hit and destroyed the World Trade Center, another crashed onto the Pentagon in Washington, and a fourth was forced to crash land in a field in Pennsylvania. Major East Coast airports were immediately closed and all flights to destinations east of Chicago were either grounded or diverted.

Lizzie and I heard about it all as the news unfolded on National Public Radio at breakfast time, around 8 a.m. in California. It was worse than unbelievable. It was nightmarish. I think everyone I know can remember where they were, when they heard about it, much as the older ones among us remember where they heard about the shooting of President Kennedy. We decided not to put the television on, largely because of the children. When they got to school, all normal lessons and activities had been suspended, and the teachers were planning to explain to the children as gently as possible what was going on.

Lizzie had sadly become resigned to my frequent flights around the US and the world, to promote or produce films, leaving her alone with the children. I was habituated to it. I was well on the way to becoming a "Million Miler" on United Airlines alone. But this shocking news did stop me in my tracks. Was the era of the Frequent Flier finished for good? But if so, how could I do my documentary work? (In fact, it took the scourge of the Coronavirus, nearly 20 years later, to virtually shut down air travel and the film industry).

One week after 9/11, however, I did catch an eastbound flight, when new security inspections had been put in place. I flew into a New York that was scarcely recognizable. The airport had only just been reopened and was almost deserted. The cabbie driving me into Manhattan could not stop talking about the events. Even in Brooklyn, as we drove in, you could smell burning and dust, a week after the catastrophe. People walking along the sidewalk seemed to move like zombies – slowly, their heads down. The New York swagger and brio had disappeared completely.

The meetings went ahead as planned, but nobody's mind was on the business of making films, unless the subject was the tragedy itself. As it happened, I had been in contact with a Professor Naihua Duan at the Medical Department of the University of California, Los Angeles. His specialty was dealing with trauma. I phoned him from New York and asked whether he would be in a position to fund any coverage of the aftermath of 9/11. He immediately agreed to find the funds for a half-hour film, telling me exactly what he needed: survivors of the event, who had been close to any of the buildings, which had been hit: people suffering from trauma.

It turned out to be all too easy to find such people. Within a few hundred yards of the World Trade Center was the historic Trinity Church, which I had contacted while researching *Pulling Out All the Stops*, the pipe organ film we had made in the 1990's. The church ran a crèche, where mothers could drop off and pick up their children throughout the day, and they put me in contact with several of these mothers. Their stories were true nightmares.

Only a few weeks later, we made the film, with our new Associate Producer Victoria Simpson doing much of the research, the camerawork and the subsequent editing. We concentrated on just two stories. One African American woman was walking along the street with her daughter, away from the World Trade Center and towards the Church, when the first plane hit the building.

"There was an enormous explosion", she said. "I turned around to see the building erupt like a volcano, out of its side. Fire and smoke were pouring out of it. My four-year-old daughter and I were just transfixed, watching in horror. Then I saw the second plane. Another huge explosion. Everyone on the street beside us was standing there, eyes wide open, looking up: this was like a disaster movie, but for real. We had no idea of the danger we were in.

"Fire trucks started arriving from all over town: you couldn't hear yourself think for the sirens and the shouting and the chaos. I grabbed my daughter and held her to me as tightly as I could, but we hadn't moved an inch since it all started. There was a crowd of us, and we were all mesmerized by the whole thing. We couldn't stop watching. Then there was this tremendous rumbling, like an earthquake: a deep, dark sound like the end of the world, and the first building started to collapse. It all happened like a movie in slow motion.

"Then I realized that people were running away. Someone shouted 'Get out of here' as they ran past us. I looked and saw this giant cloud of dust and smoke coming down the road towards us. And then I started running, with my daughter in my arms. But somehow, she wriggled free, screaming as the dust cloud caught up with us. I kept running, shouting her name, but I couldn't see anything, and I couldn't hear anything either. The roaring, rumbling sound was so loud. I started running around in circles, looking for my daughter, but hundreds of people were now running past me. I realized I had no hope of finding her.

"Somehow, I did find Trinity Church, and I started sobbing and calling my daughter's name like a mad woman. The Church was taking everybody in, like it was a place of refuge where we'd be safe. Inside the Church was a huge crowd of people, some on their knees praying, some screaming hysterically, but mostly just shocked and silent. But I must have gone on shouting my daughter's name, because quite soon, an elderly man came up to me, holding my daughter's hand, and said 'Is this who you're looking for?'

"I grabbed my daughter and said 'Thank you, Sir. And thank you, thank you, Lord!' a dozen times, as I held her, and we both broke down into tears. The old man just nodded and smiled. 'I saw her on the sidewalk, and scooped her up as I ran,' he said. 'It was the least I could do, though it's the first time in many years that I've run like that.' And then he moved away and was lost in the crowd. To this day, I've never been able to trace him and thank him properly for saving my daughter."

The resulting half-hour film was quickly edited and soon transmitted on the PBS network nationally. It was one of the shortest, simplest and least expensive films that InCA Productions has ever made, but it seems to have had a lasting impact. UCLA was still using it to illustrate the short and medium-term effects of trauma, ten years later. For all of us involved in making it, it brought back the horrifying memories of that day. When I looked at the film again, a few days before writing this, it brought tears to my eyes: the simple courage and kindness of human beings, in the face of terror, is a miraculous thing.

• •

9/11 had several other unexpected reverberations in our lives. Months later, we received a large brown envelope from the Immigration and Naturalization Service (INS), with a letter calling us to an interview at their offices in San Francisco. Here, we would apparently be cross-questioned about all aspects of American life, to make sure that we were fit to become citizens.

Also inside the envelope was a hefty fifty-six-page document, printed on the cheapest off-white government paper you can imagine. These were the Cliff Notes (or cheat sheet), listing the arcane knowledge we would have to master, to pass the face-to-face test during the interview. We tried to remember all the factoids: how many states were there? Easy. Explain the different structure and function of the House of Representatives and the Senate: less easy. Who was Paul Revere, and why should we care? Who knew, if you were a non-native who had not sat through civics class in an American high school?

Lizzie and I did our best to remember it all. We felt as if we were going to the most important job interview in our lives, when we went to the INS office in San Francisco. We were given a number and sat in a large waiting room, with Filipino, Mexican and Chinese families, each chatting in their respective language. If the test was going to be tough for us, how much tougher would it be for them?

A buzzer sounded, and a green light was illuminated beside our number on a display board. We walked down a long corridor and knocked on a door. A friendly voice invited us to come in. Behind a big desk sat a smiling, gray-haired African American officer.

"Please sit down," he said, and opened the only item on his desk: a fat file, full of papers.

My heart sank: was my speeding ticket there, from Manhattan Beach in 1984? What damning evidence had been collected, describing my past misdeeds in the US? Was it considered subversive to subscribe to the British satirical magazine *Private Eye*? The smile on the face of the INS officer slowly died.

"Oh, my goodness," he said. My heart sank further.

"Oh, Good Lord," he said. Lizzie and I looked at each other in panic.

"I can't believe it!" he said, and then looked up and beamed at us.

"Do you realize when these documents were processed?" he asked. We had no idea.

"They were processed on 9/11," he said, "On that very day, at 9.30 in the morning." He turned over a couple of pages. "That's only an hour before the plane hit the Pentagon and all the government work in Washington stopped."

He looked up at us with the largest grin you can imagine. "Someone must have meant you to be citizens," he said. "Do you still want to become an American,, with terrorists flying planes into our buildings?"

We assured him that we certainly did: better to be playing on the home side, if we were going to be living here. He apologized for the fact that he still had to ask us a few questions, then looked down at the paperwork again. Another big grin. He looked up at Lizzie.

"So your family name is Ross?" he asked. Lizzie agreed that it was. "Elizabeth Ross..." he said thoughtfully, and then beamed again.

"Oh, my goodness…" We still did not get it. "Betsy Ross!" he exclaimed.

"Oh yes," said Lizzie, like a schoolgirl who has learned her lines properly. "She's the one who sewed the first American flag, isn't she? My mother's known as Betty Ross – she's an Elizabeth too."

The INS officer slowly stood up, all smiles. He invited us both to stand as well. He shook us warmly by the hand.

"Betsy Ross!" he said again. "I don't believe it. Welcome to America. I can't see there's much point asking you folks any more questions. This was meant to be!"

And so it came to pass. A few weeks later, we found ourselves with two thousand others in the vast Masonic Hall on the top of San Francisco's Nob Hill, across the road from Grace Cathedral. In front of us, on the stage, was another INS officer, this time from eastern Europe. He was the warm-up man for the citizenship ceremony. He told us that he had only become a citizen himself two years before.

"And look," he said, "I've already got a job, and they give you the uniform free. No charge!" The audience laughed nervously. Most of them did not speak much English.

"The next bit's the serious stuff," said the warm-up man. "A judge will come into the room, and she'll ask you to hold up your hands and swear allegiance to the United States of America. You just say 'I do' to whatever she asks you. Try it out for me. It's like getting married. Say 'I do.'"

"I do," we all said, a little self-consciously.

"Louder than that!" we were told, and we tried again. "I DO!!!"

 "Right," said the warm-up man. "From the moment you say that to the judge, you're American citizens, and nobody on earth can take that away from you. And by the way, from then on till the day you die, the IRS is going to tax you, so you'd better take it seriously. Anyone want to back out? Now's your last chance."

You could have heard a pin drop.

"Good," he said. "Now here's the judge."

Right on cue, a door opened at the side of the stage, and in walked a diminutive African American woman, with a black academic gown and a kind but serious expression. She took center stage.

"I may not look like a judge, but I am," she said, smiling. "Are you ready to become Americans?"

There was a roar of approval. Of course we were. Who else but the Americans could stage-manage a civil event this well? And these were government employees! Within five minutes, we had all said "I do" multiple times, and we were married to the United States.

As we walked out – all two thousand of us – dozens of officials met us, handing us all passport application forms and other information. Surrounding us were dozens of families, having their pictures taken, grinning and laughing. We felt very proud and rather tearful. We had become part of the huddled masses of immigrants, which America, traditionally, has welcomed.

What's more, we still had our British passports, in case things went "tits-up" in the US of A, as they say here. Nearly twenty years later, under the Trump regime, we were glad about that.

• •

My trip to New York after 9/11 had another quite different outcome as well. While in the city, I was unexpectedly invited to a party, to meet a publisher who was interested in TV tie-ins. In fact, I discovered that the party had been converted into a fund-raising event for the survivors of 9/11, including the families of those who were in the buildings and the firemen who lost their lives trying to rescue them.

Just after I arrived at the fund-raiser, I heard a loud English voice and the sound of hearty laughter. This was just about the first laugh I had heard in the three days I had been in the city, which was still in shock and deep mourning. I moved towards the group and introduced myself: I felt I could do with a laugh or two.

"Hallo, I'm Edwina Sandys," said the loud English voice. In front of me stood a good-looking woman of about my age, with flaming red hair. "What do you do?"

I told her and asked her the same question.

"I'm an artist," she said. "I do paintings and sculptures and all sorts of stuff. I've got one of my pieces near here, in the grounds of the United Nations School."

I mumbled something rather inadequate about how appalled and sorry I was at the events of the past ten days, and her response was immediate.

"We've got to stand up to these people!" she said. "If we allow them to knock the stuffing out of us, they've won the war already. Have a drink!"

"She's one of Winston Churchill's grand-daughters. A chip off the old block," said the man beside her. This turned out to be Richard Kaplan, Edwina's husband, a noted architect and city planner.

"And she's a redhead, as you've noticed," he continued, "So she speaks her mind!"

"Oh, come on, Richard!" said Edwina. "When have you ever not spoken *your* mind? You're a Jew, and this is New York!"

Richard's big, booming laugh came rolling out again. This friendly sparring was obviously par for the course. Edwina turned to me.

"Where are you from?" she asked – the inevitable question that all expatriate Brits put to each other within minutes of meeting.

"I was born in central London," I ventured. "Chalk Farm, actually."

Now it was Edwina's turn to laugh heartily.

"*Chalk Farm?*" she said. "That's hardly *central* London, is it? It's miles from central London. I doubt if a black cab would even *take* you there."

There was a friendly twinkle in her eye as she said this, so I had to believe she was not just being rude. It turned out, of course, that she had lived in the most fashionable part of London's Belgravia, a stone's throw from Buckingham Palace. Her mother was Diana Churchill and her father was the former cabinet minister Duncan Sandys. I vaguely remembered that he was a man so devoid of charm that he had been known as Sunken Glands in *Private Eye.*

"You're a documentary film-maker, are you?" asked Richard, more constructively. "Do you know Peter Foges? He used to be at the BBC and he's a friend of ours."

I told them that Peter had been a serious boyfriend of my first wife's twin sister Catherine Jay – wheels within wheels. So I certainly did know him, and so did my wife Lizzie, from her time at the BBC.

"Well, he's coming to dinner tomorrow night," said Edwina. "Why don't you come too? In fact, why don't we turn the whole thing into a dinner party, Richard? We could all do with some fun after this dreadful business."

And thus I entered the magical world of Edwina Sandys. Picture, if you will, the most perfect loft apartment in New York's SoHo district: high ceilings, lazily turning fans, huge space, great light from enormous windows. They owned the entire second floor. Half of it was Edwina's studio – the more public half, because this was where potential purchasers of her art would be invited, and this is also where she created it. The other half was Richard and Edwina's apartment. Designed by Richard, it had multiple levels, with bedrooms and study areas cantilevered out across part of the space, but allowing the main living area to be both intimate and spacious.

As a visitor, you pushed the button beside the exterior door on Broadway, three blocks south of Houston Street, right opposite Dean and Deluca, the fashionable grocers. It was the ideal place to be, as an artist catering to the taste of New York's wealthy liberals – and even a few conservatives, for goodness' sake: this was art created by Winston Churchill's grand-daughter!

Then you took a ramshackle freight elevator a couple of floors up, and it opened onto their private hallway, which was entirely painted in bright vermilion red – one of Edwina's favorite colors – and stuffed with bright red, surreal sculptures. There were only two exits from this Alice-in-Wonderland entrance hall: to the flat, or to the studio.

Edwina's art is so varied and so multi-faceted, that it has in some ways served her badly. She has no single easy-to-define style. She has created works in almost every medium:

sculpture (bronze, stainless steel, marble and wood), oil paints and acrylics, comic strips and multi-material concept pieces like *The Marriage Bed* (a full-size bed, half a bed of roses and half a bed of nails – literally). She has created myriad cut-outs, reminiscent of Matisse, in wonderful colors and flowing, suggestive shapes. The columnist and author Peregrine Worsthorne said of Edwina, "If it's not suggestive, then she's not concentrating." But her talent goes much further than that.

Did I mention bronze sculpture? She has created many of these: some of her earliest pieces were minimalist, including a clever *trompe-l'oeil* piece of a woman's arm and hand, appearing to hover in space, holding a mirror – in which you can see the woman's face, as she does her make-up. A more serious piece is her *Christa* – a beautifully executed female Christ figure, nailed to a cross: a feminist crucifixion. In the 1970's, this caused a furor in the Episcopal and Anglican Church, when it was exhibited in one of New York's most fashionable churches.

But on my first visit, I had no idea what I was walking into. I was best known for my science and technology related films – *Cosmos, Connections, The Ascent of Man.* What could I contribute to the dinner party of a celebrated artist and her *coterie* of followers?

The dinner was memorable. Peter Foges was indeed there, on form as the witty *bon viveur* he has always aspired to be. So were a dozen other people, a marvelous mix of New York's arty society and talent. The long teak table was illuminated by dozens of tiny tea lights. The food was simple, quick to prepare and delicious. The jokes crackled and fizzed like fireworks. I commented on the recurring images of Adam and Eve in Edwina's art.

"Oh, that's Richard and me," she said, grinning mischievously. "We've always wanted to have an Adam and Eve party here, and call it Eden, and have everyone arrive naked under their raincoats."

Richard laughed. "We'd have a big snake," he said, "and luscious temptations."

"Has anyone ever done a film about you?" I remember asking, naively. The conversation at the table stopped. Edwina grinned.

"No," she said. "What fun it could be. You're a producer. Does that mean you have access to lots of money?" I had to admit that this was not the case.

"Well never mind," said Richard, "I'm sure we could phone a few people and rustle up the first hundred thousand."

He was as good as his word. Within a few weeks, I found myself directing an art film, with no previous experience. Named after one of Edwina's Adam and Eve pieces, I proposed that we should call the film *One Bite of the Apple.*

Edwina proved to be a splendid personality on camera, both on location (Florida, Minnesota, London – wherever her art was on public display) and in her studio, while she was working. She also turned out to be a wonderful and generous friend. She and Richard invited Lizzie, James, Pippa and me to stay with them at their classic house in the Hudson River Valley. They took us out on the river in their powerboat, during a record-breaking heat wave. That same evening, their house was invaded by what looked like a plague of locusts.

"Oh yes, this happens once or twice a year," said Edwina, brushing thousands of dead crickets from the ground, below the windows. "You chose the wrong weekend." Upon which, more champagne was opened, and the incident all but forgotten.

Richard was as good as his word, on the money front. Pulling all available strings to family foundations, the National Trust and others, sufficient funds were found to complete our modest video biography. Victoria Simpson shot the film on the same Panasonic consumer camera that we had used undercover in India, on the Amelia Earhart film. The quality was good enough to be accepted by PBS. Victoria's boyfriend (and, later, husband) Monte Vallier composed and played the music. We all had a ton of fun, and the film was widely distributed, riding on the Churchill name and Edwina's bubbly personality.

She had remained doggedly British. Much like my wife Lizzie and I, she had managed to keep her British accent intact, even after twenty-five years of marriage to a New Yorker and a vivid, busy life, traveling all over the US. She never forgot her roots. Some of the most moving scenes in the film were shot with Edwina in London, nostalgically wandering through the back streets of Belgravia, remembering her childhood. She found a tiny hair salon, which she had patronized, decades before – and discovered that one of the original owners was still there. She wandered around the gardens of Chartwell, Winston Churchill's rambling country house outside London, where he used to paint in his old age.

"I always think of him, when I'm painting," she said. "It was art therapy for him, of course, but he loved it, particularly after he finally left politics. It was practical work: mix the paints, choose the brush, start the groundwork on each canvas. He'd hoist me on his knee as he sat at the easel and ask me what I thought about his progress. I was quite scared of him, really, because I knew he was famous. But I always noticed the brandy glass on one side, and the paints on the other.

"'Ah yes,' he'd say, 'Inspiration has to be encouraged, you know.' And perhaps that's what I learned from him. I've never said no to a drink, when I'm in a creative mood."

As I write these words, I remember my own first and last personal contact with Winston Churchill. When he died in January 1965, I was halfway through my second year at Oxford University. Britain went into a week of mourning. After many solemn ceremonies in London, his body was transferred in a simple coffin to a railway train, hauled by a fine streamlined steam locomotive, which had been named *Winston Churchill* many years before. Travelling at a stately forty miles an hour, it took him from London, through Oxford station, to the tiny village of Bladon, where he was laid to rest in the ancient churchyard, near the family seat of the Marlborough family – his family – at Blenheim Palace.

On a cold January day, more than a thousand students went down to Oxford station, to pay their respects and watch that train pass by. There was total silence. People took off their caps and hoodies, if they were wearing them. And bowed their heads. This was the mid-sixties in Britain – the time of the Beatles and Stones, the height of the satire boom

– but there was not a sound from the onlookers. Just the mournful whistle of the train, as it disappeared into the distance. I will never forget it.

So you can well imagine what a privilege it was for me to make a film with Edwina, one of Churchill's five grand-daughters. I have been told subsequently that the other granddaughters inherited much of the self-regard and serious demeanor of Churchill. Thank God, I worked with the one who inherited the wit, the artistic talent and the warm heart.

● ●

As the new millennium unfurled and various film projects came to fruition one way or another, my elder children began to hit milestones of their own.

In 1996, Amanda had chosen to go to Bristol University, in South-West England. It was known as a hotbed of fun as well as a respected seat of learning, and it certainly lived up to its reputation. On her very first evening in the Halls of Residence, she went down to the Cellar Bar, looking for a part-time job. The fact that there is an officially sanctioned bar in a student dormitory astounds most Americans, but the drinking age in England is 18, and universities (like the BBC) like to offer an in-house refuge for drinking, to somewhat reduce the number of students vomiting publicly in the city's main streets.

Amanda had worked part time the previous summer in a local London pub, to earn some pocket money. So, when the young lad in charge of the bar asked her to pull a foaming pint of draft beer, to prove she was up to the job, she passed the test with flying colors and was promptly hired. Within days, that young lad, Andy Bodley, had become her boyfriend. Exactly nine years later (after she had qualified as a lawyer and been working for a large London law firm), the two of them got engaged. Andy popped the question at the top of a mountain in Tasmania, where he had spent much of his childhood. Exactly ten years after they met, on 28 October 2006, they were married in the most charming village in the English Cotswolds. They designed the entire event themselves, and the family danced the night away in a huge marquee on the village green of Minster Lovell.

And where did they spend the first night of their honeymoon? In the Old Swan Inn, in the very same room that Helen and I had occupied, to celebrate our nuptials, back in March of 1975! The Jay family are certainly creatures of habit…

Juliet, meanwhile, had followed Amanda to Bristol University and studied Economics and Social Sciences. She went to work with a London marketing firm, specializing in the rather dry and specialized field of Econometrics, and it wasn't long before she was snapped up by the Rupert Murdoch empire. A shrewd tactician, she rose through the ranks at speed, working behind the scenes at the Times and Sunday Times, out in London's Docklands. She also managed to persuade Rupert's minions that she would be even more valuable if she had an MBA, a Master's in Business Administration. Why not, if they would pay for it?

The real coup was to persuade them that the only place to get a really impressive MBA was in the US (like her Dad had done, 35 years before). No, better than that: to get the MBA in New York. Hey presto! Within a couple of months, she had gained entry to

Columbia Business School, and The Sunday Times had agreed to keep her on salary, while she spent her two years, gaining the degree. I had the great pleasure of celebrating my 60th birthday in 2005, with Lizzie, Juliet and her boyfriend Cabe, at an open-air café in Greenwich village.

Juliet and Cabe came to visit us in San Francisco twice, en route to the wildly spectacular Burning Man festivities, out in the Nevada desert. But that relationship didn't last, and she finally agreed to marry another successful businessman, Thijs Bauer. He is Dutch, and together they chose a suitably European venue for their wedding: the island of Ibiza. On 21 May 2011, they rented a spectacular house, with its own pool and extensive garden, and threw a jaw-dropping party for more than 100 guests, including my first wife Helen, most of the Jay family, half the population of Amsterdam, plus Lizzie, myself, James and Pippa. Wow!

● ●

22. KEEPING SCORE WITH MICHAEL TILSON THOMAS

Keeping a small production company going – paying the staff, covering the overhead, all that dull but essential stuff – is not easy. If you want to focus on top quality films, so that you can really pay attention and make them as good as possible, you cannot just go out and solicit any old production jobs. That is the *modus vivendi* for many documentary studios, which hope to get bigger and bigger, employ ever more staff, and create more and more "product."

But what do they produce? Mostly, I suggest, second and third-rate stuff with low technical standards: minor corporate promos, quick videos for online and website consumption or cheap shows for cable networks, quickly churning out a multi-part series like a sausage machine. Well, we are always warned not to investigate too closely how sausages are made.

Of course, the downside to trying to be a real "quality house" is that there can be awful gaps in the company income. It is a bit like being an architect, who disdains designing public toilet blocks and insists on waiting for the next commission to design a cathedral: a risky strategy. There can come a day when you realize you can't meet payroll at the end of the week.

Joan Saffa, the heroic co-director of *The Heart of Healing* and many other InCA shows, is a good friend as well as a great producer, director and editor. She was on the payroll when we faced one of those moments. We were working with a valiant and well-meaning would-be producer called Ellison Horne, who had raised some modest sums of money to develop a project called *Celebrating Solutions*. His hope was to tell local Bay Area stories about people who were creating new opportunities in their local community, through their own ingenuity. Many of them were people of color, homeless or living with a disability, and Joan and I felt that this was a worthy cause. It could lead to some good local storytelling and be tied into an active website, where people could exchange ideas.

The trouble was that we just could not raise sufficient funds to go into full production. Excellent and kindly local funders, like the Wallace Alexander Gerbode Foundation, had given us sums of up to twenty-five thousand dollars, but productions – let alone whole series – need a rather larger budget than that, to be of acceptable quality for broadcast.

One day, on our quest for funds, Joan and I went to see the Gordon and Betty Moore Foundation. It had been launched by the wealthy founder of the Intel corporation, Gordon Moore, after whom Moore's Law is named: the well-known phenomenon that the number of transistors per square inch on integrated circuits tends to double every year. We had interviewed him for *2001: HAL's Legacy*, and I was optimistic that his people would be interested. The foundation had plenty of money and had backed similar Bay Area initiatives. Best of all, the Program Officer we were due to meet with was a friend of Joan's: Janette Gitler, herself a former TV producer.

"Aha!" we thought, "If Janette can't wield the can opener on the Moore Foundation and dig out some funds for *Celebrating Solutions*, who can?"

It turned out that she could not. The senior officers of the foundation – as is often the way with plump, fully-staffed foundations – had recently been on a retreat and come up with a whole new raft of priorities and initiatives, and our kind of television show was not going to fit in with them.

"But wait," said Janette, "I think I might have something else you'd really like. But it's not a Moore Foundation project. Let's take a walk outside, and I can tell you about it. These walls have ears."

It turned out that Janette was very good friends with a board member of the San Francisco Symphony (SFS). She had confided to Janette that the Symphony was desperate to find a producer, who could create a new kind of show, which would make classical music more appealing to children.

"How about you guys?" asked Janette. "InCA's got the track record – big projects, big budgets, big impact."

Joan and I looked at each other and gulped. Neither she nor I could read music, nor had we ever played a musical instrument. The last time I had been to a live classical music concert was... I couldn't even remember. Help! How could we possibly be convincing candidates?

I couldn't help thinking of all the patronizing musical tosh I had seen created for children: Danny Kaye's version of *Tubby the Tuba*, for example, still sets my teeth on edge. Even Wynton Marsalis's award-winning PBS music series of 1995 seemed to me an embarrassing, self-conscious affair, with perfectly dressed eight-year-olds scattered around the set like ornaments – even posed neatly up in the rafters of a barn, desperately trying to look interested.

Janette reminded us that Leonard Bernstein's *Young People's Concerts* had been a huge feature of CBS back in the era of black and white TV. Incredibly, for three years in the late 1950's and early 60's, they were broadcast at the prime time peak of 7.30 p.m. That's what the Symphony wanted to achieve. But that was 40 years ago!

But nothing ventured, nothing gained, so Joan and I agreed to meet with John Kieser, the Director of Media for the SFS. As it happened, John and I were both fathers of children who had recently started to attend the French American International School in San Francisco. He was part Canadian, part American, part English, and he had a great sense of humor. Most important of all, this was going to be his last, best attempt to get something big off the ground, in the television arena. He had already tried working with two other producers and the local PBS station (KQED), and the results had been, he said, "underwhelming, to put it mildly."

The acid test was for us to meet the Music Director and Principal Conductor of the SFS, Michael Tilson Thomas – known to everyone, including himself, as MTT. We should share any bright ideas we had with him, John suggested. We should all go to MTT's house and beard the dragon in his den.

For some two hundred years, anywhere in the world, the Music Director and Principal Conductor of a renowned orchestra has been basically God Almighty within His Realm. Although the board members of a Symphony might need to restrain Him gently, if the financial situation became too dire, or His advisors might whisper a gentle warning in His ear if His proposals became too outlandish, the basic fact is this: whatever God wants, He gets. Whatever He hates is dead meat.

So it was with no little trepidation that Joan and I accompanied John to a neo-Gothic gabled mansion in San Francisco's Pacific Heights, the home of MTT. But I had the germ of an idea, and the following forty-five minutes would determine if that idea would fly.

Happily, MTT could not have been more welcoming, as was his manager, partner and (later) husband, Joshua Robison. We were invited up to Michael's top-floor "Eagle's Nest", a glorious room with views across San Francisco Bay and a first-class grand piano. We were offered delicious drinks and snacks. Indeed, we were welcomed as if we were old friends. Michael lounged around in casual clothes and sneakers.

"So, what's the new idea?" he asked.

I think it helped that his previous position had been Music Director and Principal Conductor of the London Symphony Orchestra. He had had seven years of listening to Brits and understanding British humor and understatement. When I am nervous, I tend to resort to both of these, which by this stage in the book may not come as a surprise to you.

I explained what I believed: that it was fruitless to target an audience of children alone. The target audience had to be whole families – indeed, people of all ages from eight or ten upwards. I suggested that MTT's favorite music seemed to be romantic and emotional – and people of all ages understand these feelings.

Joan and I went on to explain our proposal for an introductory documentary: to take one much loved symphony (MTT's choice which one, of course) and do four things. We would show how MTT prepared his score in his own mind and how he re-introduced the work to the orchestra. We would see how they all rehearsed the piece and finally show them performing at least a part of it to a live audience.

At the same time, we would explain, with the help of the musicians, how an orchestra works behind the scenes: what percussionists have to do with the animal hides that cover their drums; how the wind section carve or modify their own mouthpieces; how the violins look after their strings; and the endless requirement to practice, practice, practice. Finally, we would interweave an interview with MTT, sitting at the piano and explaining what the chosen symphony meant to the composer, and what that composer was trying to say to us, movement by movement.

Michael listened intently. We had been warned that he was not always receptive to ideas that were not his own. But he seemed to like what we were proposing. Indeed, by the end of the session, which eventually lasted well over an hour, he had already added his own thoughts and thereby made it his idea after all. Things were looking good.

He showed Joan and me his vast collection of scores, kept on shelves in a special room nearby. Each one of them was dog-eared from use, covered with his own colored pencil marks, which indicated the special emphasis he had wanted to give each piece in separate performances over the years. We suggested that we might be able to film a great scene of him selecting a symphony, taking the score to the piano, marking it up, humming parts of it out loud, and then playing some favorite or specially tricky passages, to reacquaint himself with the composer's voice and spirit, and to find a fresh interpretation.

By the time we left, it was virtually a done deal. Michael was excited, we were excited, even John was excited - and somewhat relieved, I think. By admitting our musical ignorance and playing the "useful idiot" role, we felt we could get MTT to talk to the camera as if he was talking *to us personally*. He would be explaining, in real time to Joan and myself, what the music meant.

This is an old trick that many makers of documentaries use. You cannot be deeply knowledgeable about everything. You have to learn just enough about a subject to ask the right questions. I am not an astronomer, yet I had to learn how to talk to Carl Sagan usefully. I knew nothing about China, yet I helped create *The Heart of the Dragon* by listening to the experts we had gathered. I knew even less about the American Constitution and Bill of Rights, but Peter Jennings could talk to the camera (behind which I always stood) and explain it *to me.* That way, he would not sound like a professional reporter on assignment, or a famous person giving a lecture, but like a friend talking to another friend, explaining something important. That, I believe, is the key to connecting on camera with a television or film audience: have the presenter talk to them as if he or she is talking to one single person - indeed, to a friend.

The funding strategy for the project was remarkable. The Haas Junior Foundation (associated with family money from the Levi Strauss fortune) had put up a "challenge grant": basically, they had offered $500,000, and the San Francisco Symphony was required to match it - i.e. raise the same amount from other sources. Then Haas would put down a further million pounds, and again it had to be matched... and so on, up to a potential total of - amazingly - over twenty million dollars. The dream was to produce a full suite of media: multiple documentaries, live concert performances, DVDs, CDs, a radio series, training for music teachers and - most important of all - an award-winning website that would tie them all together and really teach people what classical music could mean.

But everything would hinge on the success of the first documentary, for which the SFS already had the necessary funds. If it was no good, or even just routinely ho-hum, there would be no "greatest media music project ever made" or "greatest non-fiction budget ever raised." So Joan and I felt a certain sense of responsibility to get it right, as you may imagine. Indeed, we were scared witless!

Right from the start, MTT was a pleasure to work with, however. He had a wonderful on-camera presence. He never needed a script or cue cards: he knew what he wanted to say. No two takes were ever quite the same - which could mean problems with the editing - but each one was fresh, crisp and often remarkably witty and deft.

The foundation for each of the films was his personal copy of the conductor's score of the symphony in question. Hence his proposal for the title of the project – *Keeping Score*. However clever this name was, it certainly must have confused readers of the TV listings. *Keeping Score?* It sounded like some sort of sports program – detailed statistics for baseball nuts, perhaps. But being God in the realm of the classical orchestra, MTT insisted, and the series name was never changed to something more obvious and direct. In retrospect, I think this was a pity, because many potential viewers and music lovers, we learned later, had never heard of the project, or never imagined it had anything to do with music.

MTT decided that the pilot one-hour show would feature Tchaikovsky's Fourth Symphony: "an old war horse" was what he called it. Something easy to digest – a real crowd pleaser. We found that, on camera in the Eagle's Nest in his home, Michael could hum or sing any passage from the score, as if he was the entire orchestra. Then he would turn to the piano, mark up the score and pound out a few bars. And then he would turn to the camera and say:

"*That* is what the composer was trying to evoke – the pathos, or the joy, or the fear..." It was heady stuff. He truly made the music come alive, right then and there, on the first take, even for musical idiots like myself.

At the first rehearsal with the orchestra, he told the musicians:

"What we have to do is to breathe new life into this piece, as if we'd never played it before. We have to re-think it, even if it is an old chestnut. So let's try something different, shall we?"

Over a few days, we filmed the rehearsal process with multiple cameras. Michael cajoled, enticed and occasionally almost threatened the orchestra. He teased out new subtleties. He insisted on a roaringly fast climax to the Fourth Movement.

"It's got to be 'Wham, Bam, Thank'ee Ma'am'", he told the musicians, and they knew what he meant. After three rehearsals of the grand finale, they were bathed in sweat – and so was Michael.

Earlier, we had filmed many of the lead musicians at home, practicing the piece, making evocative points about what the music meant to them personally, and why they loved the particular instrument they played. For John Englekes, the Principal Trombone was almost an extension of his manhood, the way he described it. Plus, he said, the trombone case was ideal for carrying bottles of the very best California craft beer to Europe, when the orchestra toured.

The brass section have a certain reputation as the bad boys and girls of the orchestra – any orchestra, not just the SFS – and they were not going to be bested by any member of – say – the Vienna Philharmonic's brass section who might suggest that all American beer was "gnat's piss, like Budweiser," as Engelkes put it. So they always took along specimens of our best local brews – often Lagunitas IPA – to impress the Austrians and the Germans. They swaddled the bottles in cotton, velvet and plastic bags, and smuggled them into the spacious travel cases of the larger brass instruments.

"You see," Englekes liked to joke with his foreign hosts, "We can play your music better than you do, *and* we can make superior beer."

The final event to be filmed was the first live performance in San Francisco's Davies Hall, with the orchestra in evening dress and MTT in all his conductor's finery. John Kieser had decided wisely to bring a special live-event crew up from Los Angeles to tape the performance. They brought two huge trucks with them: one full of equipment, cables and cameras, and the other a fully-fledged live director's suite. The trucks were usually used for football games and big open-air rock concerts. They were truly impressive.

The director for the taping of the live performance was Gary Halvorson, a master of capturing fast-paced live events. Remarkably, he could also read music like a pro, because – long ago – he had been trained at the Julliard School of Music. His deft intercutting between ten cameras, spliced in with sequences of our own documentary footage, gave a huge sense of immediacy and excitement to our finished film, as well as making a brilliant stand-alone concert DVD of its own. 'Wham, Bam, Thank'ee Ma'am' it certainly was.

I think it was the idea of Joyce Wessling, John Kieser's colleague, to have a camera follow MTT as he walked offstage after this premiere performance of Tchaikovsky's Fourth, and tape his immediate response to how it had gone. Anyway, the results were spectacular. Michael gave us one of his best ever interviews – standing, perspiring, in his dressing room, still jazzed and hyped by the thunderous finale of the symphony he had just conducted, the applause and standing ovation of the audience still ringing in his ears. The sheer thrill of it all quite overwhelmed him. He had tears in his eyes as he said, about Tchaikovsky:

"Thank you, Peter Ilyich, for giving us this wonderful experience." And, implicitly, thank you to the orchestra for bringing Peter Ilyich's spirit back to life.

I was quite hooked by the whole experience and could hardly wait to get into post-production. Joan worked with Blair Gershkow to edit the show. I worked on the structure and sketched out recommended pieces of narration for MTT to voice, to link the ideas together. Then we went back to that Gothic house in Pacific Heights, to show Michael the "rough fine-cut" – the almost finished show – for him to react and pass judgment. Our hearts were in our mouths. He hadn't seen a single minute of cut footage yet. What if he hated it?

We sat in one of MTT's formal sitting rooms for some time, before he made himself available. He did not seem totally focused on what we were going to show him, and with Michael, it is very important to get his full attention. But finally John Kieser felt the time was right to press the DVD play button, and the show unfurled. It ran for the whole fifty-seven minutes (a PBS hour) without interruption. The end credits were laid over the final triumphant bars of the symphony and the huge applause from the live audience. Fade to black.

Complete silence in the room.

Michael sat motionless for several seconds, still looking at the now-dark screen. Then he looked round at us all, got up, and simply said:

"Bravo!"

This, from any musician, is the highest compliment. He thanked everyone, shook Joan and me and John by the hand and smiled broadly.

"Bravo. Bravissimo," he said, several more times.

Personally, I was thrilled. We had done it! MTT is famous for demanding the very best out of everyone, including himself, and a bravo from him is worth a dozen from many other people. As an unexpected punch line, he said he was driving downtown and would be pleased to give anyone a lift. I did not specially need to go downtown, but the prospect of being driven anywhere by Michael Tilson Thomas in person was too unusual to turn down. Joshua usually drives him everywhere. En route, Michael and I chatted like old friends. It was clear that, as far as MTT was concerned, we had a success on our hands, and we could reasonably hope for more funding and more films.

In a postscript to the story about the Tchaikovsky film, PBS liked it so much that they extended the run of the national series *Great Performances* by one further show, to accommodate *Keeping Score*, billed simply as *The Music Show from San Francisco*. Later that year, the film won the prestigious ASCAP Deems Taylor prize for the best musical film of the year in any of the media.

I recalled a summer from my childhood, when I used to sit at a grand piano in Croydon, aged about eight. My draconian Aunt Hilda Mary was trying to teach me to do proper scales and quite literally rapped me on the knuckles whenever I messed up, which was frequently. One particular afternoon, I looked out of the French doors in her elegant house, saw the sunshine, the trees and the bright green lawn, and had a desperate urge to run outside and play soccer or ride a bike instead. I am not naturally a sporty person, but *anything* was better than Aunt Hilda Mary and her classical piano scales. How surprised she would have been to see what I was doing in San Francisco, fifty years later. Heavens above, how surprised *I* was!

•••

More funding did eventually appear. The Haas Junior Foundation put up around three million dollars for three more films, plus the website and other outreach activities. That money was matched by the James Irvine Foundation, the National Foundation for the Arts and some very generous Symphony Board members like Nan Tucker McEvoy (mother of Nion, who later funded James's film, *The Book Makers*). We started work with our television team and were joined by groups of other producers and writers who created the award-winning website, the radio series and the teaching initiatives.

The first question facing us was: which composers and which symphonies would MTT choose, to follow the opening Tchaikovsky pilot? He decided to dive in at the deep end: the first would be Beethoven's third symphony, *Eroica*, the work which arguably was the first to fully define the composer's unique talent. MTT's early mentor and close friend, Leonard Bernstein, had led the way along the path that Michael was now treading: from Beethoven to Mahler, and Mahler to Copland – though Mahler's work (Michael's special favorite) had to wait till the grand finale of our series, several years later. For *Keeping Score*, it was clear that Michael had set his sights on conveying the depth of feeling of the world's greatest romantic music.

The Beethoven film has always been one of my favorites, out of the nine films we created for the series. Michael really meant every word that he said, as he sat at the piano and pounded out the great moments from the symphony: the anger, Beethoven's rage at losing his hearing, the suicidal urges – and the light, airy, almost flippant tune, which Beethoven used again and again during the work, and eventually turned into the magnificent, stately finale.

The hero of *Eroica*, MTT argued, was not Napoleon: his name had been angrily erased from the title page by Beethoven himself. Nor was it any one person in particular. It was not even that will o' the wisp, The Artist. The hero was Everyman and Everywoman, Michael said – each one of us, who has the courage to withstand the slings and arrows of outrageous fortune. The hero of *Eroica* is you, and you, and you, and you, and even me – all of us, who have the courage and the opportunity to stand up, declare our humanity and try to live a full life.

Michael's pleasure at actually being on location was also infectious. For the pilot show (Tchaikovsky's Fourth) we had a smaller budget and had stayed in San Francisco. But from then on, Europe was our oyster. To do justice to Beethoven, it meant frequent visits to Vienna – not only the stately palaces and concert halls, but some of the many, many apartments and cottages where the composer had lived. He was always being thrown out by angry landlords, who hated the "noise." The list included the modest house in Heiligenstadt, a hillside spa town (now a suburb of Vienna), where Beethoven had retreated, to come to terms first with his tinnitus and then his encroaching deafness. This little house is where he wrote a suicide note to his brother, and the way MTT told the story, right there in the low-ceilinged cottage, was deeply moving.

The second piece Michael chose was Stravinsky's *Rite of Spring* – a guaranteed winner in every way.

"This music", said Michael forcefully to camera, enjoying himself hugely, "is about sex and violence."

Again, MTT threw himself at the piano, to demonstrate just how revolutionary Stravinsky's music was. We licensed some excellent footage from the Joffrey Ballet, to show how strange were both the original costumes and the dance steps required for the ballet element. Truly, the sum total was a mesmerizing pagan festival, and this combination was undoubtedly why it had caused such a scandal at its Paris premiere, a century before.

Intercutting these elements and the piano with the orchestra's rehearsal and final performance required some brilliant editing, performed again by Blair Gershkow, under Joan Saffa's detailed and expert guidance. The secret sauce, however, was the presence from now on of Peter Grunberg in the cutting room. He was a charming Australian expert and an official pianist with the Symphony, and he prevented us from making many musical mistakes in the editing.

But the bonus extra, as ever, was the location work. MTT was fascinated to find the exact seat in which Stravinsky had sat in the *Théatre des Champs Elysées*, for the famous Paris première. Two camps of troublemakers had clashed during the performance – those who favored the new work, and those who were determined to find it profoundly abhorrent. There was a fistfight, right there in the auditorium. MTT, channeling Stravinsky, got up from his seat and rushed to the side of the stage, and into the wings. Pierre Monteux (no less) was conducting the orchestra that night in 1913. MTT demonstrated how Stravinsky had stood in the wings with dancer Vaslav Nijinsky, shouting the rhythms to the dancers, since they could not hear the orchestra above the shouting match in the auditorium.

The third composer MTT chose was Aaron Copland. Here, I have to declare a bias: as an Englishman brought up on European composers, I find Copland very hard to swallow. At his best – *Fanfare for the Common Man* – he is brilliant, in my opinion. At his worst (*Rodeo* is just one example) I find him mawkish and self-conscious. A nice Jewish boy pretending to be a cowboy? Oh, please. Give me Irving Berlin or Rogers and Hart or George Gershwin or any of the myriad of other early-to-mid 20th Century composers, who had fewer pretensions to grandeur. *Rodeo*, to me, is as stereotypical of the hokey "West" as the bronzes of Frederick Remington that we had featured in *The West of the Imagination*.

But the San Francisco Symphony needed an American composer, to please the punters, and MTT genuinely likes Copland's music, so there was nothing to be done about it. Joan Saffa did much of the work on that show. I am very grateful to her. She said it reminded her of her childhood. It certainly did not remind me of mine.

••

It was by no means certain that there would be any more *Keeping Score* films after the first four. The hugely generous Haas Junior Foundation's matching grant offer still stood, but matching it was getting really tough for John Kieser (by now the SFS's General Manager), the Development Office and the Board. The National Endowment of the Arts had kicked in a further six-figure sum, and the Board had emptied out their pockets again, but this was a mightily expensive undertaking. Each concert had to be recorded live, and that meant that, every time, Gary Halvorson and his traveling circus of highly paid technicians and shiny trucks had to travel up from Los Angeles and stay for a week. The sound of cash registers ringing was almost as loud as the music.

Then there were those (including MTT) who asked aloud why Joan Saffa, David Kennard and InCA Productions were creating all the films. Why not give someone else a chance? John Kieser maintained that it would be best to keep the style of the shows rather similar, because they'd been a big success, and to make a smoothly connected series out of the whole thing. The target for the SFS was ten films: one a year. Best not to rock the boat, John suggested, but perhaps an extra writer would bring a fresh element to the mixture? Charlie Pearson, an old friend of Joan's and an experienced scriptwriter, joined the team. It was the beginning of a great friendship.

Miraculously, the money for the second three-part series was finally raised and, without pausing for more than a couple of months, we set sail on the next three films: Dmitri Shostakovich's enigmatic *Fifth Symphony* – "music born of fear" under Stalin, as MTT described it; Hector Berlioz's hyper-romantic crowd pleaser *Symphonie Fantastique* and...

who was to be the American composer this time? MTT was adamant: it had to be Charles Ives. More about him later!

To take the smash hit first: the Berlioz work had everything necessary for a great documentary. Of course, there were plenty of great tunes and dramatic moments. In fact, the work could well have been used straight out of the box as the soundtrack for a creepy mystery or horror film with romantic interludes – though it was written eighty years before any such film was created.

The storyline was great, too. Young Hector hailed from an achingly boring French town, halfway between Lyon and the Swiss border. His father, the snobbish town doctor, sent him to Paris to study medicine, of course, and Hector, of course, hated medicine. He used to sneak out of the medical lectures, ignore the jars full of severed limbs and preserved fetuses (which we filmed, still *in situ*), and have a high old time with musicians of every sort, learning as he went. He missed the three-day revolution of 1830 because he was shut away in an Academy garret doing a three-day examination, to win the prestigious Prix de Rome. When he emerged, blinking, into the sunlight, his friend Victor Hugo told him:

"Sorry, *mon vieux*. You missed the revolution. But it's OK. Our side won."

MTT told these stories with relish. We invaded the famous French Academy in the heart of Paris and found the actual attic room where Berlioz had studied for the exam. Elderly French academicians, appalled to see a camera crew in their Holy of Holies, and to hear an American speaking to camera (*"Un Américain! Ça alors!"*), tutted and shushed us into near silence in their library. Michael had to do his final piece to camera actually whispering, which made it all the more fun.

There was even a great romantic backstory. Berlioz was besotted by a visiting Irish actress called Harriet Smithson, whom he had seen playing Ophelia in Paris in 1827. She had developed a more "naturalistic" (read: "over-the-top") style than the French drama companies thought dignified, and the role of Ophelia gave her the perfect opportunity to overact with relish. This was a scene we had a lot of fun reconstructing, in a studio in Oakland. For a few years, Harriet became the muse of a raft of French romantics. Berlioz wrote his *Symphonie Fantastique* for her, long before they had even met face-to-face. Finally, she realized how obsessed he was with her. She agreed first to become his lover and then to marry him at the old British Embassy, where we filmed MTT.

The marriage, as MTT recounted with delight and in detail, was a disaster. They had one child, but the real progeny of the relationship was the Symphony. It is an evergreen; but, as Michael explained, it also anticipated many of the musical tricks and inventions, which came to fruition much later in the century. One way or the other, it is a great story and made, I think, a very entertaining film.

At the opposite end of the emotional spectrum lies Dmitri Shostakovitch's *Fifth Symphony*. This is a very controversial work. It was composed at the height of Stalin's power in the 1930's. The big question has always been: was Shostakovich frightened into submission by Stalin's threats? Did he write a propaganda piece, to save his skin, at a time when many an artist and composer was being thrown into the Lubyanka prison? Or did he create something more subtle?

Again, we had a wonderful storyline on our hands, as well as a grimly imposing piece of music. And again, MTT attacked the story and the music with relish. We found the apartment where Dmitri was living, when he composed the piece: it had been preserved, but not yet opened as a museum. MTT stood in the gaunt stairwell, outside the front door, as the ancient gated elevator made its slow and sinister way up to the fourth floor: would it contain friend or foe? He explained that Shostakovich chose to sleep on the landing, outside the flat: if the secret police came for him, he explained to his family, they would not have to wake everyone up. They could just take the composer himself, for "questioning."

There is no room to recount all the stories, or even to list all the locations where we filmed. We had paid a previous visit to St. Petersburg for *Keeping Score*, when we told the story of Stravinsky's early life under the Czars, with glittering images of the Summer Palace. But now we were conjuring up the atmosphere of Leningrad, as the city had been renamed by the Soviets.

Our first visit was in the dead of winter: vast gray expanses of icy river and canals, with snow and slush in the gutters. Our Russian researcher found an old man who owned a large ex-Soviet government limousine, of the sort preferred by senior secret policemen in the 1930's. We filmed it at dawn, prowling along empty streets. In a surprise cut to the inside of the car, we discover MTT, clad in a warm overcoat, wearing a Russian fur hat with earflaps: the story he told of the fear that Stalin imposed on the arts was brutally effective.

Perhaps it was a reaction to this wintry aura of fear and desolation that led us to do two memorable things during our second visit to 'Leningrad,' when the weather was far better. One was to celebrate the 'White Nights' of mid-summer, when it never quite gets dark, being at such a northerly latitude. We hired a large and luxurious speedboat and invited a small group of Russians – our local fixer, researcher and crew, plus some friends and musicians – for an all-night vodka-drinking binge. It was a locally much appreciated way of saying "thank you."

We careened around the many narrow canals at a lunatic pace, singing songs and laughing wildly. It was after midnight, yet still light enough to read. Everywhere, the lifting bridges had been raised. Well after midnight, Russians of every age and income were carousing on ferries, singing as they chugged along in tiny dinghies, or falling down drunk on passing tugboats. My wife Lizzie had joined me on this trip, and says she has never had more fun, or indeed had a worse hangover the next day. We were so incapable of movement in our hotel room, having returned to bed at 4 a.m., that we entirely missed seeing the Hermitage Museum and the interior of the Winter Palace the following day. It's all a question of priorities, I suppose. I have no regrets.

The other memorable happy evening in St. Petersburg is of a long, laughter-filled dinner in a fancy restaurant, with MTT, Joshua Robison, John Kieser and the crew. Long after the restaurant normally closed, MTT and I challenged each other to a limerick-telling contest of epic proportions. I thought I knew more smutty limericks than most people, and I also believed that James Burke was the only person who knew more than me. How wrong I was: Michael Tilson Thomas won hands down – and they were all genuinely funny. Well, I suppose that, if you can memorize the entire score of Beethoven's *Eroica* and a hundred other symphonies by heart, memorizing a couple of hundred questionable limericks is child's play.

The final film in this second series of *Keeping Score* needed to feature another American composer, we were informed, to keep MTT and the Board happy. Preferably, it should be a maverick, an unusual choice, someone outside the normal repertoire. Michael's choice was immediate: Charles Ives. I am not sure whether John Kieser, our friend and manager at the Symphony, groaned out loud when the choice was announced, but it was clear that several people had some misgivings, including some members of the orchestra.

"Ives was crazy," said one of the first violins, when we interviewed her. "Schizophrenic. His Dad was, too."

That part of the interview with the violinist was vetoed. For Michael, Ives was a misunderstood genius, not a lunatic. Not at all. No way. He was offended even by the suggestion.

"Charles Who?" was my reaction, which goes to show how little I knew (and still know) about classical music.

Charles Ives was virtually discovered single-handedly by Aaron Copland in the mid-twentieth century, having languished in (some said) well-merited obscurity since around 1914. In a dynastic line of innovation, Copland had spotlighted Ives, Leonard Bernstein had championed Copland, and in turn MTT had grabbed the baton from Lenny. But what was so special about Ives?

"Well," explained John Kieser, "Much of Ives' music sounds like a train crash." This sounded fun: I knew John enjoyed trains as much as I did.

"In fact," he went on, "a series of train crashes. You'll find a weirder selection of percussion and oddball instruments onstage during an Ives work than at any other time. When did you last see a theramin?" I discovered that a theramin is a hefty cabinet-sized first-generation electronic instrument, which produces weird other-worldly sounds, reminiscent of a cat in pain, a flexible metal wood-saw played with a violin bow, or a huge Jew's Harp.

Ives was a noted businessman at the turn of the twentieth century. His day job was at a successful insurance company in New York City, which he had founded and co-owned. On his way to work, on the train from Danville, CT, he spent his time filling in the newly invented crossword puzzles in the newspaper. I started to suspect that this is what inspired him to start writing music that could be read as a series of 'up-and-down clues' as well as regular bar-by-bar left-to-right 'across' ones.

Ives' father had been the leader of the town band in Danville, a mildly prosperous manufacturing town, and had himself enjoyed musical experimentation. Long before it was possible to make location recordings, he had engaged two marching bands to march towards and then through and past each other, both playing different tunes, just "to hear what it sounded like." The worthy citizens of Danville, according to the local newspaper, thought it sounded like a grand mess, but it certainly provided an unusual afternoon's entertainment for large crowds of them.

Michael was shrewd in his choice of piece: we would feature Ives' *Holidays Symphony*. This at least gave us a structure for the film: the four seasons. Joan and a local cameraman went to work to capture some of the most beautiful photography of New England – from deep snow to the fiery orange of fall foliage – that I have ever seen. One of the four movements featured the July 4 celebrations, and so did we: we shot every classic Norman Rockwell image of the nation's Independence Day that you could find in Connecticut, from tiny tots in red, white and blue to parades, brass bands and magnificent firework displays.

The Ives music that this served to illustrate was also like all the Fourths of July you have ever enjoyed, all happening at once. Snatches of a dozen patriotic traditional tunes, marching bands, sound effects of rockets and explosions, babbling brooks and chuffing trains, everything from the buzzing of bees to the bubbling of a soda machine – it is all in there somewhere. It was as exhausting as a real day out on July 4, and that was just one of the four movements.

For the Thanksgiving movement, Ives pressed into service a piece he had written earlier for the pipe organ. Nothing daunted, MTT rolled up his sleeves and limbered up both his arms and legs. With barely five minutes of rehearsal, he sat down at the organ in the central church of New Haven, CT, just across the road from Ives' Alma Mater, Yale University, and threw himself into Ives' creation. I was glad that I had some experience of the instrument at Grandpa Kennard's knee (when I was eight years old) and with the Pipe Organ Centennial film ten years before. At least I knew where to put the cameras.

Leaving no cliché unturned, we also persuaded the Yale Whiffenpoofs to sing *a cappella* the famous ballad *At A Table Down at Morey's* – actually filming it in Morey's tavern. Ives himself, as a student, had enjoyed doing this, but the scene somehow got relegated to the DVD extras, alas. There was always just too much great material to fit into an hour's film on *Keeping Score* – a luxury not always available on many projects.

In retrospect it is bizarre to think that such a traditionalist as Ives – a great football player at Yale, an *insurance salesman* for God's sake – had concocted such very strange and revolutionary music. Was it before its time? Yes, it certainly was. It makes many of the experiments of John Cage and other modernists look tame by comparison. Of course, it may be the sort of music that will remain ahead of its time for ever.

• •

By this stage in the *Keeping Score* project, we had created seven films with MTT, at the rate of about one a year. Davies Hall, the Symphony's base in the City, felt like our second home. My monthly stipend from the project had put both my children through college.

Understandably, MTT was getting antsy: he had been loyal, but he was getting a bit sick of being directed – i.e. told what to do – by David Kennard. Joshua, his close friend and companion, told everyone that *no-one* in Michael's life consistently told him what to do, not even Joshua, with one exception: me. The honeymoon between us was clearly over, and MTT suggested to the Symphony Board that another director should be given a chance to do the final shows, however many there might be. We needed a complete change of style and pace, MTT suggested. We needed fancy animation, perhaps. We needed to do it all in a magnificent studio, perhaps. We needed to re-think the whole thing.

At issue was the fact that, in Michael's eyes, he had left the best till last: what he wanted to tackle now was Gustav Mahler. Again, here was the Copland-Bernstein-Tilson Thomas succession: each had worshipped the ground that Mahler composed on. How should these shows be made extra special?

A little bird told us that MTT phoned Martin Scorsese, the well-known movie director and a good friend of Michael's. He asked him what to do. Should he insist that the time-worn Kennard-Saffa team be replaced? New brooms were surely needed, weren't they? Could Marty give him the name of some fantastic young director in LA? But apparently, Scorsese had seen some of the shows, and he liked what he had seen.

"What's wrong with these films?" Scorsese apparently asked. "They work! They're great! Never make changes for the sake of change."

But Michael was determined to alter something. From now on, he told John Kieser, he would himself assume the role of director on location. He would decide how to choreograph the pieces to camera, where to place the camera, what would be said, and so on. And so it came to pass.

To be fair, Michael did a pretty good job, but he is so multi-talented that this should have been no surprise to me or anyone else. Why, he had even recently performed a complicated song-and-dance routine in a musical about his own family, the Thomashevskys – which, of course, he had also entirely written. So what was a little directing, to him?

His new role was made perfectly clear to our excellent chief cameraman, Ian Salvage. Ian winked at me, and we had a perfect understanding. He would make sure that MTT did not hoist himself on his own petard, as the English like to say. And of course, all the shots without Michael, including the scene-setting and the shots of the actor who played Mahler – the 'B Roll', as it is called, would be left to Joan and myself.

Good detective work from the whole team and our local fixers helped us to dig out some wonderful locations, including the house on an Austrian lake, which Mahler had owned during his ill-fated marriage and the traumatic death of his child. Now owned by a dentist from Vienna, the house was miraculously unchanged over the last hundred years. MTT prowled around it, describing Mahler's personal and private conflicts, as well as the sources of his inspiration. As ever, Vienna also provided moody backdrops for our every need. Even Budapest got into the picture, because this was where Mahler had premiered his *First Symphony*, the work that MTT wanted to feature.

This turned out to be a brilliant choice. The final season or series of *Keeping Score* consisted of just two one-hour films – after which the entire amazing budget had been well and truly spent. The first film was the story of young Mahler, growing up in the provincial Bohemian Czech town of Jihlava – not a vacation destination you need to bother with. Here he absorbed all the local influences, from Klezmer to folk bands, which later permeated his *First Symphony*.

Jewish by birth, he found it difficult to find a decent job in the Austro-Hungarian Empire's capital, Vienna, or to get his music performed there. Anti-Semitism was ingrained at every level, however elegantly or subtly. So he took a job as the Director of the Opera in Budapest. This required him to learn perfect Hungarian in less than six months, a daunting task. He later even converted to Catholicism, so that he could be considered for the most prestigious job in the musical world – Director of Music at the Vienna Opera, where Jews were still not welcome. Remarkably, he was offered the position: a testament to his enormous talent.

He composed his own music on the side, since he needed the day job, but he could not find anywhere to get it performed in Austria. Finally, the *First Symphony* was premiered in Budapest, where it was received, according to one critic, with "tepid applause and scattered boos." Its massive length and strange sounds baffled the audience.

During the course of this first Mahler film, MTT explains that the misunderstood *First Symphony* contains the seeds of all the masterworks Mahler would go on to compose during his tragically short fifty-year life. Everything resonated with his traumatic childhood and youthful experiences in Jihlava. This thought would have resonated with Vienna's *enfant terrible,* Sigmund Freud, and indeed Mahler went to see Freud on one occasion. He interrupted the great psychoanalyst's summer vacation in Holland, to share his troubles and general dyspepsia. Freud apparently told him, during a long walk along the beach, that the best treatment was to keep calm and carry on composing.

Part Two of the Mahler epic – the second film – illustrates how key passages in Mahler's later works brilliantly amplified the early inspiration of his *First Symphony*. This second film, by itself, would have been unsatisfactory, if you had not seen Part One, because there were so many haunting references to his first work. I think it was John Kieser's insight, as General Manager of the Symphony, that Joan Saffa and I should construct a bridge between the two films, so that the final DVD could be a two-hour film that rolls both parts into one new whole. Towards the end of Part Two, Joan constructed a most beautiful montage, which gently brings together many of the most moving themes in Mahler's music, to reveal the soul of the genius and give a subtle overview of his life.

For me, the result was a revelation: we had created a cinema-length movie that told a subtle, evolving and deeply moving tale. Even though it was two hours long, it could be viewed without any sense of tedium. I realized that, whatever else I had the energy to attempt, I would try to create my first feature-length documentaries. Those were to be the trilogy of wine films, *"A Year in..."* – see Chapter 24.

I look back on my nearly ten-year affair (so to speak) with Michael Tilson Thomas with great affection. He taught me to understand great music – at least, just a little bit. He could be snippy, or caustic. Some days, as they say in the trade, he would just "phone in" his performance. But at other times, he was funny, companionable and of course a genius in the interpretation of music. As Jacob Bronowski said of Isaac Newton, we should not expect great men to be constant friends or reliable party animals. They have too much going on in their heads.

I think MTT is indeed a great artist. What he has done in Miami with the New World Symphony (NWS), America's greatest teaching orchestra, is ample proof of that. Michael both founded the NWS and found the funding for it. He is at heart a teacher, who feels a responsibility to pass on precious knowledge to future generations.

I was very happy when I heard that John Kieser, who remains a great friend, left the San Francisco Symphony and went to work with Michael and the NWS in Florida. That is where MTT is creating his best work today. He even got Frank Gehry to design the new NWS building for him. But then, Frank Gehry was MTT's baby-sitter, back in Los Angeles in the 1940's. His long-term friends stay loyal.

■■

23. JOURNEY OF THE UNIVERSE:
THE HISTORY OF EVERYTHING

You might think, from reading the last chapter, that I spent the entire time from 2002 to 2012 in helping to create *Keeping Score* with Michael Tilson Thomas. Well, all work and no play make Jack a dull boy, and I was happily able to keep more than one pot boiling on the stovetop.

Back in the year 2000, as part of our work on the series, *The Promise of Play*, its executive producer Stuart Brown had suggested that we should interview the cosmologist, planetary physicist and philosopher Brian Swimme.

"Huh?" was what I thought, "A cosmologist, talking about play?"

But, being a well-brought-up English lad, I am sure I muttered something like "What an interesting idea, Stuart", and did nothing about it. As Dirk Niepoort, the witty Portuguese-German winemaker we filmed fifteen years later, remarked:

"When the English say 'How interesting', they mean exactly the opposite."

But Stuart was relentless in his ambition and determined to introduce characters to *The Promise of Play*, who had *not* been suggested by our irritating official expert, Brian Sutton Smith. So I agreed that Brian Swimme should be invited to join us at one of the filming sessions in San Francisco's hands-on science museum, the Exploratorium. And, time permitting, we would give him an interview. Why not?

The Exploratorium is a wonder to behold. Since we filmed in the year 2000, it has outgrown its premises in the 1915 Panama Pacific Exhibition building, the Palace of Fine Arts, and moved to a far more tourist-friendly location at the water's edge on San Francisco's Embarcadero. But back in the day, it was still as it had been in the 1970's: the world's first science museum to proudly announce that it had no exhibit that you could not touch, manipulate or participate in.

Brian was part of a group of people we invited to enjoy a hands-on day of exploration at the Exploratorium. The group included our son and daughter, James and Pippa, and a motley selection of fun-lovers and experts in various fields, who would throw themselves with abandon into playful experimentation.

Brian was a treat. He was also one of the handful of interviewees and on-camera experts I have worked with, who are definitely taller than me. That rather short (ha!) list includes John Kenneth Galbraith and John Cleese: they are all substantially taller than my 6 foot 2 inches. They have helped me come across as a little less of a control freak (my wife tells me) than I would do otherwise. But, back to the subject in hand...

Brian explained, for *The Promise of Play*, that the Universe itself is profoundly playful. One of the only things that Einstein may have got wrong is his suggestion that "God does not play dice." All sorts of random and unpredictable events seem to have emerged over the last thirteen billion years. Look at quarks: now you see them, now you don't. A lot of the very silly and non-functional stuff that emerges over time usually gets swallowed up by evolution, but... wait a minute. Would God – if (s)he exists – have chosen giraffes, hippopotamuses or camels to continue to survive, if (s)he did not have a sense of humor? They each occupy a defined niche in the ecosystem, however bizarre that niche is.

More seriously, Brian suggested, the randomness and joyful creativity of the Cosmos is *by definition* playful. Unless you take every word of the world's holy texts literally, the entire 13.82 billion years of the existence of the Universe has been a great game, leading to... well, who knows? The game is by no means over yet.

Brian Swimme's interview was a great tonic in *The Promise of Play*, which would otherwise have been drowned in a sea of half-baked pop psychology. It's ironic, really, that our so-called play expert, Professor Sutton Smith, should also have been called Brian. Apart from Monty Python's *Life of Brian*, where the man is confused with Jesus, I do not run into many Brians. Like Nigel, Clive and Bruce, it is a very British-sounding name that, in itself, inspires no great confidence, I find.

I had no idea in 2000 that I would meet Brian Swimme again, then go on to create an international film with him, and finally be invited to become a Distinguished Adjunct Professor, teaching graduate students in San Francisco at his side. But I am getting ahead of myself.

If you run a small documentary production company, and if you have had the same office phone number for twenty years, you get used to receiving a few strange calls out of the blue. They usually start: "You don't know me, but..." and then go on to suggest that the person calling has a very gifted son or daughter, who would benefit greatly from an internship with InCA Productions. Or else they are trying to sell us insurance. Or else they have muddled our number with that of an aggressive ambulance-chasing law firm down the road.

In 2009, I had a call from an English woman whom I will just call Caroline.

"You don't know me," she said, "But I have an idea that will interest you."

I was about to trot out the usual litany of kindly half-truths about being a bit busy just now, and so on. But then she mentioned Brian Swimme: she had attended a number of his lectures and was a big fan of his. Indeed, she sounded as if she believed he could walk on water.

"I do know Brian," I replied, but Caroline insisted on coming to see me, and on brokering my re-introduction to Professor Swimme. She felt that he was just the person to do a "Complete History of Everything": the whole shebang, all 13.82 billion years of it, in a series of films, or perhaps one blockbuster movie.

I duly met with Caroline and Brian. It found that Brian sparked all sorts of creative ideas in me, and apparently vice versa. He was both a planetary physicist by training and a philosopher by inclination, but he was also really open, charming and completely genuine. He had a natural enthusiasm and kindness, which I found infectious, and I believed he would be extremely effective on camera, if well directed. Until that date, his videos had been mostly recordings of his live lectures, and that format nearly always comes across as dull and unimaginative. But even in these simple videos, Brian plainly had star potential.

Brian and I agreed to do a long hike together – alone – on the wild hilltops of the Marin Headlands, a couple of miles from my office. We discussed ideas for a possible film. We agreed that it would have to have its feet on the ground in a central location somewhere on earth – not a studio with a make-believe spaceship, like *Cosmos*, but a real place. We kicked around the idea of a small town somewhere in backwoods California: it might work, if it had a high school and a library and a few different locations, which could trigger ideas in Brian's head. But then we agreed that it had to be somewhere more iconic: a horrible word, but justified here, I think. It had to be a metaphor for human understanding of the universe, but also a real, down-to-earth community.

Then I remembered the sequence that Adrian Malone had filmed with Jacob Bronowski thirty-five years before, on the Greek island of Samos. This was the home of Pythagoras, a figure who straddled two worlds: one was religious mysticism – he was a guru to a large bunch of followers on the island; the other was modern science – he believed in the value of unambiguous proofs. The 3:4:5 proof of the right (-angled) triangle is what most people have heard of, but his work went much deeper than that: he believed that the entire universe was governed by numbers – in other words, by mathematical rules, which were there to be discovered by humans.

"Why don't we film you entirely on Samos? Interacting with historical locations and also with the ordinary, everyday life of the people?" I asked Brian. "Then we can add special effects and archive film in post-production? It could make an amazing visual, emotional and intellectual ride."

Brian loved the idea, but our problem was Caroline. She was well-meaning, but somewhat out of her depth in these creative waters. She was also very dull to spend time with: she seemed to suck the air out of any room she was in. I am ashamed to say that I left it to Brian to tell her this, in the kindest way possible. We paid her a fee, to thank her for making the introduction, and sailed on without her. This sounds callous, and maybe it is, but I have learned that you cannot afford to sail the seas of filmmaking, when someone is acting like an anchor, dragging along the seabed behind you.

The same thing had happened with Doug, the sound engineer who had introduced me to Reid Dennis on the Amelia Earhart project. In that case, we had kept him on through the first two legs of the flight. It was my co-producer Joan Saffa who had waved the red flag: Doug had gone on ahead of the planes to set up some complicated arrangements in Brazil and had not done well. We had paid him off in the same way, gave him a credit on the film, and sailed onwards.

With Caroline gone, the issue of fund-raising raised its head, all too predictably. We needed big money, to pull this thing off: thirteen billion years to cover! But lo and behold, there was someone else waiting in the wings, who would make the entire project possible.

She seemed an unlikely candidate as executive producer and chief fund-raiser, but how wrong I was!

At my first meeting with Mary Evelyn Tucker, I got the impression that she was primarily a devoted academic. At that time, she and her husband John Grim were both itinerant teachers, lecturing for the time being at UC Berkeley on the connections between ecology and religion. Later, they both managed to score permanent positions at Yale, with almost identical job titles: Senior Lecturers and Senior Research Scholars at the Yale School of Forestry and Environmental Studies. (Yale had a school of forestry? Who knew?)

Brian respected Mary Evelyn and the contribution she could make to the project, particularly from spiritual, environmental and feminine (not to say feminist) viewpoints. They both admired the work of Father Thomas Berry, an influential writer on the links between faith and the future of the planet, and knew him personally. Even more exciting, Mary Evelyn suggested that she knew where possible treasure was buried: funding to develop and later to produce the film.

We launched a series of intensive meetings – just Mary Evelyn, Brian and myself – in the little bungalow she was renting a mile or two from the Berkeley campus. For six weeks we worked together, putting the most important concepts, locations, images and ideas onto three-by-five cards, and dividing them up into ten 'chapters,' as a way of slicing and dicing the last thirteen-plus billion years.

This was an astonishing experience. On *Cosmos*, Carl Sagan had already chewed up much of the intellectual food, and regurgitated what he felt were the tastiest morsels, before we ever started working on the programs. But this time, we were starting from scratch: what would be in the film or films and – more importantly – what would not?

It is, of course, an act of immense hubris to try and do this, but documentary producers like to hide behind those weasel words "A Personal View by..." whoever is in front of camera. That means: "It's up to Brian what's in and what's out, so take it or leave it, and if you don't like his selection, that's your problem." This approach was first tried and tested by Kenneth Clark and Jacob Bronowski at the BBC. Over the years it has saved me and many other producers from the slings and arrows of angry academics, irritated beyond measure that their favorite shard of wisdom has not been included.

Right through the process of selecting the content, it was unclear whether we were going to create one long film, or several short films. Everything depended on the success of the fund-raising. I really could not quite believe that Mary Evelyn Tucker was going to pull it off: academics are usually hopeless at making presentations and prying anything but modest research grants out of foundations. But we needed a good deal more than a million dollars to do this project, complete with galactic animations.

Long story short, Mary Evelyn did it. She raised enough money to carry us right through the production stage: we could book our tickets to Samos, way down south in the Greek islands, just a mile from the Turkish coast. Within a few weeks, we were on a series of planes to London, Athens and Samos, for the scouting trip: Brian, Mary Evelyn, myself – and Lizzie.

This was the last major InCA production that involved Lizzie, so it has a special place in my heart. She had always been a superbly well-organized Associate Producer and Production Manager, trained by the BBC. She had graduated to full Producer rank while working with me on various projects, but in reality, her heart was now in her new studies and subsequent profession: psychology. She was well on her way to her second Master's degree, and our children were already at college in England. The Samos project was just too tempting, however: she loved Brian's wit and wisdom, and she wanted to help launch us into the production in a professional way.

We spent three fascinating weeks on Samos, guided by a young English-speaking student who was a native of the island. Lizzie had found her through that wonder of the new millennium, the internet. We became a team of friends, enjoying both laughter and insight. We struggled up mountain paths to Pythagoras's cave, we visited monasteries and markets, ancient Greek sites and museums. We looked for impressive vistas, we discovered tiny rural churches, barely twelve feet square, with ceilings covered in stars. Each place was a possible metaphor for some part of the story of the universe.

The pleasure of that first trip, on reflection, was partly the pure thrill of discovery and of creative improvisation. It was also partly the fact that a scouting trip avoids the everyday worries of actual filming. It is such a pleasure to absorb a culture and build a script without constantly thinking:

"Are we on schedule? Is it going to start raining? How soon? Can we afford to bribe this shepherd into taking his damn sheep somewhere else? Do we have to give the camera crew a lunch break? Is that plane going to ruin the soundtrack?"

It turned out that there was another factor at play: we were two men and two women – a balanced team, with an all-round perspective. Best of all, Lizzie was there to say honestly "I simply don't understand that," when Brian or Mary Evelyn got too abstract or intellectual. My problem is that I am sometimes too tactful or too uncertain (or too afraid) to say what I really mean, after the first take on a film shot, or the first sketch of a piece of script.

On our return from the scouting trip, we set to work. Lizzie was constructing schedules. Brian and Mary Evelyn were planning exactly where on the island of Samos to say what. I was working up a budget with InCA's long-time business manager, Cheryl King, who knew how much such ventures really cost.

We then had some bad news: the student who had been our guide on the scouting trip was now back at college and no longer available, so Lizzie had to find someone else. She discovered Evangelia Agadaki – "Vange", as she insisted on being known: a Greek woman who lived on Samos but had spent much of her life in South Africa. She spoke perfect English and ran a small travel company with her husband Kirk, so she knew every inch of the island. She also knew exactly how to get permission to go anywhere and do anything on Samos: when to get an official permit from Athens, and when to ignore protocol and press a One Hundred Euro bill into some official's hand. She was completely truthful, dependable and accurate – and also, a very kind and loving person. Bravo Vange, and bravo Lizzie for finding her. Having a great local fixer can transform filming from a grueling endurance test into a real pleasure.

Lizzie also recommended a great London-based cameraman, who was an old friend of hers: Mike Fox. He had shot some of *The Heart of the Dragon,* for director Mischa Scorer. Mike was a legend. He agreed to put together a team of three technicians for the film, including his favorite soundman, Mike Lax, also a veteran of the industry. Mike Fox plus Mike Lax? It sounded like a comedy duo or a cure for constipation – Fox'n'Lax. But they were the best we could wish for. As it turned out, however, neither one of them was able to help us.

Almost at the last minute, Mike Fox called us in California: he was on contract for a feature film, which he had reckoned would never be green-lighted for production. Unexpectedly, they had completed their funding and were ready to start. So Mike Fox could not come with us. This was a terrible blow. A good cameraman can make or break any film, particularly one that was designed to be as moody, beautiful and evocative as the scripts we had planned.

"I'm really, really sorry," said Mike, "But I've found you someone who's every bit as good as me – honestly. I can guarantee that you'll like him. He's called Ian Salvage."

Well, what could we do? There seemed to be an ominous ring to Ian's family name: would we be forced to salvage what he shot from the wreckage? But it was too late to do anything else: Ian was hired, and Mike Lax was still contracted to be the sound recordist. We took Simon Muriel, a former InCA intern and already an accomplished associate producer, as the third member of the crew.

In April 2006, we all traveled to Samos to start the first shoot. As usual, the production people – Lizzie and I – went first, to meet Vange and make sure things were set up properly. Then came Brian Swimme and Mary Evelyn, with a couple of days to discuss plans and get over jet lag. Finally, Simon Muriel escorted the film crew from London to Samos, where we met them at the airport.

The sun was shining. It was a glorious spring afternoon. We had planned just one hour of filming that first day, without Brian or Mary Evelyn, to get to know the camera crew as a team. We filmed at a potter's studio in a rural village. Everyone was in high spirits.

"Great to see you again, Dave," said Mike Lax, in his Cockney London accent. "It's been a few years. So you can still find work, can you?"

He had always been a joker, since I had known him at the BBC. This kind of friendly joshing is all part of the fun of working with British crews, who tend to take themselves less seriously than their opposite numbers in the US. That evening, we had a grand celebratory dinner, organized by Lizzie and Vange, to launch the filming.

"Welcome to Samos" said Vange and Kirk, her husband. They toasted us in the wine of the island, which is excellent. There was roast lamb, every sort of Mediterranean seafood and grilled vegetables, Greek music and of course Ouzo. Ouzo is the Greek equivalent of the Chinese liquor, Mou Tai – and the effect of Mou Tai is lethal, as I describe in Chapter 9.

We had our celebration dinner at the start of the trip in part because Lizzie needed to get back to California, to continue the studies for her Master's in Organizational Psychology, and to see James and Pippa. Once the arrangements were firmly settled with Vange, she felt she was no longer needed on Samos, and wanted to get back home. So the next morning, we got up at dawn, and I drove her thirty miles to the island airport. While I was away, we had planned an early morning shoot of some scenic vistas, which Simon Muriel would direct, with Ian Salvage and the team.

I will never forget the next few hours. I was just kissing Lizzie goodbye and watching her walk towards Passport Control, when her mobile phone rang. She answered it, and her face went white. After a fairly short conversation, she came back out.

"Oh my God," she said, "Mike Lax is dead."

I took the phone from her. The cameraman, Ian Salvage, was on the line. He was profoundly shocked.

"We had a call time of 8 a.m. in the lobby," he said. "When Mike didn't turn up, I thought it was odd, because he is always on time, very professional. So I went and knocked on his door. No reply, so I went and found the manager, who opened the door with a passkey. Mike didn't seem to be in his room, but as we started to leave, I tried the bathroom door. Something was blocking it, but I pushed and – there he was, on the floor. He must have been in the middle of shaving, when he had a heart attack. It was not a nice sight. The manager and I looked for signs of life: no breath, no heartbeat. It must have happened less than an hour before. He was still warm."

We immediately canceled all plans for filming for that day and the day after. Lizzie and I conferred: there was nothing that she could do for us on Samos that couldn't be better done by Vange and Kirk. Since she was on her way back to London via Athens, she suggested that she should contact the British Embassy there, and ask for instructions: what should we do with the body of a British citizen? When she got to London, she would see Mike Lax's wife. Ian Salvage, meanwhile, promised to call Mike's wife immediately and personally explain what had happened.

I returned to the hotel, feeling as if I was in a dream. There was a somber mood. The police were there, with a local doctor. Everyone was being very professional. But it all seemed unreal. Just the evening before, Mike had been the life and soul of our celebration party. Now he was gone. I thought back to the event, twelve hours before: had we given him too much to drink? Had we encouraged him to overtax himself? Should we have sandwiched in that one-hour shoot on the way from the airport? I felt awful: it seemed like it was all my fault.

The police questioned all of us, and Vange called an undertaker. Brian and Mary Evelyn sat in the lobby, silent and pale-faced. We all gathered around them.

"It's no-one's fault," said Ian. "This is how Mike Lax would like to have gone – suddenly and without fuss. He was doing his job, the job he's done so well for forty years or more. I spoke to his wife, and of course she couldn't believe it. He had seemed so fit when he left. I said that Lizzie would contact her, and that we'd see her at London Airport when we returned, after the filming."

That day we all spent quietly, either alone or in little groups of two and three. Ian, ever the professional, phoned other sound men he knew in London, to find someone who could come out immediately, pick up Mike's sound equipment and allow us to resume work.

"The show must go on," he said. "Mike would have wanted that."

For Brian and Mary Evelyn, who knew very little about the toughness of film crews and the problems of location filming, this was all extraordinary, even shattering. They fretted that it seemed like a bad omen. Should we cancel the film trip, in respect for Mike? Ian told them a couple of true stories about accidents he had witnessed on film locations.

"When you're out in the real world," he said, "You can't control things. I'm desperately sorry for Mike's wife, because I think they were very close. But Mike died on location – in battle, as it were."

The following day, Ian went and quietly filmed some beauty shots of the island, with Vange and Simon Muriel. They did not need sound for these. I went to the airport to meet the replacement sound technician. Brian spent some time alone, thinking no doubt about the meaning of life, and re-writing some of his pieces to camera. He and Mary Evelyn went for a long walk, and no doubt talked about spiritual and philosophical things.

The third day, we started filming, and Brian was brilliant on camera. Somehow, Mike's death had focused all of us. It gave added resonance to Brian's fundamental message – that humankind was responsible not only for learning about the universe ("we are the way the universe is conscious of itself"), but also for acting as the stewards of the planet. He called for compassion and insight. Miraculously, he was able to memorize perfectly what he wanted to say, and then deliver it to camera without any notes, word perfect, as if he had just thought of each idea. The day ended with our filming the Midnight Mass at the cathedral in the town of Karlovassi.

The fourth day, Sunday, was the Greek Orthodox Easter. We dedicated it to the memory of Mike Lax and did not work that day.

■■

It took three trips to Samos, in three different seasons, to complete all the filming. Brian's to-camera pieces covered everything from the Big Bang (or "The Flaring Forth", as Brian preferred) to the current despoiling of the earth by careless, greedy human beings. All told, we filmed more than ten hours of material with Brian alone, so that we could make a full ninety-minute feature film, and a longer educational series as well.

In addition, we filmed all the daily activity of the island: music and folk-dancing at a tiny open-air tavern on a hilltop, country markets full of fish and vegetables, everyday life in the port, Pythagoras's cave, mysterious ruined castles, and massive twenty-foot statues of ancient Greek gods in the museum. Each location was a metaphor for some part of the Universe's thirteen-billion-year history, or provided some allegorical connection with, say, the formation of planets from stars, or the development of the simplest life forms.

The structure of the film, we had agreed, would run from pre-dawn, through an entire day, visiting a wonderful range of different locations, with special emphasis on beaches, streams, mountains – all the natural wonders of Samos – as well as on the colorful inhabitants of the island. The climax of the film – as we entered the modern era, was to take place late in the evening, as the hands of the Samos City church clock moved inexorably towards midnight. Thirteen billion years would be compressed into one earth-day.

Brian and I had created this structure to give an elegant conceptual framework to the show. The first scene would be shot at night, introducing Brian on the deck of the local inter-island ferry, a lone figure, staring out at a dark sea. At first light, he would arrive at the Karlovassi ferry port. During the day, he would slowly tell the story of *The Journey of the Universe*. Of course, that "day" took many weeks to film. But when cut together, as the church clock advanced to noon, and onwards to afternoon, sunset, and the evening, we would be following the unfolding of the universe – from the Big Bang to the formation of galaxies, the stars, our sun, the planets, our Earth, the emergence of life and the evolution of Homo Sapiens. The film would end, looking into the future, on the stroke of midnight.

It would be quite a tall order to fit all this into a ninety-minute film. We also had to leave room for animated sequences – mostly depictions of galaxies and star systems – and archive film, to depict the wild and irrepressible growth of life on earth, from single cells to complex creatures. But, nothing ventured, nothing gained. Back at InCA's offices in the Bay Area, we started on the daunting task of editing – at first, on paper, while we sorted out the best takes and the most promising material.

For six years, InCA had in fact been located in our house in Mill Valley. When it was time for James and Pippa to go to high school, Lizzie and I had decided that we should try to get them into the bi-lingual French American International School in San Francisco. After four years, they could sit for the International Baccalaureate, a golden key to getting into a top-rated university anywhere in the world. For a year, James commuted from Mill Valley into San Francisco, but this didn't work: having to run for the bus home each afternoon, he was making no friends in the city.

Lizzie had the bright idea that we should rent an apartment in San Francisco to live in for the duration, but also keep the house in Mill Valley and move InCA into it. So it was to our house that Mary Evelyn and Brian came one day, to look at some of the first assembled sequences for the film, and to give us some bad news.

One of the family foundations, which had promised to support us, had already given us the first half of a major two-part grant. But now, they had just told Mary Evelyn that the second half would not be available: the foundation's priorities had changed, and support for films and education had been canceled. That meant that we were several hundred thousand dollars short of our full budget. Suddenly, there was very little money left.

I was aghast. We had many months of editing in front of us. We had to create expensive animations, license extensive archive film, commission up to an hour of music, sweeten and mix the soundtrack, do the titles, develop the final online prints, wrap up the paperwork... All this would require the full budget. So I proposed that we should halt all work until the missing money was replaced by grants from other sources.

At this point, Mary Evelyn stepped up and assumed full responsibility as the Executive Producer, since she had raised all the money so far. She announced that the project simply could not wait until further funds were raised.

"Who knows when that will be?" she asked. "The film has to be drastically shortened and completed as a one-hour special for PBS."

Now I really was aghast. I felt that this would make the movie a joke. The history of the universe in fifty-seven minutes? It sounded like a speeded-up, Benny Hill sketch. I resisted, and begged Brian and Mary Evelyn to think again. But Mary Evelyn was implacable.

"If you don't like it, David," she said, "We'll have to find someone else to finish the film."

Luckily for me, InCA was still producing the *Keeping Score* series for the San Francisco Symphony, so we had no problem with paying the staff. But it was a real kick in the gut for me to be asked to walk away from a show in which I had invested so much effort and thought. I tried remonstrating with Brian, but he reluctantly backed Mary Evelyn's decision: better to get the show finished than to leave it hanging in mid-air, with no clear assurance that it would ever be completed.

So I was effectively fired from my position as Senior Producer (though I kept the Director credit) and the project was withdrawn from InCA. This was the first time this had happened to me, I think, since I had co-founded the company in 1984, more than 25 years before. It was a shock.

In due course, the project was given to a very capable local editor, Patsy Northcutt, to complete. I have no doubt that she accepted quite a modest fee to do the work, and Mary Evelyn and Brian spent a lot of time, entirely unpaid, helping to shoehorn the content into a fifty-seven-minute sized slipper.

To be honest, I was pretty upset about all this: it is a blow to one's professional and personal self-regard, to be replaced in this way. I thought I had helped to create some fabulous material: I was one of the parents of this squalling child, and I hated losing custody of it. But, not being one to nurse grievances, I tried to forget about it and concentrate on other projects.

Less than a year later, the show was completed. It had been named *The Journey of the Universe* – a title I disliked, at least in part because it made no sense to me. A journey suggests a point of departure, a linear trajectory and a planned destination, surely? "Journey" was one of those silly words that had become fashionable for no good reason: everything had to be seen as a journey, particularly in some academic circles. I could understand that a lifetime might be seen as one, but the entire history of everything? That seemed a bit of a stretch.

I heard all about this, and indeed about everything else, through Patsy, because Mary Evelyn had cut off all direct contact with me. She had not even invited me to comment on the final cut of the film. I tried my hardest to think charitable thoughts.

But finally I had to admit that Mary Evelyn Tucker, whom I had once dismissed as a hidebound academic, was a brilliant Executive Producer. She single-handedly rescued the project from the jaws of defeat. She has dedicated much of her life to the film since its premiere, and to the many spin-offs which have come from it: the website, the book (written by Brian), dozens of foreign-language versions and screenings throughout the world, an educational interview series and an online college course. The project is still developing and "complexifying" (as Brian likes to say about the universe), even today.

Mary Evelyn even persuaded the San Francisco PBS station (KQED) to run the show in four parts, interrupted by fund-raising pitches, as what they call a Pledge Special, and it did so well that PBS distributed it nationally as a fund-raising show. It went on to win a Regional Emmy for Outstanding Achievement: Documentary. The whole world seemed to love it.

By now, I have sat through many screenings of the fifty-seven-minute version and have come to like the final film quite a bit. I was happy enough to share the credits with Patsy Northcutt, who is a very nice person, besides being a real professional. But deep down, I still mourn the film that could have been made: a real blockbuster gee-whizz ninety-minute big screen experience, with a little more majesty and spectacle, and a little less sense of hurry and fluster.

Happily, I am now back on speaking terms with Mary Evelyn Tucker and have become great friends with Brian. He invited me to co-teach a graduate course with him at the College where he is a Professor – CIIS, the California Institute for Integral Studies in San Francisco. Using excerpts from some of the shows I had produced during the previous forty-five years, he and I encouraged our students to consider the relationship between Cosmology and the Modern Media.

The students were so excited by the opportunity to think visually and in story-telling terms, instead of preparing academic papers, that they began to create their own ideas for documentaries. We incorporated these ideas into the class. Suddenly, we found that we were teaching a class in creativity, and the students were loving it. Three of them went on to make their own feature documentary film on the future of energy. It was then that I realized that I was doing for the first time what I had secretly always wanted to do – teaching.

"Come on, David," said Brian, over one of our regular lunches at a restaurant in downtown San Francisco. "That's what you've been doing for more than forty years: teaching. So have I. But you've taught tens of millions of people, and I've probably only taught a few thousand."

It was a typically generous thing for Brian to say. He is one of the warmest, cleverest, most insightful and yet humble human beings I have ever known. He is also a ton of fun, and I am privileged to be able to call him a friend. It was he who encouraged me, based on the classes we co-taught, to write this book of memoirs. Thank you for everything, Brian.

24. THE WORLD OF WINE: FROM JOHN CLEESE TO GEVREY CHAMBERTIN

In Spring 2003, InCA Productions occupied quite fancy and expensive premises on Miller Avenue, the boulevard leading from the freeway into the heart of Mill Valley. The trees rustled quietly, and the sun shone into the office through big, California windows. We were busy with *Keeping Score*, the Symphony series, but not so busy that we couldn't produce another project at the same time. One day, the phone rang.

"Hello. InCA Productions", said our new paid intern, a young woman with high hopes of becoming a filmmaker one day. There was a pause.

"Yes, I'm sure you are," she said, "And I'm the Queen of England." She put the phone down and laughed.

"Who was that?" I called out, from my office.

"Someone who said he was John Cleese!" she said. "As if!"

I rushed out of my office. "No, no, it probably *was* John Cleese," I stammered.

"I thought it was *you* for a minute," said the girl. "Having one of your jokes. But it couldn't have been you, because you're *here*!"

The phone rang again, and this time it was me who answered it. "John!" I said, "How nice to hear from you! Just one moment…"

I stepped back into my office to take the call and closed the door, while the staff looked at each other in bewilderment. Were they going to be working with the Monty Python team?

In fact, Lizzie and I had met Cleese about three months earlier. He was the star guest speaker at a predictably dull convention of lawyers, in the bowels of San Francisco's Hilton Hotel.

"I was hired to give them a bit of a laugh at the end of their three days of torture," Cleese explained afterwards, when we took him out to supper. "I only do that sort of thing for the money, you understand." It was quite a lot of money, we learned later.

After the meal, we drove John to the airport, having had a really enjoyable time. He was flying back to his new home in Santa Barbara, having recently moved from London to California. He was fed up with England, he told us, and particularly fed up with the London press, which was obsessed with the idea that he had lost his sense of humor.

"Small-minded bloody people, the English," he said. "I'm glad to be out here in the sunshine."

John and I had a mutual friend – Karl Sabbagh, who had co-founded InCA Productions with me back in 1984. He and his wife had met John, while all three had been students at Cambridge University, and were involved in producing comedy shows with the famous Footlights group. When John told Karl that he was moving to California, Karl suggested that he should contact me, if he was ever in San Francisco.

"You never know, John," Karl had said. "You might want to do a documentary one day." And so it had come to pass.

"I've been approached by the Food Channel," John told me on the phone. "They want me to do a whole series about wine. Well, they can forget that. I might do a single special, perhaps. But I'm not going to do it with the director they sent me from Los Angeles. Are you interested?"

My second self, the prankster who had always been lurking just beneath the façade of the serious documentary maker, could hardly believe it. The chance to create something with John Cleese? Yes, indeed – in a heartbeat!

"What's your schedule like?" asked John. "I think I need to give them an answer fairly soon."

"I'll drop everything," I said, not even pretending to be cool or diffident. "I could drive down tomorrow."

"Oh great," said John. "You can stay at my place if you like. We should be able to work something out in a day or so. You write, don't you?"

Somewhere in the background, I could hear a heavenly choir singing on the soundtrack of my life.

"Yes, I did bits and pieces with Mike Palin and Terry Jones of the Pythons, when I was at Oxford," I said, stretching the truth a little. All I had done was to walk onstage and give them a tray of custard pies, one of which was planted in my face. "And I've written few sketches since then. And been in the Oxford Christmas Pantomime, as Idle Jack." I was chattering nervously by now. "But we'd be doing a documentary, wouldn't we?"

"Yes, we would, but there's no harm in having a bit of a laugh as well," said John. "Try and make it down here by lunch-time and I'll have something to eat standing by. Something to drink as well. It's a wine film, isn't it? We might as well start doing the research as soon as possible."

The five-and-a-half-hour drive south seemed to pass in a flash. I spent the time thinking about a short film I had created for the Napa Valley visitor center, in 2001. It was an introduction to winemaking, featuring Robert Mondavi (in person – he was not just a brand) and other stars of Napa. It had been my own brief crash course in how wine is created. But I still knew very little about the subject in hand – as ever!

"Welcome to paradise," said John, as he came out to greet me on arrival at his ranch in Montecito, the upmarket suburb of Santa Barbara. "Oh no, I forgot, you managed to escape from England too. God, it feels good, doesn't it?"

He was very friendly – a little older, a little grayer and a little plumper than I had remembered, but he had lost none of his humor, so far as I could see. He took me round the grounds of his house. There was a stable block, "for my daughter's horses", he explained, and there was a small zoo, which had a colorful assortment of exotic birds and a random selection of small to medium-sized mammals.

"I love zoos," he said. "Always have, ever since I was a boy in Weston-super-Mare. Of course, that's what led to my biggest disaster so far."

I politely enquired what that disaster was.

"It was *Fierce Creatures*," he explained. "Immediately after I did *A Fish Called Wanda*, with Jamie Lee Curtis and Kevin Costner, I decided to go ahead and put up the money for a sequel. We shot most of it in Jersey Zoo, in the Channel Islands, and we had a great cast – Ronnie Corbett, all sorts of classic British comedy actors – but it sank with all hands, and I lost a fortune. Which reminds me, you know the old winemaker's joke, don't you?"

I shook my head.

"How do you make a small fortune in the wine business?" He paused for the requisite beat. "You start with a large fortune." He paused for two further beats. "Well, it's the same thing with funding films. But worse."

As I came to realize in the next twenty-four hours, John Cleese is a master of timing. He can transform a fairly funny line or a mildly promising idea into a bombshell of hilarity, simply by the pacing of his delivery and his tone of voice. But before we could get down to the script, we felt we ought to do the boring bit: the business deal and the budget. We sat outside at a shady table, sipped wine and jotted down figures. It was all settled in less than ten minutes.

"I'll take my fee," he said, "And that'll leave a bit more than $100k for everything else. I'm sure we can shoot it in under a week – it's only forty-five minutes, a cable-network hour – and you can all stay here at my place. We'll stick to the script, more or less, and wrap it up with a few weeks of editing. I'll come up to San Francisco to do the narration and fill in any gaps. I won't charge any expenses."

And that is exactly what happened: John, with his experience at Video Arts, the industrial and commercial film company he had co-founded in the 1970's, was the world's most efficient on-screen host. He got it right on the first take, virtually every time.

Our next job was to decide on the content of the film. It is no exaggeration to say that it took us just one afternoon to do this. A cable-TV hour has to be planned round half-a-dozen commercial breaks, so that is how we structured it. I proposed that we tipped our hat to Monty Python by starting the film with what appeared to be the wrong opening – as if the cinema projectionist had loaded the wrong reel by mistake. John loved the idea.

"Yes, let's do something way over the top," he said. He put on an exaggerated French accent: "Wine, Nectar of ze Gods," he said.

"We could get local wine makers to dress up in togas," I suggested.

"Right," said John, warming to the task. "Have an orgy of wine-drinking and excess, with pompous music, and then cut to my finger pushing the Eject button on a DVD player, and then a wide shot, and I'll take the DVD out and say 'Well, that's enough of that!' and throw it out the window."

We plotted out the structure from there on, and it only took a few hours. First, John would ask why wine evoked such snobbery, when it could and should offer such simple pleasure. Then, he would visit three or four good local wineries in the Santa Barbara area, introduce the six most famous grape varieties, and see how the stuff was made. Then he'd ask how you should choose what to drink:

"Simple," he said. "It's whatever you like and can afford. Don't listen to the experts and don't buy it just because it's expensive."

He suggested that we should hold a party at his house. He would ask some famous friends, some wine experts and some neighbors and ordinary folk to a wine-tasting, to see who could guess which were the expensive wines and which were not. We would then do a scene in a fancy restaurant, where he could play both the snobbish and bullying sommelier and also the anxious diner, who is being bullied into overpaying. I could be the stand-in/stunt double for the sommelier, whose shoulders and arms you would see from the back, as he poured the wine. Imagine – the chance for me to play a scene with John Cleese!

Finally, he suggested, we could shoot a scene in his kitchen, where he would appear with his American wife, and they would talk about how to keep wine cool, and how best to serve it at home. This scene later proved to be the commercial undoing of the film. His then wife, Alice-Faye Eichelberger, was a therapist who spoke with a strange mixture of South London and broad Texan accents. He had met her in England, and as far as the crew and I could tell, they made a happy couple. John had been married twice before: to Connie Booth – with whom he had produced a daughter and written and co-starred in the brilliant *Fawlty Towers* – and to Barbara Trentham, with whom he had produced a second daughter, and who was not often mentioned. But Alice-Faye seemed there to stay.

I thought we had a sure-fire international hit on our hands, because the final product was fresh, crisp and fast-paced. But alas, it was not to be. For starters, John placed restrictions on our distribution of the film: it was not to be shown in Britain, to punish those ungrateful people who said he'd forgotten how to be funny. But there was worse to come. A few short years after *John Cleese's Wine for the Confused* premiered on the Food Channel in the US and went into highly successful distribution as a DVD, he split up with Alice-Faye. That meant that he refused to allow the film ever to be sold again, with its cozy scene with Alice-Faye in the erstwhile Cleese family kitchen. Since I had a generous slice of the back-end revenue, this embargo was a bit of a blow.

However, it all turned out to be a bigger blow for John. Hell indeed hath no fury, as we men are often warned. Alice-Faye hired an attack-dog divorce lawyer called (behind her back) 'The Steel Magnolia,' who took him to the cleaners for nearly $20 million. He later went on tour in the UK and around the world, doing a one-man stage show that he called *The Alimony Tour,* ostensibly to scare up the money to pay Alice-Faye and her lawyer. During this show, according to Karl Sabbagh, who saw it in England, Cleese told the world that the two most appalling financial catastrophes to befall him in his life had been *Fierce Creatures* and Alice-Faye Eichelberger. As you may imagine, in the UK at least, all this did not enhance his reputation: perhaps the newspapers had been right, and he didn't have so much of his old sense of humor left after all.

Personally, I am very fond of the film we created. *John Cleese's Wine for the Confused* proved very popular on Amazon, and second-hand copies of it are still available. People seem to think it is a good general introduction to the world of wine, with many smiles, several chuckles and at least a couple of guffaws.

I have happy personal memories too. John was always the most generous host: he took Lizzie and me out to a sumptuous dinner on my birthday and welcomed Victoria Simpson (Camera) and Monte Vallier (Sound) to stay at his home with us, as if they were family. He hugely enjoyed his visit to San Francisco to complete the post-production. We were the last patrons standing at one of San Francisco's most excellent restaurants, at 2 a.m. Personally, I think our little film is one of the sweetest combinations of education and entertainment that it has been my pleasure to produce and direct.

So, thank you John, and I hope you find a more lasting happiness with Wife Number Four, Jennifer Wade. We shall see.

••

John Cleese's Wine for the Confused left me with a lingering thirst for more. Somewhere in my subconscious, over the next few years, I was turning over the possibilities of creating my own film – or perhaps a series – about wine. *Keeping Score* with Michael Tilson Thomas, plus two films about creativity (in children and in adults) had led me to wonder what made a truly creative winemaker. Was that person an artist, just as a painter or composer was an artist? Did they have a particular vision of what they wanted to create, long before they had the newly picked grapes in their hands? What made one winemaker greater than any of her neighbors, who owned similar vines in similar locations?

As usual, there were three things to be done: develop the concept, find the expert and raise the money. My first instinct was to approach a local living legend, Kermit Lynch, to be our wine expert: he had founded a small wine-importing operation in Berkeley in the early 1970's and grown it into a powerhouse in the American market. I knew him through his monthly newsletter, which was delivered to the posh San Francisco apartment we were renting, while our children went to High School in the city. I met him and his photographer wife Gail Skoff, when they invited Lizzie and me to dinner, to discuss the idea. It was an evening to remember: Gail's cooking plus Kermit's cellar make a stunning combination. But when we came to discuss details over dessert, the project hit the rocks.

"I've been thinking," I said, "That perhaps you could help me raise the money – from some of your wealthier clients, maybe?"

"Oh", said Kermit. "You don't have the funding yet?"

"No," I explained, "I need to have the star before I can raise the money, and that process would be much quicker if you were interested in helping."

"Hmm," said Kermit. "I'm not sure about that. How much do you need?"

"Well, I'd like to do a series of films."

"Ah", said Kermit. "Well, I'm not sure I've got the time to do a series. I'm not just running the wine business. I've written a book, and I'm launching a musical career, you know. I have just issued a CD. Also, we spend half the year at our property in France."

"Well, what I had thought," I said, "Is that we might feature you in the first episode, and then some other wine experts in the subsequent films." There was an ominous silence.

"Other people?" asked Kermit. "You mean it would not just be about me?" His interest vanished. We were shown to the door.

"Thank you for the most excellent dinner," we said.

"Think nothing of it," said Kermit politely, and thereafter that is exactly what I did. We obviously had to find someone else.

I pulled together a small dinner party with a few wine-savvy friends, including Josh Nossiter, whose brother had made what Josh himself described as "that dreadful film" *Mondo Vino.*

"Surely we can do better than that, can't we?" he said.

He suggested I should meet the co-owner of San Francisco's well-regarded Ferry Plaza Wine Merchants, Debbie Zachareas. She, in turn, agreed that the people I needed to meet were top-class wine distributors like Kermit, with perhaps a tad more humility: they would have long-lasting relationships with premium growers in the world's best wine regions. She suggested Terry Theise, an expert on German and Austrian wines, based in Washington DC; Jorge Ordonez, who imported many of the best Spanish wines; and Martine Saunier, who knew more about Burgundy than anyone else in the US. I met them all, but the pick of the bunch was Martine.

Debbie had described her as "elegant, wise, witty and typically French." The last of these descriptions could mean several things, but my doubts were put to rest the moment I met her. She was conducting a wine-tasting fund-raiser for the international school that our children had attended. A sprightly lady of indeterminate age and a twinkling eye, she had the sort of French accent that Maurice Chevalier put to such good use, a generation or two ago. She was smart both in dress and in mind, and her smile was to die for. It took me less than five minutes to decide: here was the star of our show. Afterwards, I helped her to clear up the glasses, by finishing great mouthfuls of wonderful wine.

"I can't put it back in the bottles," she said, "*Santé!*"

She swallowed a generous mouthful of Gevrey Chambertin – a twenty-year-old vintage, I noted. She sighed and licked her lips.

"Ah yes. The Pinot Noir is the king of grapes. Do you like wine, David?"

"Well, yes," I responded, "But I can't afford anything like this."

"That's the great thing about being in the wine business," she said, "You have to keep sampling the best. If we do a Burgundy film together, you will discover some wonderful things."

I went through my spiel about needing to find the funding, and, in contrast to Kermit's lack of interest in the subject, she said:

"No problem! I meet people all the time, who could afford to fund such a film."

I said that we would need at least half a million dollars, to do it right. And then there'd be distribution and promotion costs, on top of that.

"That's nothing, for some of my clients. Leave it to me!"

I told Lizzie about my encounter, and prepared for the long, hard slog to raise the money. It would probably take months of meetings, phone calls and proposals. I just hoped that we could get in front of a few philanthropic donors, before they had made their year-end decisions about where to put their tax-free donations. I was thinking in terms of a one-hour film for PBS. But, a few weeks later, the day after Thanksgiving, Martine called me at home.

"I think I've got the money," she said.

I nearly dropped the phone.

"How, Martine?" was all I could say.

"I was invited as a guest for Thanksgiving to Blackberry Farm. It's a beautiful resort in the Blue Mountains of Tennessee." she explained. "We supply all their wine. I sat next to this nice man at dinner, and I said to him, 'Do you happen to know anyone who might be interested in funding a film about Burgundy wines,' and he said 'Yes, I think I do.'"

"Well, who does he know?" I asked.

"It was *him. He's* interested in funding it."

Something like this very rarely happens, so I was determined not to count my grapes before they were picked. What is said over dinner can easily be forgotten or unsaid the following day. But the mystery man was as good as his word.

Todd Ruppert was the model of the perfect funder from a filmmaker's point of view. He had recently retired from a very senior position at the well-respected investment company, T. Rowe Price, and was now investing his personal fortune into the widest possible range of activities, from bauxite mines to classic photography collections, from China to South Africa, Switzerland and the Cayman Islands. He was stylish, had good taste and – happily – a much-treasured cellar of very fine wines.

He was also unimaginably busy, constantly flying round the globe to meetings, with occasional weekends of R & R with his family in Baltimore. The first date he could manage for a serious meeting was ten weeks away, in mid-February 2011. But he promised to bring "a special guest", if Martine and I would make the pilgrimage across the country to his home.

We arrived in Owings Mills, Maryland, to a warm welcome from Todd's entire family. Martine had contrived to have a very special bottle of Burgundy shipped to his house, to help seal the deal: a 1945 Vosne Romanée. Todd gasped, as he opened the wooden box.

"Oh, wow," he said. "That's quite something. One of the best vintages ever." So he certainly knew his wine.

And then the special guest arrived: Robert Parker, the notorious wine critic who had invented the '90+ Points' system of judging wines, and whose taste for big, strong, meaty reds had shaped the entire world's wine production. It turned out that he was a neighbor and an old friend of Todd's. We were certainly going to be closely vetted, that evening.

All's well that ends well: our concept of a wine film based on repeated visits to Burgundy during the different seasons of one year was approved. Parker thought it would help people to understand the amount of work it took, to create good wine. Todd said he didn't see why we had to make it a PBS film: he saw the project as an investment, not as a piece of philanthropy.

"Hey," he said, "Let's make it a real movie! If it earns its money back, that's great. If it doesn't, it'll be a tax write-off down the road." We shook hands that evening and agreed to draw up a contract.

We hit the ground running. I planned our first visit to Burgundy in April: I saw it as a scouting trip but luckily decided to take our small semi-professional Panasonic camera along, just in case there were a few unmissable shots. Little did I know what was in store for me.

∙∙∙

It was a whirlwind trip. I flew from San Francisco to London, saw Juliet and Amanda (plus Amanda's bonny new baby Tom), then took the Eurostar train through the Channel Tunnel to Paris. A hectic cab-ride across the city to the Gare de Lyon was followed by two hours on the TGV Express, at 150 miles an hour. I got off at the first stop, Macon, with my head spinning. I was greeted by Martine in the pale afternoon sun.

"Quick," she said, "There's not a moment to be lost. Do you have a camera?"

"Yes," I said, "But what's the hurry?"

"It's the weather," she said. "It's perfect today, but it may break any time now. The old castles and villages will look perfect in this light. Jump in the car. Let's go!" We roared out of the station yard and onto the backroads of Burgundy.

I was exhausted from the travel. I had not had a chance to discuss what we should film. I had not even brought a tripod with me. But Martine was implacable.

"It's the spring in Burgundy!" she said. "It's perfect. Look!"

Up on a hilltop, to the right of the road, I saw one of the most romantic castles you can imagine. We pulled into a small driveway. I jumped out and fired up the camera. With no tripod, I had to balance it on the roof of the car and wedge it with a road map. Panning shots were out of the question. I tentatively tried a zoom out, with the camera locked down.

For the next two weeks, I had to perform like a one-man band: I was cameraman, lighting gaffer (using whatever lamps, spotlights and halogen work-lights came to hand) and sound recordist, as well as director and interviewer. Martine took me to see most of her best Burgundy winemakers, and it was clear that we had to do interviews, both out in the fields and back at the wineries. Everyone was anxious to explain how worried they were that frost would damage the new young buds, which had appeared much too early in the year. The only microphone I had was the built-in mike on the camera. I just had to make sure that the camera was never more than six feet from whoever was speaking, or else they would sound like they were talking in a bathroom.

This was obviously not the best way to do things. A two-person crew is the minimum you need, even with miraculously compact modern equipment, to do a professional job. But I was astonished to find, at the end of the first trip, that I had recorded more than ten hours of material. The entire opening *Spring* sequence of *A Year in Burgundy* was filmed by me. It was really exciting: thanks to the miracle of the automatic settings on the Panasonic camera, I was a complete one-man filmmaker for the first and only time in my life.

Later, in the editing room, Jamie Lejeune did a heroic job, making up for my shortcomings. Clever software helped him to steady my wobbly shots, sharpen up the focus where necessary, colorize the images with more subtle shades, and eliminate the rumble of the camera and other extraneous noises on the soundtrack. Without his skill and the newly available range of software, we could never have achieved what we did, in-house at InCA. This was the key to being able to create our wine films within our budget: it allowed us to make four visits to each region for each film and truly reflect *A Year in Burgundy* and later, *A Year in Champagne* and *A Year in Port*.

Of all the characters we featured in our first film, the star had to be Lalou Bize-Leroy, now universally recognized as the Queen of Burgundy. Born in 1932, she was at the height of her powers when we filmed her in June 2011. Truly a legend in her own lifetime, she was one of the pioneers of bio-dynamic (fully organic) winemaking. She has always hated publicity but had been friends with Martine (someone almost her own age) for many years, and finally consented to give us an interview. After all, Martine imported her wine into the US.

To meet her in her cramped office, then out in the fields, was really extraordinary. She believes completely in the teachings of Rudolf Steiner and the Waldorf school. The vines, she explains, have to be treasured and spoken to and even physically caressed; we filmed her sensuously stroking her "children," as she called them. Vines should never be trimmed or ruthlessly pruned, she said, pointing to the Romanée-Conti vineyard right next door to her own, which routinely trims back its vines, like everyone else in Burgundy. The grapes have to be picked at the right phase of the moon, Leroy explained, and then gently cooled and brought back to the winery in tiny wicker baskets, like raspberries, to be individually sorted, one by one. Then they must be left to mature for many years in complete silence, in ancient oak barrels in a very deep cellar…

Romanée-Conti, let me remind you, used to be the world's most famous, revered and expensive wine. Its vineyard encompasses just four and a half acres, and bottles have sold for anywhere up to… (wait for it!) half a million dollars. Sotheby's broke all records in 2018 by selling a 1945 Romanée-Conti for $558,000, seventeen times the auctioneer's estimate. But second place on the list of all-time wine sales records till that date (according to Wine Searcher) was a bottle from Domaine Leroy next door: a bottle of her Musigny Grand Cru was sold the same year for $551,314. To put this in perspective, number three on the list of highest price wines in 2018 (a Riesling, surprisingly) was knocked down for a mere $33,883.

What is even more incredible is that Lalou Bize-Leroy's wines claimed up to four places in the various top ten lists of the "world's best" that year. And then, the next two years, Lalou outdid herself. Her wines shot up in value by a further 40 to 50%. Her glorious product has now taken over the title of the world's most expensive wine. She is truly a wizard – and I was very, very fortunate, thanks to Martine, to get the chance to meet and interview her.

For the summer and harvest visits to film *A Year in Burgundy*, I had been careful to take Jamie Lejeune along with me. He had been discovered by Lizzie, on a small commercial shoot we were doing at a San Francisco restaurant, where he was a waiter. He joined InCA Productions as the researcher on a planned *History of Food* series that never happened. He had then taken on the hair-raising job of Assistant Editor to Blair Gershkow on the technically complex *Keeping Score* series. He had always been fascinated by photography, and I am proud to say that our three wine films established his reputation as a brilliant cameraman, as well as a great editor and a superb post-production colorist. During post-production on *Burgundy*, our son James joined the team as well, to help edit and to create stylish, eye-catching graphics: another bonus, for all of us. He learned a lot from Jamie.

As the Burgundy film came together in the cutting room, it was clear that we really did need to make a final visit in winter, to wrap it up and give it a sense of completion. We needed to cover all four seasons. But the budget was almost spent. So I decided to venture out to Burgundy by myself once again. I was invited to stay with our favorite Burgundian wine-making family, the Morey-Coffinets, spending as little money as possible. I was not over-ambitious this time: I filmed simple, static scenes and landscapes in the late autumn mists, as village winemakers pruned their vines and burned the dead twigs. The smoke rose into the mist. Ancient stone crosses stood, gaunt and gray, against the horizon. Each image was like a painting – a medieval scene that the Cistercian monks, the original winemakers of the region, would have instantly recognized.

The final touch to the film, for me, was the music. Thibault Morey-Coffinet, the young winemaker of the family business, volunteered to compose and play four new piano pieces, to reflect the seasons of Burgundy. They created the perfect atmosphere for the film and were complemented by much of the music that my son James had selected, particularly the *Gnossiennes* of Eric Satie. As in our Amelia Earhart film, fifteen years before, a solo piano provided the film with a specially personal, intimate atmosphere.

In retrospect, I feel that *A Year in Burgundy* is one of the small handful of films of which I am most proud. With Martine's wisdom at my disposal, I was able to write and narrate it myself. Although I could not have done it without the huge input by Jamie and James, and other professionals like our great English-born sound mixer, Mark Escott, this was the first time I had ever created a film that was so completely my own work: the credits were embarrassingly short. I could sense that this might be, in some ways, the high point of my career. Time was ticking: by the time the film was finished and released, I was almost seventy.

- -

While we were shooting *A Year in Burgundy*, we had been discussing with Todd Ruppert whether we should aim for a sixty or a ninety-minute film. None of us was entirely sure that it would hold up for a whole cinema-length hour and a half. But we had our first feedback at a screening that winter at Blackberry Farm, where Martine had first met Todd.

Todd invited us to pull together a thirty-minute reel of our favorite scenes from the movie, to test the waters. He invited a couple of dozen friends to celebrate his birthday with us and view the reel, as an entertainment between the main course and dessert. The response was electric: his friends clapped and hollered and stamped. They loved it.

The following morning, Todd invited Martine and me to his cottage on the estate.

"OK," he said, "What's going to be our next one?"

Martine and I looked at each other. We had secretly discussed this possibility.

"Champagne?" she suggested. Todd smiled.

"Perfect," he said. "Same budget? Same deal? You've got it! Let's do it!"

We were stunned and could hardly believe our good luck. He had been the perfect Executive Producer, making helpful suggestions from time to time, but never getting in the way of the creative process. But we still had something important to resolve about *A Year in Burgundy*. How long should it be? We still were not certain. So we cut two versions: both a sixty *and* a ninety-minute film.

When it came time to organize a premiere, Todd booked the fashionable BAFTA theatre in London's West End, home of the British Academy of Film and Television Arts. We invited two hundred people to a lavish Burgundy tasting, with food and speeches to complement the film. Friends, family, investors, celebrities and people from the media were all there. But Todd felt that the sixty- minute version would be quite long enough for people to sit through, if they were also going to eat, drink and be merry, so that is the one that we screened. Happily, it was very well received.

For the New York premiere, I persuaded Todd to run the ninety-minute version. First, a VIP group of around thirty people were treated to tip-top Burgundies at the home of our friend Edwina Sandys (see Chapter 21, "Churchill's Granddaughter and the New York Scene"). Then, we chartered a luxury bus to transport the VIPs to the Tribeca Film Festival Theatre, where an audience of about a hundred people were already excitedly waiting for the film. Many of them were wine-loving friends of our publicists, Alisha Lumea and Polly Legendre: they knew half the sommeliers and chefs in New York, or so it seemed.

We ran the movie. The eighty-six minutes seemed to flash past, and at the end we got a standing ovation. Todd, whose Wall Street investor friends made up more than half of the VIP contingent, was beaming. As the audience left, he came up to Martine and me.

"OK," he said. "Great. We've got to release this as a full-length movie. Forget about TV. Forget about PBS. It works so well on the big screen. Oh yes, and, um, by the way: what's going to be our third film?"

This time, Martine and I did not have a ready answer.

"Let's talk it over," she said diplomatically. "There are so many interesting choices."

We finally settled for Portugal's Douro Valley, but not before we had made the second film, on Champagne.

· ·

Our team – Martine, Jamie, myself, and now my son James – became a tight-knit little family on the shoots for the *Champagne* and *Port* films. Besides starring in many scenes with the winemakers, Martine would also book our accommodation, usually in vacation rental cottages, and go to the local markets, to buy delicious food, which she would cook for our evening meals. It was in many ways an idyllic arrangement: based at a house in the country, with two cars, the camera guys could come and go as they pleased. Jamie and James would be up before dawn to catch the magical shots of early morning and return for delicious breakfast omelets. We seldom took days off – it was all too much fun. Even rain could produce unforgettable scenes, as filmed by Jamie's camera.

There simply is no space to tell all the stories about the filming. We learned that the winemakers of Champagne are a very different species from those in Burgundy, even though they are separated by less than two hundred and fifty miles. Where almost everything and everyone in Burgundy seem simple, time-honored and relaxed, the people of Champagne are often reserved, tight-lipped and suspicious. They believe that the world has unfairly stolen the secrets of their specialized winemaking: every wine region in the world now seems to turn out some sort of pseudo "champagne."

They have also been invaded too many times to trust outsiders easily: since Attila the Hun was finally defeated here by the Romans and Gauls in the fifth century, this has been a battleground of choice at a crossroads in Northern Europe. One of World War I's grimmest battlefields, the Marne, lies at the gates of Champagne. In World War II, Hitler smashed through the region en route to Paris, leaving behind a "*Champagne Fuehrer*", to seize the best bottles and ship them to Berlin. Happily, the local winemakers built false walls in their cellars, hid the good bottles behind them, put false labels on the dross and sent that off to the Fatherland, to tickle the palates of the Nazis.

All this made for a very different and, I believe, equally fascinating wine film. Back in the cutting room, a whole new atmosphere reigned, incorporating war and death as well as the celebrations for which Champagne is a vital ingredient. This time, we had two editing suites: Jamie in one, and James in the other. I was delighted to discover that James was a natural editor, and rapidly became a first- rate translator of sub-titles (having studied French at school), as well as a writer of script and all-round producer. How good can it get, when you have the chance to work with your own son?

A Year in Champagne, like *A Year in Burgundy*, was entered for the well-respected Santa Barbara Film Festival. The Burgundy film had won an Audience Favorite award there, as well as the Jury Prize at the French Oenovideo Wine Film Festival. So we were hoping for great things. What we did not expect was a call from Hollywood. Two days after the Santa Barbara premiere of *A Year in Champagne*, my office phone rang. It was Alisha, our publicist.

"Have you seen *The Hollywood Reporter*?" she asked. "They've given us a fantastic review."

Less than an hour later, the phone rang again.

"This is Samuel Goldwyn Films," I was told. "I have Peter Goldwyn for you. Hold the line, please."

"Hello. David?" said Peter, as if we had been friends for many years. "Who's distributing the Champagne film for you? If it's not signed up, we'd be pleased to take it."

The Burgundy film had been distributed thus far by FilmBuff, an organization of bright young people based in New York. They had scored us a Netflix deal, besides getting us onto iTunes, Hulu and the many other digital outlets newly available. They had also found an outfit, which would distribute the film as a DVD – Kino Lorber, whose efforts in that regard eventually left a lot to be desired. But FilmBuff did not have the magic of the Goldwyn name.

"We've had some success with our film about sommeliers," said Peter. "It's called *Somm*. You may have seen it."

I had indeed and was not very impressed: it felt like reality TV on the big screen. But apparently it was making money for Goldwyn.

"Well, that's great, Peter," I said, evidently trying to ingratiate myself with him. "Of course, I'll need to ask Todd, our Executive Producer, but I'm sure he'll be happy to go ahead."

Todd enjoys mingling with the big names of any industry, and discovered that he was going to be in LA the following week, at a party to launch a new portfolio of famous photographs he had just bought.

"Hey, this is great," he told me. "I'll invite Peter Goldwyn to the party, and we'll shake hands right there."

That is exactly what happened. Samuel Goldwyn Pictures became the distributor of all three of our wine film trilogy: *A Year in Burgundy, Champagne* and *Port.* It has to be said that the percentage they demanded from the sales was more than twice as large as that required by FilmBuff. It also has to be said that the paperwork involved in doing a deal with Goldwyn is ludicrously complex and runs to over fifty pages: it is mostly boilerplate legalese, more suited to a $50 million feature film than a modest documentary. However, as Jamie Lejeune said when he edited their logo onto the front of the films:

"I never thought I'd see the day when I put the Goldwyn name on a film I'd cut."

That old black magic of Hollywood – all the razzmatazz of Tinseltown – still exerts its power.

∙∙

In August 2016, we launched our final wine film, *A Year in Port.* This featured Portugal: the Douro Valley, where evidence of human civilization goes back more than 5,000 years. Stunningly hot in summer, freezing cold in winter, this rugged terrain produces the most amazing range of wines: not only the warm, sweet dessert wine which carries the name of the regional capital, Oporto, but a huge variety of blends from the many vine varieties that grow on its steep terraces.

The hidden bonus is the charm of the Portuguese people – unfailingly friendly and welcoming, in sharp contrast to some of the champagne makers we encountered. Our favorite character was probably Dirk Niepoort – part German, part Dutch, part Portuguese, and the sixth generation of his family to create remarkable wines. His kindness and puckish sense of humor remain vividly in the memories we all have. Thank you, Martine Saunier, for having introduced us to him and to so many other lovable winemakers!

In sharp contrast to the indifference of the French authorities towards our previous two films, set in Burgundy and Champagne, the Portuguese government was the answer to a maiden's prayer. Nuno Mathias, their consul in San Francisco, single-handedly achieved more than a team of publicists could have done. We have had premieres of the Port film in embassies in London, Paris, Berlin and Washington DC; we have been featured in the airline magazine of TAP, the Portuguese airline, and we have had numerous parties at the consulate in San Francisco. No wonder that the alliance between Portugal and England – the world's oldest, lasting for more than 600 years already – has been so strong.

Happily, this last film in our three-film series won a Joint First Prize at the Rhode Island Film Festival – New England's oldest and biggest such event. James flew across to a stifling hot theatre to introduce the film and be interviewed by the press – and in particular, this time, by the Portuguese press. We decorated the film's website with the festival's laurels and a month later held a New York premiere in the United Nations International School's main auditorium, the night before the opening of the General Assembly.

To be honest, there is nothing more satisfying than watching one of your films with a live audience. For more than forty years, I had made films for television, and the only live-audience events were press previews, often in small viewing rooms. But the thrill of hearing a couple of hundred people laugh at the jokes, or gasp at the moments of drama – as when two sailing barges collide during a hectic race on the River Douro in Oporto – well, there is nothing to beat it. We toil away to weave our work together, never really knowing whether the world will love, hate or (worse) be utterly indifferent to the result. Hearing the applause when the end credits roll is a guilty pleasure, which makes it all worthwhile.

A Year in Port will be my last film, as Producer, Director and Writer. It speaks with my voice, and not only because I narrated it. It mixes drama and facts, strong story arc and bright jewel-like moments, arts and science, happy optimism and mind-boggling oddities. Why do the major port producers still choose to tread grapes by foot? Do they really still play cricket in Porto, on the grounds of the only full-time Cricket Club in continental Europe? How can there possibly be over two hundred grape varieties in the Douro? And how can you get port from a bottle without pulling out the cork?

The answers to all these questions are in the film. Roll up, Ladies and Gentlemen! Buy or rent your copy now. Always available, 24/7, on iTunes, Amazon, YouTube or elsewhere. Ah, the miracle of modern distribution! More than 75% of the films I have made are still available in one venue or another. It seems a long time since the days of *Germany 1870-1970,* when I was directing films in black and white on celluloid. Back then, even the VHS tape format was still in the future: there was no way to keep a personal copy of the film you had just made. The BBC Archive appear to have wiped the Germany series, by the way, as well as most of *The Sunday Debate, The Age of Uncertainty* and others. Luckily, the books accompanying most of the projects survive, to bring back happy memories.

If *A Year in Port* is indeed my last hurrah (apart from my modest contribution to James's film, *The Book Makers* – see the *Epilogue*), it will be, for me, a happy finale to the one hundred and forty-something shows that I have helped to create. That is an improbable number, but (just to check) I made a list of all those longer than fifteen minutes, and it is included at the end of this book.

• •

25.   THE ONES THAT GOT AWAY

In all honesty, I could not let this book conclude with the stirring trumpet fanfare and sentimental adieu at the end of the previous chapter. From the book so far, you might have got the impression that my professional life has been a seamless succession of projects, each one leading to the next with nary a pause between them, let alone a yawning gap in my income.

When I look at the pile of boxes in our basement (mementos from 1945 onwards) and the complete project files on my office computer, covering the years 1980 to 2020, from the end of *Cosmos* to the present day, I am reminded of all the might-have-been films and series that crashed and burned before takeoff.

In every case, many people put in months of effort, often unpaid, to develop them – often at the same time as we were making films that had actually been funded. This is par for the course, if you are an independent documentary maker, whether or not you have invented a company shell (like InCA Productions) to try to protect you from the fates. As the old song says, you have to constantly "pick yourself up, dust yourself down, and start all over again." Not that it is easy to move on, particularly when you are fond of a project.

Michael Gill, the charismatic producer of the *Civilisation* series, who became a good friend, warned me about this when I was first venturing out into the big, cold world, after full-time employment at the BBC and on *Cosmos.*

"Always have half a dozen projects in development. Better still, have ten. You never know which one will get funded. In fact, you may well be offered something you haven't been trying to do at all or didn't even know about."

That is what happened initially with Michael's own series, *The Buried Mirror,* a history of the Hispanic peoples written and presented by the Mexican diplomat and poet Carlos Fuentes. Michael got funding for the development – $200,000 from the Smithsonian Institution, no less – and that is what paid for my first "honeymoon" in Mexico with Lizzie, as I recounted earlier. But could he get the production money? Not for years, by which time I was busy on another project and, alas, could not find time to create even one film for Michael's series.

Then there was *The Blue Revolution,* the project that Belgian producer Luc Cuyvers initially brought to InCA. The development money helped to pay for Lizzie's and my trip to Tahiti, the Great Barrier Reef, Hawaii and Japan: our second honeymoon, in effect. But the production? After many years of struggling to find funds, Luc took the show to the Discovery Channel and had to hire a cheaper production company to create it. Another might-have-been.

All this on-again off-again uncertainty was for some reason – for me – very often associated with projects about the future. As I described in Chapter 14, I have had a bee in my bonnet about the future ever since working with James Burke. The final show in the *Connections* series allowed James to do a little mild speculation about the way change happens and will continue to happen. It is largely serendipity, he maintained. You can point to fields that seem promising, like colloid chemistry or cold fusion, but they often go nowhere. Monorails and magnetic levitation trains have been promoted as the solution to all our transport needs for 70 years, but where are they now?

On the other hand, who foresaw the Internet? Not even Arthur C. Clarke, as he willingly admitted. Clarke reminded me in 2000 that George Orwell had imagined a world where you could address a screen and find the answer to any question from a Universal Brain of some sort, but that was an intimation of Google and Bing, rather than a universal web of connectivity, potentially linking every human being on earth with every other, in living color and sound.

So, is futurism for suckers? Maybe so, but I think there is no harm in imagining things or roughing out possible scenarios. That is what propelled James Burke, George Colburn and I to develop a project called *You and the 21ˢᵗ Century* in the early days of InCA. Stephen Bankler-Jukes, a plausible entrepreneur based in London, persuaded us that he had friends with plenty of money and influence in high places, and that a raft of future-oriented films would go down a treat with Britain's Channel 4 and similar forward-looking TV networks in Europe. Better still, SBJ, a natural-born publicist, had lavish print materials produced, to promote himself in cahoots with all of us – and to display our half-baked ideas. Of course, Bankler-Jukes explained, he would become part owner of all the intellectual property, before the series was even sold.

"Hang on a minute," said James Burke, who always jealously guarded his rights as an author. "That won't work."

And, of course, it didn't work: the project collapsed, though I salvaged some of the ideas I had contributed and put them into *Things to Come* (see Chapter 14).

In the 80's and 90's I just couldn't stop trying to invent one-hour science shows about the future for series like *Nova,* Channel 4's *Equinox* and the BBC's *Horizon.* Perhaps because the Nanotechnology film had been funded (again, see Chapter 14), I thought that any film about a future technology that was based on some evidence of current scientific achievement would be commissioned or funded immediately. Well, dream on, Kennard...

I had made friends with Howard Rheingold in Mill Valley, soon after arriving there in 1988. He is a great character, renowned for his colorful clothing, bright mind and exotic parties. He is also a much-respected non-fiction author, with a long string of provocative future-oriented books to his credit, including prescient tomes about mobile phones, crowd sourcing and mob violence (presaging the era of Trump, 30 years before it happened). Long before the subject was well known or fashionable, he wrote a thought-provoking book about virtual reality (VR).

He introduced me to another perennial wizard of new media, Jaron Lanier, and we put together a succinct proposal for a *Nova* film on VR. It is once again in the news today, and perhaps the technology of the headsets has improved sufficiently to make it entrancing rather than nausea inducing. Indeed, I am told that they really like VR in China

– perhaps because 'real' reality has become somewhat dystopian there. But back in the late 1980's, VR seemed to be science fiction that was coming true, before our very eyes.

Well, that futuristic project died a sudden death too. Paula Apsell of WGBH Boston, who seems to have been the senior Executive Producer at *Nova* since the dawn of television, turned her thumbs down very swiftly. She has always been notoriously difficult to reach by phone, much like the grander theatrical agents. You had to call her exactly when she told you to, however inconvenient. I remember standing beside a freeway with Howard Rheingold, shouting into a payphone above the roar of passing traffic, trying to persuade her that our film was based on fact and really rather interesting.

"Virtual reality?" said Paula. "It doesn't exist. It's nonsense. It'll never happen, David. It's science fiction. Who needs it? I can't afford to have *Nova*'s reputation damaged by that kind of film."

I noted at the time that she had refused to run our film on Nanotechnology on *Nova*, because she thought that was nonsense too. Luckily, Britain's Channel 4 had more imagination than Paula.

Many years later, the same thing happened with another futuristic project. I was given an inside look into the world of 3-D printing by a friend, the designer and lecturer Geoff Hollington, long before the general public had ever heard of the idea. Until around 2010, 3-D printing, or 'additive manufacturing', had been used only for making prototypes and scale models. If successful, the objects would later be made using injection molding and other established techniques.

But what would happen if everything from lampshades to machine tools and body-parts could be made to a unique specification, one by one, in a friendly neighborhood 3-D print shop? Could this herald the end of traditional hammering, banging, chopping, welding and soldering and, indeed of factories and mass-production? If so, the number of objects being transported halfway round the world in container ships, or across the US by UPS, would dwindle remarkably – and that couldn't be bad, could it?

Nova flatly rejected the whole idea as nonsense once again. The Alfred P. Sloan Foundation of New York, which had entirely funded the futuristic *2001: HAL's Legacy*, also refused to support a film on the subject of 3-D printing. However, I persuaded Doron Weber, the Chief Executive, to offer me a $40,000 matching grant, if we could persuade a mainstream publisher to put up the same sum as an advance for a book on the subject.

Could we find such a publisher? No. It is amazing how many people are keen to be the second funder of a project, provided someone else has had the bravery to plunge in first. Yet, today, authoritative sources like *The Economist* run leading articles and special supplements on additive manufacture and 3-D printing, and there is much speculation about building molecules the same way. We were, again, ahead of our time.

We were certainly ahead of the curve with *Now What?* – a concept that I developed in 1998 with Jim Gollub, during the glory days of our jointly-owned marketing company, IDeA (Information Design Associates). Jim's previous day job at SRI International (the Stanford Research Institute think tank) had been to create strategic scenarios for public and private clients, to help guide their decision making. As Jim explained it:

"It's OK to think about the future if you don't forecast what *will* happen, only what *could* happen or *might* happen. You have to say: 'If X happens, then what might be the consequences? Y? Or Z? Or what?' Then you ascribe a probability ranking to each scenario." He made the future sound like a fascinating chess game, with an almost infinite number of possible moves.

Jim and I decided to create a television series based on this idea. First, we would convene a small group of multi-talented experts on a subject – say, sex and marriage. We would encourage them to describe some of the many possible implications and trends that might develop from (say) emerging genetic technology.

But instead of creating a straight documentary from this material, like an illustrated business presentation of scenarios, we would frame the discovery of the alternative outcomes as an adventure, taking place inside a fictitious, animated cityscape. The television viewer, following the point of view of a roving camera, would enter buildings and be transported into live-action pre-recorded scenes, where actors, with dialog, were making decisions. Depending on those decisions, the story (and the journey around the city) then followed one path or another, till eventually there was a more-or-less satisfactory *dénouement*: a story structure, in other words. We would be demonstrating what James Burke had always maintained: that any action, invention or decision has multiple consequences, many of which we cannot foresee.

What made our idea for *Now What?* unique, however, was the fact that you could also play the game online, immediately after the program had aired on TV. At a *Now What?* website, you would be able to travel around the animated city at your leisure and revisit the locales and scenes that were featured in the TV show. But online, you could be an active participant. You'd be encouraged to make different decisions than the ones the actors had made in the original scene. That would allow you to follow a different path through the city to different locations, where new scenes would play out. And so it went: a series of new adventures and new discoveries would unfurl. We shot a couple of test scenes, to demonstrate the idea. People seemed to like them.

Jim Gollub and I seriously thought that this was an innovative, not to say groundbreaking way of linking a cable-TV channel to a website. But when we took it to Discovery and its subsidiary, The Learning Channel (TLC), the idea went down like the Hindenburg. Ironically, the program executive we were allocated was Richard Wells, with whom I had worked twenty years before on *Cosmos*. I liked him, and I think he liked me, but he simply did not understand the potential of our idea, and once he had partially understood it, he liked it even less. He felt it would make lousy television and was much too complicated to handle on TLC's existing website. I asked for a development grant, to shoot some specimen scenes and a demo-reel of the animation. No, said Richard, this was not possible. End of story.

••

So there have been many projects that never got off the ground, because they never received funding. A series on San Francisco history, *The Barbary Coast Trail,* led to development funds, glossy brochures and the chance for Lizzie and I to commission a

Kennard Family Memorial brass plaque, let into the sidewalk at the side of the Powell Street cable car line just south of Union Square. The plaque is still there, largely ignored and trampled on by tourists rushing for the cable cars, but production funding never materialized.

On a very different subject, I was contacted by my old Oxford college in the 1990's, with a request to collaborate with their then Chaplain, Robin Griffith-Jones. He had a remarkable idea about creating a television series, which asked why there were *four* Christian gospels: why not more? Why not less? The Jewish and Muslim faiths rely on one single authorized holy text, not four different and often conflicting personal stories, after all.

The Four Witnesses, as I mentioned in Chapter 12, was planned at one time as a documentary series for Peter Jennings to present. After his death, we recast it as a drama. Soon after Robin had left Lincoln College to become Master of the Temple Church (the original Knights Templars' headquarters in London), we interviewed Jeremy Irons, for the role of Christ. He came to a meeting at Robin's new house, right in the middle of the Inner Temple Gardens, home to London's most distinguished barristers and legal eagles. What is more, he came on his motorbike, and strode into the meeting wearing impressive black leather pants and gauntlets – like a modern-day Jesus, preparing to throw the money changers out of the Temple, I thought. He loved the project, too: when could we begin? Surely, I imagined, this would be the clincher: how could anyone refuse to fund such a project, with Irons in the fire?

But nobody did – not even the Christian-based Eli Lilly Foundation, the fabulously well-endowed philanthropic arm of the big American drug company. My friend and Public Television collaborator, Polly Kosko of South Carolina Educational Television, was convinced we had a winner, particularly for the American market. But no, apparently it was just a little too provocative for many Americans, and not sufficiently evangelical for others. It finally saw the light of day as a book, still titled *The Four Witnesses,* and was published internationally by Harper San Francisco, with great success.

Most frustrating of all are the projects that start production with a first tranche of money, and then falter and collapse for one reason or another – usually something personal. *Unforgivable?* was one of these, and as my long-time colleague and co-producer Joan Saffa wrily remarked, what happened to us may well have justified the title. But first, a short backstory.

Ian and Victoria Watson were old friends of Lizzie and me in Marin County. They were enjoyable company – Victoria presenting herself as a classy, upper-class Brit, and Ian as a no-nonsense Canadian investor. Our children had learned to ride horses and enjoy other such upmarket pastimes with their children. They also threw excellent parties at their ranch-style house by the Belvedere lagoon, a few miles from the InCA office. It was all very agreeable. Professionally, they had always been interested in 'New Age' ventures and vaguely spiritual projects. They were generous board members of the Institute for Noetic Sciences, which had co-produced *The Heart of Healing* with us.

When Ian contacted me and said he wanted to introduce a business colleague, one Paul Dietrich, I was interested. Ian had money and I assumed he was quite likely to fund at least part of a film on a subject which intrigued him.

Lizzie and I met with Ian and Paul, and Paul took the lead in outlining their proposal: a one-hour film, possibly a ninety-minute film, about forgiveness. I was immediately interested, because there were plainly many extraordinary stories of people who had forgiven others for crimes that were horrible – from embezzlement to murder. What made people able to forgive? Should you forgive but remember, rather than forgive and forget? Why was the inability to forgive – like the inability to be playful – so corrosive to the soul? What did the endless tales of family feuds, revenge and hatred teach us?

Lizzie, ever the inquisitive psychologist as well a television researcher, was more interested in why our prospective donors were so interested in the subject.

"I wonder what they've done that requires forgiveness?" she asked, after our first project meeting. "Paul talked a lot about his Catholic faith and working with Mother Theresa in Calcutta, but I bet there's more to it than that. What has he been up to? Is there anything else he has done, for which he feels he needs forgiveness? Or who has he needed to forgive? And for what? What was his childhood like?"

She threw herself into a detailed Google search, trying to dig up Paul Dietrich's past. In 2002, Google had just started to become a mainstream research tool and was revolutionizing the task of digging up hidden details. She found some interesting stories. What Mr. Dietrich had omitted to share with us on his CV was that, for some years, he had been deeply involved with Big Tobacco, in their ceaseless quest to persuade the public that cigarette smoking did no harm. He cannot have been proud of that in retrospect, but was that enough to motivate a forensic investigation into forgiveness?

Lizzie dug further, but found nothing conclusive, except for some periods in Paul's life which seemed curiously opaque: he seemed to disappear and reappear in an odd way. But she was right to look for clues. People often support projects for reasons known only to themselves. Lizzie and I could never forget that Brendan O'Regan had championed *The Heart of Healing* ten years before because, without our knowing it, he was desperately searching for mental and spiritual strategies to outwit HIV and AIDS.

With Ian and Victoria, the motivation seemed simpler. They were both attracted to Buddhism, which, along with Catholicism, places forgiveness high on the list of spiritual priorities in life. Indeed, they had contacts, which could lead us to both the Dalai Lama and the actor Richard Gere, who was a committed Buddhist. When she heard this, Lizzie's ears pricked up.

"Never mind the Dalai Lama," she said. "Joan Saffa can go and film him. I want to meet Richard Gere. David, you've got to do the filming with him, and I'll be your Associate Producer."

Lizzie has always maintained a carefully curated shortlist of men whom she really fancies. It includes Bill Clinton, Paul McCartney and, yes, Mr. Gere. She hastens to assure me that, being a faithfully married person, all she wants to do is to shake their hand, gaze into their eyes and perhaps give them a hug. Normally, she does not get the chance to get that close to any of her heroes, but here was an opportunity, presented on a plate.

With initial funding from Paul and Ian, we set off for New York, picked up a camera crew, and suddenly, there we were, in Richard Gere's office – and there he was, smiling his special smile. Lizzie's knees nearly buckled. She says she cannot remember a thing he said in the interview, but afterwards he posed for photos, and Lizzie made sure to get several that featured just her and her pin-up. Happily, Richard seemed quite taken with my wife and put his arm around her, smiling broadly. She was in heaven. The best of the photos we took still graces our living-room mantelpiece and draws incredulous remarks from visitors

Meanwhile, Joan Saffa and a film crew were doing the heavy lifting: they went to Dharamsala, the Dalai Lama's Indian home, in exile from Tibet. That is the opposite side of the planet from California and getting there was only half the fun. Paul Dietrich, Ian Watson and their entourage had also come along for the ride – for the chance to ingratiate themselves with the Dalai Lama, of course.

As Joan tells the story, Paul was exceptionally keen to get photographs of himself with the holy man. He instructed the crew that the first order of business, once they were in the Presence, was to get group shots and then separate two-shots, particularly of himself with the His Holiness. When they were finally ushered into the reception room, the Dalai Lama was his usual charming, smiling self, but showed an iron will.

"No photographs till we have done our work!" he reprimanded Paul. "First, let us talk about forgiveness."

With his tail between his legs, Paul sat down and did as he was told, Joan says. But he finally got his photos with the Dalai Lama. I hope he enjoys them as much as Lizzie enjoys hers with Richard Gere.

Joan also filmed and edited the astonishing story of Marietta Jaeger, an American woman who had forgiven the man who had murdered her seven-year-old daughter. It packed an enormous emotional punch, as affecting as anything Joan had filmed for *The Heart of Healing.* As Marietta put it on camera:

> *"Forgiveness is not for wimps. Try it. It takes daily, diligent discipline. I still grieve and I will always grieve for Susie, but I now have absolutely no anger or hatred towards David [the murderer]."*

We were all convinced that our early production material would persuade many foundations and philanthropists to open their purses and fund the project fully. Everyone seemed to believe that the material we had created for this film, by now titled *Unforgivable?*, was unbeatable – both thought-provoking and profoundly moving. Then, one morning, I had a phone call out of the blue from Paul Dietrich.

"Oh, David," he said, "We've decided to give the project to WGBH Boston. They have promised to get it onto PBS nationally, and we have no such guarantee from anyone else."

In vain, I explained to Paul that InCA had an unblemished record of getting every show it had produced in the (then) twenty years of its existence onto a national network. We had helped him to create some vivid and compelling stories and would be sure to create more, so why reject us at this stage?

"We've found another producer, whose credits are just as good as yours," said Paul with icy indifference. "She always works with WGBH, the Boston PBS station, and guarantees that they'll take the film. Ian and I retain the right to do what we like with the project. It's our copyright material, as per our agreement with you."

And that was that. No thanks for what we had created – essentially, no thanks for turning a vague concept into a compelling sizzle reel, within budget and on time. We were disposable assets – just another bunch of "creatives", to Paul.

By including this story here, I suppose that I have never really forgiven Paul or indeed Ian, who was, I thought, my friend. To be treated in such a cavalier way is par for the course in our industry. But to be treated like this by putative do-gooders, who were touting the benefits of forgiveness and the spiritual life – well, that was more than ironic. It seemed to me a piece of plain old-fashioned hypocrisy. Was it, indeed, *Unforgivable?* Lizzie certainly thought so.

∎∎

One final project will serve to demonstrate how big projects can get away from you, even when you think you have got them in the bag. This was the snappily titled *Global Warming – the Signs and the Science.*

The story of this production unfolds shortly after our debacle with *Unforgivable?* My old friend, Polly Kosko of South Carolina ETV called me, to ask whether I had any spare time. Thanks to Paul Dietrich, I suddenly did.

"Well, David, I've just come back from a Program Fair in Canada", said Polly, in her inimitable Southern drawl. "And I stumbled on a good show that's been created for the Discovery Channel up there. It's four half hours on Global Warming, a bit rambling and unfocused, but I think we could re-purpose the footage and shoot some new scenes with an American on-camera host. We could get a great two-hour special out of it. Are you interested?"

This was at least two years before Al Gore's definitive film *An Inconvenient Truth* was premiered. I had read about the theory of global warming, but I had not realized how much solid evidence was being collected by climate scientists: interesting stuff, though I worried that it could all be a bit dry and might not hold up longer than an hour.

"Who are you thinking of for the host?" I said. "Not Jim Lehrer again?"

Lehrer had been the host of the PBS evening *NewsHour* since time immemorial. Polly had persuaded him and his then colleague Robin MacNeil to co-host the American version of *The Heart of the Dragon* some twenty years previously.

Polly laughed. "Not Jim Lehrer. Try again," she said. "Someone a little younger." I made a few stabs in the dark.

"You'll never get it," she said. "It's Leonardo DiCaprio."

This was amazing news. Leonardo had become a global superstar in 1997, when he romanced Kate Winslet in *Titanic*, the highest grossing picture in movie history at that time. Why was he considering an association with PBS, which has trouble paying minimum Equity rates?

"He's an eco-warrior," said Polly. "He wants to be known as something more than a romantic lead. He's got his own foundation, somewhere in Santa Monica. Why don't you go and meet him?"

When I told Lizzie that I would be going down to LA sometime soon to meet DiCaprio, she thought it was a joke. She had never fancied Leo like she fancied Richard Gere, but Leo might fit the bill nicely, as a new casual acquaintance: someone to mention in our Christmas letter, perhaps.

"Apparently he's dating the model, Gisele Buendchen, so don't get too excited," I told her. She gave me an old-fashioned look.

"David, you know I'm not being serious," she assured me. "It's just nice to, um, meet these people, you know?" She explained that she might somehow be able to find time off from her studies in Organizational Psychology, to accompany me.

First, however, I had to meet the Canadian producers, who worked out of Montreal, and thrash out a deal. How could we use their footage, to make a new show? How much creative control did they want? I booked a passage on Air Canada via Toronto and set off to the wintry north.

The mercury fell precipitously. It was well below freezing by the time we got to Toronto. Traveling further north and east up to Quebec was going to place me right in the middle of an arctic nightmare.

"Welcome to Montreal," said the first officer, shortly after we landed, and were taxiing across the frozen concrete. "It's quite chilly out there, folks. In fact, it's that temperature where the two thermometers agree: it's forty degrees below zero, whether you measure it in Fahrenheit or Celsius. And then there's the wind chill factor. Wrap up well."

In the ten steps it took me to get from the terminal building to a taxi, the cold slashed my face like a knife. I slammed the door and settled back into the warmth of the cab.

"Eh!" said the cabbie, with a strong Québecois accent, "what are you *wearing*?"

I had put on my heaviest formal overcoat and a large scarf, with jacket and pullover beneath. I thought it was both smart and serviceable in cold climates.

"Hah!" said the cabbie. "You need a good fur hat with ear-flaps. Then wrap your body up with a full-length quilted coat, like the lagging on a boiler. Or you'll freeze to death. Where are you from? England? That figures. It just rains there."

Over the next forty-eight hours, I negotiated terms for the production, watched some good footage, and tried to keep warm. I started to understand why Montreal is a city linked by a maze of underground passageways and shops: more than a few minutes in the open air, and you get frostbite and your nose drops off. Never have I been happier to wing my way back to balmy California.

Next stop was Santa Monica. I had decided that the first meeting with Leonardo DiCaprio and "his people" should be something I did by myself. Lizzie could join me as Associate Producer when we filmed. As I had been instructed, I hired a car and drove up the coast to Malibu. Right there on the Pacific Coast Highway was an unremarkable beach house. I parked and rang the bell. An older lady answered the door.

"I'm David Kennard," I said.

She turned and called out, "Leo!" as if she was his mother. It turned out that she was! A moment later, he appeared, wearing a beanie, cargo pants and loafers.

"Hi," he said. "This is my mother. Mother, this is Mr. Kennard from PBS." He led the way to the kitchen. "Do you want something to drink?"

Like many people, I have dreams where famous people play brief supporting roles. Stephen Fry, Michael Palin and Her Majesty the Queen have all figured occasionally in my dreams. But this seemed even more dreamlike than any scene I could remember from my sleeping hours. Leonardo DiCaprio was tossing me a can of iced tea and wandering out onto the deck, overlooking the ocean in the soft winter sunlight. No agents, no Hollywood fluffers, no hangers-on…

"So, what's the plan?" asked Leo.

I told him about all the excellent footage I had seen in Montreal.

"Sounds great," he said. "Why don't you come by my office tomorrow morning, and we'll rough out a structure for the picture. You want me to do some on-camera stuff, right?"

Driving back to my hotel, I wanted to pinch myself. It had been like hanging out with an old friend. The next morning, the same atmosphere prevailed. Two busy young women, who could have been his cousins, started drawing schedules and film structures on a whiteboard. Leo wandered in, wearing a hoodie and the same knitted woolen hat that he had worn the day before.

"Don't people recognize you in the street?" I asked him, wondering where his chauffeur or bodyguard was, and whether his limousine had darkened windows.

"Not often," he said casually. "The trick is to hide in plain sight. Wear everyday clothes. Drive a Prius. That way, no-one thinks I'm anything special. So I'm not."

Planning the script was both pleasant and efficient. The two women turned out to be vigorous environmental groupies, who were the principal staff of his foundation. They knew their stuff, and we soon had a number of to-camera pieces worked out. Then we discussed locations. DiCaprio insisted they should all be within easy driving distance of his office, because his movie-shooting schedule did not allow for travel, and we did not have the budget for it anyway. We agreed on several set-ups that were relevant to the subject: near a runway at the airport, up in the hills near a reservoir, on the roof of an office building with giant solar panels, and... We needed to find someplace where he could look down on a Los Angeles freeway, choked with traffic. I had a flash of inspiration.

"Do you know that strange, tall octagonal hotel, just up the road, at the intersection of Sunset Boulevard and the 405 Freeway?" I asked. "Those rooms have balconies. I bet you can get a good view of the road from the top floors."

"Oh yeah," said Leonardo. "It's a Holiday Inn, I think. Or it used to be. Real classy locations you're picking!"

I thought of the scores of set-designers, scenery-shifters, grips, clapper-loaders, make-up artists, camera assistants and costume people who would normally surround him on location.

"It's a documentary," I said, "We'll just be hiding in plain sight."

He smiled and seemed to accept the situation: filming on a shoestring was going to be quite a novelty for him.

The dates for the shoot were set for some three weeks later. Lizzie would come down with me from San Francisco, to help produce the scenes, and I would direct. We would pick up a local LA crew – just three of them, compared to the cast of thousands on Leonardo's feature films. The biggest question to resolve was: should we tell the hotel that we wanted to film in one of their bedrooms? If we did, they would doubtless charge us a hefty facility fee. They would also get wind of the fact that they had Leonardo DiCaprio as a transient guest, even if only for a few hours. That would mean unwelcome attention from paparazzi and the press. So we decided to film undercover.

I went in with Lizzie and asked for a room in our family name, as high up the building as possible. We specifically asked for a room on the side facing the freeway. Using my most exaggerated British accent, I explained that we enjoyed the idea of looking down on Los Angeles and its traffic.

Our luggage consisted of several odd-shaped items, which were part of the filming kit, but we had tried to conceal them inside suitcases and carry-on bags. The desk clerk gave us the key with a suspicious look on his face.

"We may be having visitors," I said.

"Not after 6 p.m., you won't," said the clerk.

We went upstairs. Half an hour later, the camera crew arrived, with a mysterious gaffer wearing a hoodie and a woolen beanie. The tripod case gave them away.

"Are you going to be taking pictures up there?" the clerk asked them. He called our room. "Are you expecting four people?" he asked.

I agreed that we were.

"You're not making a porno film, are you?" he asked. I asked him to wait and went down to the lobby. Once again, I assumed my prissiest British accent.

"We're doing an educational interview," I said, "And we need to make a recording of it. Here's a printed release, which you could ask the manager to sign, if you would. It's for PBS, and it covers you and the hotel for insurance. Two copies please, one for you, one for me."

The clerk still looked suspicious. "There's no partying allowed," he explained, and grudgingly allowed everyone upstairs.

Once the elevator doors had closed, we all burst out laughing, Leonardo included.

"Whoa," he said. "A porno film? I hadn't been planning on that."

Once in the room, the crew had to set up the camera out on the balcony. Lizzie and Leonardo sat on the bed together and discussed the script. There was nowhere else for them to sit, and I took a few photos of them, propped against the pillows, to memorialize the occasion. Leo was fine with this.

"Just don't use them for promotion," he said. "We don't want people to get the wrong idea."

After a few minutes, there was a knock on the door. It was the desk clerk again. He was carrying the signed release. I took it and thanked him, but he just stood there, looking over my shoulder at Lizzie and Leonardo, lounging on the bed, with scripts in hand.

"What kind of video did you say you are making?" he asked again.

"It's a film about global warming," said Leonardo, in a strange Germanic accent.

"It's educational," said Lizzie, looking rather fetching in her tight jeans.

"Ah," said the clerk, obviously not believing a word of it.

"But we need to get on with it," I said, "We haven't got all day. So, since we've got the release now, would you mind if we got down to work?"

The clerk turned on his heel and walked away. We were quite concerned that he was going to call the manager, but no-one else arrived, and we shot Leo's piece to camera without further problems, until we were wrapping up.

"I need to keep the video tapes," said Leo to me. "I haven't signed the deal with PBS yet."

This was unusual, but I had no option. I was not the executive producer – that was Polly Kosko. So I handed Leo the tapes and he went downstairs with Lizzie, who was escorting him to his car. As they passed the clerk, they thanked him profusely for his help. Leo was no longer wearing his disguise. The clerk looked at him in disbelief, and then with dawning recognition.

"Aren't you, er...?" said the clerk.

"I'm often mistaken for him," said Leonardo. "Thanks again," and he left.

The same thing happened on the other shooting days: no more hotels or bed scenes, but the same issue with the tapes. Leonardo insisted on keeping everything we had shot. I called Polly Kosko and asked her what I should do.

"Well, I suppose you've got no option," she said. "Maybe he wants to review them at home."

Ten days later, we found out what he was up to. Polly and I both received a stern letter from DiCaprio's lawyers, a big firm based in Century City, just down the road from where we had filmed the hotel balcony scenes. Apparently, Mr. DiCaprio would not be signing the final deal with SCETV and PBS, and would not be releasing the tapes, unless they agreed to give him editorial control of the entire film and credited him as Executive Producer.

If they failed to agree to this, his lawyers threatened InCA, SCETV and the Canadian producers with a "forensic audit" of all the accounts and funds relating to the project. This is a standard Hollywood ploy: forensic audits can eat up thousands of hours of staff and lawyers' time on both sides, while every tiny receipt is checked and analyzed. Frankly, I was worried, and called Polly Kosko to discuss our strategy. She was blithely unconcerned.

"The heck with Leo," she said. "We don't need him. I'll call the Governor."

SCETV - South Carolina Educational Television - is a state agency, under the ultimate control of the State Governor. Polly, being an accomplished socialite as well as the consummate professional, knew him very well.

"He won't allow Hollywood to screw around with us," she said confidently.

A few days later, one of the briefest letters I have ever seen was sent to Leonardo's lawyers, under the impressive Great Seal of the State of South Carolina and the strapline "Founded in 1729," when it became a separate Royal Colony. The letter was signed personally by the Governor. Polly sent me a personal copy, with the word "Hah!" written in her own hand, across the top.

My legal friends have recommended that I shouldn't quote the exact text of the letter, but basically it made clear in a single sentence that the State had no further use for Mr. DiCaprio's contributions. Its pointedness and brevity suggested that the Governor knew exactly where Mr. DiCaprio could put them.

And that was it. We never heard from the lawyers, or from Leo, again. The Canadian producers suggested that the popular singer Alanis Morissette, a devoted Canadian environmentalist, would do a very good job as the host and narrator of the show, which indeed she did. End of story. Well, almost.

A couple of years after *Global Warming: the Signs and the Science* premiered nationally on PBS – to a warm reception – Leonardo produced and launched his own public television documentary on the same subject. It was good, but somehow it seemed two years behind the curve, we felt. We had got there first.

And the personal punch line? Well, in 2004, the year we filmed Richard Gere, Leonardo DiCaprio and John Cleese (see Chapter 24), we created a special Christmas card to send to our family and friends. The card featured three separate photos of Lizzie, with her arm round each of the three stars we'd worked with during the year, and they were all smiling – as was Lizzie. The message inside said "It has been a busy year for us." I'm afraid that that self-serving card lost us more friends around the world than anything else we've ever sent by mail.

■■

EPILOGUE: *The Book Makers*

So what?

By which I mean, does the fifty-plus years I've spent churning out radio and television documentaries amount to (as my American friends might say) a hill of beans? Should I, instead, have spent my time working for Yellow Van Lines and similar excellent enterprises, as my International Business Professor at the Indiana University School of Business recommended in 1968?

Well, I'd certainly be richer if I'd done so, as my wife frequently reminds me. But I'm profoundly glad I chose the path I took. To illustrate why, here's one final anecdote about the impact non-fiction television and films can have.

On May 16, 2017, Lizzie and I found ourselves in the charming northern city of Riga, the capital of Latvia, just down the road from the Russian border. We were there on a four-day vacation from our temporary base in London, to take pictures of the astonishing Art Deco architecture, to meet as many Latvians as possible and to discover one tiny corner of the world that neither of us had yet visited. The Spring sun was welcoming, the food was surprisingly good and the Latvians we met were lovely. This was back in the pre-Covid-19 era (remember?), when serendipitous trips to exotic places were just the ticket.

We had both promised not to think about work – no worries about psychiatric patients for Lizzie, and no ruminations about our son James's new InCA film *The Book Makers*, which had started production (see below). But you know how easy it is to sneak a quick look at your emails just before cocktail hour on vacation, just to make sure that things are OK back at home base.

I found I had received an email from a certain Callum G. Brown, Professor of Late Modern European History at the University of Glasgow. I had never heard of him, but he had certainly heard of me, thanks of course to Google. He was researching a new book, to be called *The Battle for Christian Britain, 1945–1980*. It was to be published by Cambridge University Press in late 2019, as the capstone to a series of books on the secularization of Britain.

Two of the chapters in the book were going to be devoted to what Callum described as "The Battle at the Beeb." The first of these chapters dealt with the "Heyday of Christian Vigilance 1945–1965", when the BBC largely toed the establishment line. 'Religious Programmes' on BBC Radio and Television were almost 100% in step with the views of the officially established Church of England, headed by Her Majesty the Queen. There was the occasional Jew or Humanist thrown into the mix, but only to add a little spice to discussions.

"The Battle at the Beeb – Part Two" was the concluding chapter of the book – one might even say, the climax of Callum's argument that Britain's spiritual and social norms were utterly transformed in the fifteen years between 1965 and 1980. To gather evidence for his thesis, he had cast far and wide, scarcely expecting, almost 50 years after the events, that he would find a useful Producer/Director from that far-off era, who was still alive and coherent.

Callum set up a series of telephone interviews with me during 2017. I burrowed deep into my paper archives, finding old copies of the *Radio Times*, (the BBC's official listings and features magazine), reviews of programs I had produced and newspaper features on the subject. (See Chapter 4 – From Science to Religion).

"Is it true that Cardinal Heenan had a heart attack within days of appearing on your *Sunday Debate*?" Callum asked me. "How did you ever get permission to do a three-part series attacking the Roman Catholic church?"

"It wasn't an attack per se," I explained, "Our host, Robin Day, simply asked the question '*On balance, is the Roman Catholic Church a force for good in society?*' And then we got the most eminent and watchable people to present the pro's and con's."

I explained the prestigious internal BBC firepower we had at our disposal, to protect us from political repercussions: Robin Day himself (later Sir Robin), the Walter Cronkite of British television, as Debate Chairman; Oliver Hunkin, the bravest of Heads of Religious Programmes (Television); and the loyal mandarin John Lang, Head of all Religious Broadcasting. Callum was fascinated.

"So they let you have your way? They backed you up!" He could hardly believe it.

He became even more interested when I told him that I had worked as a young Director/Producer on *The Ascent of Man*, with Jacob Bronowski, immediately prior to *The Sunday Debate*. "But that was a landmark of humanist programming," said Callum. "Bronowski was a secular Jew presenting a scientific view of human history, in complete contrast to Kenneth Clarke's *Civilisation* series, which was deeply in thrall to the achievements of Christianity."

Callum then discovered that Helen (my first wife) and I had produced the first film ever made at the BBC about Muslims in Britain; that I had then quit Religious Programmes to help produce and direct, one after the other, three profoundly agnostic BBC series – Galbraith's *The Age of Uncertainty*, James Burke's *Connections* and, to cap it all, Carl Sagan's *Cosmos*. Sagan was particularly fond of reminding his audience that belief in God was a foolish self-indulgence.

In short, my career from 1970 to 1980 had provided, in Callum's words to me on the telephone, "A series of nails in the coffin of Established Christianity in Britain." Who knew? I was quite taken aback. In his book, on page 283, he says:

"In 1970, religion was still in a position of considerable power within the [BBC] and thus in British culture as a whole. By 1980, it was much mocked, maligned and side-lined. ...... The churches' leaders were ... left wringing their hands at the passing of a Britain dominated by Christian culture."

Of course, it's flattering to imagine that a single producer-director can play even the tiniest role in the history of a nation's culture. I'm sure my contribution is vanishingly small. But, cumulatively, I believe that the work of honest, imaginative documentary-makers and wise broadcast journalists who strive to tell the truth is of vital importance today. We need more and more of them, in the era of Fake News and Anti-Social Media.

Professionally, the BBC taught me what fair, ethical, constructive, imaginative, enjoyable filmmaking is all about. I feel a responsibility to pass that on and to share it with others. Even now, the BBC still remains, for me, the essence of Public Service Broadcasting. In every western democracy – indeed, all over the world – we need to defend and preserve such institutions. Or invent them, where they don't yet exist.

As I bring this book to a conclusion, I can't help reflecting on the state of the world I am leaving. 2020 has been dominated by the Coronavirus, as well as by a global drift towards more authoritarian government. As an Anglo-American, I see my two countries facing a highly uncertain future. It all feels like an epochal change, the long-term results of which are hard to imagine. It will be up to other filmmakers than me to describe, interpret and imagine what lies ahead of us.

That is why it is a particular pleasure for me to watch my son James flourish as a documentary filmmaker himself. He took a Master's in Modern History at Oxford, where he designed and edited the university's student magazine, *Isis* – the oldest such publication in the UK. Then he returned to San Francisco, to start learning about animation and filmmaking in general. In the last seven years I have had the pleasure and privilege of working with him on four of our InCA Productions feature documentaries, three short films for the San Francisco Symphony and a 15-minute video portrait of the Arion Press. (See *incafilms.com* and *jameskennard.com*).

James consumes knowledge voraciously, but his natural talent is art of all sorts. He has become an excellent animator, graphics designer, cameraman, editor, director and producer. The final 90-minute film we set out to create together, *A Year in Port,* won First Prize for Documentary Features at New England's oldest and largest film festival, in Rhode Island, in 2016.

As I write this, James's own one-hour documentary, *The Book Makers* has recently been launched. Created with generous funding from our old family friend, Nion McEvoy (Pippa's godfather, inter alia), this is in every way James's baby, as Nion wished. My role has been that of the graybeard Senior Producer, who made a few suggestions about the content, the editing and the distribution, but basically tried to stay out of the way.

Happily, after premiering at a handful of film festivals in New England and on the West Coast, *The Book Makers* was accepted by American Public Television for national distribution to 90% of PBS stations across the United States and is now in international distribution. One of the many complimentary reviews it has received was published by *The Economist*'s Prospero arts blog in October 2020. This reflects all the hard work James put into the film, and I'm very proud to be associated with it. Here's an extract:

OPEN SESAME
A new documentary explores the remarkable resilience of the book

One is made entirely of lead. Another dances when opened. A third includes images of Mount Fuji fashioned from foam sponges, and a children's book weaves together pictures and strands of text from classic tales. All pose the same fascinating question: what, in a digital age, are physical books still for?

Some answers emerge in "The Book Makers", an enchanting new film that probes the form and function of the codex, that hunk of paper between two boards that has evolved over millennia into the ideal reading device. The film is not just a dazzling introduction to the art of the book. It is also a passionate tribute to this extraordinary invention that renders the intangible – ideas, thoughts, feelings – tangible.

James Kennard, who conceived and directed the film, is a Californian who learned the filmmaking trade from his father, David Kennard, a director of legendary documentaries on Joseph Campbell and Carl Sagan, among many others. After working as cameraman on a trilogy about the world's wine regions, the younger Mr Kennard has now struck out on his own.

Books made by hand immediately appealed as a lively art to explore, filled with clanking machines and luscious visuals. By happy chance he was able to follow one book artist, Mark Sarigianis, from the start of a monumental printing of Charles Bukowski's novel "Ham on Rye" to its completion 626 days later.

"The Book Makers" travels across the world to meet other leading book artists, including Peter Koch, a fine printer and bookmaker in Berkeley, California, Russell Maret in Brooklyn, Christian Robinson, a children's book illustrator in Sacramento, and Veronika Schäpers in Germany's Black Forest. The camera lovingly dwells on the extraordinary artistry involved in making books by hand, from typecasting to printing to painstaking painting, cutting, sewing and writing...

The film argues that digital technology, paradoxically, has liberated the physical book from its original function of conveying information. Gone is the obligation to impart lists of facts and quickly outdated data. Freed from the "burden of doing so many tasks that digital information does better", the book in the 21st century is "being totally reborn and reinvented", says Abby Smith Rumsey, a historian. The physical book today can glory in its ability to communicate using all five senses...

In the midst of a pandemic, when so many spend their days in front of a screen, the humble book has proven a godsend, as bookshop sales show. Beyond such fabulous works of art, any book "is finite, which means it's manageable and digestible," says Sam Winston, an artist based in London. "If you're living in an age where hyper-stimulation is very apparent, books are one of the ways you can get back into a different sensory plane."

Just looking at and touching such works – at fine-book shows or the world's leading artist book fair, Codex, which closes the documentary's tour – can revive the spirit. Failing that, this film is an excellent substitute.

As I approach the end of my career and of my life, I take great pleasure in the fact that my four children and my wife Lizzie are all following exciting paths, which demand all their talents plus a lot of hard work.

Lizzie has reinvented herself several times: once a BBC secretary, then a production manager, a researcher and an independent TV producer, she is now Dr. Elizabeth Kennard, PsyD., with a grueling but impressive career as a psychologist and therapist at Kaiser Permanente, a big hospital group in the San Francisco Bay Area. She has been the most loyal, most capable, most adventurous, most intelligent, most sexy, most loving wife I could ever have wished for. And she is my best friend. What more can I say?

Amanda, my eldest daughter, is now in her mid-40's. After taking a BA and MA at Bristol University, as I have recounted, she became a successful lawyer with a high-powered London law firm, Olswang. When it came time to have children with her husband Andy, she reinvented herself, like Lizzie: she trained to become an elementary school teacher, joined the staff of the historic and eminent St. Paul's School (where she had studied 25 years before) and now balances that job with bringing up Tom, Charlie and Daisy in West London.

Juliet, Helen's younger daughter and also a graduate of Bristol, has had a high-flying career as a senior marketing executive. After taking her MBA at Columbia University, she was made responsible for the management, design and successful launch of the paid websites of The Times and Sunday Times newspapers in London. After two further jobs, she was head-hunted to manage the entire Online Customer Experience for Britain's National Health Service, the fifth largest employer in the world. Currently, she runs UK operations for a European-based health software company. With her husband Thijs, she has two daughters – Lara and Sophie – and they also live in West London.

Pippa, my youngest daughter, chose to follow her elder half-sisters to Bristol University, where she studied French and Spanish. She managed to organize a year abroad to study these languages, half on the tropical island of Réunion (a tiny dot in the Indian Ocean) and half in the elegant Spanish city of Seville. Naturally adventurous, she then launched a high-tech adventure-travel start-up company in London with a group of friends. But the call of home was too great, and she returned to California, where she has been a Human Resources executive for the online ride company, Lyft, then with Pinterest and currently with Asana, which creates software to enable remote teams and groups to work together.

On 12 July 2019, (as it happens, Lizzie's and my wedding anniversary as well), Pippa married Alex Goldis, a bright young engineer working on super-secret new projects for Apple. They chose the Pelican Inn as the venue – an extraordinary reproduction of an English country pub, in rolling hills near the ocean, just twenty minutes' drive from our house in Mill Valley. We thought they might be rushing a little too quickly into marriage at the time, but as it turned out, the event would have been impossible in the Coronavirus summer of 2020. They live with their fine dog Rufus in a charming house in Pacifica, near the coast, 15 miles south-east of San Francisco.

So... four children, five grandchildren and counting, not to mention my extended family in England and my many kind friends in Europe, America and around the world. I am indeed, as I said at the beginning, very, very lucky.

But, Carpe Diem, as dear Reed Dennis used to say, when he piloted his Grumman Albatross plane around the world, to make our Amelia Earhart film. He was seventy-two at the time. To me, aged just over 50 when we made the film in 1997, that seemed ridiculously old to be gallivanting around the globe. But now, in my seventy-sixth year and faced with various health worries from cancer to the lurking Coronavirus, I think I understand why he felt the need to do something spectacular – immediately!

Seize the day, indeed... Live your life to the full! When you hear the clock on the time-bomb ticking, like Sergeant Hambrook in my 1969 film, *Seven Seconds to Run,* just enjoy yourself and achieve as much as you can – and try not to think about what follows. If you have had as much love and as much fun as I have had in my life, every extra day is just a bonus.

To all those who have given me that love and that fun – thank you!

So... that's a wrap.

▪▪

Acknowledgements

Many friends, family and professional colleagues gave me advice about the pleasures and the pitfalls of attempting to write a memoir. "Beware the wrath of those who don't get mentioned," I was told on several occasions. "Beware the glee of those, who keep better records than you, and will point out every mistake." But primarily, the message was: "People will think you're far too big for your boots to write a memoir, if there's no money to be made from it."

Nonetheless, I persevered. I was helped enormously by Mary Jay – properly, of course, Lady Jay, but such a good friend that I sometimes find it hard to remember that she is thus entitled, as well as being my former stepmother-in-law. Mary is a recently retired professional publisher with a long history in every aspect of books, from encouraging new writers in Africa to proof-reading, editing and distributing what they have written. As a result of what she called "a fortunate accident," (she broke her leg), she found she had several immobile weeks at her disposal, and very kindly devoted most of them to reading and editing this tome. Thank you, Mary, for a heroic effort! You saved me from many a stupid mistake and suggested many a felicitous improvement.

Charlie Pearson, a good friend and professional writer who divides his time (when Covid restrictions aren't in place) between Northern California and the West Coast of Mexico, strongly advised me to dump the original concluding chapter. This recounted in painstaking detail the medical trials and tribulations that hit me after the age of 70. He said it was a downer and too self-serving by far, even though my intention had been to show how fate can deal some bad cards from the bottom of the pack, after a run of good luck through most of my life. How right he was! The advent of the Coronavirus has put my adventures with cancer into sharp perspective. Thank you, Charlie!

Dick Gilling, my elder colleague on *The Ascent of Man* and *The Age of Uncertainty*, patiently reviewed my assessment of the BBC in the 1970's, and what happened thereafter. He decided long ago to emigrate with his wife Annie to Australia, and for a time ran an InCA Productions office in Sydney. He reminded me that it was a huge privilege and great pleasure to work with John Kenneth Galbraith, and that the accompanying book to *The Age of Uncertainty* was a great success, even if the TV series wasn't too well received. Thank you for all your gentle suggestions, Dick. I am so pleased that we have remained good friends, albeit separated by 6,000 miles or more.

Many others have read part or all of this book. At one extreme, Jim Gollub, data analyst supreme, put the sections that referred to him under a microscope, and pointed out various errors in my story of the birth and death of IDeA, InCA's short-lived sister company, in the 1990's. He also correctly noted that I had given inadequate attention to the wonderful video-editing work that his kindly wife Charlotte Grossman had provided on several major InCA projects.

At the other extreme, my dear friend Brian Swimme, cosmologist extraordinaire, said he read the whole book, and then refused to give me any detailed comments at all. When we met for a lunch in San Francisco, he just described how much the book had made him laugh: "sometimes a smile, sometimes a chuckle, sometimes a real guffaw." For this to be the principal critique coming from a philosopher and planetary scientist was a delightful surprise. Brian is a superb writer himself, who manages to express cosmic insights in a few sentences. This book is exactly the opposite, drawing only modest conclusions after 180,000 words. It was generous of Brian to give up all the time necessary to read it, but he said he enjoyed the gossipy bits as much as the factual record.

Finally, my unbounded thanks to my dear wife, Lizzie. With her feet up on a sofa and a gin and tonic in her hands, she worked her way through the first draft of this book over a month of cocktail hours, more or less one chapter per working day. Like me, she keeps great detailed records of her life in neat year-by-year boxes. We met at Christmas, 1980: 40 years ago, so that's a lot of boxes (and she had plenty already filled by the time she met me!). But she remembered most of the events since then without even opening the boxes – BBC highlights, our arrival in America, forensic details of our family life, and all the projects she has helped me with, as well as her own triumphant metamorphosis into a professional psychologist. Best of all, she knows me well enough to be able to tell instinctively when I'm exaggerating or reaching too far, to get a cheap laugh. Or even an expensive one.

Thank you, dearest Lizzie, for all the happiness in my Second Life.

■■■

David Kennard: Principal Credits as Director and/or Producer

Germany 1870-1970 (1970)
The Sky at Night (1970)
So You Think You're a Good Husband/Wife (1970)
Seven Seconds to Run (1971)
The Ascent of Man (1973)
A Chance to Meet (1973)
The Sunday Debate (1973/74)
Through the Looking Glass (1974)
Children of the Way (1974)
The Age of Uncertainty (1976)
Connections (1978)
Cosmos (1980)
The Communications Revolution (1981)
The Hero's Journey (1982)
The Heart of the Dragon (1984)
The Living Body (1985)
The West of the Imagination (1986)
We the People (1988)
Minidragons (1989)
Little by Little (1990)
Imagine This World (1990)
Things to Come (1991)
Dangerous Years (1992)
The Heart of Healing (1994)
Our Fragile Fortress (1995)
Pulling Out All the Stops (1997)
Africa's Children (1999)
The Promise of Play (2000)
2001: HAL's Legacy (2001)
Stories of Hope (2002)
Surviving September 11 (2002)
One Bite of the Apple (2003)
Keeping Score (2004-2012)
John Cleese's Wine for the Confused (2005)
The Power of the Sun (2006)
Global Warming: The Signs and the Science (2006)
Recreating America (2009)
Reinventing Yourself (2012)
Journey of the Universe (2013)
A Year in Burgundy (2013)
A Year in Champagne (2014)
A Year in Port (2016)
The Book Makers (2020)

....

Made in the USA
Coppell, TX
16 November 2020